OCR GCSE (9–1)

GEOGRAPHY B

Geography for Enquiring Minds

OCR GCSE (9–1)

GEOGRAPHY B
Geography for Enquiring Minds

Jo **Debens**
Alan **Parkinson**
Jo **Payne**
Simon **Ross**
Editor: David **Rogers**

An OCR endorsed textbook

This resource is endorsed by OCR for use with specification **J384 OCR GCSE (9–1) Geography B (Geography for Enquiring Minds)**. In order to gain OCR endorsement, this resource has undergone an independent quality check. Any references to assessment and/or assessment preparation are the publisher's interpretation of the specification requirements and are not endorsed by OCR. OCR recommends that a range of teaching and learning resources are used in preparing learners for assessment. OCR has not paid for the production of this resource, nor does OCR receive any royalties from its sale. For more information about the endorsement process, please visit the OCR website, **www.ocr.org.uk**.

Acknowledgements

pp. 3, **19** and **21** The Met Office, www.metoffice.gov.uk; **p.77** *Sidmouth Herald*, 5 August 2014, Beachgoers warned after huge Sidmouth cliff fall, www.sidmouthherald.co.uk/news/beachgoers_warned_after_huge_sidmouth_cliff_fall_1_3709172; **p.82** © North Norfolk District Council; **p.138** *The Economist*, www.economist.com/node/21642053?fsrc=scn/tw/te/dc/brightlightsbigcities; **p.139** United Nations, Department of Economic and Social Affairs, Population Division (2014). World Urbanization Prospects: The 2014 Revision, Highlights (ST/ESA/SER.A/352) http://esa.un.org/unpd/wup/highlights/wup2014-highlights.pdf, © 2014 United Nations. Reprinted with the permission of the United Nations; **p.141** UN World Urbanisation Prospects 2014/LSE Cities © 2014 United Nations. Reprinted with the permission of the United Nations; **p.153** Lymperopoulou, K (2015) Geographies of deprivation and diversity in the Leeds City Region. Local Dynamics of Diversity: Evidence from the 2011 Census, Centre on Dynamics of Ethnicity, The University of Manchester, UK; **p.172** © Philip's; **p.189** Horn Affairs, http://hornaffairs.com/en/wp-content/uploads/sites/9/2011/07/ethiopia-food-security-conditions-projected-for-august-september-2011.jpg; **p.199** © Philip's; **p.200** The Met Office, www.metoffice.gov.uk; **p.201** Environment Agency; map of UK water stress based on: http://webarchive.nationalarchives.gov.uk/20140328084622/http:/cdn.environment-agency.gov.uk/geho1208bpas-e-e.pdf; **p.209** Office for National Statistics, a population pyramid from the ONS website; www.ons.gov.uk/ons/rel/census/2011-census/population-and-household-estimates-for-the-united-kingdom/stb-2011-census--population-estimates-for-the-united-kingdom.html#tab-The-structure-of-the-population-of-the-United-Kingdom; **p.210** Cool Geography, www.coolgeography.co.uk/GCSE/AQA/Population/Demographic%20Transition/Demographic_Transition_Model.jpg; **p.211** © Philip's; **p.213** Office for National Statistics (ONS) National Statistics website: www.statistics.gov.uk, www.ons.gov.uk, Crown copyright material is reproduced with the permission of the Controller of OPSI HMSO; and Welsh Assembly Government Statistical Directorate. Lincolnshire Research Observatory (LRO), www.research-lincs.org.uk; **p.236** *The Guardian*, 30 August 2006, Mixed blessing, www.theguardian.com/society/2006/aug/30/communities.guardiansocietysupplement; **p.243** ONE, 14 Surprising stats about global food consumption, www.one.org/us/2014/11/12/14-surprising-stats-about-global-food-consumption/#; **p.246** Shiklomanov A. (1999) World Water Resources and their Use, a joint SHI/UNESCO product, http://webworld.unesco.org/water/ihp/db/shiklomanov/summary/html/figure_8.html; **p.256** Global Forest Watch, www.globalforestwatch.org; ; **p.261** Max Roser, http://ourworldindata.org; **p.278** *t* Environment Agency showing flood risks of various areas; https://flood-warning-information.service.gov.uk, *b* Google Earth Pro

Maps on **pp. 18, 77, 79** and **222**, reproduced from Ordnance Survey mapping with the permission of the Controller of HMSO. © Crown copyright and/or database right. All rights reserved. Licence number 100036470.

Every effort has been made to trace all copyright holders, but if any have been inadvertently overlooked, the Publishers will be pleased to make the necessary arrangements at the first opportunity.

Although every effort has been made to ensure that website addresses are correct at time of going to press, Hodder Education cannot be held responsible for the content of any website mentioned in this book. It is sometimes possible to find a relocated web page by typing in the address of the home page for a website in the URL window of your browser.

Hachette UK's policy is to use papers that are natural, renewable and recyclable products and made from wood grown in sustainable forests. The logging and manufacturing processes are expected to conform to the environmental regulations of the country of origin.

Orders: please contact Bookpoint Ltd, 130 Park Drive, Milton Park, Abingdon, Oxon OX14 4SE. Telephone: +44 (0)1235 827720. Fax: +44 (0)1235 400454. Email education@bookpoint.co.uk Lines are open from 9 a.m. to 5 p.m., Monday to Saturday, with a 24-hour message answering service. You can also order through our website: www.hoddereducation.co.uk

ISBN: 978 1 4718 5309 8

© Jo Debens, Alan Parkinson, Jo Payne and Simon Ross 2016

First published in 2016 by
Hodder Education,
An Hachette UK Company
Carmelite House
50 Victoria Embankment
London EC4Y 0DZ

www.hoddereducation.co.uk

Impression number   10 9 8 7 6 5 4 3 2

Year   2020 2019 2018 2017 2016

Cover photo © Getty Images/iStockphoto/Thinkstock

Illustrations Aptara and Barking Dog Art, Design & Illustration

Typeset in India by Aptara, Inc.

Printed in Italy

A catalogue record for this title is available from the British Library.

Contents

Introduction

This book has been written specifically for the OCR GCSE Geography B: Geography for Enquiring Minds specification to be first examined in September 2018. The writers are all experienced teachers and subject specialists who provide comprehensive and up-to-date information that is both accessible and informative.

The authors have written this book for those with enquiring minds, for those that wish to know and find out about the people and places that make our world so fascinating. By working through the enquiry questions running throughout each topic and each chapter, it will help you to take an enquiry-based approach to your learning. You will find out about the world by thinking, studying and questioning like a geographer.

This book includes a range of features designed to give you confidence and make the most of your course in a clear and accessible way, as well as supporting you in your revision and exam preparation.

Features in the book

→ Learning objectives

At the start of each section is a list of what you will cover to help you track your learning. At the end of each section, you can return to this feature and check whether you feel confident that you have covered everything required.

Key term

Key terms are highlighted in red throughout the book. You will find definitions of these key terms in the glossary on pages 286–290. You should learn these key terms and definitions so that you can use them effectively in your exams.

Activities

Throughout each chapter you will find activities designed to help you think about the content on the pages. These are made up of different question types:

- activities that help you analyse and understand the information and illustrations contained within the pages, including individual, paired and group work
- activities that help you prepare notes and summaries to help you with your revision
- questions that are similar to those you will find in your exams
- questions that help you to develop and practise your geographical skills.

→ Take it further

Take in further questions are included for students aiming for the higher grades, and may ask questions that require you to go beyond the information found in this student's book.

⚔ Geographical Skills

Geographers need certain skills in order to be able to process information from maps, graphs or text extracts. These skills include being able to read an Ordnance Survey map, or describe the trend on a graph. The Geographical skills boxes in this book will help you to develop these important skills and will help you tackle the activities on each page.

👣 Fieldwork ideas

Possible ideas for fieldwork projects appear in boxes throughout the book. Chapter 17 will help you to pull all these ideas together and plan for fieldwork, including how it will be assessed in your exam.

Practice questions

Although you will work through lots of exam-style questions in the activities throughout the book, at the end of each topic is a dedicated page to these question types, which also show you how many marks each question is worth. You can use these as an end-of-topic test to check that you can understand and remember what you need to know for this topic in the exams.

Case study

Case studies of real-life places will help you to put the geographical concepts that you learn into context. For your exams, you need a detailed and thorough knowledge of some places to help you answer some of the case study questions. The UK map on this page and the World map on page viii show you the location of the case studies found in this book.

Tips

Throughout the book and alongside the practice questions you will find tips to help you relate the content to the assessment questions.

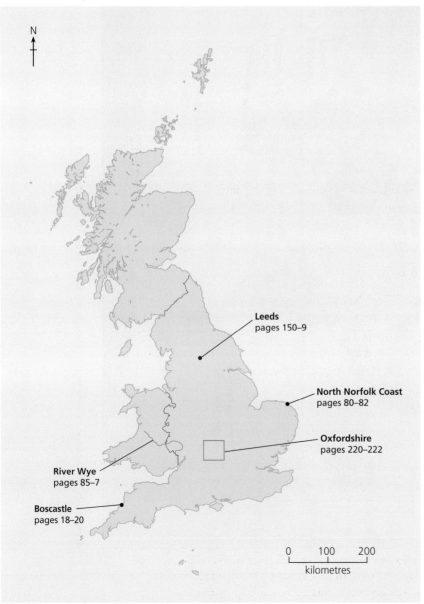

N

Leeds
pages 150–9

North Norfolk Coast
pages 80–82

Oxfordshire
pages 220–222

River Wye
pages 85–7

Boscastle
pages 18–20

0   100   200
kilometres

▲ **Figure 1:** The location of case studies within the UK that are used in this book

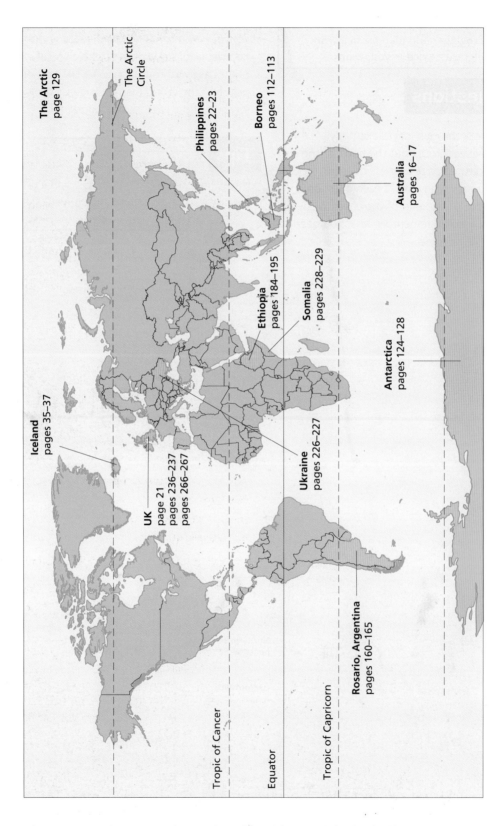

The Arctic
page 129

The Arctic
Circle

Philippines
pages 22–23

Borneo
pages 112–113

Australia
pages 16–17

Ethiopia
pages 184–195

Somalia
pages 228–229

Antarctica
pages 124–128

Iceland
pages 35–37

UK
page 21
pages 236–237
pages 266–267

Ukraine
pages 226–227

Rosario, Argentina
pages 160–165

Tropic of Cancer

Equator

Tropic of Capricorn

▲ **Figure 2:** The location of case studies outside the UK that are used in this book

Global Hazards

Chapter 1: How can weather be hazardous?

By the end of this chapter, you will know the answers to these key questions:

→ Why do we have weather extremes?

→ When does extreme weather become hazardous?

→ Case study: The 'Big Dry' – is El Niño to blame for Australia's drought issues?

→ Case study: Why did Boscastle experience a flash flood on 16 August 2004?

→ Case study: Was there really a heatwave in the UK in summer 2015?

→ Case study: Super Typhoon Haiyan: a physical or human disaster?

Chapter 2: How do plate tectonics shape our world?

By the end of this chapter, you will know the answers to these key questions:

→ What processes occur at plate boundaries?

→ How can tectonic movement be hazardous?

→ Case study: How was the eruption of Eyjafjallajökull hazardous?

→ How does technology have the potential to save lives in hazardous zones?

There are a variety of hazards that impact human lives. How dangerous do you think the place shown in this photograph is? How can we protect people from hazards like this?

How can weather be hazardous?

Why do we have weather extremes?

→ In this section you will:

- → examine the global circulation system, including the effects of high and low pressure belts in creating climatic zones

- → explore the extremes in weather conditions associated with wind, temperature and precipitation in contrasting countries

- → consider the causes, distribution and frequency of tropical storms and drought, and whether these have changed over time.

What is the global pattern of air circulation?

There are large-scale, circular movements of air over the Earth's surface. These circulations of air transport heat from the tropical regions at the Equator, where the Earth gets more heat from the Sun, to the polar regions at the poles.

The imaginary lines that surround the Earth are known as lines of **latitude**. The Equator is at the 0° latitude line and the region spanning it is known as the 'low' latitudes. The polar regions are towards 90° north and south of the Equator line and are known as the 'high' latitudes.

The world is divided into two at the Equator line to create the northern and southern **hemispheres**. In each hemisphere there are three specific 'cells' of air called Hadley, Ferrel and Polar (Figures 1 and 2). Within these cells, air circulates within the **troposphere**, an area of the atmosphere from the Earth's surface up to 10–15 kilometres high. The troposphere is the part of the atmosphere where the Earth's weather takes place. The three cells of air play an important role in creating the distinct **climate zones** that we experience on Earth.

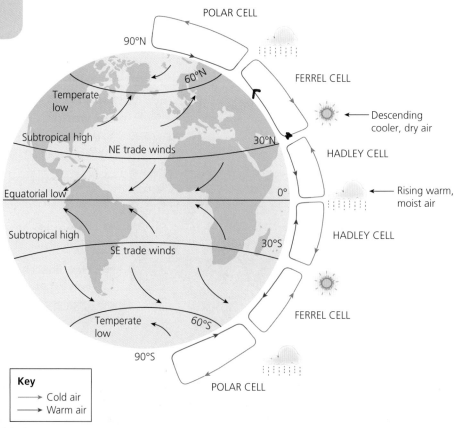

Key
→ Cold air
→ Warm air

▲ **Figure 1:** Global circulation system

	Where is it?	What happens?
Hadley cell	The largest cell which extends from the Equator to between 30° and 40° north and south.	• **Trade winds** are winds that blow from the tropical regions towards the Equator. They usually travel from an easterly direction. • Near the Equator, the trade winds meet and the warm air rises and forms thunderstorms. • From the top of these storms air flows towards higher latitudes where it becomes cooler and sinks over subtropical regions.
Ferrel cell	The middle cell, which generally occurs from the edge of the Hadley cell to between 60° and 70°.	• This is the most complicated cell as it moves in the opposite direction from the Hadley and Polar cells, similar to a cog in a machine. • Air in this cell joins the sinking air of the Hadley cell and travels at low heights to mid-latitudes where it rises along the border with the cold air of the Polar cell. • This occurs around the latitude of the UK and accounts for the frequently unsettled weather. • Air then flows back towards the low latitudes, in the direction of the Equator.
Polar cell	The smallest and weakest cell, which extends from the edge of the Ferrel cell to the poles at 90°.	• Air in this cell sinks over the highest latitudes, at the poles, and flows out towards the lower latitudes.

▲ **Figure 2:** Differences between the three circulatory cells

What happens in areas of high pressure and low pressure?

What we know as wind is air moving from high to low pressure. **Atmospheric air pressure** is the force exerted on the Earth's surface by the weight of the air. It is measured in millibars. The normal range of air pressure is 980 millibars (**low pressure**) to 1050 millibars (**high pressure**). Where the air in the Hadley cells rises at the Equator, low pressure is created. However, where the Hadley and Ferrel cells meet at 30° north and south of the Equator, air descends, creating high pressure on the ground below (see Figure 3). The contrasts in air pressure associated with the different cells, combined with distance from the Equator, creates regions with distinctive average temperature and rainfall patterns (see pages 4–5).

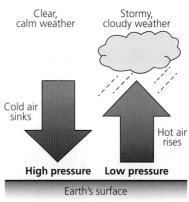

▲ **Figure 3:** The difference between high and low pressure

What happens in areas of low pressure?

A low-pressure system occurs when the atmospheric pressure is lower than that of the surrounding area. It is usually associated with high winds and warm, rising air. As the warm air cools and condenses as it rises, it forms clouds. **Condensation** is the process whereby this rising vapour turns into a liquid. Eventually, moisture falls from the atmosphere as rain, sleet, snow or hail, collectively known as **precipitation**. Daytime ranges of temperatures are unlikely to be large, as the cloud cover reflects solar radiation during the day and traps heat during the night.

What happens in areas of high pressure?

When air cools it becomes denser and starts to fall towards the ground, increasing the air pressure. This cool air is subjected to warming, which causes any clouds to evaporate. Also, heavy rain at the Equator means that most of the moisture in the atmosphere is removed before the air reaches the sub-tropics. At 30° north and south of the equator high pressure systems are usually associated with clear skies and dry (possibly hot), calm weather.

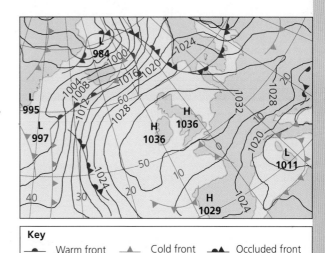

Key
— Warm front   — Cold front   — Occluded front

▲ **Figure 4:** A synoptic weather chart showing an area of high pressure over the UK recording 1036 millibars

What is the relationship between the global circulation system and the major climate zones of the world?

A number of climate zones, or belts, can be traced between the Equator and the pole in each hemisphere as a result of the global movements of air and the atmospheric pressure that this generates.

▼ **Figure 6:** Peak District, Derbyshire, England

TEMPERATURE CLIMATE

In the mid-latitudes, 50°–60° north and south of the Equator, two air types meet, one warm from the Ferrel cell and one cold from the Polar cell. Low pressure is created from the rising of the warm, sub-tropical winds over the cold, polar winds at a front. As this air rises and cools, it condenses to form clouds and ultimately frequent rainfall. This is typical of the UK.

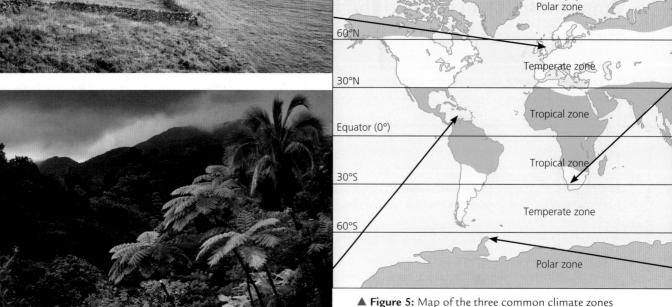

▲ **Figure 5:** Map of the three common climate zones

▲ **Figure 8:** Windward Islands, Dominica, Caribbean

TROPICAL CLIMATE

This is a belt of relatively low pressure, heavy rainfall and thunderstorms as a result of rising air in the Hadley cell. Places such as northern Brazil in South America and Malaysia in South East Asia experience this climate.

	Jan	Feb	Mar	Apr	May	Jun	July	Aug	Sept	Oct	Nov	Dec
Average temp (°C)	12.4	15.4	19.3	25.1	29.0	31.7	31.5	30.8	29.0	23.8	17.7	13.1
Rainfall (mm)	3.2	2.9	2.2	1.6	2.5	1.1	0.0	0.7	2.1	1.4	1.8	1.6

▲ **Figure 10:** Climate data for Djanet, Algeria

SUB-TROPICAL (DESERT) CLIMATE

At 30° north and south of the Equator there is high pressure as a result of sinking, dry air as the Hadley and Ferrel cells meet. This creates a belt of desert regions. These include the Sahara in northern Africa and the Namib desert in Namibia, southern Africa. Daytime temperatures can exceed 40 ° C, while at night, due to a lack of cloud cover, temperatures can fall to below freezing.

60°N

30°N

▲ **Figure 7:** Namib desert, Namibia, Africa

▼ **Figure 9:** Antarctic Peninsula

Equator (0°)

30°S

60°S

POLAR CLIMATE

At the highest latitudes, cold air from the Polar cell sinks, producing high pressure. This is characterised by dry, icy winds caused by the spin of the Earth. In some places in Antarctica, the average annual wind speed is nearly 50 miles per hour!

Activities

1. Multiple choice:
   Which two cells meet to bring high pressure to the sub-tropical region?
   a. Hadley and Hadley
   b. Hadley and Ferrel
   c. Polar and Ferrel
2. Describe the difference between high and low pressure.
3. Use the climate data in Figure 10 to draw a climate graph for Djanet, Algeria.
4. In which climate zone is Djanet located? How do you know this?
5. With the help of Figure 1 on page 2 which shows the global circulation of air, and pages 4 to 5, explain why the rainfall in Djanet is so low.

→ Take it further

6. Why is the **average** daytime temperature for a high pressure region misleading?

✝ Geographical skills

A climate graph (Figure 11) shows the average temperature and rainfall for a place during a year. It is measured using months of the year on the x axis and both y axes are used to plot the rainfall in bars and the temperature as a line.

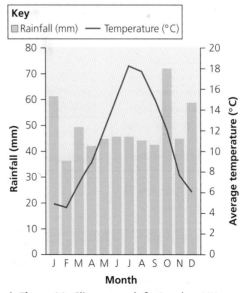

▲ **Figure 11:** Climate graph for London, UK

Weather extremes: where are the coldest, hottest, driest, wettest and windiest places in the world?

DEATH VALLEY: Driest place in North America with an average rainfall of 500 mm. Storms coming from the Pacific Ocean must travel over a series of mountain ranges on their journey eastwards. This means that many of the clouds have already cooled, condensed and fallen as rain before they reach Death Valley.

MOUNT WAIALEALE: Located on the island of Kauai in Hawaii, this is the wettest place in America with an annual average rainfall of 9763 mm.

PUERTO LÓPEZ: A small fishing village in Colombia is one of the wettest places on Earth. It has an annual rainfall of 12,892 mm. In the mid-1980s, it rained every single day for two years!

URECA: Located on the southern tip of Bioko Island in Equatorial Guinea, this is the wettest location in Africa with an average annual rainfall of 10,450 mm.

ATACAMA DESERT: Coastal mountains to the west block moist air from the Pacific and the Andes block rain from the Amazon in the east (see Figure 13). The prevailing wind (most frequent wind direction) comes from the south-east and carries moist air from the Atlantic.

As the air is forced to rise to cross the Andes it cools, condenses and turns to rain on the eastern side of the Andes. This leaves the Atacama in the rain shadow, which means that it receives little rainfall as high land shelters it from rain-producing weather systems. This creates a 'shadow' of dry conditions on the western side of the Andes.

On its western side, the Atacama lies close to the ocean where a cold current flows northwards along the coastline. As it is cold, onshore winds do not have enough warmth to pick up moisture from the ocean surface. This lack of rising air prevents precipitation from forming.

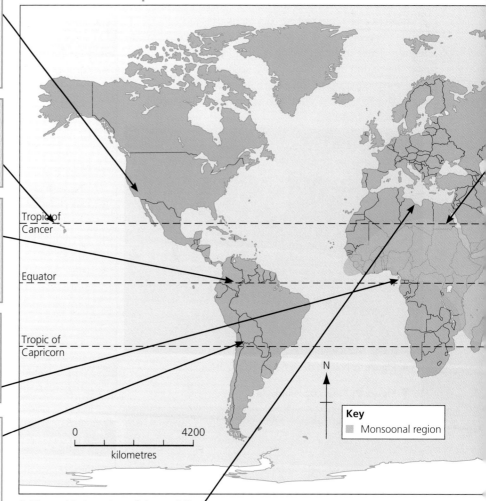

▲ **Figure 12:** Location of the world's weather extremes

AL–AZIZIYAH, LIBYA: The hottest place on Earth is Al-Aziziyah in Libya. 40 km south of Tripoli, Al-Aziziyah is where, on 13 September 1922, the world experienced its hottest air temperature ever recorded at 57.8 °C.

VOSTOK, ANTARCTICA: The coldest place on Earth is Vostok in Antarctica. At a height of around 3500 m above sea level, the Russian research station at Vostok is always cold. On 21 July 1983, the coldest air temperature on the planet was recorded here at –89.2 °C.

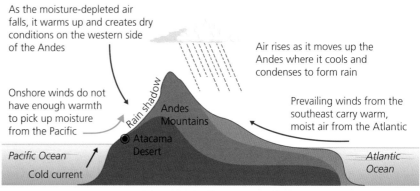

As the moisture-depleted air falls, it warms up and creates dry conditions on the western side of the Andes

Onshore winds do not have enough warmth to pick up moisture from the Pacific

Air rises as it moves up the Andes where it cools and condenses to form rain

Prevailing winds from the southeast carry warm, moist air from the Atlantic

▲ **Figure 13:** Why is the Atacama Desert so dry?

ASWAN: Located in the driest region of Egypt, it has a rainfall of only 0.861 mm per year! Its proximity to the Tropic of Cancer contributes to the high temperatures and dry weather.

MAWSYNRAM: The 10,000 villagers of Mawsynram cope with 11 metres of rain per year. That's 20 times the average rainfall for London! 80 per cent of all of India's rain arrives in the seasonal monsoon deluge from June to September. During this time, more heat from the Sun (solar radiation) is hitting the northern hemisphere. The monsoon is powered by the difference between land and sea and the ways that they respond to the Sun. The sea is cooler than the land as there is both more of it to be heated and it is always on the move due to the winds. The land therefore heats quicker than the sea. As the Sun bakes the land in India, the warm air above it rises and draws in cooler air from the sea. With the triangular shape of India and the long coastline, there is a powerful and sustained current of air moving northwards through India, which bring rains known as the monsoon.

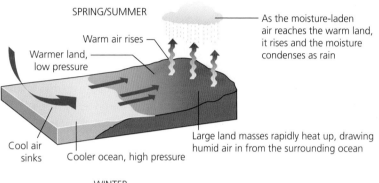

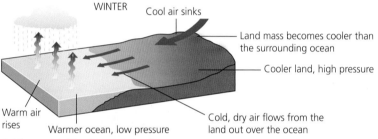

▲ **Figure 14:** The formation of monsoons

COMMONWEALTH BAY, ANTARCTICA: This is the windiest place on Earth with winds regularly exceeding 240 km/h, with an average annual wind speed of 80 km/h. Storms are causes by katabatic winds, which are winds that carry air from high ground down a slope due to gravity.

WELLINGTON, NEW ZEALAND: The highest gust of wind ever recorded in Wellington was 248 km/h and the average annual wind speed is 29 km/h. Gusts of wind exceed gale force (75 km/h) on 175 days of the year. The mountainous landscape either side of Wellington acts as a funnel for the winds, increasing their speed.

	Location	Rainfall (mm per year)
	London, UK	558
1	Mawsynram, India	11,871
2	Cherrapunji, India	11,777
3	Tutendo, Columbia	11,770
4	River Cropp waterfall, New Zealand	11,516
5	Ureca, Bioko Island in Equatorial Guinea, Africa	10,450
6	Debundscha, Cameroon, Africa	10,229
7	Big Bog in Maui, Hawaii	10,272
8	Mt Waialeale in Kauai, Hawaii	9,763
9	Kukui in Maui, Hawaii	9,293
10	Mount Emei, Sichuan Province in China	8,169

▲ **Figure 15:** Top ten wettest places in the world

Activities

1. Choose three of the locations of weather extremes in the world. **Analyse** the reasons why the weather is so extreme. Use the information from other areas of this chapter to help you, including Figure 1.

→ Take it further

2. To what extent would you agree that Antarctica is the 'most extreme' place in the world? Use evidence from pages 6–7.

✝ Geographical skills

Create a bar graph of the data in Figure 15. Colour code the bars according to the continent. Label the axes and give your graph a title.

What is El Niño?

El Niño was the term first used for the appearance of warm surface water around the coast of Peru and Ecuador. It was originally spotted by a group of Peruvian fishermen who relied on the usually colder waters swelling up from beneath the sea surface to bring up nutrient-rich waters from the deep ocean. This in turn improved their catch of small fish called anchovies. They noticed the unusually high sea surface temperatures occurring about every two or three years around Christmas.

How does El Niño and La Niña in the Pacific Ocean cause extreme weather?

What causes El Niño?

Scientists continue to study the exact causes of El Niño. There is a strong interaction between ocean and atmosphere in the Pacific, so even small changes can be enough to have a large-scale impact across the region and cause global changes to weather and climate.

For a brief time, seafloor heating as a result of volcanic activity became a popular theory. It was noted that two separate eruptions in the region were followed closely by El Niño events. For example, Mount Pinatubo erupted in 1991, the same year in which an El Niño event began. However, this is not a likely theory.

A more probable cause is small changes in sea surface temperatures. This could be caused, for instance, by tropical storms in the western region of the Pacific. If they are violent enough, or last long enough, they could start the movement of warm water eastwards across the Pacific.

What are the normal conditions in the Pacific Ocean?

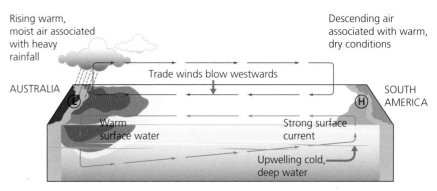

▲ **Figure 16:** A normal year

- The surface winds over the Pacific Ocean, known as the trade winds, blow towards the warm water of the western Pacific, off the coasts of Australia and Indonesia.
- Rising air occurs at this location as a result of water heating up the atmosphere. The trade winds across the surface of the Pacific push the warm water westwards from Peru to Australia.
- In the eastern Pacific, off the coast of Peru, the shallow position of the **thermocline** allows winds to pull up water from below. The thermocline is the point at which the temperature changes from warmer surface waters to deeper, colder water. It is this that creates those optimum conditions for fishing, which have already been mentioned, as there is an abundance of phytoplankton within the cold water, supplying the fish with food.
- As a result of the pressure of the trade winds pushing the water westwards, the sea levels in Australasia are about half a metre higher than Peru, with sea temperatures 8°C warmer.

Activities

1. Summarise the conditions in the Pacific Ocean in 50 words for each of the following; a normal year, El Niño and La Niña

2. In pairs, sit with your backs against each other. One of you needs the textbook open on this page and one of you needs a blank piece of paper. The student with the textbook needs to describe the diagram of a normal year to the other student who then has to draw the description on their piece of paper. Continue the exercise for as long as it takes to have a complete diagram. Swap roles for the El Niño diagram.

What happens during El Niño?

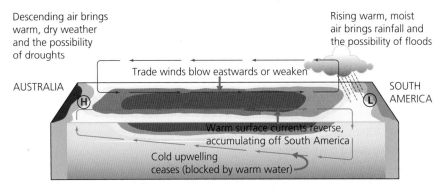

Descending air brings warm, dry weather and the possibility of droughts

Rising warm, moist air brings rainfall and the possibility of floods

Trade winds blow eastwards or weaken

AUSTRALIA

SOUTH AMERICA

Warm surface currents reverse, accumulating off South America

Cold upwelling ceases (blocked by warm water)

▲ **Figure 17:** El Niño

- During El Niño, the trade winds weaken, stop or even reverse in the western Pacific.
- The piled up warmer water around Australasia makes its way back eastwards across the Pacific, leading to a 30 cm rise in sea level around Peru. This prevents the usual cold upwelling.
- As a result, there is more warm water over the coast of Peru leading to rising air and low pressure. The water becomes 6–8°C warmer in the eastern Pacific.
- Peru would therefore experience more rainfall than normal.
- In Australasia, however, the water becomes cooler and there is less air rising resulting in high pressure and stable, dry conditions.

What happens during La Niña?

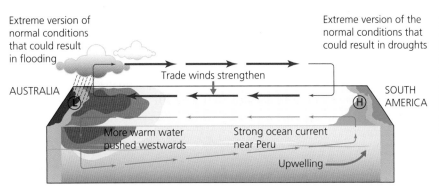

Extreme version of normal conditions that could result in flooding

Extreme version of the normal conditions that could result in droughts

Trade winds strengthen

AUSTRALIA

SOUTH AMERICA

More warm water pushed westwards

Strong ocean current near Peru

Upwelling

▲ **Figure 18:** La Niña

A La Niña event may, but does not always, follow an El Niño event. La Niña refers to unusually cold sea surface temperatures (3–5°C colder) found in the eastern tropical Pacific. Broadly speaking, the impacts of La Niña are the opposite of El Niño, where Australia would experience **droughts** during El Niño, there could be increased risk of flooding during La Niña. Likewise, Peru could experience droughts during La Niña. La Niña could also be described as a more exaggerated version of a normal year in the Pacific Ocean.

El Niño and La Niña are among the most powerful phenomena on Earth, affecting climate across more than half of the planet. Their consequences are, in fact, global.

How do we know if it is an El Niño year?

Many techniques have been used to identify and predict the occurrence of El Niño.

- Better satellite coverage looking for oceanic patterns.
- Design of buoys has improved. They can now measure sea surface temperatures, surface winds, air temperature and humidity.
- Buoys can be used in mid-ocean or in shallow water and can remain active for one year.
- Buoys transmit to weather forecasting systems, sometimes every hour.
- Sea levels around the world can be measured and recorded.
- Biological recordings. For example, during El Niño, phytoplankton does not grow as there is no upwelling of cold water in the eastern Pacific.

Activities

1. Spot the difference! What are the key differences between the three weather patterns? Use the following table design to help to structure your notes.

	Normal Year	El Niño	La Niña
High pressure			
Low pressure			
Rainfall			
Flooding			
Droughts			
Trade winds			

→ Take it further

2. Represent the information about a normal year, El Niño and La Niña in a flow diagram.

▲ **Figure 19:** Satellite image of Typhoon Haiyan approaching the Philippines

Tropical storms are found:

● over tropical and sub-tropical waters between 5° and 30° north and south of the Equator
● where the temperature of the surface layer of ocean water is in excess of 26.5°C and at a depth of at least 50–60 m
● at least 500 km away from the Equator where the **Coriolis effect**, or force, is strong enough to make the weather system spin.

Tip

There are many specific facts on this page. Using these numbers makes your answers more precise and accurate. In reference to the formation of a tropical storm, rather than saying 'the water needs to be warm and the sea fairly deep', say 'sea temperatures need to be approximately 26°C and the ocean depth 50–60 metres'.

Tropical storms: what, where and when?

What is a tropical storm?

A **tropical storm** begins as a low-pressure system originating in the tropics, known as a tropical depression, and can develop into a tropical cyclone (also known as a hurricane or typhoon). It is a circular storm originating over warm water and is characterised by high winds and heavy rain. A tropical storm has maximum wind speeds ranging from 63 kilometres per hour to 118 kilometres per hour. When wind speeds are in excess of 119 kilometres per hour, the storm becomes a tropical cyclone.

Tropical cyclones are known by different terms depending on where they are in the world:

● In the north Atlantic Ocean and east Pacific they are known as hurricanes. An example is Hurricane Katrina in 2005, which caused the death of 1836 people and led to 80 per cent of the city of New Orleans being under water.
● In the northwest Pacific, they are known as typhoons. In November 2013, Typhoon Haiyan (see Figure 19) hit the Philippines as well as southern China and Vietnam. It was one of the strongest tropical cyclones ever recorded, affecting 11 million people and causing US$2.86 billion of economic damage.
● The term 'tropical cyclone' is most frequently used in the northern Indian Ocean, around countries like Bangladesh. In May 2008, Cyclone Nargis made landfall, causing the worst natural disaster in the history of Myanmar. More than 138,000 people lost their lives, many of whom lived on the densely populated Irrawaddy Delta.

Where in the world do tropical storms occur?

Tropical storms are found in very specific parts of the world, from the Gulf Coast of North America to the northwest of Australia, and from the Indian Ocean island of Mauritius to Bangladesh (Figure 20).

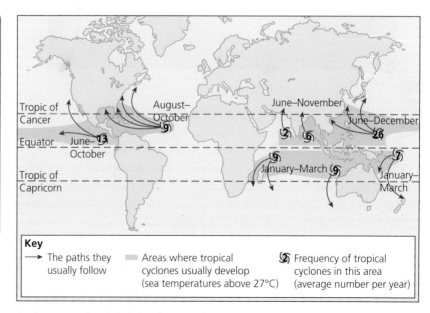

▲ **Figure 20:** The global distribution of tropical storms

How does the Coriolis effect help in the formation of tropical storms?

Notice how the clouds form a swirling, circular pattern in Figure 19. This is the result of the Coriolis effect, which acts on winds because the Earth is spinning. Pilots flying long distances have to alter their flight path to allow for the Coriolis effect. The Earth spins faster at the Equator because it is wider than it is at the poles. In the northern hemisphere, winds are deflected to the right and in the southern hemisphere winds are deflected to the left (see Figure 21).

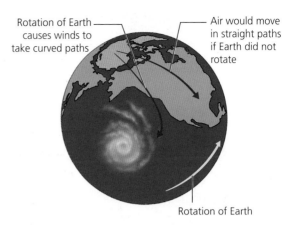

▲ **Figure 21:** Model of the Coriolis effect

What causes a tropical storm?

The conditions need to be perfect for a tropical storm to form. There needs to be a movement in the air near the surface of the water. In the troposphere, the temperatures need to cool quickly enough for tall clouds to form through condensation. The wind speeds need to change slowly with height. If the speeds are greater in the upper atmosphere, the storm could be sliced in two. Fuelled by the warm ocean, water vapour is evaporated. As warm, moist air rises it expands, cools and condenses to form the clouds. It maintains its strength as long as it remains over warm water.

Wind speeds increase towards the centre of the storm, around the eyewall (see Figure 22). This is typically 15–30 kilometres from the centre of the storm. Deep clouds rise from the Earth's surface up to a height of 15,000 metres. This, combined with the heaviest rainfall, makes the eyewall the most destructive and dangerous part of the storm.

When the vertical winds reach the top of the troposphere at 16 kilometres the air flows outwards, deflected by the Coriolis effect.

Inside the eye of the storm is a different story. Wind speeds decrease rapidly and the air is calm. There is a central area of clear skies, warm temperatures and low pressure (typically 960 millibars).

You can recreate the Coriolis effect on a merry-go-round on a children's playground. While standing at the edge of a spinning merry-go-round, try throwing a ball towards the centre and see how it deflects to the left or right.

Tip

Practise being able to reproduce models and diagrams from memory. Study a diagram for one minute, then look away and draw everything you can remember. Study the diagram again and add details that you did not remember. Keep practising until you can reproduce a diagram, map or model confidently without looking.

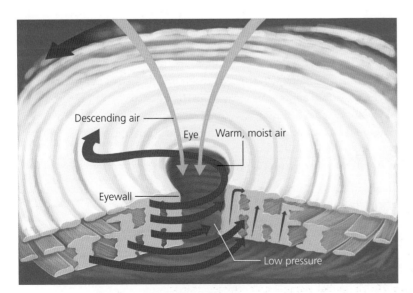

▲ **Figure 22:** Cross section of a tropical storm

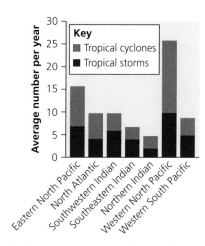

▲ **Figure 23:** Frequency of tropical storms and cyclones

How frequently do tropical storms occur?

Tropical oceans generate approximately 80 storms per year. The greatest number is in the Pacific Ocean, followed by the Indian Ocean and the Atlantic ranking third (Figure 23). The most powerful storms occur in the western Pacific. Tropical storms occur every year during the late summer months from June to November in the northern hemisphere and from November to April in the southern hemisphere.

Has their frequency changed over time?

The number of storms in the Atlantic has increased since 1995, but there is no obvious global trend. There is, however, some evidence to suggest that they are becoming more intense. It has been calculated that the energy released by the average hurricane has increased by 70 per cent in the past 30 years.

During El Niño, winds high over the Atlantic tend to be stronger than normal. This change in the vertical differences of wind speeds decreases hurricane activity as the storm is likely to be torn apart. Elsewhere, more tropical storms occur in the eastern part of the South Pacific during El Niño and less during La Niña.

Scientists are in disagreement about whether climate change has made tropical storms more frequent. Chapter 3 has more information on the impacts of climate change.

Activities

1. Annotate a blank map of the world with:
   a. The locations in which tropical cyclones occur.
   b. The names of tropical cyclones in different parts of the world.
   c. The months in which they occur.
2. Why might tropical storms be more frequent in particular months?
3. Using Figure 22 to help you, work in pairs to create a model of a tropical storm. Consider using materials such as card, sticky notes and cotton wool. Make sure your model has clear labels.
4. When does a tropical storm become a tropical cyclone? Choose your answer from the list below.
   a. When the water depth is less than 50 metres.
   b. When the sustained wind speeds reach 63 kilometres per hour.
   c. When it is 500 kilometres away from the Equator.
   d. When it reaches land.
5. Explain in the form of a recipe how a tropical storm develops. What are the key ingredients and processes?
6. Has the frequency of tropical storms changed over time?

→ Take it further

7. To what extent are the data on tropical storm frequency from 1995 reliable?
8. Why are tropical storms often given names? Find out if there is a tropical storm (or hurricane; cyclone or typhoon) in *your* name. When was it? Did it cause a lot of damage?

Droughts: what, where and when?

What is a 'drought'?

Defining a drought is not easy as it can vary from place to place. They develop slowly and it can take weeks, months or even years for the full effects to appear. In some places a drought might be declared after as few as fifteen days! In general, a drought occurs when a region experiences below average precipitation. It is a period of time with abnormally dry weather leading to a shortage of water, which can have a negative effect on vegetation, animals and people over a large area.

Where in the world do droughts occur?

Recent severe droughts have occurred around the world in countries including Australia, Brazil, China, India, parts of the USA and Mexico, as well as the Sahel region of Africa (Figure 25). Large parts of these countries and regions already have a dry climate and receive low amounts of rainfall per year, so a period of time with less rainfall than usual can have a significant impact on the people and the environment. Less typical places, such as the tropical Amazon basin, can also experience drought if they receive significantly less rainfall than usual over a long period of time. Figure 26 summarises some of the key drought events of the 2000s.

▲ **Figure 24:** Dry lake bed in São Paulo, 17 October 2014

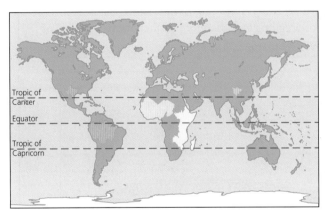

▲ **Figure 25:** Location of key drought events in the 2000s

✝ Geographical skills

You will often be required to deconstruct, interpret, analyse and evaluate visual images such as photographs. Look at Figure 24. What question could you ask to the man in the photo that would help you to interpret the situation?

When?	Where?	What?
2002–2005	Amazon Basin, South America	• Parts of the basin experienced the worst drought in 100 years. • Towns lacked food, medicine and fuel as there was no access for boats. • The drought affected 1.9 million km² of rainforest. • 5 gigatons of carbon was released into the atmosphere as a result of dead trees fuelling forest fires. Usually, the Amazon actually absorbs 1.5 gigatons of carbon in a typical year.
2006	Sichuan Province, China	• 37.5 million people were affected. • Nearly 8 million people faced water shortages. • 129 million livestock died.
2010–2013	Texas, USA	• 2011 was the driest year in the state's history. • By 2013, 95% of the state was dealing with drought. • $5.2 billion in agricultural losses.
2011	East Africa including Somalia, Ethiopia, Kenya, Eritrea, Djibouti and South Sudan	• Caused by falling rains – the area received 30% less rain than the average. • 50,000 to 100,000 deaths. • 12 million people in need of food aid. • Crop failures and livestock deaths. • Increases in malaria and measles.
2012	Western Sahel including Niger, Mali, Mauritania and Burkina Faso	• 10 million people at risk of famine after a month-long heatwave. • Over 50% of the crop yield was lost.

▲ **Figure 26:** A summary of key drought events in the 2000s

What causes a drought?

The physical causes:

- Most droughts occur when the regular weather patterns have been disturbed. There might be an above average presence of dry, high-pressure systems.
- El Niño brings descending air and high pressure over Indonesia and Australia, leading to drought (see pages 8–9).
- As global temperatures increase, more water is needed to grow crops and more water is lost through evaporation.
- The **intertropical convergence zone** (ITCZ) has been linked the occurrence of drought, particularly in Africa.

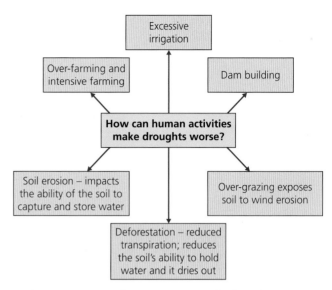

▲ **Figure 27:** How can human activities make droughts worse?

What is the intertropical convergence zone (ITCZ)?

The ITCZ is a low-pressure belt which encircles the globe around the Equator. It is where the trade winds from the northeast and southeast meet. The Earth is tilted on its orbit around the Sun, causing the ITCZ to migrate between the Tropics of Cancer and Capricorn with the seasons (Figure 28). Around 20 June each year, the Sun is overhead at the Tropic of Cancer and around 20 December each year, the Sun is overhead at the Tropic of Capricorn.

Winds and pressure are shifted annually from north to south. The point where the two trade winds meet at the ITCZ results in heavy precipitation and thunderstorms as hot, dry air and warm, moist air combines. Consequently, Africa has parts of the continent that are in a cycle of dry and wet seasons.

In some years, the ITCZ might not move as far northwards or southwards to reach some of the driest areas, and so not relieve them of the dry conditions they have experienced for half of the year. Local people in those regions may therefore be faced with a period of drought.

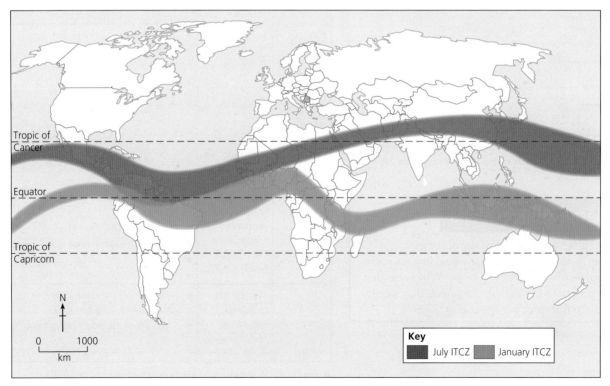

▲ **Figure 28:** The location of equatorial and tropical low-pressure systems (ITCZ)

How frequent are droughts?

Many regions of the world, such as California in the USA, experience drought every year. A report by NASA in 2013 predicted that warmer worldwide temperatures will lead to decreased rainfall and more droughts in some parts of the world.

At a national scale, the Met Office has conducted a study on how climate change could affect the frequency of drought in the UK. The worst case scenario predicts that extreme drought could happen once every decade, making them ten times more frequent than they are today.

'Severe droughts such as the one seen in 1976 have a big impact – causing water shortages, health risks, fire hazards, crop failure and subsidence. Understanding how the frequency of these events will change is therefore very important to planning for the future.'

Eleanor Burke, Climate Extremes Scientist, Met Office.

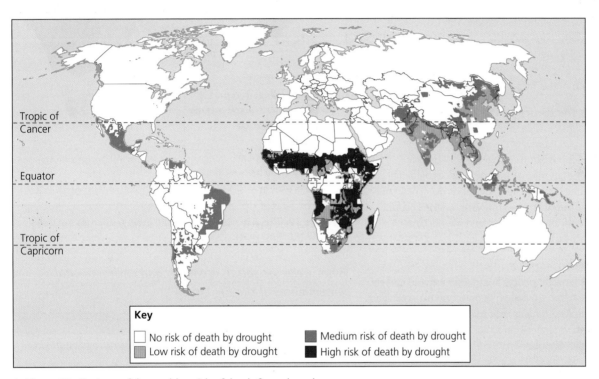

Key

☐ No risk of death by drought   ▨ Medium risk of death by drought
▨ Low risk of death by drought   ■ High risk of death by drought

▲ **Figure 29:** Regions of the world at risk of death from drought

Activities

1. Describe the physical processes that are responsible for drought.
2. Referring to Figure 29, describe the distribution of the risk of death by drought.
3. Working in groups, use a piece of string and sticky notes to create a giant timeline of droughts in the 2000s across your table.
   a. Use the information from Figure 26 (page 13) to add key facts from each drought event.
   b. Research three to five more drought events that have occurred since 2000 and add them to your timeline.

4. Compare your timeline to Figure 29. Which places experience drought but are not at risk of death? Why is this?

→ Take it further

5. Read the quote from the climate scientist above. What happened in 1976? Think like a geographer! Why is it so important for you to study extreme weather events?

Case study: When does extreme weather become a hazard?

The 'Big Dry' – is El Niño to blame for Australia's drought issues?

Which regions of Australia are affected by drought?

Australia is part of the driest inhabited continent and has lived with drought throughout its history. From 2002 to 2009 it experienced the driest period in 125 years, which became known as the Big Dry.

Australia is drought prone because of its geography and changeable rainfall patterns. Australia is located in a sub-tropical area of the world that experiences dry, sinking air leading to clear skies and little rain. For most of the country, rainfall is low and irregular. In 2006, the annual rainfall was 40–60 per cent below normal over most of Australia south of the Tropic of Capricorn.

What were the causes of the Big Dry?

El Niño

When El Niño is present (see pages 8–9), Australia becomes drier than normal and the chances of rainfall decrease. During El Niño, the trade winds over the Pacific Ocean that normally bring warm water weaken, causing the water to cool and the rainfall to diminish. Eastern Australia thus heats up and gets drier.

Other causes

In Australia, 23 million people live in a similar land area to the USA, which has 320 million people. This may not seem like a high number, but it cannot maintain its current population growth in relation to access to water, making the country overpopulated.

Eastern Australia is home to the Murray–Darling river basin. The Murray River is the longest river in Australia, draining an area the size of France and Spain combined! The river basin covers part of New South Wales, Victoria, Queensland and South Australia. The basin is home to two million people and is under a lot of pressure to provide the water needed to support agricultural production in the region. 40 per cent of Australia's agricultural produce comes from this region and it contains 70 per cent of irrigated cropland and pasture.

Tip

The Geographical Exploration exam requires you to carry out a decision-making exercise. Practise this skill using the drought in Australia case study.

1. Outline the social and economic impacts of drought in Australia.

2. Propose the best response to drought in Australia from Figure 32 and justify how the response would help people in Australia in the long term. [12 marks]

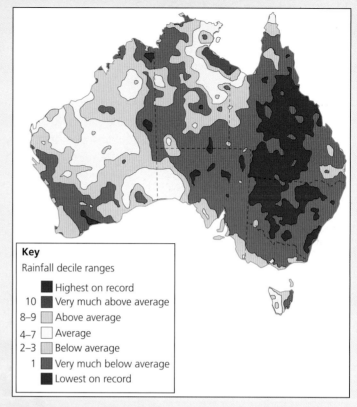

Key

Rainfall decile ranges

	Highest on record
10	Very much above average
8–9	Above average
4–7	Average
2–3	Below average
1	Very much below average
	Lowest on record

▲ **Figure 30:** The distribution of rainfall averages across Australia, 2002–03 (El Niño year)

What were the social, economic and environmental consequences of the Big Dry?

	Consequences
SOCIAL	● People in rural areas left due to a lack of water, putting greater pressure on the population of cities. ● Rural suicide rates soared.
ECONOMIC	● Farmers had to sell cattle as they could not afford to feed them. ● Food prices rose as Australia became more dependent on imports. ● Water bills rose 20% in 2008. ● Tourism was negatively affected. ● Agricultural production was severely affected. ● 10,000 people directly employed by the cotton-growing industry were affected. ● The number of dairy farms reduced by more than half.
ENVIRONMENTAL	● Loss of vegetation, wildlife and biodiversity as well as soil erosion. As the soil dries out, it becomes looser and it is easier for the wind to blow it away. ● Grassland turned to scrubland. ● Energy from HEP was reduced leading to more pollution as Australia resorted to the use of fossil fuels. ● Water quality reduced as toxic algal outbreaks occured in depleted rivers, dams and lakes.

▲ **Figure 31:** Consequences of the Big Dry drought on people, the economy and the environment

How have different stakeholders responded to the drought problems of Australia?

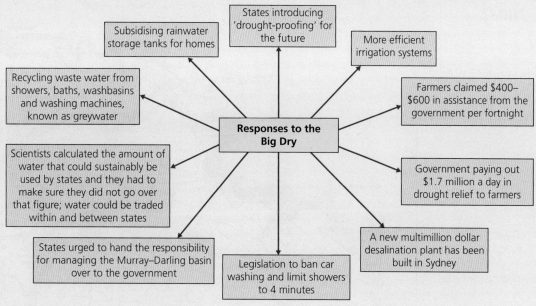

Responses to the Big Dry

- Subsidising rainwater storage tanks for homes
- States introducing 'drought-proofing' for the future
- More efficient irrigation systems
- Recycling waste water from showers, baths, washbasins and washing machines, known as greywater
- Farmers claimed $400–$600 in assistance from the government per fortnight
- Scientists calculated the amount of water that could sustainably be used by states and they had to make sure they did not go over that figure; water could be traded within and between states
- Government paying out $1.7 million a day in drought relief to farmers
- States urged to hand the responsibility for managing the Murray–Darling basin over to the government
- Legislation to ban car washing and limit showers to 4 minutes
- A new multimillion dollar desalination plant has been built in Sydney

▲ **Figure 32:** Responses to the Big Dry

The end of the drought was officially declared by the prime minister on 27 April 2012.

SIR JOSEPH BANKS DR
DESALINATION PLANT

▲ **Figure 33:** Desalination plant in Sydney

Activities

1. Using Figure 30 describe the pattern of rainfall in 2002–03.
2. In pairs, take on the role of expert geographers. Create a news bulletin that explains how El Niño causes droughts in Australia. Don't forget to include diagrams, photographs and place-specific details.
3. To what extent is El Niño to blame for the problems of drought in Australia?
4. Read the information about the impacts of drought. Which do you think was the most devastating impact and why?
5. Organise the consequences of the drought into a table with two columns to show short-term (immediate) and long-term consequences.

6. Create a mind map that explains how each of the following stakeholders responded to the drought.
   - Individuals
   - Farmers
   - National government
   - Local government
   - Environmentalists
7. Where else in the world has used desalination plants in response to droughts? Why are they located in these places?

→ Take it further

8. What is the problem with allocating an amount of water that states can use sustainably?
9. The BBC reported a story from Australia with the headline 'Australia Cyclone Yasi roars into Queensland Coast'. Find the article on the internet. Using pages 10–11, suggest why Australia was experiencing cyclones rather than floods.

Case study: When does extreme weather become a hazard?

Why did Boscastle experience a flash flood on 16 August 2004?

Where is Boscastle?

On 16 August 2004, the idyllic Cornish village of Boscastle, on the north Cornwall coast, was transformed into a scene of utter devastation.

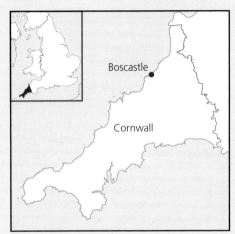

▲ **Figure 34:** Location map for Boscastle

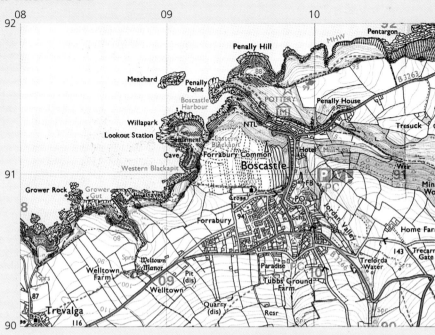

▲ **Figure 35:** Ordnance Survey map of Boscastle, scale 1:25,000 © Crown copyright OS 100036470

What happened?

A huge flash flood, consisting of two billion litres of water travelling at 65 km per hour wrecked the village at the height of the tourist season.

What were the extreme weather conditions that led to the flash flood?

A flash flood is caused by heavy or excessive rainfall in a short period of time, generally less than six hours. In the case of Boscastle, seven centimetres of rain fell in only two hours; unprecedented in the month of August. This 1-in-400 year flood event occurred as a result of a combination of exceptional circumstances, see page 19.

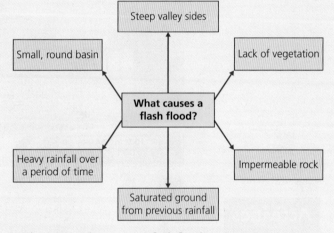

▲ **Figure 36:** What causes a flash flood?

Steep valley sides

Small, round basin

Lack of vegetation

What causes a flash flood?

Heavy rainfall over a period of time

Impermeable rock

Saturated ground from previous rainfall

◀ **Figure 37:** The scene in Boscastle the day after the flood

👣 Fieldwork ideas

- Primary data: if you have an accessible local river, collect data on the speed of the river flow. What were the limitations of your technique?
- Secondary data: use the Environment Agency website (http://watermaps.environment-agency.gov.uk) to explore your local area further. Does the river have a history of flooding?

What were the causes of the flood in Boscastle?

Physical causes:

● Torrential rain and a rising high tide caused the river levels to increase by 2.15 metres in only one hour.

● Heavy thunderstorms had developed across the southwest by midday. The unusually heavy rainfall had been linked to the remains of Hurricane Alex travelling across the Atlantic Ocean to the UK.

● At Boscastle, the high land in the area caused warm, moist air from the sea to rise rapidly. This cooled and condensed into towering cumulonimbus clouds 12,000 metres high. An estimated 1422 million litres of rain fell in two hours. This is the equivalent of nearly 570 Olympic swimming pools!

● There had been above average rainfall for the previous two weeks, which meant that the ground was already saturated (it could not absorb any more water). Any later rainfall became surface runoff, flowing straight into the rivers.

● Boscastle is at the meeting point, or confluence, of three rivers: Valency, Jordan and Paradise. Therefore, on the day of the flood, huge volumes of water from these three rivers converged at Boscastle, overwhelming the village.

● The topography had a significant part to play. The steep hillsides caused water to travel quickly to the valley floor. The valley floor is also very narrow and therefore funneled the water of the Valency and Jordan through a small area of land.

● The term 'river basin' refers to the area drained by a specific river. In the case of Boscastle, the river basin is only 23 km² which is very small.

Human causes:

● People were not to blame for the flood, but the pattern of the streets and some of the man made features of the village made it worse.

● Cars and vegetation became trapped under the low-lying bridge through the village. This acted as a dam and water quickly found an alternative route around the bridge, causing more damage to the village and its buildings.

● Old sewer systems were inefficient and quickly became overwhelmed by the volume of water.

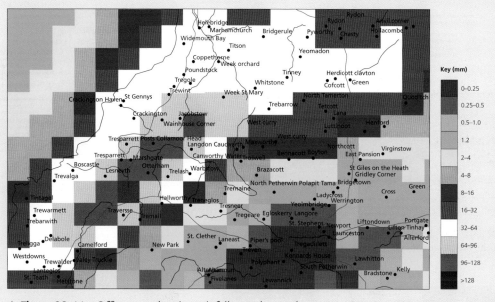

▲ **Figure 38:** Met Office map showing rainfall over the southwest on 16 August 2004

Key (mm)

	0–0.25
	0.25–0.5
	0.5–1.0
	1.2
	2–4
	4–8
	8–16
	16–32
	32–64
	64–96
	96–128
	>128

▲ **Figure 39:** Trees and debris blocked the bridge through the centre of the village

What were the social, economic and environmental consequences of the flood?

Social	Economic	Environmental
● Cars were left wrecked in the harbour or scattered throughout the village; 84 cars were recovered from the harbour and streets and 32 were never found. ● 1000 residents and tourists were affected. ● There were no major injuries or loss of life. ● 58 properties were flooded.	● 90 per cent of the economy in Boscastle is dependent on tourism. More than 20 hotels and B&Bs were forced to shut. ● Infrastructure damage to roads and services was predicted to cost North Cornwall District Council £2 billion. ● 25 businesses were destroyed. ● The Visitors Centre and Museum of Witchcraft were severely damaged.	● Four bridges were washed away. ● Trees were uprooted and carried downstream.

▲ **Figure 40:** The consequences of the flooding for people, the economy and the environment

How did different stakeholders respond to the flood?

▲ **Figure 41:** Rescue operation in the hours following the flood

Seven helicopters from the RAF and Royal Navy were used in the rescue operation, the largest joint rescue since 1979. People found their way to the roofs of buildings, awaiting rescue. In total, 120 people were winched to safety. Rescue efforts were hampered by heavy rain and lightning.

Shop owners and residents used sandbags to keep as much water out of buildings as possible. Local accommodation providers opened up their properties as shelter for tourists who were unable to return to their place of stay as their cars had been swept away.

Within a few days, diggers and other machinery had cleared the streets of debris and uprooted trees, and the village was also visited by the Deputy Prime Minister, John Prescott, and Prince Charles.

The Environment Agency improved flood defences, carrying out over £10 million of improvements (see Figure 42). The river channel was widened and deepened and the car park was raised in an attempt to reduce the impacts of any future flood events. A flood culvert was also installed to improve the flow of the River Jordan.

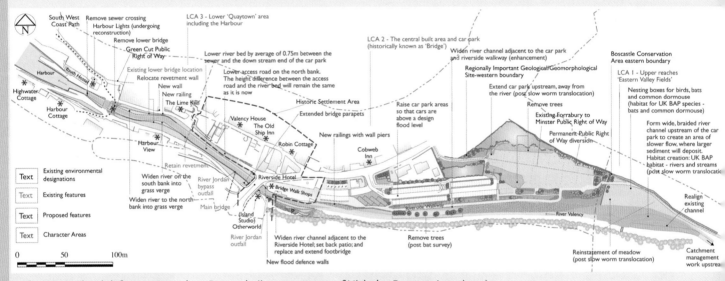

▲ **Figure 42:** Flood defence proposals at Boscastle (image courtesy of Nicholas Pearson Associates)

✝ Geographical skills

Draw a sketch map to show the case study location. Draw a frame in which to produce your sketch. Draw the outlines of the location as if you are looking down on the location.

Add the following features to your map:

- River Valency and River Jordan
- The main road, B3263
- The Witchcraft Museum
- Boscastle Harbour

Annotate your map with the physical and human causes of the flash flood. These could be colour coded.

Activities

1. Describe the weather conditions on the day of the flood.
2. Assess the causes of the Boscastle flood against the six causes of flash floods in Figure 36 (page 18). Why was a flash flood at Boscastle inevitable on that day?
3. Describe how human activity made the flooding worse.
4. Create a mind map for each of the stakeholders who responded to the flood and explain how they helped. Colour code each explanation according to whether it was a short-term or long-term response.

Case study: When does extreme weather become a hazard?

Was there really a heatwave in the UK in summer 2015?

In the UK, a **heatwave** is defined by the Met Office as when daily maximum temperatures exceed the average by 5°C for more than five consecutive days. In 2015 there was a heatwave in the UK at the end of June and the beginning of July, when temperatures were hotter than they were in Rome and Athens. This was considered as the second heatwave in just a few weeks. On 1 July 2015 temperatures hit 36.7°C at Heathrow, making it the highest July temperature on record in the UK.

What extreme weather conditions caused this event?

As you can see from Figure 43, there was a low-pressure system over the west of the UK and high pressure across Europe and the UK. A heatwave had already been declared in Spain. This allowed light, southerly winds to draw in hot air from the high-pressure system dominating parts of central and southern Europe. The result was sweltering heat in the UK. The heatwave ended with thunder and lightning storms that delivered more than half a month's worth of rain in an hour to parts of Dorset and East Anglia.

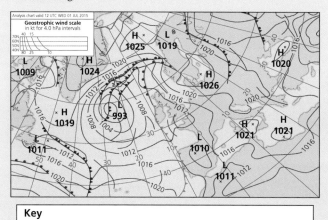

Key
- ● Warm front
- ▲ Cold front
- ●▲ Occluded front

▲ **Figure 43:** Synoptic chart for 1200 GMT 1 July 2015 showing high pressure over Europe

What were the positive and negative consequences of the heatwave?

As this was a heatwave with a very short duration – only a few days – the impacts were relatively limited. However, there were both positive and negative consequences of the unusually high temperatures.

- Wimbledon spectators were advised to wear hats to protect themselves from the heat.
- Some schools cancelled their sports day.
- Struggling train services and heavy traffic on the roads as road and train track surfaces began to melt in the heat.
- Car breakdown 'call outs' were up 14 per cent due to overheating cars.
- Retailers reported a 1300 per cent increase in the sale of fans compared with the same time in the previous year; barbeque sales were up 67 per cent and sunglasses up 39 per cent.

How did people respond to the heatwave?

- Network Rail set speed restrictions on lines that were vulnerable to buckling in the heat.
- Virgin Trains cancelled 20 trains.
- A health alert known as a Level 3 'heatwave action' was issued by the government.
- 999 calls doubled in one day, particularly those involving the elderly.

Activities

1. Using page 3 and Figure 43, suggest which extreme weather conditions caused the UK heatwave in July 2015.
2. How would the impacts have been different if the heatwave had continued for:
   a. a further week
   b. two months?

◀ **Figure 44:** Brighton beach was packed with sunbathers during the July 2015 heatwave

Case study: When does extreme weather become a hazard?

Super Typhoon Haiyan: a physical or human disaster?

What happened?

Typhoon Haiyan hit the southeast coast of the Philippines with winds of up to 195 mph recorded on 8 November 2013. It was the strongest tropical typhoon on record and was classed as a **super typhoon**. The regions of Leyte, Tacloban and Samar were hit first before the storm continued on its journey westwards through six central Philippines islands before weakening into a tropical storm as it reached Vietnam and southern China (Figures 45 and 46).

Super typhoons

A super typhoon is defined by the National Oceanic and Atmospheric Administration (NOAA) as a typhoon that has sustained winds speeds of more than 150 mph for at least one minute.

What were the causes of Typhoon Haiyan?

The Philippines is an **emerging and developing country (EDC)** that experiences an average of 20 typhoons each year. It is made up of 7000 islands in the middle of one of the most disaster-prone regions on Earth.

The key ingredients needed for the formation of a tropical storm are present in this region (see page 11). The Philippines are vulnerable to typhoons because of the vast expanse of warm water and the large number of small islands, which are not concentrated enough to slow the pace of a typhoon. Furthermore, there is low wind shear, keeping the structure of the typhoon intact. Typhoon Haiyan caused a 5 m storm surge with waves up to 15 m high. It was so large in diameter that it affected two-thirds of the country, which stretches more than 1850 km. Some scientists attributed the typhoon to global warming as a result of increased sea levels and ocean temperatures.

There is no doubt that this typhoon was exceptional in its scale and intensity. However, the impacts were worsened by the level of development of the country. Much of the population live in extreme poverty and there has been rapid population growth, particularly in vulnerable coastal areas. Buildings are poorly constructed, as are the storm shelters. In Tacloban alone, the population had grown from 76,000 to 221,000 in the space of just 40 years.

What were the social, economic and environmental consequences of the typhoon?

There was catastrophic damage throughout much of the island of Leyte, with cities and towns destroyed. There were fears of flash floods and landslides as a result of the 400 mm of rain delivered by the typhoon. The UN was very concerned about the risk of rising death tolls through secondary causes: a lack of medical care and food, and diseases spreading following the disaster. The people who survived the typhoon itself were at risk of dying by other means that were inherently linked to the economic status of the country.

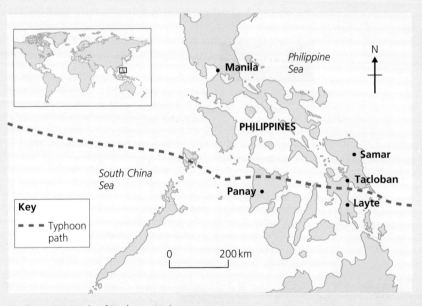

▲ **Figure 45:** Path of Typhoon Haiyan

When?	Where?
2 November 2013	Started from an area of low pressure several hundred kilometres east-southeast of Micronesia
4 November 2013	Tracked westwards, becoming a tropical storm; given the name Haiyan
5 November 2013	By 6 pm it was classed as a typhoon
6 November 2013	Assessed as a super typhoon, the equivalent of a Category 5 on the Saffir–Simpson Scale
8 November 2013	Made landfall, hitting the coastal region of Guiuan in eastern Samar
10 November 2013	Struck northern Vietnam as a severe tropical storm

▲ **Figure 46:** Timeline for Typhoon Haiyan

The Philippines is still heavily reliant on **primary industries** (industries that collect raw materials from the land and sea): the country is the world's biggest producer of coconut oil. However, many coconut plantations were levelled by the typhoon. Thousands of hectares of rice were also destroyed, as were fishing boats.

Key impacts

→ 11.5 million people affected (ten per cent of the population)

→ Estimated economic damage of $2.86 billion

→ At least 6300 dead and a large number missing

→ 670,000 people made homeless (55 per cent living in evacuation shelters)

→ $85 million lost from farm damage

→ 130,000 tonnes of rice destroyed

→ 90 per cent of the houses in Tacloban were destroyed or damaged

→ 130,000 houses were destroyed.

How did different stakeholders respond to the typhoon?

● The region was still recovering from an earthquake in October 2013, which killed 222 people and injured 1000, when the typhoon struck. The British charity ShelterBox was already in the region and provided people with water purification equipment, blankets, cooking implements and solar-powered lights.
● 1215 evacuation centres were set up.
● Britain sent *HMS Daring* as part of the emergency response.
● Widespread looting and violence in Tacloban led the government to deploy soldiers to restore law and order.
● The UN and countries such as the UK, Australia, Japan and the USA donated millions of pounds and sent medical teams. The UK government alone donated £50 million.
● The Philippine Red Cross delivered basic food aid including rice, canned goods, sugar and cooking oil.

Various factors made the relief effort challenging. The damage to roads and infrastructure hindered the distribution of aid. Heavy rain persistently hampered rescue attempts. Due to the number of small islands, it was difficult to assess the damage and to determine which communities were most in need of help. Helicopters were used to survey these areas as they could not be reached easily by relief teams.

Activities

1. On a blank map of the South East Asia region, label the countries and islands affected by the typhoon. Annotate the map with information about the track of the typhoon.
2. Study Figure 47. What would the place have looked like one year before the photo was taken? What would it look like one year after?
3. Categorise the consequences into social, economic and environmental impacts.
4. Give an example of long-term and short-term aid given to the people of the Philippines, and explain how it helps.
5. Why was Typhoon Haiyan so devastating?

→ Take it further

6. Why do you think the impacts of Typhoon Haiyan were less severe in Vietnam and China?

▲ **Figure 47:** The aftermath of Typhoon Haiyan in the port city of Tacloban

CHAPTER 2

How do plate tectonics shape our world?

What is going on in the Earth beneath our feet?

No matter where you are on Earth, you are affected by what is happening beneath your feet, from the Earth's crust to its core. The Earth is made up of a number of different layers. You could compare the structure of the Earth with that of an egg which has a yolk, white and shell. The Earth has the **core**, **mantle** and **crust**. These layers behave in different ways and are formed from different materials.

At the core of our planet, temperatures can rise as high as 6000°C. This is the same temperature as the surface of the Sun. Figure 1 shows the structure of the Earth in more detail.

The core is the hottest part of the Earth. Heat energy is **radiated** outwards from the super-hot core to the Earth's surface, with heat energy spreading out through the mantle, where it creates the molten magma.

If you've ever seen a road being laid with tarmac, you will have some idea of the consistency of magma. The hot magma churns around in the mantle due to a process called **convection**. This is the same process that happens in a pan of boiling water; the water at the bottom is heated by the hob and rises through the pan, as hot material is less dense than cooler material. In the Earth, the mantle is heated by the core and the heated magma rises towards the crust. Here it begins to cool, so it becomes more dense and sinks again. Once it reaches the core, it is reheated and the process repeats to continuously churn and move mantle magma around. This is illustrated in Figure 1b. These convection currents are responsible for forcing the floating **tectonic plates** to move, due to the friction of the plates upon the magma.

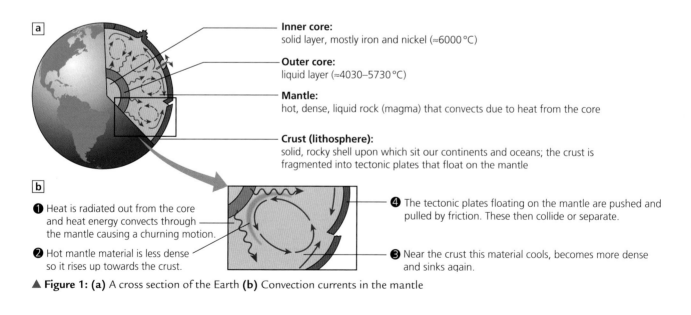

a

Inner core:
solid layer, mostly iron and nickel (≈6000 °C)

Outer core:
liquid layer (≈4030–5730 °C)

Mantle:
hot, dense, liquid rock (magma) that convects due to heat from the core

Crust (lithosphere):
solid, rocky shell upon which sit our continents and oceans; the crust is fragmented into tectonic plates that float on the mantle

b

❶ Heat is radiated out from the core and heat energy convects through the mantle causing a churning motion.

❷ Hot mantle material is less dense so it rises up towards the crust.

❹ The tectonic plates floating on the mantle are pushed and pulled by friction. These then collide or separate.

❸ Near the crust this material cools, becomes more dense and sinks again.

▲ **Figure 1: (a)** A cross section of the Earth **(b)** Convection currents in the mantle

How do tectonic plates move?

The surface of the Earth (the crust) is relatively thin compared with the entire depth of the Earth (the crust is between 10 and 100 km in thickness). We can compare it with a loaf of bread: there is a thin, cracked crust over the surface of the thicker, denser bread inside.

The Earth's crust is broken up into seven large sections and 12 smaller sections, which are called tectonic plates. There are two types of plate: the heavy, dense **oceanic** plates and the lighter, less dense **continental** plates.

● Oceanic crust (plate) is found beneath our oceans and is between 5 km and 10 km thick. Example: the Pacific Plate.

● Continental crust is found beneath our land and is between 25 km and 100 km thick. Example: the North American plate.

The plates are moving constantly due to the convection currents in the mantle. The hot liquid mantle creates friction against the underneath of the plates, which in turn either pushes plates forward or drags them backward depending on the direction of convection beneath. This has been happening for millions of years. As a result, the relative positions of the plates are very different today from where they were in the past. This process of plates moving over time, causing the changing relative positions of the continents, is called **continental drift**.

A **plate boundary** is where two (or more) plates meet. Different hazards, landforms and features can be found at different plate boundaries. Some plates move towards each other (destructive or collision), some move away from each other (constructive) and some slide past each other (conservative). Figure 2 shows the location of these plates on the Earth.

Activities

1. What is continental drift and why does it occur? Draw a diagram to explain your answer.
2. Study Figure 2.
   a) Which places in the world have the most rapid plate movement?
   b) Where are destructive plate boundaries mostly found?

→ **Take it further**

3. Research evidence for continental drift. Rank this evidence in terms of what you think is most reliable to least reliable.

Mount Everest, created by collision plates in the Himalayas, is 8848 m tall. How many times would you have to climb the stairs in your school to reach the height of Everest? How long would it take?

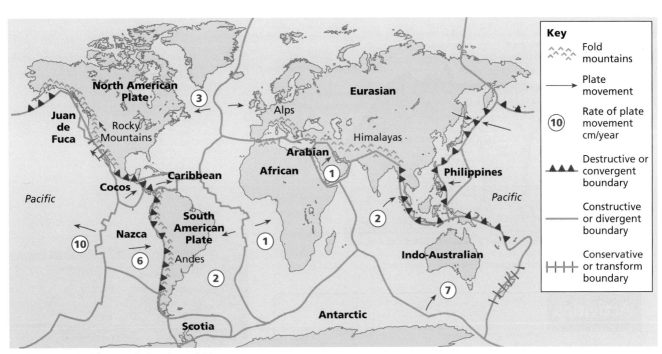

▲ **Figure 2:** World map of plate boundaries

What happens at the battleground where plates meet?

Tectonic plates are always on the move in different directions. Some move towards each other, others move away and some slide alongside each other. Each plate boundary behaves differently and causes different **landforms** and **hazards** for that place.

Figure 3 shows that there are four main types of plate boundary.

Type of margin: destructive boundary (also called convergent)

Description of plate movement: two plates push together or converge and, when they do, land is destroyed. Denser plates (oceanic) will **subduct**, meaning they sink below less dense (continental) plates.

What hazards are created and how: as the denser plate sinks into the mantle it rubs and causes friction, which melts the plate and creates magma. This can lead to volcanic eruptions as the magma reaches the surface as lava. Earthquakes are also felt due to the stress caused by the friction of the plates. Example: eruptions from Mount Pinatubo in 1991 caused global temperatures to drop by 1°C.

Example: Philippine (oceanic) plate and Eurasian (continental)

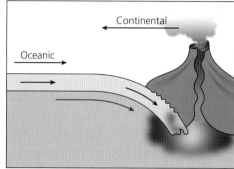

Destructive (convergent) boundary
When a heavier oceanic plate meets a lighter continental plate, it is forced to subduct (sink) into the mantle, which causes friction as the plates rub and leads to melting and the creation of volcanic ridges.

Type of margin: collision zone (also a convergent destructive boundary)

Description of plate movement: two plates push together or converge, but they are both the same density (for example, both are continental), so they just collide and push up against each other (there is no subduction).

What hazards are created and how: the collision causes land to squeeze upwards and fold mountains to form, like the Himalayas, as the ground buckles and reshapes under pressure. Severe earthquakes can occur in the process. Example: Nepal earthquake in 2015.

Example: Himalayas

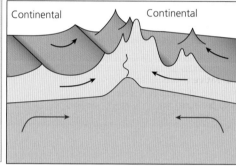

Collision (convergent) boundary
If two continental plates collide, neither one will subduct since they are both the same density. Instead, the plates push together and are forced upwards, creating fold mountains such as the Himalayas.

▲ **Figure 3:** Types of plate boundary

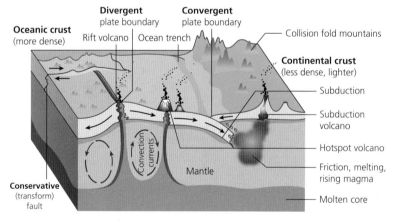

▲ **Figure 4:** Convection currents drive plate movement

Activities

1. Explain what convection is and how it drives plate movement.
2. Study Figures 1a, 1b on page 24 and Figure 4. Create a step-by-step diagram or flowchart using key terms to explain why plates move.

▲ **Figure 5:** Iceland – a land on two continents

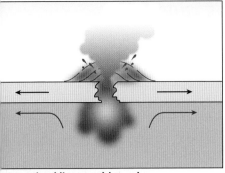

Type of margin: constructive boundary (also called divergent)

Description of plate movement: plates are separating by moving away from each other.

What hazards are created and how: as plates move apart, magma from the mantle can reach the surface and erupt through **fissures** and **faults** (splits in the ground that allow magma to vent out) causing volcanoes and creating new land as lava emerges and spreads out. Example: Eyjafjallajokull eruption in 2010.

Example: Iceland, Mid-Atlantic Ridge (see Figure 5)

Constructive (divergent) boundary
When two tectonic plates are pulled in opposite directions, this divergence allows magma from the mantle to reach the Earth's surface through spreading volcanic ridges.

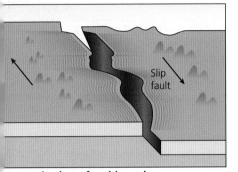

Slip fault

Type of margin: conservative boundary (also called transform)

Description of plate movement: plates slide past each other slowly. The plates may be moving in the same direction but at different speeds, or moving parallel to each other but in opposite directions.

What hazards are created and how: as the plates move past each other, their rough edges snag and stick like Velcro, which causes friction and stress to build up until one plate 'snaps' and jolts forward. This causes violent earthquakes and some rifts in the land. Example: Lake Kivu earthquake in 2008.

Examples: East Africa Rift or San Andreas Fault, California, USA.

Conservative (transform) boundary
As two plates 'slip' past each other they will snag and build up pressure until they finally jolt past each other, creating earthquakes and rifts in the Earth's surface.

Activities

1. Draw and annotate a comic strip that shows each of the four plate boundaries in action.
2. Look back at Figure 2 on page 25. Try to identify where earthquakes and volcanoes are most likely to be found. Describe the distribution, for example, 'Tectonic hazards occur in bands that follow the edges of ...'
3. Explain why volcanic activity is not found at conservative plate boundaries.
4. Copy and complete the following paragraph: Destructive plate boundaries cause _____ because the movement of plates allows _____ to reach the surface. _____ plate is denser than _____ plate and so it is forced to sink or _____. The plates rub to cause _____ and this melts the _____ and can lead to volcanic _____. At _____ plate boundaries you only find earthquakes.

Constructive boundaries allow _____ to reach the surface when the plates _____ from each other. Mountains are formed by _____ boundaries when plates do not sink and just _____ up together.

5. Use an atlas or the internet to research an example location for each of the four plate boundaries. What landforms can you see here? What risks are there? Why do people live there? For example, in Indonesia, locals use the sulphur from Kaweh Ijen for mining.
6. How can Iceland be part of two continents? Analyse Figure 5 and the map in Figure 2 (page 25) to make suggestions for this and explain why Iceland is so volcanic.

→ Take it further

7. Use www.discover-geography.co.uk to find out about tourism and living in volcanic areas. How sustainable is living in Iceland or the Azores?

▲ **Figure 6:** Earthquake damage in Morocco

How does plate movement cause earthquakes?

What is an earthquake?

An earthquake is a violent shaking of the Earth's crust. Earthquakes can cause vast damage and loss of life and are very difficult to predict.

What causes earthquakes?

On pages 24–25 we saw that plate movement is driven by convection within the Earth's mantle and that there are four key types of plate boundary: constructive, destructive, collision and conservative. Earthquakes can be found at any plate boundary, as any time the ground deforms and moves (like for a volcanic eruption) it will create earthquakes. However, conservative boundaries are the ones that cause *only* earthquakes.

Unlike climatic hazards, there is no season or time of year when earthquakes are most common. They are geological hazards created by plate movement and can occur at any time, often with very little warning. In fact, earthquakes are very difficult to predict for that reason; they do not exhibit as many signs or symptoms as volcanoes do (see page 30).

Area of greatest destruction

Damage decreasing

Damage decreasing

Seismic wave

Plate movement

Plate movement

Focus

Epicentre

Shock wave

▲ **Figure 7:** Conservative plate movement causes earthquakes

Tectonic plates are not smooth; they are jagged and rocky. Their edges grind together and stick. Think of it a little like 'Velcro'. If you try to move two pieces of Velcro across each other, they will snag and catch on each other. In the tectonic plates, this snagging creates stress and **friction** between the plates. This friction will build up until it reaches a point when the rocks can no longer cope with the stress they carry. At this point the rocks will suddenly jolt and move forward. This sudden movement is the earthquake and it releases energy through **seismic waves**, which radiate out like shockwaves through the rock. The point where the ground snaps and moves is called the **focus** and this can be at different depths within the plate. If an earthquake has a shallow focus, it means that it occurs quite close to the Earth's surface and is therefore likely to cause more surface damage. A deep-focus earthquake may cause less damage because the energy has to travel further before reaching the surface (think of it as being cushioned). The point on the surface of the land directly above the focus is called the **epicentre**. This is the place on the surface of the Earth where the earthquake is felt at its strongest (see Figure 7).

The seismic energy is concentrated at the focus and then radiates outward in waves, getting weaker as it gets further away from the focus. So damage is worst at the epicentre where the most energy is felt; further away, the damage gets less. Two factors control how much more strongly the earthquake will be felt at the epicentre:

● how deep the focus is
● how violently the 'snapping' was at the focus.

Tip

Try to draw links between the different units you study. For example, link how developed a place is (see Chapter 11) to how severely a hazard can impact it. Use place-specific facts to compare and contrast.

Did you know?

When the Tohoku earthquake occurred off the coast of Japan in 2011, it was so violent that the whole Earth wobbled on its axis. This meant that the day was shortened by 1.8 microseconds and the land near the epicentre shifted 2 metres. So if you had jumped into the air directly above the epicentre at the exact moment of the earthquake, you would have shifted in place and in time.

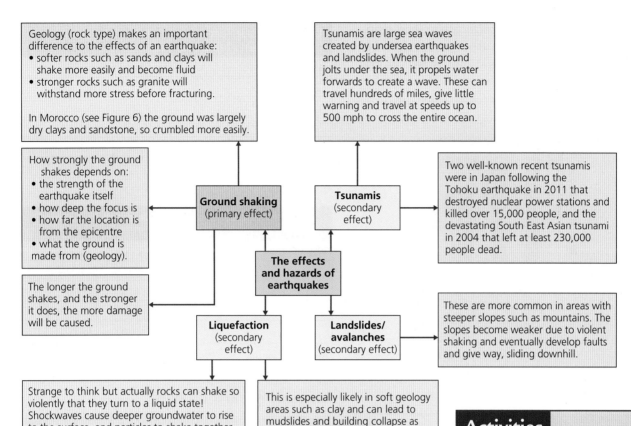

Geology (rock type) makes an important difference to the effects of an earthquake:
• softer rocks such as sands and clays will shake more easily and become fluid
• stronger rocks such as granite will withstand more stress before fracturing.

In Morocco (see Figure 6) the ground was largely dry clays and sandstone, so crumbled more easily.

Tsunamis are large sea waves created by undersea earthquakes and landslides. When the ground jolts under the sea, it propels water forwards to create a wave. These can travel hundreds of miles, give little warning and travel at speeds up to 500 mph to cross the entire ocean.

How strongly the ground shakes depends on:
• the strength of the earthquake itself
• how deep the focus is
• how far the location is from the epicentre
• what the ground is made from (geology).

Ground shaking (primary effect)

Tsunamis (secondary effect)

Two well-known recent tsunamis were in Japan following the Tohoku earthquake in 2011 that destroyed nuclear power stations and killed over 15,000 people, and the devastating South East Asian tsunami in 2004 that left at least 230,000 people dead.

The effects and hazards of earthquakes

The longer the ground shakes, and the stronger it does, the more damage will be caused.

Liquefaction (secondary effect)

Landslides/ avalanches (secondary effect)

These are more common in areas with steeper slopes such as mountains. The slopes become weaker due to violent shaking and eventually develop faults and give way, sliding downhill.

Strange to think but actually rocks can shake so violently that they turn to a liquid state! Shockwaves cause deeper groundwater to rise to the surface, and particles to shake together to become fluid.

This is especially likely in soft geology areas such as clay and can lead to mudslides and building collapse as ground sinks and gives way.

▲ **Figure 8:** The effects and hazards of earthquakes

The effects of earthquakes

There are two types of effect that can result from a hazard.

● **Primary effects** occur instantly and as a direct result of the hazard. A primary effect of an earthquake, for example, could be that buildings collapse due to shaking.

● **Secondary effects** are a consequence of something else happening. A secondary effect of an earthquake could be people injured by falling debris such as breaking windows.

An earthquake can create various associated hazards. These are illustrated in Figure 8.

So how much damage can an earthquake cause? It depends on factors such as:

● distance from epicentre (further from the epicentre, seismic waves are weaker)
● geology (softer geology will shake more easily and lose more strength than stronger geology)
● building design and infrastructure (e.g. quality of materials, foundations, support)
● level of economic development of the area. (Advanced countries generally have a lower death toll but higher economic losses, whereas this is reversed in low-income developing countries; see Figures 10 and 11 on page 30.)

Activities

1. Make a simple sketch of Figure 7. Add annotations to each of the key terms to explain what they are.
2. If an earthquake has a deeper focus, how will this influence the impact on structures near the epicentre?
3. For each of the effects of earthquakes in the mind map (Figure 8), list the possible primary and secondary impacts of the event.

Impacts will either be short term or long term: **short-term impacts** are those that the area and people can recover from relatively quickly, whereas **long-term impacts** are more long lasting. For example, a short-term impact could be a broken leg, whereas a long-term impact could be homelessness.

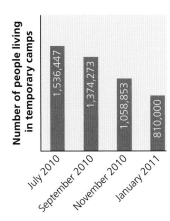

▶ **Figure 9:** Lack of housing can be a long-term impact of earthquakes. These figures show how many people were forced to live in temporary camps after the 2010 Haiti earthquake

✚ Geographical skills

Using a range of data to compare and contrast is a geographical skill. Use development data such as $GDP per capita or HDI to compare which areas have the highest death toll and why. For example, consider the difference in death toll between the Japanese and Indonesian tsunamis.

Activities

1. Analyse the information in Figures 10 and 11.
   a. Identify whether there is a link between earthquake size and impact.
   b. Which areas are most likely to suffer higher death tolls? Why?

→ Take it further

2. Plot the earthquakes from Figures 10 and 11 onto a world map.
   a. Is there a geographic pattern for where the deadliest or strongest earthquakes are?
   b. What is the level of development of these locations?
3. Use the internet to find out what the economic damages were for the top ten earthquakes listed in Figures 10 and 11. Compare your data with those from the tables. How reliable are the results?

Year	Magnitude (Richter)	Intensity (Mercalli)	Death toll	Location
1960	9.5	12	1,655	Chile
1964	9.2	12	131	Alaska, USA
2004	9.1*	12	230,000	Indonesia
2011	9.0*	12	15,884	Japan
1952	9.0*	12	4,000	Kamchatka, Russia

*Associated tsunami

▲ **Figure 10:** Top five largest earthquakes

Year	Magnitude (Richter)	Intensity (Mercalli)	Death toll	Location
2010	7.0	10	316,000	Haiti
2004	9.1*	12	230,000	Indonesia
2008	7.9	11	87,587	China
2005	7.6	10	80,361	Pakistan
1990	7.4	10	50,000	Iran

*Associated tsunami

▲ **Figure 11:** Top five deadliest earthquakes

Measuring earthquakes

There are different ways to compare how severe an earthquake is (see columns two and three on Figures 10 and 11).

The **Richter scale** measures the *power* of the shaking itself, based on measurements made by a **seismometer** (a piece of equipment that measures tremors sensitively). The scale shows how violently the ground shook and is therefore called a 'magnitude scale'. The scale is logarithmic, which means that for every whole number of increase, the power of the shaking has increased by ten times. So a 7.0 magnitude quake is 10× stronger than a 6.0 quake, 100× stronger than a 5.0 quake and 1000× stronger than a 4.0 quake! This scale is open-ended and could keep going well beyond the highest recorded earthquakes to date.

In contrast, the **Mercalli scale** measures the *intensity of the impacts* of the earthquake. It is based on perception of the effects upon humans, buildings and the environment. Using this scale, an earthquake can have different magnitudes depending upon how far away from the epicentre the measurements are made. So while the Richter scale might state that an earthquake was a 7.0, nearer to the epicentre the Mercalli scale might be a 10 and further away it might be a 9. The limitation with this scale is that it can be subjective because it is based on perception and not measurable data. However it is useful for comparing the impacts felt. A smaller earthquake might look insignificant on the Richter scale but if it occurred in a densely populated area with weak buildings, it might register highly on the Mercalli scale. Figure 12 demonstrates the links between the scales.

Mercalli scale (impacts)		Richter scale (magnitude)	Feels like
1	Detected only by seismometers	1.0–3.0	1–20 kg of dynamite
2	Felt by a few people at rest, especially on upper floors or if hanging objects swing		600 kg of dynamite
3	Felt noticeably indoors but may feel like passing trucks or mechanical vibrations		10,000 kg of dynamite
4	Felt indoors by most; may wake some at night; objects and doors disturbed and rock		20,000 kg of dynamite
5	Felt by most indoors and outdoors; some small breakages of dishes and windows	4.0–4.9	60,000 kg of dynamite (like a small nuclear bomb)
6	Felt by all; frightening; falling plaster and chimneys; small damage to buildings	5.0–5.9	20,000,000 kg of dynamite
7	Everybody runs outside; damage to buildings will vary; noticeable while driving		40,000,000 kg of dynamite
8	Walls shake; pictures fall off walls; chimneys fall; glass cracks	6.0–6.9	60,000,000 kg of dynamite
9	Buidings shift in foundations and crack; ground fractured; rails bent; landslides	7.0–7.9	20 billion kg of dynamite (would create enough energy to heat New York city for a year); felt worldwide
10	Most brick and wooden structures destroyed; ground fractured; rails bent; landslides		
11	Very few structures remain standing; bridges and roads destroyed; large landslides	8.0+	30 billion kg of dynamite
12	Damage is total; seismic waves are seen on the ground; objects thrown in the air		20 trillion kg of dynamite (would power an average UK household for 2,104,226 years)

▲ **Figure 12:** Measuring earthquakes

4/5

6/7

9

12

▲ **Figure 13:** The Mercalli scale

Activities

1. What is the difference between the Richter and Mercalli scales? Which one is most useful for comparing the impact of earthquakes in different places? Justify your choice.

How does plate movement cause volcanic activity?

What is a volcano?

A volcano is an opening in the Earth's crust through which lava, ash, steam, rock particles and gas are erupted from the mantle. Volcanoes occur along plate boundaries and occasionally at **hotspots** (see Figure 16). A destructive or constructive plate boundary can lead to volcanic activity where there is a supply of molten magma beneath ready to be released.

▲ **Figure 14:** Mount Pico, a stratovolcano in the Azores. Can you think why humans still choose to live near volcanoes?

What causes volcanoes?

Composite volcanoes

Composite volcanoes (also called **stratovolcanoes**) are found at destructive plate boundaries where the plates are moving towards one another (see page 26). The magma is much more viscous or sticky than found at constructive plate boundaries, moves more slowly and can lead to more explosive eruptions. Steeper-sided volcanoes are built up in layers every time an eruption occurs, a bit like layers in a cake. Most of these volcanoes are found along the infamous 'Ring of Fire' around the Pacific Ocean, in places such as Indonesia.

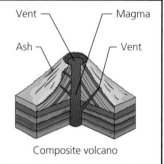

Composite volcano

Shield volcanoes

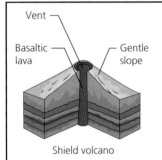

Shield volcano

Shield volcanoes are found at constructive plate boundaries where the plates are moving away from each other, allowing hot liquid magma from the mantle to flow up (by convection) and be erupted to the surface (see page 27). Often the magma erupted at a constructive boundary is more fluid than at other boundaries and spreads out from the cone or through fissures. This builds a gentle volcano shape. You can see these in places like Iceland and under the oceans where new oceanic plate is being formed.

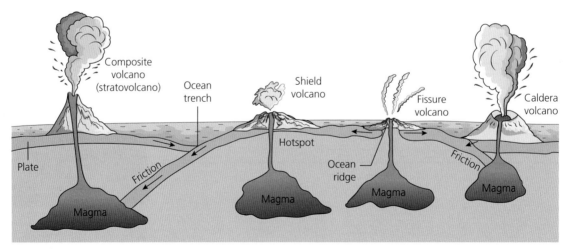

▲ **Figure 15:** Different types of volcano

Fissure volcanoes

Fissure volcanoes occur at constructive plate boundaries when the plates separate to leave a rift or fissure. The eruption does not from a cone but lava flow out along a fault line and builds up, for example in Iceland or at the Mid-Atlantic Ridge.

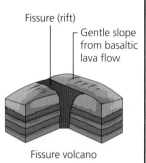

Caldera volcanoes

A **caldera** volcanoe occurs when a volcano erupts so explosively that the magma chamber empties and the crater collapses into itself. Eventually as magma rises again, a new cone will grow. Calderas can be over 1 mile in diameter, for example Yellowstone in the USA.

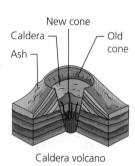

Hotspot volcanoes

Almost all volcanoes occur on plate boundaries; however there are exceptions at places called **hotspots**. These hotspots occur when an oceanic plate is moving over a particularly hot area of the mantle, which creates a super-heated plume of hot magma rising up towards the crust. Eventually this can 'punch through' the plate when it becomes heated enough or thins, or fractures are found in the rock, and magma will erupt to the surface. This leads to volcanic islands appearing – sometimes overnight! Famous examples of hotspots include Hawaii and the Azores. As the oceanic plate keeps moving away from the hotspot, the material will stop being fed to the volcano and it will become extinct. So the further away from the hotspot an island is, the older it is.

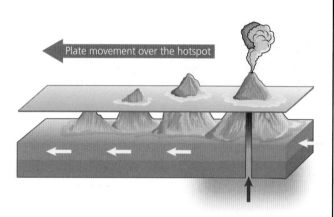

▲ **Figure 16:** Hotspot volcanoes, such as the Azores archipelago or Hawaii, appear as islands

Activities

1. What is a hotspot? Why does volcanism happen here?
2. Explain how subduction can lead to a volcanic eruption. Make reference to a real location as evidence.
3. Make an annotated sketch of each of the main types of volcano: stratovolcano, shield and fissure. Include details of how the lava and behaviour vary between the types.
4. Investigate what is meant by the 'Ring of Fire'. Why does it have this name? Explain the distribution of volcanic eruptions from your research.

Active, dormant or extinct?

→ **Active:** a volcano that has erupted recently and can erupt at any time.

→ **Dormant:** a volcano that has not erupted for a long time but still could.

→ **Extinct:** a volcano that can no longer erupt.

Effects of volcanic activity

Volcanoes can produce various effects, both primary and secondary. Some of the effects of an eruption can be seen in Figure 17.

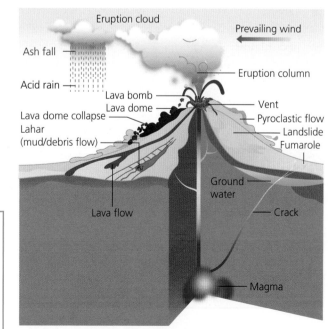

▲ **Figure 17:** Some of the effects of an eruption

The kind of eruption you will get depends upon various factors, but particularly the chemistry of the magma. The amount of silica (an acidic natural element) and gas content (particularly sulphur dioxide) in magma controls how runny or fluid it is and therefore how explosively it will erupt. This influence can be seen in Figure 18.

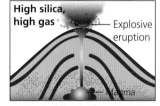
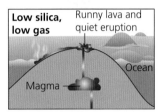
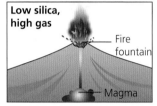

▲ **Figure 18:** How the chemistry of magma influences eruptions

Once the magma erupts it can be seen as one of two types of lava: *pahoehoe* lava is thinner, runnier and flows faster (this usually leads to shield or fissure eruptions), whereas *aa* lava is thicker, more viscous and slower (this usually leads to stratovolcanoes and explosive eruptions). There are exceptions, but this is usually the case.

Measuring volcanic eruptions

The severity of an eruption can be measured on the **volcanic explosivity index (VEI)**. This scale runs from 0–8 and looks at how far the ash plume travelled, the volume of material ejected and how often that type of eruption occurs. Just like with the Richter scale for earthquakes, each step of the scale means a ten-fold increase in severity. There hasn't been a VEI-8 eruption in the last 10,000 years. The largest in human record was Mount Tambora in Indonesia in 1815. This eruption registered 7 on the VEI and the explosion was so loud that it was heard 1200 miles away and ripped apart the volcanic cone to leave a collapsed caldera.

- **Tephra:** fine volcanic dust; this tends to deposit near the volcano but can blow in the winds across nations and can interact with the atmosphere to link to climate change
- **Lava bombs:** 'bombs' of ejected lava that cool on the outside to form a crust are propelled through the air and explode as liquid rock when they land
- **Volcanic gases:** primarily sulphur dioxide, carbon dioxide, water vapour, nitrogen; these gases can poison soil and water, cause respiratory problems in humans and interact with weather
- **Lahars:** mudflows occur when ash and mud mix with rain water; they can be very fast and bury areas beneath mud
- **Jökulhlaups:** glacial melt can occur in sub-glacial eruptions such as in Iceland; ice is melted by volcanic heat and creates floods and mudflows
- **Ash clouds:** combined with volcanic glass and debris, these can travel miles high in the atmosphere and interfere with aircraft or even reduce sunlight
- **Sulphur deposits:** solid sulphur rock can be ejected or deposited from fumaroles; this can then be used for industry; sulphur mining provides jobs e.g. the Kawah Ijen volcano in East Indonesia
- Sometimes volcanoes can bring long-term benefits; there can be an increase in tourism, they can create **geothermal power** and volcanic ash will erode to form fertile soil for agriculture
- **Pyroclastic flows:** hot rocky gas and ash clouds from explosive eruptions that can travel at up to 200 mph and reach 800°C
- **Lava flows:** *pahoehoe* or *aa* lava can usually be outrun but will destroy what it touches

▲ **Figure 19:** Some of the effects of volcanic eruptions

Activities

1. Classify the impacts of eruptions into local, international, short term and long term. Which impact do you think is the most serious? Why?
2. Why do people live near volcanoes? Consider real places such as Iceland and the Azores and explain the potential benefits, the push (negative) and pull (positive) factors that mean people live here.

→ **Take it further**

3. Find out what a VEI-8 eruption would be like. Is there anywhere on the planet that might produce such an eruption? Why here? What would the impacts be?

Eyjafjallajökull, Iceland

Where and what is Eyjafjallajökull?

▲ **Figure 20:** Where is Eyjafjallajökull located?

The infamous Eyjafjallajökull eruption occurred on 15 April 2010 in Iceland. Iceland is an advanced country and is very experienced with tectonic hazards since it has an eruption on average every five years. It is an island created by volcanic activity and sits astride a constructive plate boundary between the North American and Eurasian plates where they are moving apart at the Mid-Atlantic Rift.

Eyjafjallajökull is actually the name of the **glacier** (a slow-moving frozen river in the mountains) that the volcano is under. The real volcano is Fimmvörðuháls, which is a stratovolcano (unusual for Iceland). The name Eyjafjallajökull actually means 'islands mountain glacier' and it is the fact that the volcano is **sub-glacial** that made it so problematic due to the interaction between hot magma and cold ice.

What were the causes of the eruption?

On 19 March 2010 scientists began monitoring an increase in seismic activity at Fimmvörðuháls using seismometers. They noticed that earthquakes were beginning to increase and become shallower, meaning that magma was rising to the surface. As the magma chamber filled up inside the volcano, pressure increased and magma rose towards small cracks or fissures in the surface.

The first lava erupted through fissures as fire fountains (lava bursting up like a hot fountain) on 20 March (Figure 22) and ash began being deposited on the surface of the glacier as lava broke through the ice. At first the eruption created dramatic lava flows and many Icelanders and tourists flocked to the site to have a look. It became known as a 'Volcanic Disneyland'!

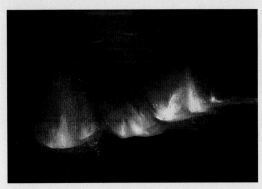

▲ **Figure 22:** In March 2010 fire fountains began erupting from a fissure near Fimmvörðuháls (Eyjafjallajökull), forcing the evacuation of local people

The eruption quietened down for two weeks and many thought it was over. However, in the magma chamber below, another source of magma from deeper in the mantle was rising and mixing. This caused chemical reactions and an increase in silica and gases, which meant the magma became more viscous and explosive. On 12 April, a second fissure ripped open and lava began flowing again. Finally the vents below the glacier Eyjafjallajökull itself were filled with magma and on 15 April the glacier burst open. A fissure cut through 200 m of thick glacial ice, which immediately caused

▲ **Figure 21:** Eyjafjallajökull glacier before and after the eruption

flooding or jökulhlaups that flowed downhill through the Thorsmörk valley towards the coast and destroyed parts of the Route 1 highway and its bridges.

Imagine extremely hot lava meeting extremely cold ice. What would happen? If you pour cold water over hot coals it will create huge amounts of steam. When the lava mixed with water, huge plumes of tephra (volcanic dust) were created, which rose 30,000 feet into the atmosphere. Figure 23 shows the movement of this tephra across Europe's atmosphere. The dark red areas show where the ash was at its most concentrated.

As a result of Iceland's location in the northern hemisphere, when northwesterly winds blew they swept this tephra, volcanic ash and gases across northeast Europe. The eruption lasted for two weeks with ash slowly being dispersed. One of the biggest consequences of this was that international air travel was affected and many flights were grounded. Iceland itself escaped any loss of life (largely due to the rural location of the volcano and small population, as well as prediction methods), but the economic and international impacts were severe and prolonged.

▲ **Figure 23:** Meteosat false colour image showing the spread of ash and volcanic particles across Europe

> Trouble pronouncing the name? Try this: 'Aye-ya-fiat-la-yo-kult'.
>
> In fact, the name is hard even for Icelanders to pronounce!

What were the consequences of the eruption?

In Iceland itself, the consequences were predominantly short term and of low severity. Local farm residents and animals were at risk from the ash cloud and were evacuated, and there was some damage to these farms and loss of livestock due to ash inhalation.

However, the most severe impacts were on the international community and were economic. While the local economy benefited in some ways from increased tourism revenue, the international economy, particularly that of Europe, suffered due to the cancellation of flights worldwide as a result of the ash cloud (see Figure 24).

The ash cloud was dispersed across major international airline routes and at the same altitude as commercial planes. Over 95,000 flights were cancelled when the UK Meteorological Office declared the atmosphere unsafe to fly in. It was decided that there was a risk of engine failure if ash was drawn into the engines, and so aircraft and their cargo or passengers were stranded (see Figure 25). This earned the eruption a nickname: the 'ash-pocalypse'!

Tip

Just use 'Iceland 2010 eruption' or 'E-16' for short in your exam.

Airspace closed across much of Europe. At least 95,000 flights were cancelled, leaving 'volcano refugees'	Stock market shares in air travel agencies dropped 4%	Less demand for air fuel – 1.87 million barrels of oil not needed = loss of money for oil industry, which led to an increase in petrol costs in the UK and Europe
The disruption cost airlines more than $200 million a day ($2 billion in total)	20 farms destroyed	Health impacts: some respiratory problems as ash settled for both animals and humans
Increased use of Eurostar, train services, ships and ferries		200 m of ice melted and jökulhlaups destroyed parts of Route 1
	Could possibly trigger a future major eruption at Katla volcano	For months the glaciers were covered in dark ash, which increased melting
In Iceland, flash floods, damaged fields and homes, but increased tourism	Increased, spending by tourists stranded away – hotels, food, etc.	Grounded air cargo flights stopped delivery of items such as food, flowers, medicines and mail

▲ **Figure 24:** The impacts of the E-16 Eyjafjallajökull eruption

Since nations are interdependent and rely upon trade networks, and since the world economy was entering a recession phase and Icelandic banks were in collapse, this eruption caused very serious long-term problems. For example, Kenya (an LIDC) lost $3.5 million due to cancelled trade and perishable foods decaying; this would have long-term impacts upon the population. Europe as a whole lost $2.8 billion in insurance costs and lost trade.

A further long-term impact is what this might mean for the future. Since volcanoes are often connected underground, it is likely that this eruption will trigger more eruptions in the future in this area. For example, last time Eyjafjallajökull erupted, it triggered Katla to erupt and led to a 'year without a summer'!

▲ Figure 25: The ash cloud caused travel chaos across Europe

What were the responses to the eruption?

Iceland has very sophisticated monitoring mechanisms throughout the country utilising satellite imagery, thermal cameras, gas chromatography, seismometers, tiltmeters and computer modelling. The Iceland Meteorological Office (IMO) co-ordinates information to share with the public, and a local text message warning system as well as radio, television and internet alerts all ensure that the population is aware of the risks.

The country also has a well-trained National Emergency Agency which co-ordinates recovery and response tactics, such as replacing bridges immediately with temporary pre-built structures, dredging blocked rivers and clearing away tonnes of ash – which is now sold to tourists!

Other nations had to respond to the disaster independently, with aircraft being grounded according to weather predictions in each area. Long-term responses may include having volcano insurance for travel.

In 2014, another sub-glacial volcano named Bárðarbunga began erupting beneath the Vatnajökull glacier. The lessons learned from the Eyjafjallöjökull eruption meant that the area was heavily monitored by the Iceland Met Office with gas emissions being made public, helicopter flights tracking ash and lava flows, and predictions made about possible explosive eruptions. In the end, the eruption remained as a small fissure eruption and because it was in a remote rural area, there was no loss of life or direct impact on humans. This is despite the fact that the lava flow grew to the size of Manhattan in New York!

Activities

1. Describe the causes of the Icelandic eruption through a flow chart.
2. Why do people continue to live near volcanoes in Iceland? What are the benefits? What risks do they face?
3. Classify the impacts of the eruption into long term and short term. Which impacts were the most severe – local or international? Why?
4. Icelandic volcanoes were named in 2014 as one of 'Europe's biggest worries for the future'. Why should the European community worry about volcanoes so far away? Are these fears justified? Back up your answer with evidence.
5. Investigate an LIDC earthquake or volcanic eruption. Build a case study and compare it with the Iceland eruption. How does the level of development influence the impact of a hazard? Link your response to data. Write persuasively.
6. Have you ever been a55ffected by a volcanic eruption? If so, how?

→ Take it further

7. Bárðarbunga volcano began erupting in August 2014 and the eruption lasted for months. It was also sub-glacial. Investigate the impacts of this eruption and compare them with those of Eyjafjallajökull. Why did this event not make international news?

Tip

To write a good case study answer you need 'place-specific facts'. Choose key facts that you can describe fully and explain and learn these. Practise using 'Point–Evidence–Explain–Link' to make developed points.

How does technology have the potential to save lives in hazard zones?

→ **In this section you will:**

→ explore how technological developments can have a positive impact on mitigation in areas prone to earthquakes or volcanoes.

How does technology have the potential to save lives in hazard zones?

Plan, predict, prepare

Modern technology has reduced the impacts of tectonic hazards, particularly in places with a high level of development and income that can afford a range of methods to plan for, and protect against, hazards.

How severely a hazard will impact a place depends upon:

- the conditions before the event (for example, building structure, health, access to emergency services, infrastructure)
- advanced warnings from predictions
- whether there is an organised system for disaster relief.

The decision to **mitigate** (reduce the impact) against a hazard will be based on an analysis of the risks, the costs and the benefits.

Earthquakes: plan, predict, prepare

It is very difficult to predict earthquakes since they are a sudden event with little warning. Seismologists study areas carefully and use sophisticated seismometers and computer modelling, but this has not led to a successful prediction yet. Attempting to predict an earthquake relies upon:

- **radon gas emissions:** this radioactive isotope *may* be released by seismic stress before rock fractures
- **electromagnetism:** passing electromagnetic shocks or waves through rocks might detect fractures beginning to develop
- **historic trends:** looking at the history of past events might identify patterns such as timescales.

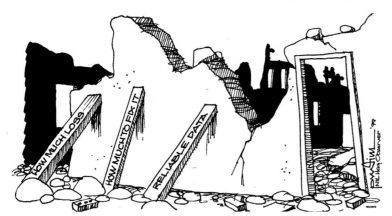

▲ **Figure 26:** The decision to mitigate considers risk, cost and benefit

- **animal behaviour:** it is alleged that certain animals, including dogs, rats and birds, can sense the seismic waves vibrating in advance and start to exhibit unusual behaviour

Since it is difficult to predict earthquakes, it is essential to have an excellent network of seismometers around an area to detect the very first rumbling and trigger an alarm.

Planning and preparation is key. In Japan there is a National Earthquake Awareness Day every year to practise evacuations and educate the population on warnings and what to do so that panic is avoided. Homes and businesses may well keep an 'earthquake survival kit' just in case, or have a safety shelter or bunker to escape to. It is crucial to have well organised plans for evacuations and for emergency services. Nowadays, media (particularly social media such as Twitter or Google Person Finder) are essential for distributing information. It is possible to design buildings to be 'earthquake-proof' (see Figure 28). Japan is a world leader in terms of earthquake (and tsunami) mitigation by considering how to protect, predict and prepare using technology for humans ... and even pets!

Protect yourself and your property – reduce earthquake risk.

BE QUAKESMART

1 Identify Your Risk

2 Make a Plan

3 Take Action
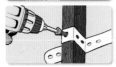

FEMA   Need help? Get your free QuakeSmart toolkit at www.fema.gov/hazard/earthquake

▲ **Figure 27:** FEMA warning posters in the USA

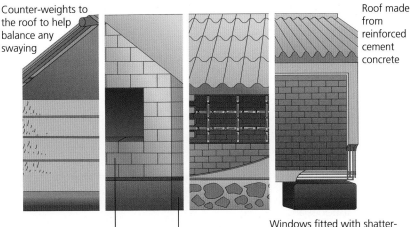

Counter-weights to the roof to help balance any swaying

Roof made from reinforced cement concrete

Hollow concrete bricks that cause minimal damage if they fall during an earthquake

Foundations made from reinforced steel pillars, ball-bearings, rubber, etc.

Windows fitted with shatter-proof glass or automatic window shutters to reduce breakage

▲ **Figure 28:** Earthquake-proof building design: a luxury for the rich?

Volcanoes: plan, predict, prepare

Scientists are able to make quite accurate predictions of volcanic eruptions, provided enough data are collected. Volcanoes give off a range of signs or 'precursors' before an eruption, which can be measured using techniques such as:

- **seismometers:** measuring the pattern of earthquakes near the magma chamber
- **gas emissions:** particularly sulphur dioxide and carbon dioxide; these increase as magma rises
- **soil or water pH:** soils and water sources may become more acidic as the sulphur content increases
- **tiltmeters:** measure the shape of volcanoes to detect 'bulges'
- **satellite imagery:** particularly thermal scanning to show whether magma is rising up
- **historic records:** to identify whether there are patterns, e.g. Hekla in Iceland erupts on average every ten years.

This information can be used in computer modelling to make predictions. For example, looking at the historic records can give an estimate of frequency of eruptions. Then chemical measurements, such as soil and gas, can be analysed to see whether acidity is changing. When added to seismic measures, the result can be a computer-aided simulation that estimates the chances of a volcano erupting.

There is little that can be done to protect against damage. We can do little to stop lava or pyroclastic flows. Attempts to 'divert' lava and artificially cool it using sea water were successful once in Heimaey, Iceland, but such examples are extremely rare. In general, the main mitigation against eruptions is planning and preparing the area for evacuation. Buildings can be insulated and barriers put in place to reduce ash entry and gas masks can be made available. Roofs can be reinforced to cope with the weight of ash without collapsing. Iceland has a complex range of instruments in place that can make predictions in advance. This is co-ordinated by the Iceland Meteorological Office (IMO) to provide warnings via text message, the internet, television and radio. The focus then is on safe evacuation and the recovery phase.

Using computer modelling to predict earthquakes

At the Delft University of Technology in the Netherlands, scientists have created an algorithm which has produced a digital model of the North Anatolian Fault, a major fault line in Turkey.

The model aims to predict where an earthquake might hit by simulating underground flows of mantle in order to detect where the friction between the plates is greatest. The scientists hope that the model will be able to provide warnings for earthquakes in the future to help minimise loss of life. They are already planning to model the tectonics of the entire Earth!

Activities

1. What is meant by 'mitigation'?
2. Why is it so difficult to predict earthquakes?
3. Describe in detail two methods of predicting volcanic eruptions.
4. Research earthquake-proof buildings. What are the best features? Draw your own design and explain the features carefully. If you can, try to make a model and test it!

→ Take it further

5. Often the highest risk is long term, with the highest death tolls coming from secondary impacts. Conduct research into different tectonic hazards, decide whether this is true and suggest why.

Practice questions

1. Define the 'global circulation system'.   [2 marks]
2. Why do we find deserts at 30° north and south of the Equator?   [3 marks]
3. Describe the climate where Hadley cells meet at the Equator.   [3 marks]
4. Suggest a cause of the El Niño phenomenon.   [1 mark]
5. Which of the two statements below is true for an El Niño event?
   a) The trade winds blowing westwards over the Pacific
      Ocean weaken or reverse.
   b) There is a risk of increased flooding in Australia.
   c) There is more warm water around Peru, suppressing the
      upwelling of cold water.
   d) Rising warm and moist air over Australia and Indonesia
      brings reliable rainfall.   [1 mark]
6. Describe the global distribution of tropical storms.   [3 marks]
7. State two conditions that are needed for a tropical storm to form. [2 marks]
8. To what extent are tropical storms becoming more frequent?   [4 marks]
9. Define the term 'drought'.   [1 mark]
10. Explain how the inter-tropical convergence zone affects
    the distribution of droughts.   [4 marks]
11. Extreme weather conditions vary in contrasting countries.
    Discuss the differences in extreme weather conditions in
    contrasting countries. You should develop your ideas fully.   [6 marks]
12. Case study for either a flash flood or a tropical storm.
    Evaluate how successful attempts were to reduce the impacts
    of the event.   [6 marks]
13. What is meant by 'continental drift'?   [1 mark]
14. Where is molten rock found?
    a) In the inner core
    b) In the mantle
    c) In the magma
    d) In the crust   [1 mark]
15. Look at Figure 3 on page 26. Explain why a convergent
    boundary is also called a 'destructive boundary'.   [2 marks]
16. Using data from Figure 10 on page 30, describe and compare
    the link between earthquake magnitude and death toll.   [4 marks]
17. For the information on death tolls in Figure 11 page 30, state
    which graphical technique would be most suitable.
    a) Venn diagram
    b) Bar chart
    c) Scatter graph   [1 mark]
18. Explain why the type of lava (*pahoehoe* or *aa*) produced in
    an eruption can affect how explosive and dangerous an
    eruption becomes.   [3 marks]
19. What scale is used to measure volcanic eruptions?   [1 mark]
20. What is a 'primary impact'? Give an example of a primary
    impact of an eruption.   [2 marks]
21. Describe how technology can be used to prepare for tectonic
    hazards.   [4 marks]
22. Tectonic hazards can have different impacts, both long and
    short term. Discuss the primary and secondary effects of a
    tectonic event that you have studied.   [6 marks]

> **Tip**
>
> Look at question 11. You need to include well-developed ideas about the weather conditions *and* the differences in weather conditions in contrasting (that means varying or different) countries. Extremes are likely to include temperature, wind and precipitation, and you should discuss at least *two* contrasting countries.

> **Tip**
>
> Look at question 16. If a question says 'use data' it means you need to quote facts from the resource. Use statistics to prove your point.

> **Tip**
>
> For a 4-mark 'describe' question, you should write in detail using full sentences and keywords. Check the focus of the question – for example, question 21 says 'to prepare' – and keep your answer focused on this.

Climate change campaigners take part in a demonstration in Central Paris. Climate change is perhaps the greatest environmental challenge facing humanity. Since 1880 the average global temperature has risen by 0.85°C. Most of this increase has occurred since the mid-1970s. Amazingly, fourteen of the world's fifteen hottest years have occurred in the twenty-first century, with 2015 being the hottest yet. What do you think the impacts of climate change will be on the UK and the world?

Chapter 3: What evidence is there to suggest climate change is a natural process?

By the end of this chapter, you will know the answers to these key questions:

→ What evidence is there for climate change?

→ Is climate change the result of natural processes or can it be linked to human activities?

→ What are the likely impacts of climate change, both globally and in the UK?

What evidence is there to suggest climate change is a natural process?

What evidence is there for climate change?

➜ **In this section you will:**

→ look at how the climate has changed during the Quaternary geological period

→ study the evidence for climate change.

How has climate changed during the Quaternary geological period?

Climate change is nothing new. Over geological time, measured in hundreds of millions of years, climate has changed constantly, affecting the distribution and development of life on Earth. Look at Figure 1. It shows the pattern of global temperatures for the last 5.5 million years using evidence from deep ocean sediments. The graph shows how temperature has changed over time compared with today's average temperature (shown by the dashed line at 0°C).

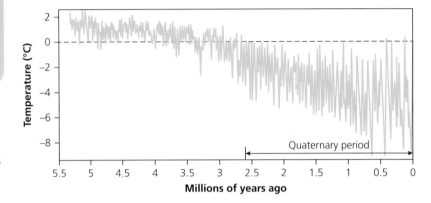

▶ **Figure 1:** Average global temperatures for the last 5.5 million years

Tip

When describing a graph, remember to make a **general comment**, describing the overall trend and **use data** to support your statement. Mention any **anomalies/exceptions**.

Remember:

G ⎤ **General Comment**
C ⎦

S- **Specific data**

E- **Exceptions**

Notice that the last 2.6 million years is known as the **Quaternary geological period**. During this period of time, temperatures have fluctuated wildly, although there has been a gradual overall cooling. The cold 'spikes' in the graph are **glacial periods** when ice advanced over parts of Europe and North America. In between are warmer **inter-glacial periods**. Notice that today's average temperature is higher than almost all of the Quaternary period. The current warm period that began some 10,000 years ago may turn out to be another inter-glacial period, with ice returning at some point in the future.

Now look at Figure 2 which shows temperature changes during the last 400,000 years. The temperature values on the graph are in comparison to today's global average temperature placed at 0°C. To help you appreciate this time scale, the human species evolved about 200,000 years ago.

The graph shows clearly how the cold glacial periods have alternated with warm inter-glacial periods.

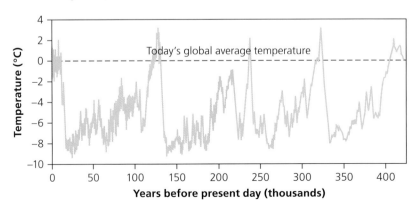

▶ **Figure 2:** Trends in average global temperatures (400,000 years ago to the present day)

43

Chapter 3 What evidence is there to suggest climate change is a natural process?

Figure 3 shows the most recent changes in average global temperatures from 1880 to 2013. It suggests clearly that in the last few decades, average global temperatures have increased relative to the 1901–2000 average. It is this current warming trend that has become known by the term **global warming**.

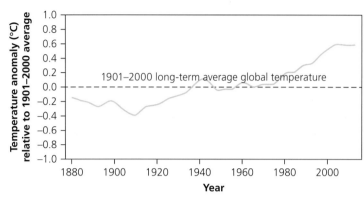

▲ **Figure 3:** Average global temperatures, 1880–2013

Activities

1. Study Figure 1. Which of the following statements are true?
   a. The Quaternary period started 2.6 million years ago.
   b. Before the Quaternary period, global temperatures were mostly higher than today's average temperature.
   c. The lowest temperature occurred about 0.5 million years ago.
   d. The highest temperature was +2°C.
   e. Temperatures fluctuated more before the start of the Quaternary period than during the Quaternary period.
   f. Temperatures have fluctuated the most during the last 1 million years.
   g. During the Quaternary, there has been a general increase in temperatures.

2. Study Figure 2.
   a. We are currently in a relatively warm period. Roughly how long has this lasted?
   b. During the most recent cold (glacial) period, how low did temperatures drop compared with today's average?

   c. The last warm (inter-glacial) period occurred about 125,000 years ago. How high did temperatures reach during this period compared with today's average?
   d. What do you notice about the length of time of cold periods compared with the length of time of warm periods?

3. Study Figure 3.
   a. Describe the average global temperature trend from 1880 to 1940.
   b. From what date did the average global temperature start to rise rapidly above the long-term average?
   c. Describe the trend in average global temperature since 2000.
   d. What is the difference in average global temperature between 1880 and 2013?
   e. Do you think this graph provides strong evidence for global warming?

What evidence is there for climate change?

The reliable measurement of temperature using thermometers goes back about a hundred years. In the UK, for example, reliable weather records began in 1910. So, how do we know what the temperatures were in the distant past?

What evidence do we have of climate change in the past?

Informed judgements about ancient climates can be made using fossil evidence. Scientists can also use data that have accumulated over long time periods and been trapped and stored within ice or deep-sea sediments.

1. Geological fossil evidence

Plants and animals are good indicators of the environment as different species tend to favour particular climatic conditions. Evidence of past climates can be suggested by the presence of living organisms preserved as fossils. For example, the discovery of 60-million-year-old crocodiles in North Dakota, USA, suggests that the climate of the past was much warmer than it is today.

Elephant-like mammals called mastodons (Figure 4) were widespread across the USA during cold, glacial periods. Their thick woolly coats enabled them to survive the very cold conditions. Fossil mastodons have been found from Alaska to Florida, indicating that these cold periods extended across the whole of the USA.

2. Ice cores

Ice cores extracted from the Antarctic and Greenland ice sheets have proved to be an important source of information about past global temperatures. When snow falls in cold polar environments it gradually builds up layer upon layer, year upon year. The buried layers of snow are compressed and gradually turn to ice. The Antarctic ice sheet is nearly 5 km thick in places and the oldest ice – at its base – is thought to be 800,000 years old.

Scientists are able to drill deep into the ice to extract cylindrical cores (Figure 5) from ice that is many thousands of years old. The layers of ice within a core can be dated accurately. By analysing the trapped water molecules, scientists can calculate the temperature of the atmosphere when the snow fell.

This information about accurate dates and temperatures has enabled scientists to create graphs of temperature changes over the last 400,000 years. The results of this research show the fluctuating temperatures that indicate past glacial and inter-glacial periods (see Figure 2, page 42).

▲ **Figure 4:** Mastodons were widespread across the USA during cold glacial periods

3. Ocean sediments

In the same way that layers of snow build up over thousands of years in a cold environment, layers of sediment do much the same thing in deep ocean basins. Scientists have been able to drill into sediments that are over 5 million years old. By studying oxygen isotopes trapped within these sediments, it has been possible to calculate past atmospheric temperatures (see Figure 1, page 42).

▲ **Figure 5:** An ice core extracted from the Antarctic ice sheet

45

Chapter 3 What evidence is there to suggest climate change is a natural process?

4. Historical records

Historical records can provide additional evidence of climate change.

- Ancient cave paintings of animals in France and Spain depict nature as it was between 40,000 and 11,000 years ago, a period of time when the climate changed significantly. The problem with cave paintings is dating accurately when they were drawn.
- Records of extreme weather events such as floods and droughts have been used to suggest that in recent decades extreme weather events have become more frequent.
- Some studies have suggested that the timing of natural seasonal activities, such as tree flowering and bird migration, is advancing. (The study of natural cycles like these is called phenology.) A study of bird nesting conducted by the British Trust for Ornithology in the mid-1990s discovered that 65 species nested an average of 9 days earlier than they had in the 1970s. Swallows are arriving in the UK some 20 days earlier than they did in the 1970s. Could this be evidence of a warming world?
- Diaries and written observations can also provide evidence of climate change, although personal accounts can lack objective accuracy.

The Little Ice Age (1300–1870)

The Little Ice Age is the name given to a period of time when parts of Europe and North America experienced much colder winters than today. The coldest periods were in the fifteenth and seventeenth centuries. Much of the evidence of the Little Ice Age comes from diaries and written observations made at the time.

- The price of grain increased and vineyards in much of Europe became unproductive.
- Sea ice engulfed Iceland, preventing ships from landing. As crops failed many people decided to emigrate. Iceland lost half its population during the Little Ice Age.
- The sea froze around parts of the UK and regular winter 'Frost Fairs' were held on the frozen River Thames.
- Throughout Northern Europe, rivers froze and people suffered from intensely cold winters when food supplies were limited. Several painters of the time captured this winter landscape (Figure 6).

Despite these harsh climatic conditions European culture and technology flourished. Huge innovations occurred in agriculture, land was reclaimed in the Netherlands and the UK and sea trading expanded. Did the Little Ice Age perhaps trigger these human responses in the face of the harsh climatic conditions?

Activities

1. Look at Figure 4. How can fossils provide useful evidence about past climates?
2. Study Figure 5.
   a. What do you think the scientist is doing in the photo?
   b. What are the challenges of working in such a hostile environment?
   c. Describe briefly how ice cores provide scientists with data about past temperatures.
3. Suggest advantages and disadvantages of historical records in providing reliable evidence for climate change.
4. Look at Figure 6. It shows a typical winter scene during the Little Ice Age.
a. What is the evidence in the painting that this is a severe winter?
   b. What are the daily problems facing the people?
   c. Can you suggest any advantages of this severe winter weather for the people in the painting?

→ Take it further

5. Use the internet to discover more about mastodons. How were they well suited to living in cold environments? How have they been useful to scientists researching past climates in the USA?

▲ **Figure 6:** *Winterlandschaft mit Vogelfalle* ('Winter Landscape with Skaters and Bird Trap') by Pieter Brueghel the Elder (1601)

What is the recent evidence of climate change?

Evidence of climate change over the past hundred years or so, particularly the recent warming trend, comes from a number of sources.

1. Global temperature data

Look at Figure 7. It shows temperature anomalies (variations from the long-term average) for the period 2008–12. This map was produced by NASA (National Aeronautics and Space Administration) using data collected from over 1000 ground weather stations together with satellite information.

If you study the colour key, you should notice that there is a warming trend for most of the world. This is consistent with earlier maps produced over several decades. NASA suggests that average global temperatures have increased by 0.6°C since 1950 and 0.85°C since 1880.

Weather stations are not evenly distributed across the world and some regions, especially in Africa, have a fairly sparse network. Computer programmes have been used to produce global maps such as Figure 7 but this does not make them absolutely accurate and reliable.

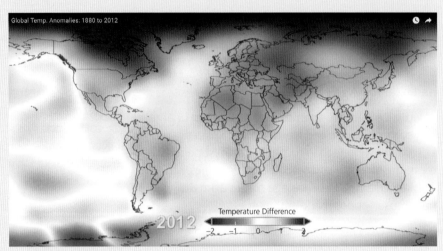

▲ **Figure 7:** Global temperature anomalies, averaged 2008–12

2. Shrinking ice sheets and glaciers

One of the most striking effects of the recent warming trend has been the retreat of ice sheets and glaciers. Maps and photos show that many of the world's glaciers are retreating (Figure 8).

There is plenty of evidence from around the world of melting ice.

- The snows of Kilimanjaro have melted by 80 per cent since 1912.
- Glaciers in parts of the Himalayas could disappear by 2035.
- Arctic sea ice has declined in volume by 10 per cent in the last 30 years.
- Monitoring of the Greenland ice sheet by NASA suggests that it is shrinking.
- In 1910 Glacier National Park (USA) had about 150 glaciers; there are now fewer than 30.
- Low-level ski resorts in Europe have suffered economic hardship and some businesses have had to close due to increasingly unreliable snowfall.

▲ **Figure 8:** The Muir Glacier and inlet, Alaska (mid-1890s and 2005)

- The Muir Glacier (Alaska, USA) has retreated by 50 km in the last 120 years (Figure 8).

47

Chapter 3 What evidence is there to suggest climate change is a natural process?

Retreat of the Columbia Glacier, Alaska, USA

The Columbia Glacier has its source in the Chugach Mountains in southern Alaska. It flows for some 50 km to the sea in Prince William Sound. Its maximum thickness is 550 m. The glacier is known as a 'tidewater glacier' because it flows directly into the sea.

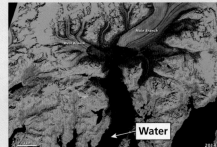

▲ **Figure 9:** Satellite photos of the Columbia Glacier (1986 and 2014)

The Columbia Glacier is one of the most rapidly changing glaciers in the world. It has been retreating at an alarming rate since the 1980s. Between 1982 and 2014, the snout (front) of the glacier retreated by about 16 km and lost half of its thickness and volume. In the early 2000s the glacier was retreating at a staggering rate of around 30 m a day, producing huge icebergs as the snout broke apart.

Scientists believe that the thinning of the ice may well be due to warming global temperatures. If global warming continues, it is likely that the glacier will continue to shrink. As it does so, the meltwater will contribute towards sea level rise.

The extremely fast rate of retreat at the snout may be due largely to mechanical factors associated with the glacier extending into the sea, although global warming may well have played a part in making the snout unstable in the 1980s.

3. Sea level change

According to the Intergovernmental Panel on Climate Change (IPCC), the average global sea level has risen between 10 cm and 20 cm in the past 100 years. There are two reasons why sea levels have risen:

- When temperatures rise and freshwater ice melts, more water flows to the seas from glaciers and ice caps.
- When ocean water warms it expands in volume; this is called thermal expansion.

Interestingly, during the warmer interglacial periods in the Quaternary, temperatures were some 1–2°C above the current levels, resulting in the sea level being 15–25 m higher than it is today. Imagine what would happen to coastal regions of the world if they were faced with this kind of sea level rise.

Activities

1. Study Figure 7.
   a. Which areas of the world recorded the highest temperature anomalies?
   b. Which areas of the world recorded the lowest temperature anomalies?
   c. How can this map help to explain the shrinking extent of the Arctic sea ice and the melting of Greenland's ice sheet?
   d. How does this map provide evidence supporting the idea of global warming?
2. For this activity you will need a blank world outline. Look back to the section on shrinking ice sheets and glaciers. Plot the location of the examples listed onto your world map. Use text boxes to write a few words about each example. Use the internet to find a few additional examples of melting ice sheets and glaciers and add these to your map.
3. Study Figure 8.
   a. Describe the changes that have taken place in this landscape between the mid-1890s and 2005.
   b. How do these changes provide powerful evidence of global warming?
   c. In many parts of the world, people rely upon annual supply of glacier meltwater for their drinking water and irrigation. How will they be affected in the future if rapid glacier melting continues?

→ Take it further

4. Read the information about the Columbia Glacier and look at Figure 9. Further information together with a sequence of satellite images can be found at http://earthobservatory.nasa.gov/Features/WorldOfChange/columbia_glacier.php. Put together your own study of the Columbia Glacier, describing how it has retreated since the 1980s. Use annotated photos to support your study. To what extent may climate change be responsible for its retreat? What effect is its melting having on sea levels?

Is climate change a natural process?

→ **In this section you will:**

→ study the natural causes of climate change

→ investigate the natural greenhouse effect and the impacts that humans have on the atmosphere.

Activities

1. Study Figure 10.
   a. What are the Milankovitch cycles?
   b. Briefly describe each of the three cycles. Include the time periods involved.
   c. What is the evidence that the Milankovitch cycles may have affected the Earth's climate in the past? Use a simple sketch of Figure 2 (page 42) to support your answer.

Is climate change a natural process?

Climate change is often in the news. The question is, how much of the measured increase in global temperature is due to natural causes and how much is related to the actions of people?

● **Natural causes:** some changes in climate can be explained by natural factors such as sunspot activity, volcanic eruptions and Milankovitch cycles.
● **Human activities:** scientists consider that the rapid rise in temperatures since the 1970s can be linked to human activities, such as burning fossil fuels, deforestation and waste disposal.

What are the natural causes of climate change?

1. Milankovitch cycles

You have already seen how there have been regular patterns of cold (glacial) and warm (inter-glacial) periods throughout the Quaternary period (Figure 2, page 42). But how were these caused?

The **Milankovitch cycles** are cyclical time periods that relate to the Earth's orbit around the Sun (Figure 10). Scientists believe that these cycles affect the timings and seasonality of the Earth's climate. In particular, the 100,000 year eccentricity cycle coincides closely with the alternating cold (glacial) and warm (inter-glacial periods) in the Quaternary period. Look back to Figure 2 (page 42) to see how the spacing between warm inter-glacial periods was about 100,000 years.

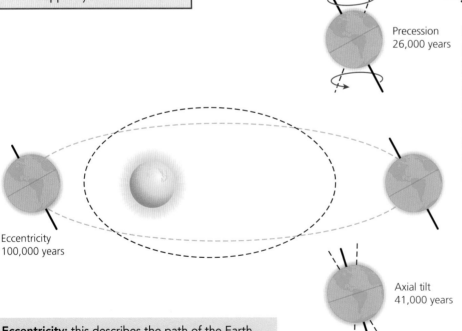

◀ **Figure 10:** The Milankovitch cycles

Precession 26,000 years

Eccentricity 100,000 years

Axial tilt 41,000 years

Precession: this describes a natural 'wobble' that occurs with the Earth rather like a spinning top. A complete wobble cycle takes about 26,000 years. The Earth's wobble accounts for some regions of the world experiencing very long days and very long nights at certain times of the year, such as northern Norway.

Eccentricity: this describes the path of the Earth as it orbits the Sun. The Earth's orbit is not fixed; it changes over time from being almost circular to being mildly elliptical. A complete cycle from circular to elliptical and back to circular again occurs about every 100,000 years. It appears that colder periods occur when the Earth's orbit is more circular and warmer periods when it is more elliptical.

Axial tilt: the Earth spins on its axis, causing night and day. The Earth's axis is currently tilted at an angle of 23.5 degrees. However, over a period of about 41,000 years, the axial tilt of the Earth moves back and forth between two extremes: 21.5 degrees and 24.5 degrees. A greater degree of tilt is associated with the world having a higher average temperature.

49

Chapter 3 What evidence is there to suggest climate change is a natural process?

2. Volcanic eruptions

Violent volcanic eruptions blast huge quantities of ash, gases and liquids into the atmosphere. Fine particles of ash can block out the Sun, leading to a reduction in surface temperatures. This is called a **volcanic winter**. Ash can be carried by winds across the globe, transferring these cooling conditions to many regions far beyond the location of the volcano.

Ash does not usually stay in the atmosphere for more than a few weeks so is unlikely to have a long-term impact on climate. Sulphur dioxide, however, can lead to longer-term cooling. The fine aerosols that result from the conversion of sulphur dioxide to sulphuric acid act like tiny mirrors reflecting radiation from the Sun. This results in the cooling of the lower atmosphere.

The eruption of Mount Pinatubo in the Philippines on 15 June 1991 was one of the largest eruptions of the twentieth century.

An enormous cloud of ash and gases, including sulphur dioxide, was ejected more than 20 miles into the stratosphere.

Satellites recorded the highest concentration of sulphur dioxide since observations began in 1978.

The aerosols cooled the world's climate for a period of three years by up to 1.3°C.

▲ **Figure 11:** The eruption of Mount Pinatubo, Philippines, 1991

3. Sunspot activity

Sunspots are spots or dark patches that appear from time to time on the surface of the Sun. The number of sunspots increases from a minimum to a maximum and then back to a minimum over a period of about 11 years. This 11-year period is called the **sunspot cycle**. Sunspots are associated with strong magnetic fields and often give rise to large explosions on the Sun's surface causing solar flares. You can see this in Figure 12.

The origin of sunspots is not fully understood but scientists have suggested connections between sunspot activity and climate change. For example, very few sunspots were observed between 1645 and 1715, a period known as the Maunder Minimum. This coincided with the coldest period during the Little Ice Age (see page 45). So, despite the fact that sunspots are dark areas on the Sun, it seems that the more sunspots there are, the more effective the Sun is at giving off heat.

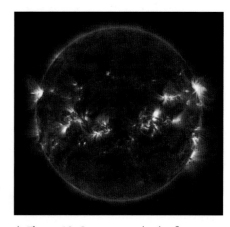

▲ **Figure 12:** Sunspots and solar flares on the surface of the Sun

Activities

1. What are sunspots and how do they affect the Earth's climate?
2. **a.** What is meant by the term 'volcanic winter'?
    b. Why does volcanic ash not have a long-term impact on climate?
    c. Explain how the emission of sulphur dioxide during a volcanic eruption can cause cooling of the lower atmosphere.
3. Describe the effects of the eruption of Mount Pinatubo on the world's climate.

→ Take it further

4. Use the internet to find out more about the eruption of Mount Pinatubo and how it affected global climates. Present your work in the form of an information poster. They should be captioned or annotated. Your poster should also include:
    - the location of Mount Pinatubo
    - brief details of the eruption
    - a description of how the eruption affected the world's climate.

What impact have human activities had on climate change?

Many scientists believe that human activities are at least partly to blame for the rapid rise in temperatures (global warming) since the 1970s. To understand how this is possible we need to consider a natural feature of the atmosphere called the **greenhouse effect**.

What is the greenhouse effect?

A greenhouse is a 'house' made of glass. If you have been inside a greenhouse you will know that it is warm at night and even during the winter. This is why people often grow vegetables and fruit such as tomatoes in greenhouses. The reason why a greenhouse is warm is because it retains the heat from the Sun. Look at Figure 13. Notice that heat from the Sun passes through the glass into the greenhouse but does not escape.

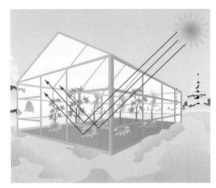

▲ **Figure 13:** The greenhouse effect ... in a greenhouse!

The Earth's atmosphere behaves in a similar way (see Figure 14).

- Heat in the form of short-wave solar radiation travels some 93 million miles to reach the Earth's outer atmosphere.
- As it passes through the atmosphere some is absorbed by gases and liquids and some is reflected off the tops of the clouds.
- Radiation that reaches the Earth warms up the surface.
- This warmth is then released in the form of long-wave infrared radiation (like heat given off by a radiator).
- The heat is easily absorbed by liquids and so-called 'greenhouse gases' in the atmosphere, particularly carbon dioxide, methane and nitrous oxides (Figure 15).
- Some heat escapes to space.

The warm atmosphere acts like a blanket over the Earth, keeping us warm. Without the greenhouse effect, it would be too cold for life to exist on Earth.

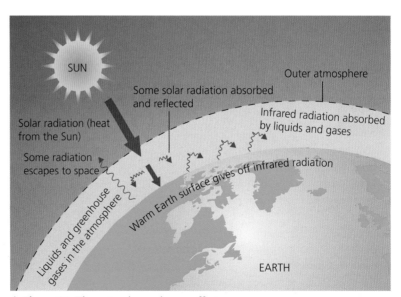

▲ **Figure 14:** The natural greenhouse effect

51

Chapter 3 What evidence is there to suggest climate change is a natural process?

What is the enhanced greenhouse effect?

Many scientists believe that in recent decades the natural greenhouse effect has become more effective at retaining infrared heat given off from the Earth. The 'blanket' around the Earth has in effect become warmer.

The main reason why this has happened is because human activities such as burning fossil fuels, deforestation and emissions from vehicles have increased the concentration of the greenhouse gases in the atmosphere (Figure 15). Scientists name this the **enhanced greenhouse effect.**

Gas	Causes
Carbon dioxide (CO_2)	• Burning of fossil fuels (coal, gas and oil) • Deforestation (burning wood) • Industrial processes (e.g. making cement)
Methane (CH_4)	• Emitted from livestock and rice cultivation • Decay of organic waste in landfill sites
Nitrous oxides (NO_x)	• Vehicle exhausts • Agriculture and industrial processes

▲ **Figure 15:** The main greenhouse gases

Gas	Percentage
Carbon dioxide (burning fossil fuels)	57%
Carbon dioxide (deforestation, decay of vegetation)	17%
Carbon dioxide (other)	3%
Methane	14%
Nitrous oxide	8%
Fluorinated gases	1%
TOTAL	**100%**

▲ **Figure 16:** Global greenhouse gas emissions

✛ Geographical Skills

Use the data in Figure 16 to draw a pie chart to show global greenhouse gas emissions.

● Remember that you will need to multiply each percentage figure by 3.6 to convert it to degrees.
● Check that your total adds up to 360 degrees.
● If it doesn't add up, round the largest figure up or down. What is the total percentage for carbon dioxide?

Tip

When drawing a pie chart, start with a vertical line and work clockwise around the 'pie' (circle).

Activities

1. Draw your own diagram based on Figure 14 to show the enhanced greenhouse effect.
   a. Consider the following points before starting:
      • Think about the various causes of the greenhouse gases (Figure 15); you could use simple sketches or thumbnail photos to show these causes on your diagram.
      • Consider using arrows of different thicknesses to indicate how more heat is retained in the atmosphere.
      • Draw a rough diagram to try out your ideas.
   b. Add text boxes to your diagram in the form of a sequence (1, 2, 3, etc.) to describe how the enhanced greenhouse effect works.

2. Many people blame global warming on carbon dioxide emissions. Is this an accurate judgement?
3. Methane is a very effective greenhouse gas. What are the sources of methane gas emissions?
4. How could methane gas emissions be reduced in the future?

→ Take it further

5. Use the internet to investigate fluorinated gases. What are they and what causes them to be emitted? Are they important greenhouse gases?

52

Topic 2 Changing Climate

Why is climate change a global issue?

→ In this section you will:

→ explore the worldwide impacts of climate change

→ explore the impacts of climate change within the UK.

Intergovernmental Panel on Climate Change (IPCC)

- Concentrations of greenhouse gases are at their highest levels for at least 800,000 years
- Sea level has risen by 20 cm since 1900
- Average global temperatures have increased by 0.85°C since 1880
- By 2100 the sea level will rise by another 26–82 cm
- By 2100 average global temperatures will increase by 0.3–4.8°C

▲ **Figure 17:** Selected findings from the IPCC report, 2013

What are the worldwide impacts of climate change?

Climate change is having, and will continue to have, significant impacts on people and human activities. It is possible to consider three types of impact:

- **Social:** these are the impacts on our lives and our lifestyles.
- **Economic:** these impacts are to do with money and the increasing costs of coping with climate change.
- **Environmental:** these impacts involve changes to natural ecosystems.

In 2013 the Intergovernmental Panel on Climate Change (IPCC) reported that it is 'virtually certain that humans are responsible for global warming'. Some of the report's findings are listed in Figure 17.

Sea level rise

An average rise in sea level of 20 cm since 1900 may not sound very much but it has already had a significant impact on natural and human systems. It has been suggested that the sea level may rise by up to one metre by the end of the century (see page 47).

Rising sea levels threaten low-lying coastal areas with flooding and more frequent damage from storms and tropical cyclones. Figure 18 lists some social, economic and environmental effects of sea level rise.

Social	Economic	Environmental
600 million people live in coastal areas that are less than 10 m above sea level.	Many important world cities including New York, Venice and London could be affected by flooding.	Fresh water sources such as wells could be polluted by salty seawater; this is called salinisation.
People living in vulnerable areas may have to move home or even move to different countries. Some small island states such as Tuvalu and Vanuatu are particularly at risk.	Valuable agricultural land (e.g. in Bangladesh, Vietnam, India and China) may be lost to the sea or polluted by seawater. Harbours and ports may be affected, which will have an impact on fishing and trade.	Damage could occur to coastal ecosystems such as mangrove swamps, which form natural barriers to storms.
People may suffer increased frequency of flooding and storm damage.	Transport systems, such as railways, roads and airports may be damaged or destroyed.	Damage to coral reefs by storms and powerful waves will affect fish breeding grounds and ecosystems.
People may lose their jobs, for example in fishing or tourism, and have to learn new skills.	Valuable land and property will need expensive measures of coastal defence.	The IPCC estimates that up to 33% of coastal land and wetlands could be lost in the next 100 years.
The numbers of environmental refugees – people who have lost their homes due to flooding – will increase.	Many countries depend on coastal tourism as their main source of income. Beaches may be eroded or flooded, forcing hotels to close. People may decide not to visit.	Harbours may become blocked by sediment due to increased rates of coastal erosion.

▲ **Figure 18:** Social, economic and environmental impacts of sea level rise

---

Paris Agreement 2015

At the Paris climate conference (COP21) in December 2015, 195 countries adopted the first ever universal, legally binding global climate deal. The agreement sets out an action plan to limit global warming to well below 2°C above pre-industrial levels. The agreement is due to enter force in 2020.

Governments agreed to:

- aim to limit the increase to 1.5°C above pre-industrial levels
- meet every five years to set more ambitious targets

- report to each other and the public on the implementation of their individual plans to reduce emissions (each country produced a comprehensive national climate action plan prior to the summit)
- strengthen the ability to adapt to and be resilient in dealing with the impacts of climate change
- provide adaptation support for developing countries
- the EU and other developed nations will continue to support initiatives in developing countries aimed at reducing emissions and building in resilience to the impacts of climate change.

53

Chapter 3 What evidence is there to suggest climate change is a natural process?

Tuvalu

Where is Tuvalu?

Tuvalu is a group of nine tiny islands in the South Pacific. Figure 19 shows the location of Tuvalu in relation to Australia.

What is Tuvalu like?

Most of the islands of Tuvalu are low-lying. In fact, the highest point on the islands is only 4.5 m above sea level. Around 11,000 people live on Tuvalu and the economy is based on the export of copra (dried coconut kernel used to extract coconut oil), the sale of fishing licences for tuna and the sale of its colourful postage stamps!

What are the issues facing Tuvalu?

Along with Vanuatu and the Maldives, Tuvalu is threatened by sea level rise, which could swamp the entire islands.

- Increased level of salinisation (pollution by saltwater) is affecting the soils, which is having an impact on agricultural productivity.
- There are no rivers on Tuvalu, as rainwater soaks into the coral rock. Water comes from wells but these are increasingly becoming polluted by seawater. At times, seawater actually bubbles up to the surface through the porous coral.
- Water supply is a key issue, with droughts becoming more common due to climate change.
- Coastal erosion has affected some of the islands, eroding away productive land.
- During king tides (highest tides of the year) the islands are battered by powerful waves, threatening homes and flooding roads (Figure 21).
- The main runway is under threat from flooding.

How are the people in Tuvalu responding?

The Tuvalu government has been campaigning for the international community to tackle global warming by reducing carbon emissions. Some people have already decided to leave the islands for nearby New Zealand, fearing that their homes will become uninhabitable. They are a new wave of 'environmental refugees'.

Some low sea walls have been constructed but they themselves are now suffering from erosion. Sea walls are not the long-term solution.

Japan is supporting a coral reef restoration programme to reintroduce species to damaged reefs. This could provide some protection from storms as sea levels continue to rise.

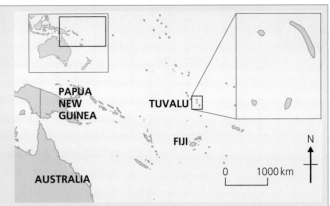

▲ **Figure 19:** Location of Tuvalu

▲ **Figure 20:** Tuvalu

▲ **Figure 21:** The impacts of a king tide in Tuvalu

Activities

1. Study the information on Tuvalu.
   a. What are the arguments for and against building a sea wall at the back of the beach?
   b. Should future developments be allowed to take place here?
2. Outline the social, economic and environmental impacts of sea level change.
3. Suggest the alternative futures for the people who live in Tuvalu.

Can extreme weather events be linked to climate change?

A single extreme weather event, such as a thunderstorm or a heavy snowfall, cannot be linked to long-term changes in the climate. Extreme weather events such as these have always occurred from time to time. However, scientists have noticed that there have been an exceptional number of these extreme events in recent decades. In 2013 the IPCC reported a clear increase in the number, frequency and intensity of heatwaves and heavy rainfall events. If this trend continues, then the link with long-term climate change may become stronger.

In a warming world, there is more energy in the atmosphere. Greater rates of evaporation from the world's oceans result in more water vapour that can in turn lead to more rainfall or snow. Climate patterns may shift, so that some areas become much drier and others much wetter.

The atmosphere is extremely complex and it is impossible to make accurate predictions into the future. But it does seem that we are now living in a world with more extreme weather events (Figure 22).

▼ **Figure 22:** Weather extremes of the early twenty-first century

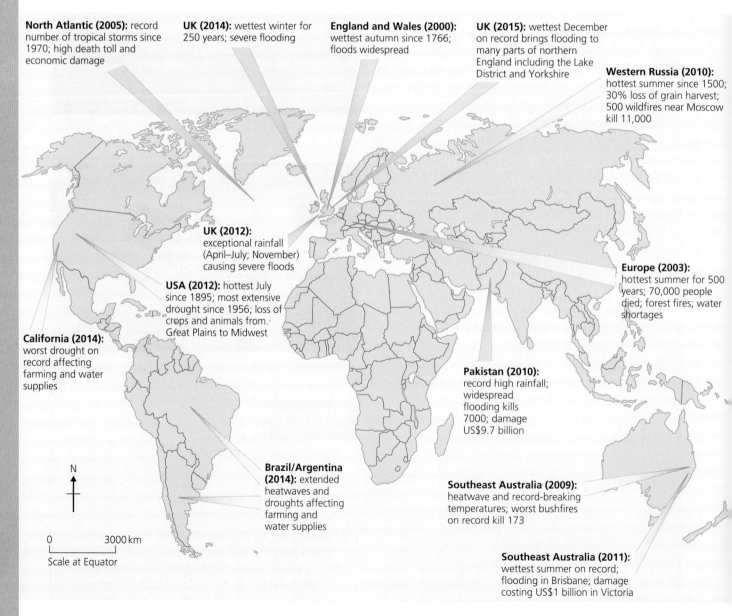

North Atlantic (2005): record number of tropical storms since 1970; high death toll and economic damage

UK (2014): wettest winter for 250 years; severe flooding

England and Wales (2000): wettest autumn since 1766; floods widespread

UK (2015): wettest December on record brings flooding to many parts of northern England including the Lake District and Yorkshire

Western Russia (2010): hottest summer since 1500; 30% loss of grain harvest; 500 wildfires near Moscow kill 11,000

UK (2012): exceptional rainfall (April–July; November) causing severe floods

USA (2012): hottest July since 1895; most extensive drought since 1956; loss of crops and animals from Great Plains to Midwest

California (2014): worst drought on record affecting farming and water supplies

Europe (2003): hottest summer for 500 years; 70,000 people died; forest fires; water shortages

Pakistan (2010): record high rainfall; widespread flooding kills 7000; damage US$9.7 billion

Brazil/Argentina (2014): extended heatwaves and droughts affecting farming and water supplies

Southeast Australia (2009): heatwave and record-breaking temperatures; worst bushfires on record kill 173

N

0   3000 km
Scale at Equator

Southeast Australia (2011): wettest summer on record; flooding in Brisbane; damage costing US$1 billion in Victoria

55

Chapter 3 What evidence is there to suggest climate change is a natural process?

Brazilian drought 2014

In 2014 Brazil faced a record-breaking dry season resulting in drought conditions across parts of the country. As water levels fell in reservoirs (Figure 23), some of Brazil's major cities including Sao Paulo faced water shortages. Many people had to collect water from water bowsers or had to endure water rationing in their homes.

Shortages of water affected industrial production (e.g. aluminium) and farming, due to the lack of water for irrigation. The exceptionally dry weather also affected the coffee industry in Brazil with beans shrivelling on the bushes in January and February due to lack of rainfall (Figure 24). Coffee production dropped significantly due to the drought.

The drought also led to a reduction in the production of hydroelectric power (HEP), due to falling water levels in reservoirs. In parts of the southeast, HEP reservoirs were operating at 30 per cent of their capacity. Alternative forms of energy such as liquefied natural gas (LNG) had to be used to maintain Brazil's energy supply.

As reservoir levels dropped to 10 per cent of their capacity and rivers dried up, levels of pollution increased, damaging natural ecosystems and killing fish.

Useful weblinks

Extreme weather in the USA:
www.ncdc.noaa.gov/billions/overview

Weather events in the UK:
www.metoffice.gov.uk/climate/uk/interesting

▲ **Figure 23:** The Cantareira reservoir that supplies much of Sao Paulo's water

▲ **Figure 24:** Coffee beans in Brazil shrivelling due to the intense heat and drought

Activities

1. Study Figure 23 which shows the Cantareira reservoir at the height of the 2014 drought.
    a. What is the evidence of drought shown in the photo?
    b. Suggest some possible environmental impacts in the reservoir.
    c. What were the economic impacts of the drought?
    d. How were the lives of ordinary people affected by the water shortages?

2. Suggest some economic and social issues associated with the failure of cash crops such as coffee (Figure 24).

➡ Take it further

3. Study Figure 22 which shows a selection of recent extreme weather events. Select an extreme weather event that interests you and use the internet to write a short report. Aim for a similar length to the information on the Brazilian drought. Make sure that you examine the social, economic and environmental impacts of your chosen event. Include a couple of captioned or annotated photos.

4. Use the internet to research other recent extreme weather events. You could use this information to draw a map similar to Figure 22 or to write additional reports. You could use the Useful Weblinks provided in the box above to help you.

What are the impacts of climate change within the UK?

Look at Figure 25. It identifies a number of possible impacts that climate change will have on the geography of the UK. While many people focus on the negatives (threats), there may also be some benefits (opportunities) (Figure 26).

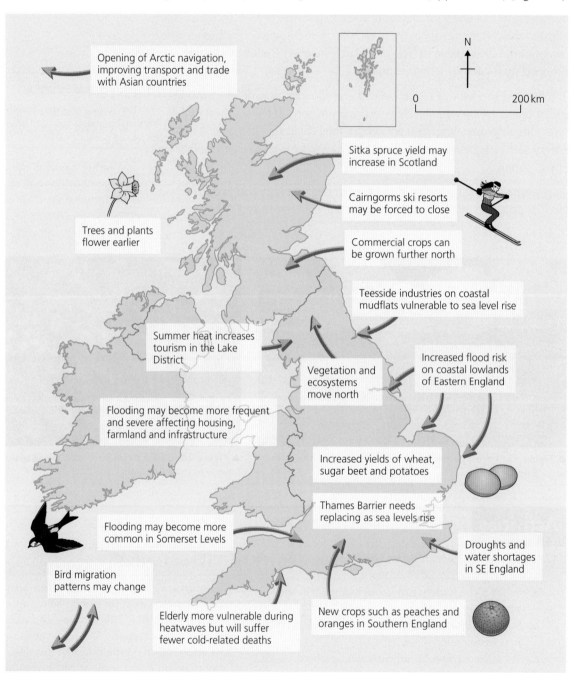

Opening of Arctic navigation, improving transport and trade with Asian countries

Sitka spruce yield may increase in Scotland

Cairngorms ski resorts may be forced to close

Commercial crops can be grown further north

Trees and plants flower earlier

Teesside industries on coastal mudflats vulnerable to sea level rise

Summer heat increases tourism in the Lake District

Vegetation and ecosystems move north

Increased flood risk on coastal lowlands of Eastern England

Flooding may become more frequent and severe affecting housing, farmland and infrastructure

Increased yields of wheat, sugar beet and potatoes

Thames Barrier needs replacing as sea levels rise

Flooding may become more common in Somerset Levels

Droughts and water shortages in SE England

Bird migration patterns may change

Elderly more vulnerable during heatwaves but will suffer fewer cold-related deaths

New crops such as peaches and oranges in Southern England

N

0   200 km

▲ **Figure 25:** Possible impacts of climate change in the UK

👣 Fieldwork ideas

Primary meteorological data can be readily obtained to investigate microclimates. Temperature, humidity, wind speed and wind direction can be measured to study small-scale spatial variations, say within a settlement, across a valley or within a woodland. The results of a microclimate study can be extrapolated to apply to a warming world and social, economic and environmental consequences can be considered.

Climate change	Threats	Opportunities
Higher temperatures – warmer summers, heatwaves, droughts	<ul><li>Heatwaves will lead to deaths among the elderly</li><li>Droughts will affect crop production and natural ecosystems</li><li>Wildfires will become more common, threatening settlements and destroying habitats</li><li>Roads and railways will need more maintenance as tarmac melts and rails buckle</li><li>Millions of people could suffer from water shortages by the 2050s</li></ul>	<ul><li>Tourism industry in the UK will probably increase, boosting the economy and creating jobs</li><li>Heating costs will fall</li><li>Industrial innovation will be encouraged to design new products to cope with the conditions</li><li>Agricultural productivity may increase under warmer conditions</li><li>Outdoor events such as festivals will become more common</li></ul>
Higher rainfall – more frequent and severe storms	<ul><li>Floods will become more common, threatening buildings, infrastructure and farmland</li><li>By the 2080s over one million properties could be at risk from flooding</li><li>Insurance costs will increase; annual damages could reach £12 billion by the 2080s</li></ul>	<ul><li>Manufacturing industry will be boosted by the need for flood defence construction and new building design features</li><li>Managed rivers may be encouraged to revert back to their natural form and new wetlands may be created, boosting wildlife</li></ul>
Sea level rise resulting from global warming	<ul><li>Sea defences including the Thames Barrier will need to be upgraded or replaced, which will be very expensive</li><li>Cliff collapse may increase, putting properties at risk</li><li>Some salt marshes may become flooded and eroded</li><li>Agricultural land may be lost due to managed retreat</li><li>Beaches may be eroded, affecting the tourist industry</li></ul>	<ul><li>Managed retreat will create new salt marsh habitats</li><li>Construction industry will be boosted by the need to build sea defences</li></ul>

▲ **Figure 26:** Threats and opportunities from climate change in the UK

Activities

1. Study Figure 25 which illustrates some of the possible impacts of climate change in the UK.
   a. What new crops might flourish in a warmer England?
   b. How might warmer conditions affect ecosystems in the UK?
   c. Why might ski resorts in the Cairngorms, such as Aviemore, be forced to close?
   d. What will be the impacts on the local economy if ski resorts have to close?
   e. How might the melting of the Arctic sea ice benefit UK trade?
   f. Trees and plants will flower earlier in a warmer UK. Is this a good thing?
   g. Production of wheat, sugar beet and potatoes may increase. Suggest how this might benefit industry and the public.
   h. Construct a table to describe some threats and opportunities from climate change. Select **four** of each using Figure 25.

2. Study Figures 25 and 26. Construct a table to identify a selection of social, economic and environmental impacts of climate change in the UK. Include both threats and opportunities.

→ Take it further

3. Conduct some research to discover why industries on Teesside might be at risk from sea level rise. Use Google Maps to zoom in on Teesside (Middlesbrough). Locate the industries (ICI is one of them) and notice how they are sited on mudflats close to the water's edge. Select maps and satellite images to investigate why these industries are at risk from sea level rise. What are the options for the future?

4. You have been asked to write a short, in-depth newspaper article on one of the impacts of climate change. Look at Figure 25 and select an impact that interests you. Conduct your own research to find out more about it. Try to include some facts and figures and a photograph. Don't forget to write a headline.

Tip

For multiple choice questions, work through the options eliminating those that are incorrect.

Practice questions

1. Study Figure A, a diagram showing the greenhouse effect. **Methane** is one greenhouse gas. Which of the following human activities produces large quantities of methane? Select the correct answer.
   a) Vehicle exhausts
   b) Burning rainforests
   c) Waste in landfill sites
   d) Making cement   [1 mark]

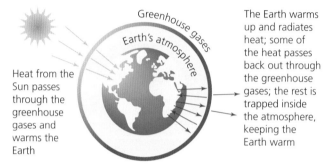

Greenhouse gases

Earth's atmosphere

Heat from the Sun passes through the greenhouse gases and warms the Earth

The Earth warms up and radiates heat; some of the heat passes back out through the greenhouse gases; the rest is trapped inside the atmosphere, keeping the Earth warm

▲ **Figure A:** The greenhouse effect

2. What are the Milankovich cycles? Select the correct answer.
   a) Changes in temperature recorded by ice cores
   b) Cycles that relate to the Earth's orbit
   c) Patterns of bird migration
   d) Cycles of nutrients in ponds   [1 mark]

3. Look back at Figure 11 on page 49 which shows the eruption of Mount Pinatubo in 1991. How can volcanic eruptions affect the world's climate?   [2 marks]

4. a) State one cause of sea level rise.   [1 mark]
   b) Assess the **environmental** impacts of sea level rise. [4 marks]

5. Study Figure B which shows people attending an outdoor festival. Explain how climate change may bring some benefits to the UK. [4 marks]

Tip

Refer to stimulus information to support your answer.

Tip

Look at question 6. Make sure you focus clearly on the demands of the question, i.e. the *economic* impacts.

▲ **Figure B:** Climate change may result in an increase in outdoor events such as music festivals

6. Explain why flooding may have significant **economic** impacts in the future.   [6 marks]

Chapter 4: What makes a landscape distinctive?

By the end of this chapter, you will know the answers to these key questions:

→ What is a landscape?

→ Where are the physical landscapes of the UK?

Chapter 5: What influences the landscapes of the UK?

By the end of this chapter, you will know the answers to these key questions:

→ What physical processes shape landscapes?

→ What are the characteristics of coastal landscapes?

→ What are the characteristics of river landscapes?

→ Case study: What are the characteristics of the North Norfolk Coast?

→ Case study: What are the characteristics of the River Wye?

The UK contains a diverse and distinct range of landscapes. What processes do you think made the landforms in this landscape?

CHAPTER

4

What makes a landscape distinctive?

What are landscapes?

▲ **Figure 1:** Durdle Door on the Jurassic Coast of Dorset

What is a landscape?

→ In this section you will:

→ consider the definition of landscape

→ explore the differences between built and natural landscapes.

▲ **Figure 2:** The flat land of the Lincolnshire Fens

▲ **Figure 3:** Flatford Valley, Suffolk – 'Constable country'

Wherever you are right now, you are located within a landscape. If you look out of the nearest window, you may be able to see part of it. Landscapes are the visible features that make up the surface of the land. We are surrounded by them and are part of them. They are where we live our lives and our lives affect them.

Landscapes are made from a combination of landscape 'elements'. Different combinations of these elements produce landscapes that may look similar at first glance, but are actually very different in their character. A closer look will also reveal differences in their geology, drainage or potential to be used by people. This chapter explains how to look for these differences or how to 'read' a landscape.

What are the elements of a landscape?

The 'elements' that make up a landscape can be placed into four groups:

Tip

In the exam, don't limit yourself to writing about landscapes that you have studied in class. If you have been somewhere exciting which you can talk about in an answer to a question, then go ahead and tell the examiner about it if it is relevant.

▲ **Figure 4:** Two Bridges, Dartmoor, Devon

Natural/physical mountains, coastlines, valleys and plains, rivers and lakes	**Biological** vegetation and other ecological areas and habitats such as marshes and hedges, along with wildlife, birds and grazing animals
Human buildings and other man-made structures, infrastructure and the way that the land is used, fences and pylons	**Variables** weather and cloudscapes, smells and sounds – these can be temporary elements, such as a dramatic storm, mist and frost in the morning or snow cover

Landscape elements

▶ **Figure 5:** Landscape elements

Describing landscapes: built or natural?

Geographers study landscapes at a range of **scales** from the **local** (a city park) to the **regional** (a range of hills like the Pennines, which extends into several UK counties). Landscapes are said to have a particular character and sometimes these extend across **national** boundaries.

Where there are more human than physical elements visible in a landscape, we use the term '**built landscape**' to describe it. This could include a city centre, a retail development or a business park on the edge of a town. Landscapes are also dynamic; they are not constant, but change over time. Familiar views can be altered by the introduction of new housing or new infrastructure such as roads, railway lines or electricity pylons. Some people feel strongly enough about the impact of changes like this that they actively campaign against proposed changes.

Where the majority of the landscape is made up of **natural** or physical elements, we can talk about a **natural landscape**. In reality, however, there are very few parts of the UK that haven't been changed by people over the centuries. An area of woodland that might look ancient was probably originally planted by people and would have been managed ever since. It may even have been chopped down and replanted several times.

Landscapes can also change from one type to the other. In reality, however, it is more likely that natural landscapes will become built landscapes than the other way round.

✝ Geographical skills

You need to be able to interpret maps including Ordnance Survey maps at 1 : 50,000 and 1 : 25,000 scales. Find a few maps covering different parts of the UK to see how the landscapes vary. You can use a digital mapping service to do this by going to www.bing.com/maps and viewing the road maps as Ordnance Survey maps.

1. Compare an upland mountain range such as the Brecon Beacons in South Wales with a flat marshy area like the Somerset Levels. What do you notice about the difference in **contour lines** and **spot heights**?
2. Compare a woodland area with an urban area. What different types of symbol are used in each location? Which different physical or human features appear in these different areas?

Close your eyes for a moment and imagine the landscape that you would most like to spend time exploring. Which of these elements can you 'see' in it?

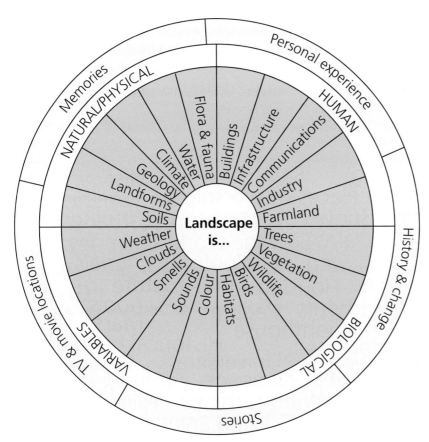

▲ **Figure 6:** What is landscape?

Activities

1. a. How would you describe the landscape in the area where you live? Is it built-up or natural?
    b. What evidence do you have for making your decision?
    c. What processes would cause it to move from one type to the other?

'Reading' the landscape of the UK

An important part of any landscape is the shape and height of the surface **landforms** that can be seen. A landform can be defined as 'any physical feature of the Earth's surface which has a characteristic, recognisable shape and is produced by natural causes'. Landforms help provide the overall character of a landscape, as well as affecting its soils and climate and the ways in which people use it. The UK has a large range of landscapes in a relatively small area.

> *'I know of no landscape anywhere that is more universally appreciated, more visited and walked across and gazed upon, more artfully worked, more lovely to behold, more comfortable to be in, than the landscape of England.'*
>
> Bill Bryson

The word cloud in Figure 7 includes some of the elements that make up the landscapes of the UK.

- Can you think of other words that could have been added?
- Which of these could be classed as landforms?
- Can you think of elements which might be less obvious, but which contribute to the way that a landscape looks and 'feels'?

By combining the words from Figure 7, we can 'make' different landscapes.

Which landscapes have you experienced?

Personal experiences are also important when thinking about landscapes. We all live *in* a landscape and will experience others at different times in our lives, such as on holiday or when visiting family and friends in other parts of the country.

- Which areas of the UK have you visited the most often?
- Which do you like to spend time in?
- Which have you never visited, but would most like to?

Fog   Salt marsh   Mist
Industry Places of worship Settlements
Follies Snow cover Transport Estuaries
Hedges Plains Sewage works Chimneys
Woodland Sand dunes Footpaths Aerials Bogs
Quarries Trees Housing Infrastructure Geology
Land use Harbours Vegetation Schools Cliffs
Mountains   Lighthouse   Marsh
Crops Rainfall Farms Universities Historical buildings
Reservoirs Valleys Drainage Smoke Beaches
Skyline Clouds Wind turbines Hills Ports
Castles Soil Grazing animals
Walls   Towers

▲ **Figure 7:** Word cloud of UK landscape elements

UK landscape factfile

- **Lowest point in the UK:** Holme Fen, Cambridgeshire, at 3 m below sea level
- **Highest points:** Ben Nevis (Scotland) at 1344 m, Scafell Pike (England) at 978 m, Snowdon (Wales) at 1085 m, Slieve Donard (Northern Ireland) at 850 m
- **Furthest point from the sea:** Church Flatts Farm, Derbyshire, at 70 miles from the sea
- **Number of National Parks:** 15 (in England and Wales)
- **Wettest city in Britain:** Cardiff (1150 mm per year)

Chapter 13 contains further information on the physical characteristics of the UK, including a relief map on page 199.

Activities

1. Re-arrange a selection of the phrases below to create a definition of landscape that you are happy with.

... can change over time	... created by human activity	... the shape of the land	... made up of natural elements
... includes physical elements	... occupied by people	... provides a habitat for animals	... is farmed and managed by humans

2. Look at Figures 6 and 7. Imagine the elements of the landscape as ingredients in a recipe.
   a. How could you combine the same elements to make different landscapes?
   b. Are there any elements missing from the word list in Figure 7 that can be seen in your local area?
   c. Identify the elements in Figure 7 that are particular to the UK.
3. Look at Figure 8. Discuss with a partner the changes that might take place in this landscape that would alter its character. Put them into three groups:
   - permanent changes which might improve its character
   - permanent changes which might change its character for the worse
   - short-term changes which might only be there for a few hours or days.

4. Look again at Figures 1 to 4. Identify the different elements that can be seen in the images and place them in the appropriate place on a copy of the table below.

Natural physical elements	Human elements
Biological elements	**Variable elements**

5. Use an Ordnance Survey map to look at the area within 10 km of your school.
   a. What landforms can be found within that area?
   b. How did you identify these landforms on the map?

▲ **Figure 8:** The beach at Whipsiderry

Where are the physical landscapes of the UK?

→ **In this section you will:**

→ identify the difference between upland, lowland and glaciated landscapes

→ look at the distribution of each of these areas across the UK

→ consider reasons for the distribution shown

→ explore the characteristics of these landscapes that may make them distinctive, including their geology, climate and human activity.

Naming mountains

Mountains over 3000 feet high are called 'Munros' in the UK, after Hugh Munro who compiled a list. Most of the 282 Munros are in Scotland. The name 'Corbetts' is given to those peaks between 2500 and 3000 feet high. Can you find out what a 'Marilyn' is?

Activities

1. Study Figure 9.
   a. Is the place where you live classed as lowland or upland?
   b. What evidence did you use to help you make your decision?

Where are the physical landscapes of the UK?

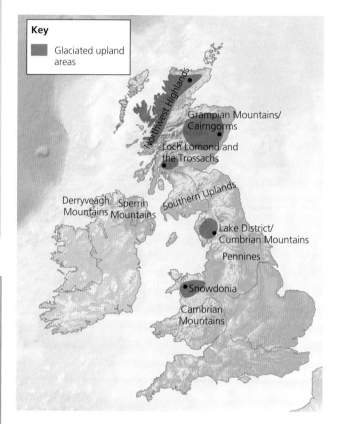

Key
Glaciated upland areas

Northwest Highlands
Grampian Mountains/ Cairngorms
Loch Lomond and the Trossachs
Derryveagh Mountains   Sperrin Mountains
Southern Uplands
Lake District/ Cumbrian Mountains
Pennines
Snowdonia
Cambrian Mountains

▲ **Figure 9:** The distribution of upland, lowland and glaciated areas in the UK

When does a lowland become an upland?

A mountain is often defined as being an area of land that rises considerably above the surrounding land, with 600 m (2000 feet) sometimes used as the height that separates mountains from hills. Upland areas can include dramatic peaks and ridges with weathered rock or moorland with heather. They include some of our most interesting landscapes.

Higher land experiences colder weather and more mist, cloud and snow. This can increase the rate of physical weathering because of the presence of water and the greater changes in temperature either side of freezing point. Temperature drops by 1°C for every 100 m of altitude. Lowland areas are closer to sea level and lie below around 200 m.

▲ **Figure 10:** Loch Brandy, Cairngorms, Scotland

▲ **Figure 11:** The Cambridgeshire Fens

How was the landscape of the UK formed?

In the UK, the most spectacular mountain ranges, such as the Cairngorms in Scotland and Snowdonia in North Wales, were sculpted by the action of ice. **Ice ages** are periods of time when the surface temperatures in temperate latitudes are lower than average. This allows ice sheets to grow in size in northern latitudes and move to cover new areas further south, including the UK. Ice ages have happened numerous times over the last two million years. As temperatures warmed, the ice melted and land was revealed again.

For the last 10,000 years, the UK has been in a geological time called the Holocene. Figure 12 illustrates the area covered by the most recent ice advance, around 10,000 years ago.

Ice has great strength and can erode and weather landscapes to create dramatic mountain scenery. **Glacial processes** may not be happening now, but many landscapes bear the scars of ice that previously scoured out deep valleys such as the Lairig Ghru in the Cairngorms. Ice also moved into the lowland areas, scraping away the soil of the Yorkshire Dales, bulldozing clay and boulders into large ridges such as the Cromer Ridge on the Norfolk Coast, or leaving piles of rocks which are different from the local geology.

Large sections of the south coast which were not covered by ice were instead covered by a mixture of boulders and sediment called drift. While less spectacular, this has also influenced the present-day landscape.

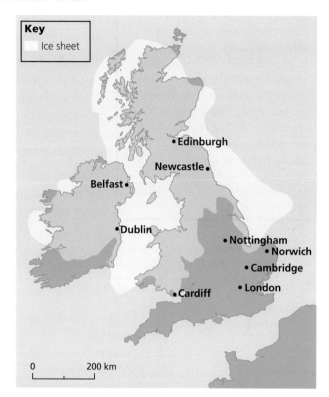

▲ **Figure 12:** Area covered by the last major ice advance over the UK

Geomorphic processes

Geomorphic processes are those that change the shape of the Earth. The 'geo' part means the Earth and 'morph' refers to the way that the shape of the Earth's surface is changed over time.

Geomorphology involves **mechanical, chemical and biological** processes which act on and alter the Earth's surface. These processes are the result of the climate and weather, chemical reactions, moving water and ice, and the force of gravity. Each has the effect of wearing away the surface in some places, moving small pieces of the surface that have broken off to other locations, and building them up into new landforms. You will find out more about how weathering, coastal processes and river processes have shaped our landscapes in Chapter 5.

✝ Geographical skills

Use Ordnance Survey maps to 'visit' some of the places the ice has covered and identify the characteristic features shown in upland glaciated areas. Look out for the steepness of the land, the absence of soil or vegetation, piles of stone and words such as corrie, tarn or cwm depending on which area you visit.

Activities

1. Study Figure 12. Was the place where you live covered by ice during the last period of advance?
2. Describe the evidence that ice shaped the land that you can still see in your local landscape?

👣 Fieldwork ideas

You can often see what the local geology is by looking at buildings, particularly churches or ones with older walls. These tend to have been built with local stone, whereas modern buildings often use bricks and concrete. These older buildings may also use local vegetation, such as the reeds used for roofing traditional thatched cottages. Survey the buildings in your local area, find the oldest buildings and look at their design and materials.

How does geology affect landscapes?

The **geology** of the rocks that lie beneath the ground influence the nature of the landscape seen on the surface. Wherever you live in the UK, the rocks beneath your feet vary, because they were created at different times, in different environments and by different processes (Figure 13).

Rocks are placed into three groups, according to their origin, as outlined in Figure 14. The three groups are: **igneous**, **sedimentary** and **metamorphic**. The shape and height of the land is partly a result of the relative hardness of the underlying rock. Relatively harder rocks, such as igneous granite and gabbro, often make up the high mountains, whereas sedimentary chalk and clays, which are much less resistant to physical processes, lie under many low-lying areas.

In mountainous areas the rock may also be easier to see as it is exposed at the surface. This may be because moving ice removed the surface covering during an ice advance (see page 65). The same ice then covered the geology in the south of England with layers of clay, producing a more subdued landscape.

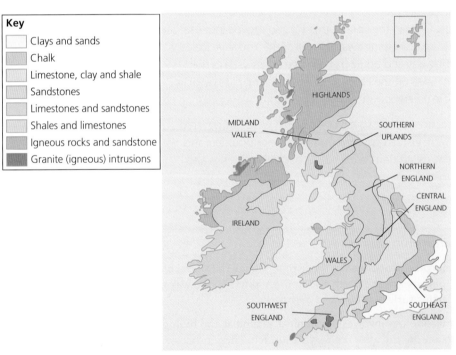

Key

	Clays and sands
	Chalk
	Limestone, clay and shale
	Sandstones
	Limestones and sandstones
	Shales and limestones
	Igneous rocks and sandstone
	Granite (igneous) intrusions

▲ **Figure 13:** A geological map of the UK

Rock type	Method of formation	Examples in the UK
Igneous	Produced when magma (molten rock) cools, either beneath the ground (intrusive) or above the surface (extrusive). These rocks were formed when the UK had active volcanoes. There are now extinct volcanoes in Scotland.	• Granite (intrusive) – Dartmoor • Gabbro (intrusive) – Cuillin Hills • Basalt (extrusive) – Island of Arran, Scotland
Sedimentary	Made from the skeletons of marine organisms (coccoliths) and other sediments, laid down and compacted at the bottom of the ocean.	• Chalk – White Cliffs of Dover; North Downs • Limestone – Yorkshire Dales; Cheddar Gorge • Gritstone – Peak District
Metamorphic	The action of heat and pressure on an existing igneous or sedimentary rock changes its structure to form a new type of metamorphic rock.	• Slate – North Wales • Gneiss – Lewis, Outer Hebrides

▲ **Figure 14:** Rock types

Soils and the landscape

Soils are created from the weathering of rocks, with the addition of organic material and water. The rocks are the parent material and influence the type of soil that develops on top of them and therefore the type of vegetation that grows in an area. This will also determine whether farming is likely to happen at all and, if it is, whether crops will be grown or animals will be kept. Areas of deep soil are often in low-lying areas whereas steep ground tends to have thin soil. The most productive soils in the UK are found in the East Anglian Fens , where the dark silty soil is the result of the land being reclaimed from beneath the sea and then drained. They are deep soils, with no stones and with a fine texture that drains well and warms up quickly.

Geology determines whether there is water draining over the surface, the density of streams and rivers, and the direction in which they flow over the ground. Where water stays on the surface, it speeds up the production of peat soils, found in upland moors and in heathland.

Deep soils can also form beneath woodland, because of the organic material that falls from the trees over time. This is less true in **coniferous** woodland and plantations. If an area of the UK was to be left untouched by people, the 'natural' vegetation that would develop over the years is **deciduous** woodland. Much of the UK was once covered with trees, but people cleared them for settlement, resources and fuel and to make way for farmland. The importance of wood was shown by the formation of the Forestry Commission in 1919 (Figure 15). This was set up to guarantee future supplies after the depletion of many woodland areas during the First World War. Large parts of the country have a landscape cloaked in woodland as a result.

▲ **Figure 15:** The logo of the Forestry Commission

Activities

1. Explain how the geology beneath an area influences the landscape that sits above it, with reference to a named location.
2. Research the age, hardness and permeability of ten rocks and make a 'Top Trumps' style card game.

→ Take it further

3. Research other national or regional organisations or charities which are concerned with the protection of landscapes. You could start by exploring the work of the RSPB, the biggest environmental organisation in the UK, or areas designated as Sites of Special Scientific Interest (SSSIs).

Geological maps

Use the British Geological Survey's map viewer www.bgs.ac.uk/data/mapViewers/home.html to explore geological maps online. You can also explore the area where you live using free apps such as iGeology or MySoil from the British Geological Survey.

Granite and the landscape of Dartmoor

Some rocks are connected to particular landscapes. One example of this is the granite that lies beneath Dartmoor in Devon, in the South West of England. This rock is **impermeable**, which means it doesn't allow water to pass through it, and so water stays on the surface, producing areas of boggy land called mires.

The weathering of the rock by slightly acidic rainwater causes the slow chemical decomposition of some of the minerals within the granite when they are exposed to it. The result is that the most resistant areas of rock stand out on the tops of hills as distinctive rounded features: the famous tors. Granite is also used to build the dry-stone walls which are employed throughout the area to fence in the sheep and the famous Dartmoor ponies that graze the moor. The moor is often used by the military as a suitably challenging place to test skills of navigation and survival. There is also an annual Ten Tors challenge, which is open to teams of young people.

▲ **Figure 16:** Tor on Dartmoor

Rainfall Amount
Annual Average
1971-2000
Met Office

Key
Average value (mm)

■ >3000	■ 800 to 1000
■ 2000 to 3000	■ 700 to 800
■ 1500 to 2000	■ 600 to 700
■ 1250 to 1500	■ <600
☐ 1000 to 1250	

▲ **Figure 17:** UK rainfall averages, 1971–2000

How does climate affect landscapes?

Climate is the long-term average of the temperature and rainfall experienced at a location. Climate has an obvious influence on the development of all landscapes, because they are exposed to it and may have been for millions of years. The UK has a maritime climate, heavily influenced by the seas that surround it. Onshore winds bring moist air and the UK's location means it is influenced by a number of different air masses which may originate over sea or land.

Temperatures drop quickly with increased altitude, which results in more cloud over higher ground to the west. The prevailing wind direction also carries air up over mountains, producing drier regions in the 'rain shadow' to the east. The climate influences the rate at which geomorphic processes occur in these areas. Upland areas have much higher rainfall totals than lowland areas and are also windier.

One main factor in how climate affects the landscape is the number of times that a rock experiences a **freeze–thaw cycle**. This is a change in temperature either side of freezing which happens on a daily (diurnal) basis. This cycle increases stress on rocks and speeds up weathering. Windy, exposed places may also weather faster than sheltered locations.

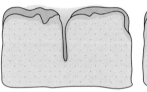 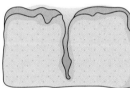 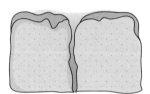

Water seeps into cracks and fractures in the rock.

When the water freezes, it expands about 9% in volume, which wedges apart the rock.

With repeated freeze–thaw cycles, the rock breaks into pieces.

▲ **Figure 18:** The freeze–thaw cycle

How does human activity affect landscapes?

There are very few areas of a densely populated country like the UK that haven't been affected by human activity, even those which remain relatively sparsely populated.

Centuries of farming and human settlement have changed the surface in many ways, including the type of vegetation that grows, the depth and health of the soil, the drainage pattern, the ability to travel through an area and the nature of the surface itself. Many low-lying areas have been drained to improve the usability of farmland, creating the fertile soils of the Fens; a landscape which lies below sea level in places.

Plantations in many upland areas of the UK, or lowland areas such as the Brecklands in East Anglia, may be no more than a few decades old. Even ancient looking woodlands were originally planted by people. Coastal marshes and windswept moorlands are also managed by people for various purposes. Many upland areas were settled in the past, when defence from attack was considered to be an important factor in settlement location.

It can be hard to escape the influence of people even in remote rural areas, whether it's a stone wall, a distant electricity pylon, the rising column of clouds above a power station or the remnants of an old settlement on a Scottish hillside.

Rural or urban?

An important distinction needs to be made between built (**urban**) and natural (**rural**) landscapes. The Office for National Statistics (ONS), which collects census data, classifies areas according to the types of houses and their density. Housing is one indicator that an area might be urban but there are others. Suburban landscapes on the edge of a town can have elements of both urban and rural landscapes in them. Some indicators of a built landscape are shown in Figure 19. Given the choice, people will often opt to live in a particular type of area and this may result in population change or migration.

Where there are people, there is a need for housing, which results in the loss of open space, woodland and habitat for wildlife. In January 2015, Boris Johnson, the Mayor of London, said that the city had reached its highest ever population, a figure of 8.6 million people.

Will the future mean more built landscapes and fewer natural ones? Some argue the opposite, and hope to 'rewild' landscapes by introducing animal species which had previously disappeared.

Indicator	Impact on landscape
Traffic infrastructure	Roads including dual carriageways and motorways create noise and act as a barrier to the movement of people and wildlife.
Street lighting	Light pollution can often be seen in areas close to urban areas. Lighting improves safety and is thought to reduce crimes, but hides the night sky.
Construction activity	Usually a sign that areas are becoming more of a built landscape, perhaps with cranes on the skyline and scaffolding being erected.
High-rise development	Usually indicating higher land values, which are a function of better accessibility.
Services which require a high population to support	Signs saying 'land acquired for redevelopment', housing developments, retail parks and warehousing and distribution centres. Open fields are removed, but trees are sometimes planted to screen the building.
Solar farms	Many of these have appeared in the last decade. While less obvious than wind turbines, they result in the loss of wildlife and change the nature of surface drainage.
Golf courses	Although they may look green and open, chemicals are used to keep the greens free of weeds, drainage is altered and there may be restrictions on access to the public.
Pedestrianisation	As traffic increases, there is pressure to remove traffic from areas with high numbers of pedestrians to reduce accidents and improve the area. There may also be changes to the high street design to increase planting and urban trees.

▲ **Figure 19:** Selected indicators that an area has a built landscape

Weblinks

Enter your school postcode here and see whether your area is classed as urban or rural: www. neighbourhood.statistics.gov. uk/HTMLDocs/urbanrural.html. How far do you have to travel before the type of area changes?

Do a place check on www. placecheck.info to identify what could be changed in your local area.

Activities

1. Name two ways that human activities have influenced the landscape of the UK.
2. Look at the signs of a built landscape shown in Figure 19. Can you suggest some other examples that you might be able to spot in your local area?
3. **a.** Over the course of a weekend, take note of the landscapes that are featured in the TV programmes or films that you watch or the games that you play. What landscapes can you identify? Are certain types of programme set in particular landscapes?

   b. Some programmes are associated with particular types of landscape and have even led to an increase in tourists visiting the locations connected with them. Northern Ireland and Iceland have benefited from their association with the filming of *Game of Thrones* and the urban landscape of London is shown in *EastEnders* and *Luther*. Which other landscapes or locations have an association with a particular TV programme or film?
4. Look at the landscape words in the table.

Soils	Apple tree
Sky	Wind
Weathering	Sand dunes
Flowing water	Coniferous trees
Clouds	Wave action
Mountains	Salt marsh
Farmland (arable)	Downs
Frost	Beach
Farm smells	Reservoir

Categorise these terms into
a. processes which shape the landscape
b. landforms (features found in the landscape)
c. landscape elements (the different ingredients which combine to make landscapes).

CHAPTER 5

What influences the landscapes of the UK?

'All too often, chasing far-away places, we forget just what beauty we have on our doorsteps'

Michael Palin, former president of the Royal Geographical Society

Figure 1: Wells-next-the-Sea, North Norfolk

Figure 2: Newquay, Cornwall

Figure 3: Groynes and surf, Tywyn, West Wales

Figure 4: Arch at Perranporth, Cornwall

Figure 5: Glen Fyne, Scotland

Activities

1. Take a look at the images on these pages.
   a. What landscape features can you already recognise?
   b. What processes do you think are active in these areas?
   c. What other sources of information would be useful to add to our knowledge about these places?
   d. How will these areas change in the short term or long term in terms of their physical geography?
   e. How do people use these areas and what impact does this have on coastlines?

✝ Geographical skills

Interpreting photographs

- Look at the features shown in the photographs on these pages. Which are human and which are natural? How do they relate to each other?
- Is the surface geology shown? Are there particular types of landscape features present?
- Look for evidence of human activity, including population, economic activity or farming. Are there any patterns to the activities shown on the photograph?
- Remember that one photo by itself can be misleading. When interpreting a photograph in your exams, use it along with other resources and information, which could include an Ordnance Survey map extract, for example.

What physical processes shape landscapes?

→ **In this section you will:**

→ learn and understand the main geomorphic processes involved in shaping coastal landscapes, including weathering, mass movement, erosion, transportation and deposition

→ learn about the formation of coastal landforms including headland, bay, cave, arch, stack, beach and spit.

Tip

Be careful not to confuse the two terms 'weathering' and 'erosion'. They are often placed at the start of exam questions. You should remember the names of the key processes involved and be able to define them.

What are the geomorphic processes involved in shaping coastal landscapes?

Geomorphic processes are the processes that change the shape of the land and they include weathering, mass movement, erosion, transportation and deposition. These processes cause changes that can be large or small; they may happen very quickly or over hundreds of years. The processes influence and shape the land found at the coast in different ways and across different timescales. They create coastal landforms which together make up the huge variety of different coastal landscapes we can see along the coast of the UK. The daily rise and fall of the **tides** changes the shape of beaches by moving beach sediment around, but it is the longer-term action of waves, wind and storms that results in some of the more visible changes in coastal landforms, combined with weathering and other processes acting on the material that makes up the coast.

Much of the coastline is not wholly natural and is managed by people to reduce its susceptibility to these processes, to reduce damage to property or the risk of loss of life. The sea is often seen as an 'enemy' to be combated, although some recent projects have allowed the sea to reclaim areas of land in a managed retreat.

Weathering

Weathering is the impact of mechanical (physical), chemical and biological processes, which act to break down the surface of the Earth *in situ*. This means without being transported. If a river, or glacier, then removes the material from the area in some way, the process is called erosion.

Mechanical weathering

Cliffs along the coastlines in places including South Devon and Pembrokeshire are subject to mechanical weathering. Mechanical weathering is due to **sub-aerial processes** which are the physical actions of rain, frost and wind.

- **Rain:** water washes away loose material and also enters cracks in the rocks. If it soaks into softer rocks such as sandstone, it adds weight to the base of the cliff, increasing the risk of collapse.
- **Frost:** when water gets into cracks in rocks and freezes, it expands in volume and puts pressure on the rock.
- **Wind:** strong winds remove fine sediment which may then be used to abrade the cliffs.

These processes create weaknesses in the rock. The weaknesses are then exploited by chemical and biological processes which further speed up the weathering and disintegration of the rock.

⊹ Geographical skills

Surveys are an important way to gather data and are useful for fieldwork enquiries. They can provide you with both quantitative and qualitative data.

1. Carry out a survey within your class of the favourite coastal landscapes of students. Ask them to bring in or gather photographs.
2. Add the locations to a map of the UK and create a picture collage. Which places have been most visited? What types of coastal landscape are featured?
3. Do the same survey for staff at the school or parents. Are there differences between the results of the surveys?

Chemical weathering

Cliffs along the coast of Kent or the Holderness coast around Flamborough Head are composed of chalk and limestone and are highly susceptible to chemical weathering.

- Water reacts chemically with certain minerals which weakens them.
- Minerals are weakened when they are exposed to the air in a process called **oxidation**.
- Some minerals are affected by water in a process called hydrolysis. This involves acidic rainfall reacting with minerals to produce material which is soluble and so is easily washed away.
- Rocks such as chalk and limestone are affected by solution, as calcium carbonate is broken down to soluble calcium bicarbonate.

Biological weathering

The rocks and land on the coast can also be broken down by the action of living organisms, which include plants and animals. Tree roots act to loosen rocks and provide crevices into which water can penetrate. Molluscs use their feet to cling to the rocks but these can also weaken the rock surface.

Ferriby chalk – susceptible to solution

Red chalk

Carstone – used as local building material

Hunstanton Cliffs are up to 18 m high and run for 1.3 km, northeast from the town. The three rocks form distinctive stripes. Erosion is caused by waves at the toe of the cliff, but also water saturation causes slumping. Heavy rain in 2012 caused cliff falls, which are still protecting the base of the cliff in places. Erosion rates are slow, but being monitored as there is a lighthouse, historical chapel and housing along the top.

▲ **Figure 6:** Hunstanton Cliffs, Norfolk

Mass movement

Mass movement refers to the sudden movement of material down a slope due to the pull of gravity. Heavy rain soaking into permeable rocks can add weight to them and the water can also lubricate the boundaries where materials meet, so that flow is more likely as the cliff 'fails'. **Rotational slumping** occurs on the soft cliffs, where the base of the cliff moves; other material then slumps down the face as the bottom moves outwards and across the beach. These can happen suddenly and have caused several fatalities in recent years, for example at Blackpool Sands in Devon in 2012 where a section of cliff collapsed onto sunbathers, and more recently on the same stretch of coastline in 2015. There may be crops planted at the top of the cliff which end up on the beach before they can be harvested. In some cases, livestock have even been carried down the cliff. Cliffs made of softer materials, including those along the east coast of the UK, are particularly susceptible to slumping.

On other cliffs, **rock slides** occur, where the failure occurs along a particular geological boundary within the cliff. A section falls down due to gravity and may dislodge other material on its way down. This can be caused by prolonged wet weather, or alternatively dry weather, which causes rocks such as clay to shrink. Cracks near the top of a cliff are a sign that it is an active area which may fail at any time.

Erosion

Erosion is the wearing away of the coast by a moving force. The main energy causing this erosive force at the coast is provided by **waves**.

- Waves arrive every few seconds and, along with the water, they also move sand or pebbles. When this sediment is thrown or rubbed against the base of the cliff as the wave breaks, the land is worn away by **abrasion**. This can sometimes result in a **wave-cut notch** at the base of the cliff where there is a greater rate of erosion than higher up the cliff.
- Water hitting a rock will compress air into any cracks within it. In the pause between waves, the air in the crack expands explosively outwards as the pressure is released by the receding water. This process, called **hydraulic action**, removes fine material and enlarges cracks, speeding up the process.
- Seawater is slightly acidic and can slowly dissolve certain rock types such as limestone by **solution**. Over time, large sediment removed by the earlier processes is broken down into smaller, more rounded sediment through attrition as particles hit each other. These smaller particles may then form the ammunition for the next wave to hit the cliff. As can be seen in Figure 6 on page 73, material that has fallen from a cliff can protect the base of it for some time before it is eventually removed.

Where hard rock occurs at the coast, you will tend to see cliffed coastlines. Softer rock is more likely to result in lower coastlines, with sand dunes or salt marshes. Where the two are found in close proximity, the result is often a more 'interesting' combination of headlands and bays, with the headlands being made of the more resistant rock.

▲ **Figure 7:** Slumped cliffs at Alum Bay, Isle of Wight

▲ **Figure 8:** Budleigh Salterton, Devon

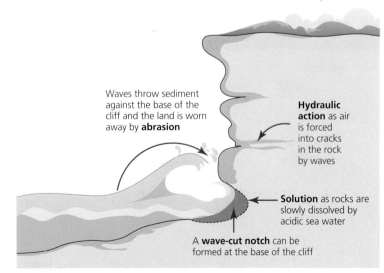
Waves throw sediment against the base of the cliff and the land is worn away by **abrasion**

Hydraulic action as air is forced into cracks in the rock by waves

Solution as rocks are slowly dissolved by acidic sea water

A **wave-cut notch** can be formed at the base of the cliff

▲ **Figure 9:** Coastal erosion

Transportation

Sediment is transported along the coast in several ways. The processes are the result of wave action and may occur at different rates depending on location.

Traction refers to the movement of larger sediment. Circular wave action rolls pebbles along the sea bed, or shifts the sediment on a beach during a storm. Smaller pieces of shingle or large grains of sand may be picked up temporarily in a process called saltation before being dropped back to the sea bed. Finer clays and smaller particles may be suspended in the water, giving it a brownish colour when seen from the air, especially after storms or along easily eroded stretches of coastline. A milky colour close to chalk or limestone cliffs may also be a sign that solution has been happening: when minerals dissolve into the seawater.

Similar processes occur in a river, see page 84.

Longshore drift

Beach sediment is moved (transported) up and down the beach profile by waves in different ways:

- The **swash** is the forward movement of water up the beach as the wave breaks.
- The **backwash** is the movement of water down the beach due to gravity after a wave breaks.

The direction of the waves hitting the coastline is dependent on the wind. If the wind is blowing at an angle to the coastline, the wave swash will be at a similar angle, transporting loose sediment along the beach with it.

As the backwash is being pulled by gravity, it always returns to the sea at 90° to the coast, which is the shortest route down the beach. This means that the sediment will be moved along the beach in a zigzag manner (see Figure 10).

Although the wind may change direction from day to day on any stretch of coastline, there will be a prevailing wind direction. This will result in a net movement of sediment in one particular direction along the beach. This process of sediment being moved along the coastline is called **longshore (littoral) drift**.

Groynes are sometimes built to slow down this movement of sediment across the beach. This might be because too much sediment would be moved from vulnerable sections of coastline. They could also be built to ensure that a sandy beach remains in place for tourist or sea defence purposes.

Deposition

When waves move material along the coast, and more sediment stays on the beach than is taken away by the backwash, this is deposition. This creates landforms such as beaches and spits (see page 78).

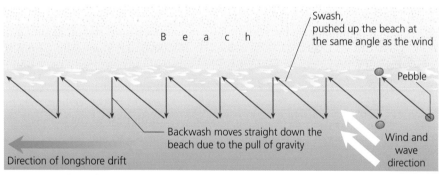

▲ **Figure 10:** Longshore drift in action

Activities

1. Carry out an internet search for the term 'cliff collapse' and click the 'News' option to see where they have been happening. Read through a few of the reports and fill in an incident report containing the following information:
   - where the incident happened
   - type of rock involved
   - how much material was lost
   - any damage or casualties
   - what was done to reduce the impact.
2. Explain the processes which cause cliffs to retreat through erosion.

3. Explain the process of longshore drift, using diagrams.

→ Take it further

4. Identify some measures which could be taken to reduce the impact of erosion along the coastline. Research the relative advantages of each of these options. Which of these methods is likely to be the most cost-effective?

How are coastal landforms formed?

Features of erosion: headlands, bays, caves, arches and stacks

A **headland** is a narrow piece of land which projects outwards from the coast. It is surrounded by the sea on three sides. Wave energy is concentrated on these locations because the waves curve towards them as they enter shallow water. The rocks making up a headland are more resistant than the rest of that stretch of coastline, but weak points are exploited as the rock does not have the same amount of resistance all over. Cracks such as vertical **joints** or horizontal **bedding planes** in sedimentary rocks allow water to enter the rock.

These cracks are also widened as a result of hydraulic action and abrasion. As these take place where waves impact the base of the cliff, there may be the creation of a **wave-cut notch** at the base of the cliff, resulting in a slight overhang. Over time, small **caves** are formed at these weak points as cracks are enlarged. These often form along the tide line.

Caves extend into the headland and may join up with another cave being formed at the opposite side, or may follow a line of weakness and extend across from one side, to create a **natural arch** which will start out as a tunnel.

These arches will start small and form close to the tide line. Water surging into these openings widens them and salt spray speeds up the process of erosion by hydraulic action and abrasion. Rock falling from the cave walls or ceiling may form a temporary barrier, encouraging water to move up and over it and increase the height further. In time, as arches grow, the weight of the 'ceiling' may become too much and collapse. The outer part of the arch will then become separated from the headland and form a tower called a **stack** (Figure 11).

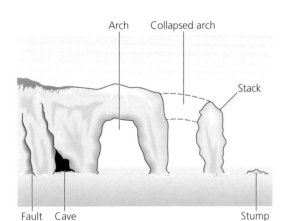

▲ **Figure 11:** Sequence of erosion of a headland

Stacks vary in height and stability. The Old Man of Hoy (Figure 12), a 137 m sandstone stack in Orkney, has stood for over 200 years, but the so-called Twelve Apostles along the Great Ocean Road in Victoria, Australia, are now down to just seven after the most recent collapse in 2009.

Stacks will eventually be worn down to form a **stump**, which may be covered over at high tide. The wearing down of the cliff to the level of the waves produces a **wave-cut platform** (also known as a shore platform) which grows in size as the cliffs retreat ever further inland. Over time, the headland will erode back towards the rest of the coastline, where the process of headland formation will start again.

▲ **Figure 12:** The Old Man of Hoy

The Sidmouth Herald

5 AUGUST 2014

Beachgoers warned after huge Sidmouth cliff fall

Police say a dramatic landslide should act as a stark message to those who walk onto the pebbles on the eastern seafront. One officer spoke of how one couple told him they had been just metres from a previous rock fall. 'The couple in question were not local and had gone onto the beach, ignoring these notices and the danger of sitting under the cliffs. They stated that they were about 20 metres away from the falling debris. One or both of them could have died.'

PC Jim Tyrrell wants visitors and residents to be aware of the dangers between Sidmouth and Salcombe Regis, where the rocks are prone to falls after wet

weather, or long spells of hot, dry weather. 'It really is becoming somewhat of an issue,' he said.

Stunned onlooker Tony Lane caught the 'spectacular' drama on camera. 'There was a huge rumble,' he said.

'It started with one or two stones falling, and then it all came down in two sections. There was a massive dust cloud.'

Dry weather causes shrinkage in the Mercia mudstone which forms part of the cliff. Wet weather also caused landslides during the previous winter, threatening clifftop properties.

▲ **Figure 13:** Newspaper extract from *Sidmouth Herald*, 5 August 2014

GIS

Some GIS software allows for comparisons of maps. *Where's the Path* is a free tool which allows users to compare present-day and historical maps side by side: http://wtp2.appspot.com/wheresthepath.htm.

Figure 14 shows the small village of Kilnsea which sits where Spurn Point meets the mainland at the mouth of the Humber estuary. There are features which can be identified on both maps, and the amount of erosion could be calculated by measuring how far the cliff has retreated, using the grids for measurement.

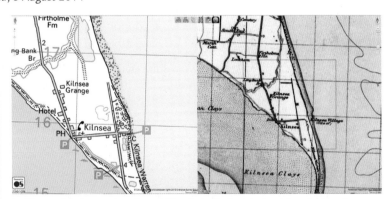

▶ **Figure 14:** Screenshot from *Where's the Path,* showing historical and present-day maps

Activities

1. Read the extract in Figure 13.
   a. What reasons are given for the cliff collapse at Sidmouth?
   b. What options do the police have for managing the risk in an area that is popular with holidaymakers?

Take it further

2. What are the options for people whose clifftop houses are threatened by coastal erosion? How can cliffs be protected?

⊹ Geographical skills

1. Draw a sketch map of Figure 16. Annotate your sketch map with the likely processes that led to its creation, including the winds that were involved and the source of sediment that helped build it.

2. Explore a stretch of coastline of around 30 km in length by looking at the area on an Ordnance Survey map. Use the map to explore the different types of landform that can be found and the way that people use your chosen stretch of the coast. If your classmates are allocated consecutive stretches of the same coastline, this could result in an interesting large-scale survey.

Features of deposition: beaches and spits

Beaches

Beaches are often found along the UK coastline. They are areas of land that lie between the storm-tide level and the low-tide level. They can be made up of sand, pebbles or a mixture of both. Some beaches are made up of mud and silt.

The charactesistics of beaches are:

- Gently sloping land; very low angle to the sea
- Stretches far inland
- Tourist resorts often have groynes to keep the beach in place
- Can be found in bays or along straight stretches of coastland

Spits

Spits are created when the coastline ends and the process of longshore drift continues, so sediment is deposited off the coast. If the conditions are right, this sediment will build up to form new land which will extend out along the existing coastline. The end of the feature will be curved by wave action and the impact of winds. Spurn Point is a spit at the mouth of the Humber.

Conditions that help the formation of spits are:

- large volumes of sediment of different sizes available
- rapid rate of movement of sediment along the coast
- shallow offshore gradient, which means that sediment is being deposited in shallow areas and can build up faster so that it comes above the surface
- sheltered from strong winds, or low wave energy
- opportunity for sediment to be vegetated which helps it become established as a permanent feature.

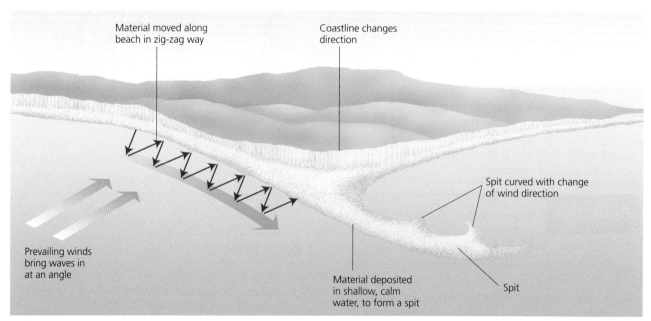

▲ **Figure 15:** Formation of a spit

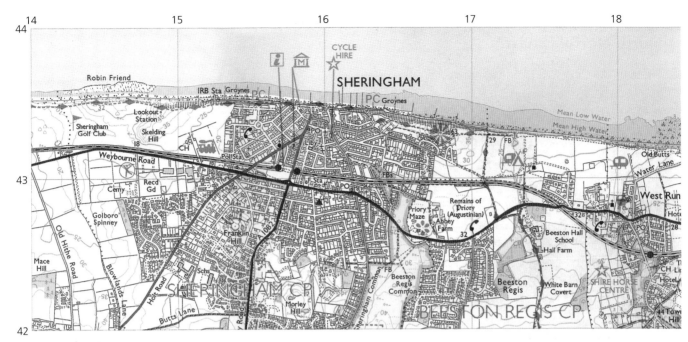

▲ **Figure 16:** Ordnance Survey map of Sheringham, scale 1:25,000 © Crown copyright and/or database right. All rights reserved. Licence number 100036470

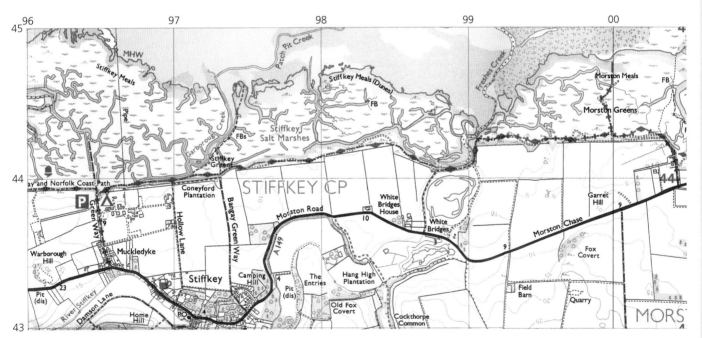

▲ **Figure 17:** Ordnance Survey map of Blakeney National Nature Reserve, scale 1:25,000 © Crown copyright and/or database right. All rights reserved. Licence number 100036470

Activities

1. Compare the coastal environments shown in the two map extracts in Figures 16 and 17.
2. Comment on the reasons for the location of the main road shown in Figure 17.
3. Explain the formation of the landform found in square 9644 of Figure 17.

4. Identify the features in Figure 16 shown at the following grid references:
   a. 157432   c. 152432   e. 178423
   b. 173431   d. 159428
   Which of these is the odd one out?
5. What types of sea defence are marked on Figure 16? Explain how these work with the aid of a labelled diagram.

Case study: What are the characteristics of your chosen landscapes?

What are the characteristics of the North Norfolk coast?

In this case study you will find out about the Norfolk coast and explore:

- the landforms created by geomorphic processes
- the processes operating at different (time) scales
- how human activity has affected these processes and the landscape that has resulted from this activity.

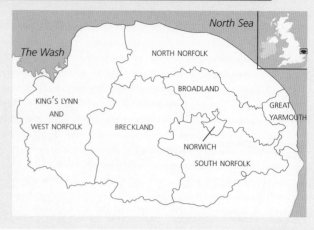

▶ **Figure 18:** Location map of Norfolk

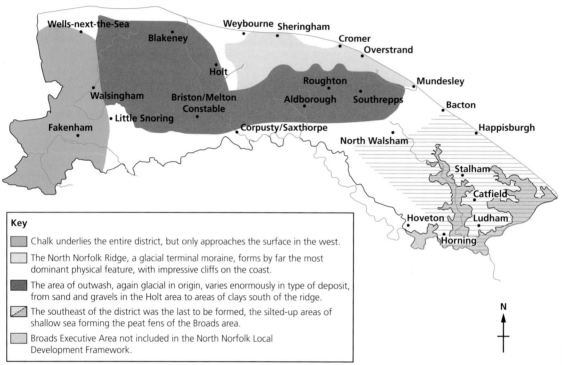

Key

☐ Chalk underlies the entire district, but only approaches the surface in the west.

☐ The North Norfolk Ridge, a glacial terminal moraine, forms by far the most dominant physical feature, with impressive cliffs on the coast.

☐ The area of outwash, again glacial in origin, varies enormously in type of deposit, from sand and gravels in the Holt area to areas of clays south of the ridge.

☐ The southeast of the district was the last to be formed, the silted-up areas of shallow sea forming the peat fens of the Broads area.

☐ Broads Executive Area not included in the North Norfolk Local Development Framework.

▲ **Figure 19:** Map of the landscape character of North Norfolk

Where is Norfolk?

Norfolk is a county in the east of England, bordering Suffolk, Lincolnshire and Cambridgeshire. It creates the southern border of the Wash, an inlet of the North Sea, into which several rivers including the Great Ouse flow. The North Norfolk coast runs for almost 70 km between the towns of Wells-next-the-Sea and Cromer, and includes all the small villages that lie between.

What makes the Norfolk coast distinctive?

It is a low-lying coastline, with a range of habitats including salt marsh, cliffed headlands and expanses of sand dunes. The gradient of the seabed close to the coast is shallow, so the tide goes out a long way. As beach sand dries out, it is blown onshore by winds to create the sand dunes. The underlying rock is chalk. A large number of flints are found

within the chalk and are used locally as a building material. At Hunstanton, the chalk appears in the famous striped cliffs seen on page 73.

The chalk is hidden by a layer of material called drift, which was laid down by an advancing ice sheet at the end of the most recent Ice Age. The ice sheet travelled from the north and also created a ridge near Cromer which provides the highest land in the whole county at just over 100 m. This produces a range of farming land and habitats including heathland and woodland.

What is landscape character?

Geographers often talk about the landscape character of an area. The North Norfolk coast has a particular character which is produced by a combination of the geology, the land use and the impact of coastal processes. The subdued relief and flinty soils are part of that character. The relief also allows people to appreciate the 'big skies' in this part of the world. Dark sky tourism is a growing activity in this area. This is possible because of the low levels of light pollution as the location is far from any large cities. The coastal area is also designated as an Area of Outstanding Natural Beauty (AONB).

The coast road used by residents and tourists follows the slightly higher land and lies inland from the coastal marshes. Some of these marshes near Holkham were drained by Dutch engineers who had previously worked locally to drain the Fens. Local landowners paid for the work, so that the peat soils could be used for summer cultivation and to prevent serious winter flooding. The wide sandy beach at Holkham is regularly named as one of the world's best beaches, known for its extensive and well-developed sand dunes. It has appeared in a number of feature films.

How does human activity, including management, affect the geomorphic processes working on the coast?

The villages along this stretch of coast sit on the slightly higher land to reduce their chance of coastal flooding, although Wells-next-the-Sea and Blakeney were among those places flooded during a storm surge in January 2013, which also left homes lying on the beach further round at Hemsby.

At Blakeney Point (Figure 20) and Scolt Head Island, spits have been produced by the transportation of sediment along the shoreline. The boat trip out to see the seals from the harbour at Morston is a popular activity for tourists and adds to the value of tourism to the local economy and for local employment. This is a coast where deposition is more important than erosion. The rapid pace at which the tide comes in and the presence of hidden hollows cause problems for those unfamiliar with the area. Local lifeboat crews have regular callouts during the summer months.

▲ **Figure 20:** Blakeney Point spit

At Stiffkey, an area of salt marsh has developed where fine material has been trapped by specialist plants which can tolerate high levels of salt to create natural sea defences. Salt marshes are very low lying, but build up as sea level rises, so

form a good natural defence. They are rare places and their characteristic plants are protected by the National Trust.

At Holkham, the estate has planted the dunes with pine trees to stabilise the dune system, and visitors are encouraged to use boardwalks rather than disturb the marram grass and erode the dunes, which can result in sand blowouts. The Holkham estate also manages the sea front at Wells-next-the-Sea where there are groynes to protect the famous beach huts, and gabion baskets below the Coastwatch lookout station (see http://www.nci.org.uk/wellsnextthesea). These try to slow down the transportation of sand from in front of the resort by slowing longshore drift, but care needs to be taken as sediment held here will not be available to protect coastline further downdrift.

The coastline has been subject to erosion in the past. Entire villages such as Shipden, Keswick and Wimpwell disappeared in the last century and now lie beneath the waves. The section near Happisburgh has become quite well known as a result of news coverage of cliff retreat. This has cost people their homes, despite battles by residents for appropriate compensation for their losses. The final house in Beach Road in the village was lost following the storm surge that took place in January 2013. This event was another reminder that this is a coast that continues to be shaped and defined by the sea.

At Cley-next-the-Sea, shingle ridges were breached and large dunes were stripped of sand at Wells-next-the-Sea. The **sea walls** and **rip-rap barriers** at Sheringham, and the **gabion** boxes at Brancaster, are a reminder that no coastal settlement is safe from potential damage, despite the generally benign nature of the waves.

The management at Cley-next-the-Sea is carried out as part of the 'Living Landscape' project. This provides a home for wildlife, but also protects the shingle ridge which forms the base of the spit at Blakeney Point. A breach in the ridge could starve the spit of shingle, and threaten its future existence.

The village of Happisburgh, further south from Cromer, is a well-known example of a settlement which has seen an increased rate of erosion as a result of a decision not to repair a damaged sea defence. Villagers have fought for years for compensation for damage to their properties, which are threatened by a receding coastline, unlike the village of Sea Palling further south, which has been protected by a sea defence scheme. At Sea Palling, a sea wall has been built to reflect wave energy back into the sea which reduces erosion from waves. Offshore breakwaters have also been constructed which reduce the intensity of wave action and therefore reduce coastal erosion. This decrease in wave energy has led to a reduction of transportation of sediment which has created a wide beach.

Sea defence systems

Rip-rap barriers: large rocks placed in front of the cliff to dissipate wave energy and protect the cliffed coastline by slowing down the rate of erosion – installed at Sheringham

Sea walls: walls usually made of concrete to reflect and absorb wave energy, to prevent erosion of the coastal landscape including areas where settlements are found – installed along promenades at Cromer and Hunstanton

Gabions: wire cages filled with stone, used to reduce erosion by absorbing wave energy, or in front of sand dune systems where they get covered with sand over time and trap sediment in front of low lying coasts – installed at Old Hunstanton

Groynes: concrete or hardwood barriers, placed perpendicular to the coastline at intervals along beaches to slow down the rate of sediment movement, and help the beach to remain in front of resorts – installed at Hunstanton and Wells-next-the-Sea

Activities

1. Visit the Environment Agency's flood mapping page to explore flood issues along this (or any) stretch of coastline. Access a Coastal Erosion map for your chosen location.
   (http://watermaps. environment-agency.gov.uk/)

→ Take it further

2. People who use an area of landscape in a specific way are often referred to as stakeholders. Some of these are landowners or manage the land for a particular purpose. Identify the range of stakeholders that would be interested in the Norfolk coast and want to have a say in its future. Some organisations to get your list started would include the Environment Agency, HM Coastguard and the RSPB.

Coastal management

For management purposes, the coastline of the UK has been split up into sections called 'littoral cells'. Each of these cells includes a stretch of coastline which lies between points that form natural boundaries. Often these represent a point where the direction of movement of sediment along the coast changes. Within each of these cells, decisions have been made by the Environment Agency and other landowners on the way that they will be managed. Coastal defence works are very costly, so need to be prioritised to areas where they are most needed.

There are four main options for any stretch of defended coastline (Figure 21). Decisions have been made for the period up to 2030 for each section of the UK's coastline.

Strategy	What this means
No active intervention	Do nothing
Hold the existing defence line	Maintenance of the existing sea defences
Managed realignment	This includes the creation of new areas of salt marsh by deliberately breaching sea defences. This approach has been used at locations such as Wallasea Island on the Essex coast.
Advance the line	Build new defences. This became necessary after the 2013 storm surge at locations such as Clacton, which has suffered from threatened cliff collapse.

▲ **Figure 21:** Management strategies to defend coastlines

The North Norfolk District Council has provided Shoreline Management Plans (SMP). These are non-statutory plans for coastal defence management planning. They look at the risks associated with the erosion processes that have shaped the coast.

Figure 22 shows the key values linked with the section from Brancaster to Brancaster Staithe and highlights the complex interactions that are needed between different groups with different interests, for example groups in the tourist industry and groups working to preserve habitats for wildlife. Shoreline management in this area consists currently of holding the existing defence lines.

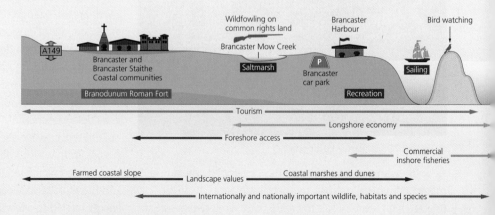

▲ **Figure 22:** Cross section from Brancaster to Brancaster Staithe

Norfolk makes an excellent location for fieldwork as it provides a variety of coastal habitats, including salt marsh and sand dunes, as well as opportunities for exploring the impact of tourism on coastal villages and towns. The cliffs are often unstable, but yield fossils at places like Hunstanton. There are also chances to explore the impact of second homes (particularly for Londoners, for example Thornham and Burnham Market), an ageing demographic due to retirement communities, and the rebranding of coastal resorts which were originally developed during the Victorian time. The Norfolk Broads are a National Park, offering scope for tourist management and ecosystem case studies. For more information on this stretch of coastline, visit: www.norfolkcoastaonb.org.uk/content/maps/mapvms.html

The Norfolk Wildlife Trust at Cley-next-the-Sea has a new educational centre which helps students to interpret the way that the coastal management works together with the geomorphic processes.

Happisburgh's Beach Road ends in a steep drop showing the impacts of rapid erosion with threatened properties, and cliff collapses can be seen in fields to the south of the village as a result of rapid erosion, and soft, unprotected cliffs.

What physical processes shape river landscapes?

Weathering

The processes involved in the weathering of river landscapes are largely the same as those which shape coastal landscapes.

Mechanical weathering

- **Rain:** water washes away loose material and also enters cracks in the rocks. If it soaks into softer rocks such as sandstone it adds weight to the river banks, increasing the risk of collapse.
- **Frost:** when water gets into cracks in rocks and freezes, it expands in volume. This puts pressure on the rock and results in the break-up of rocks on river banks.
- **Wind:** strong winds remove fine sediment which may then be used to abrade the river banks.

Chemical weathering

- Rainwater reacts chemically with certain minerals which weakens them.
- Minerals are also weakened when they are exposed to the air in a process called oxidation.
- Some minerals are affected by water in a process called hydrolysis. This involves acidic rainfall reacting with minerals to produce material which is soluble and easily washed away.
- Rocks such as chalk and limestone are affected by solution, as calcium carbonate is broken down to soluble calcium bicarbonate.

Biological weathering

Rocks in river banks are broken down by the action of living organisms, which include plants and animals. Tree roots act to loosen rocks and provide crevices into which water can penetrate. Rabbits and other animals can burrow into river banks which can lead to rocks breaking up.

▲ **Figure 23:** Biological weathering from Chinese mitten crabs, an invasive species, on the banks of the Thames

Mass movement

Mass movement refers to the sudden movement of material down a slope due to the pull of gravity. Heavy rain soaking into permeable rocks can add weight to them, and the water can also lubricate the boundaries where materials meet, so that flow is more likely as the material making up the river banks 'fails'. Rotational slumping occurs on the banks of rivers, where the bottom of the river bank slips into the river and other material slumps down the bank. Soft, clay river banks are particularly susceptible to slumping.

Erosion

Erosion is the wearing away of the river banks by a moving force. The main energy causing this erosive force is the river within the river channel.

- Water hitting the river banks will compress air into any cracks within it. The air in the cracks expands explosively outwards as the pressure is released by the receding water. This process, called **hydraulic action**, removes fine material and enlarges cracks which speeds up the erosion process.
- Water moves sand or pebbles which are then thrown or rubbed against the river banks, where the land is worn away by abrasion or **corrasion**.
- Water can slowly dissolve certain rock types such as limestone by solution or **corrosion**.
- Larger rocks in the river are broken down into small, more rounded sediment through **attrition** as the different rocks within the river hit each other.

Transportation

Water flowing downhill has the ability to carry sediment. The River Wye (see page 85) drops by around 600 metres during the first 50 miles of its course, providing a fast-flowing upper course which moves sediment in four main ways (Figure 25):

- **Traction:** large boulders and rocks are rolled along the river bed, scraping against it as they do so.
- **Saltation:** small pebbles and stones are bounced along the river bed in a series of short jumps.
- **Suspension:** very fine, light material is carried along in the water; clays tend to stick together but silts and fine sand are carried in this way and make the river 'murky'.
- **Solution:** some types of sediment, such as minerals, are dissolved in the water and carried along in solution.

▲ **Figure 24:** The upper course of a river

Traction is only likely after heavy rainfall, when the river's **discharge** is at its highest. In the upper course of a river, the bedload tends to be larger, as can be seen in Figure 24.

Deposition

When the river slows down and loses energy, sediment such as sand and pebbles are deposited, for example on the shallow bank of a river.

It is the balance of the energy of the river, the movement of water and the transport of sediment that creates all the features that are found along the course of a river (see pages 85–6).

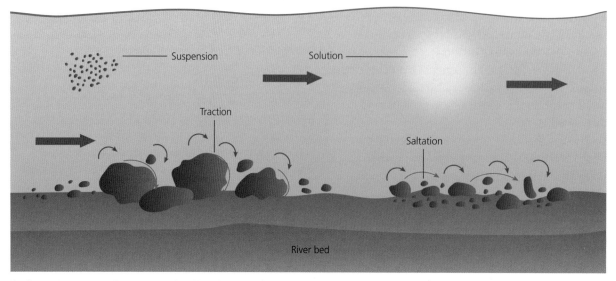

▲ **Figure 25:** Forms of transportation in a river

Case study: What are the characteristics of your chosen landscapes?

What are the characteristics of the River Wye?

In this case study you will learn about the River Wye and explore:

- the landforms created by geomorphic processes including waterfall, gorge, V-shaped valley, floodplain, levee, meander and ox-bow lake
- how human activity has affected these processes and the landscape that has resulted from this activity.

The River Wye is the fifth longest river in the UK, at over 150 miles (210 km) long. It has its source in the Plynlimon range in central Wales, just a few miles from the source of the River Severn, into which it flows, after descending almost 700 m during its course (Figure 26). Plynlimon rises nearly 2500 feet high and receives one of the highest rainfall totals of any location in the UK. Rivers work to transport water and eroded sediment, taking it from higher land to the sea (or a lake) where it is deposited.

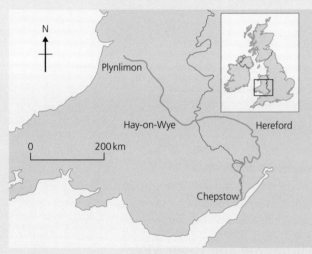

▲ **Figure 26:** The course of the River Wye

The upper course of the River Wye runs through moorlands. Its upper valley is the result of glaciations and cuts through gritstone and shales. The river descends quickly, which gives it energy to shape a typical steep-sided valley in places. At this stage it can only remove small pieces of sediment, and the bed has large stones around and over which the river flows (see Figure 24, page 84). There are bogs and heaths higher up and also some limestone areas, which provide a range of habitats for wildlife.

The Wye is a relatively natural river in that its course has not been altered too much by human activity, such as reservoir building (unlike its tributary the Elan). Its importance as a habitat is marked by its designation as a Site of Special Scientific Interest. It passes through a number of towns, which would have made use of the river for water and also as a source of power. Salmon swim up river and are fished for during the season. The removal of sediment from the slopes into the channel produces a steep-sided valley, which is usually said to be a **V-shaped valley**.

The first town the river passes through is called Rhayader, which literally means 'waterfall on the Wye', but the **waterfalls** were removed when the town's bridge was built, leaving just a short stretch of **rapids**. This area is used by canoeists, who test themselves after heavy rainfall in the faster-flowing water. Waterfalls occur when a river flows over bands of rock which vary in their resistance to erosion (Figure 27). Areas of weaker rock are eroded faster, creating a steep gradient between the hard and soft rock. This means that the river can flow faster, and as it flows over the sudden drops marked by the edge of the more resistant bands of rock, it creates rapids. With time, the softer rock is eroded more quickly and the drop becomes steeper. This creates an overhang of hard rock. A deep **plunge pool** is formed at the bottom of the drop and turbulence in the pool erodes the back wall of the waterfall further. **Gorges** can form when waterfalls retreat upstream over time. Waterfalls occur on several of the Wye's tributaries, notably at Cleddon Falls.

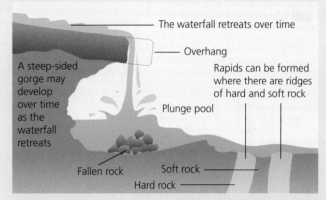

▲ **Figure 27:** Formation of waterfalls and rapids

Below the city of Hereford, the River Wye cuts down through a broad **floodplain**, a wide, flat area of land on either side of a river which is prone to flooding. This is created due to centuries of lateral erosion by a river, which widens the river floor. It is also created by the deposition of fine sediment during floods. As the river floods and flows outwards from the river channel, the flow has less energy, so it deposits the fine sediment (alluvium) being carried within it onto the surrounding area. As the water drops the heavier material first, more sediment is dropped close to the river channel. After the river has been flooded several times, this can build up to form **levees** on either side of the river.

The fertile alluvium means that the floodplain is farmed. Traditionally, this was pasture, but it is now often cultivated. Along the river's course there is farmland and a mix of woodland, making up almost 90 per cent of the Wye Valley. This is designated as an Area of Outstanding Natural Beauty (AONB).

Meanders are a natural feature of the flowing river caused by lateral erosion. As the river flows around the meander bend, the energy of the water and the sediment that it carries (Figure 28) erode the outside of the bend. Over time, the meander bends could become very large. Due to the continual erosion, the ends of the meander bend can become closer and the neck of the meander will narrow. When the river floods, the river may then cut through the neck to take a shorter route and create a new channel. The old bend will be cut off from the main channel and eventually form a curving **'ox-bow' lake**, until continued deposition of sediment fills it in.

The River Wye floods annually and these former channels become temporary pools alongside the current meandering course, and can be picked out from the air. There are few settlements close to the river at this point, because of the flood risk.

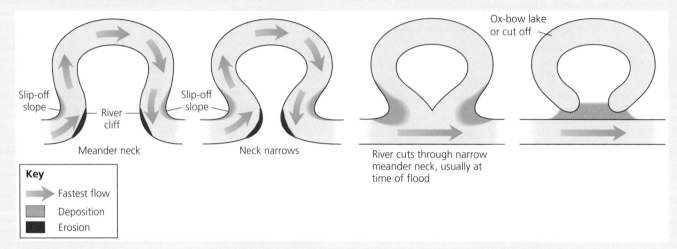

▲ **Figure 28:** Ox-bow lake formation

Settlements have developed at bridging points. These include Hay-on-Wye which hosts an annual literature festival and marks the point where the river passes from Wales into England. One of the most visited areas is the Wye Valley (or gorge). By this point in the river's course, several other tributaries have joined the main course, providing more erosive potential. The gorge runs between Goodrich and Chepstow.

One of the viewpoints looking along the river's course at Symonds Yat is a famous place for tourists to pause. It is a limestone outcrop rising over 120 metres above the river below, which winds around it, and lies down river of Goodrich Castle. Canoeists use this stretch of the river for recreation, and walkers appreciate the beautiful landscape.

The river passes the ruins of Tintern Abbey, before it widens out and flows across a flatter stretch. It then enters its tidal estuary and flows into the Bristol Estuary where it meets salt water. Salmon fishing is popular within the lower course of the river and provides employment.

Managing the River Wye

All rivers require management to ensure that they do not impact on the environments through which they run. All major rivers, including the Wye, have a management plan produced by the Environment Agency in consultation with other bodies.

▲ **Figure 29:** Symonds Yat on the Wye Valley

The Wye Valley is affected by a range of processes, both human and physical, some of which are historical, and have been in place for many years (Figure 30).

Urbanisation

Hard engineering may be required to protect settlements near to the river's channel from flooding. Over 200,000 people live in the Wye and Usk Valley, which includes large towns such as Hereford and Chepstow. These same urban environments may increase the flood risk by draining water more quickly into the channel. Around 9000 properties in the area are thought to be at particular risk of flooding. A number of strategies, including hard engineering, are used to protect these larger towns. People are also expected to be aware of methods to reduce their personal risk. Some areas of the floodplain have been zoned as being of high risk; construction is not permitted in these areas.

Agriculture

The predominant land use in the catchment is agriculture, which is a consumer of water from the river for irrigation. There are also high levels of biodiversity that need to be managed alongside the agricultural use of the land, such as controls on particular chemicals that may otherwise affect the river.

Industry

Although this is not a heavily industrialised area, the presence of the river means that some industrial activity is inevitable. Quarrying for limestone, originally to provide limestone for Llanwern Steelworks in Newport, has changed the gradient of some areas. Tintern Quarry is now

a rock-climbing activity centre but quarrying still takes place at Livox Quarry for Marshalls. The rock also contains metal ores including iron ore. Woodlands were also felled for shipbuilding and to support the charcoal industry.

Today, the tourist industry employs many people in the Wye Valley, and high-profile events such as the literary festival at Hay-on-Wye draw thousands of visitors to the area. The Forest of Dean has also been used for numerous TV and film location shoots, including the 2015 film *Star Wars: The Force Awakens*.

Geomorphic processes

The Upper Wye is steep, with mountainous impermeable landscapes, and the river responds quickly to rainfall. Some areas use the landscape to reduce the impacts of flooding, by ensuring that excess water is able to flow into areas of the floodplain that are zoned for that purpose. Further downstream, the Letton Lakes take some of the excess water during flood events to protect Hereford. Management has attempted to reduce the likelihood of flooding by slowing the rate that water enters the channel by surface runoff. Vegetation management reduces rates of runoff by increasing surface cover, and increasing interception storage. The risks of landslides or other mass movement may be reduced by planting trees which also intercept rainfall and help bind the soil surface together. There are few trees in large parts of the Wye's catchment, but other areas have seen new planting. Research conducted for the Environment Agency suggests that trees planted in the upper course of the river could reduce the height of flood water by 20 per cent by increasing interception storage. Trees also provide a local amenity for residents, as well as having an aesthetic value.

Where river banks are stabilised, they can be more widely used by anglers or walkers. Otters are also returning to the upper course of the river as a result. Stabilising the channel can assist with changing the river's response to rainfall, which ultimately helps settlements further downstream. It can also reduce the rate of river erosion, which reduces the amount of sediment being transported downstream. Soil erosion will also decrease due to vegetation reducing direct raindrop impact and overland flow. Ultimately this means that depositional features such as floodplains would have less sediment available to construct them. Artificial levees would also need to be constructed.

The flow of the river is in a state of dynamic equilibrium (it will adjust to any change, to bring it back to a natural flow where possible), and human attempts to manage the channel can upset this balance in the long term if care isn't taken to work with the natural processes acting along it during river management.

Industry
Limestone quarrying increasing gradients

SSSI (site of special scientific interest) and **SAC** (special area of conservation) as well as an **AONB** (area of outstanding natural beauty)

River Wye processes

Forestry
Trees felled for shipbuilding and charcoal, with extensive replanting since the Second World War

Wye Valley tourism
This was one of the first tourist honeypots, with visitors from the 1700s onwards; Tintern Abbey and viewpoints were popular

Transport and communications
Roads and railway follow the river valley and were built in the nineteenth century

▲ **Figure 30:** Processes affecting the River Wye

Practice questions

1. Define the term 'landscape'. **[1 mark]**

2. **a)** What are the main characteristics of a 'built' landscape? **[2 marks]**
   b) Look at Figure A below and annotate the landscape elements that you can see.

▲ Figure B

▲ Figure A

3. Which of the following is not characteristic of a natural landscape?
   a) An area of woodland
   b) A water feature such as a river or stream
   c) A shopping centre
   d) Farmland **[1 mark]**

4. With reference to a landscape that you have studied, explain what makes it **distinctive**. **[4 marks]**

5. Explain how geology can affect the landscape that forms on the surface. **[3 marks]**

6. With the aid of an annotated diagram, explain what is likely to happen to the landform in Figure B over the next 100 years. **[6 marks]**

Tip

When you are drawing an annotated diagram, use a sharp pencil, add a title and use a ruler to connect labels to the appropriate place on the diagram.

7. With reference to the Norfolk coast or a stretch of coastline that you have studied:
   a) Explain the processes of erosion that are affecting it. **[3 marks]**
   b) Explain how the different groups of people who use that stretch of coastline may have conflicting views on how it should be used. **[4 marks]**
   c) Name three different methods used to protect the coastline from erosion. **[3 marks]**

8. Which of the following is *not* a process that results in sediment being transported by rivers?
   a) Traction
   b) Solution
   c) Convection
   d) Suspension **[1 mark]**

Tip

Make sure that you are clear on what the main geomorphic processes are. Some of the terms are quite similar.

9. With reference to the River Wye or a river that you have studied:
   a) Describe the geomorphic processes that operate in the upper course of the river. **[4 marks]**
   b) Explain how human activity affects the river's natural flow. **[3 marks]**

Sustaining Ecosystems

Chapter 6: Why are natural ecosystems important?

By the end of this chapter, you will know the answer to this key question:

→ What are ecosystems?

Chapter 7: Why should tropical rainforests matter to us?

By the end of this chapter, you will know the answers to these key questions:

→ What biodiversity exists in the tropical rainforest?

→ Why are the tropical rainforests being 'exploited' and how can this be managed sustainably?

→ Case study: How is the tropical rainforest within Crocker Range Biosphere Reserve in Borneo being managed sustainably?

Chapter 8: Is there more to polar environments than ice?

By the end of this chapter, you will know the answers to these key questions:

→ What is it like in Antarctica and the Arctic?

→ How are humans seeking a sustainable solution for polar environments?

→ Case study: Small-scale sustainable tourism at Union Glacier, Antarctica

→ Case study: Small-scale conservation in Antarctica

→ Case study: Halley VI Research Station–built for the future

→ Case study: Global sustainable management attempts in Antarctica through the Antarctic Treaty System

→ Case study: Global sustainable management attempts in the Arctic through global actions?

Orang-utans in a tropical rainforest in Indonesia. What processes make different ecosystems distinct? What threats do they face?

CHAPTER 6
Why are natural ecosystems important?

What is an ecosystem?

Ecosystems are natural areas in which plants, animals and other organisms are linked to each other, and to the non-living elements of the environment, to form a natural system. Each ecosystem is made up of **biotic** and **abiotic** elements.

- Biotic elements comprise all of the living parts of the ecosystem including plants, animals and bacteria. In the natural world, plants are known as **flora** and animals are known as **fauna**.
- Abiotic elements are the physical, non-living parts of the ecosystem, including temperature, water and light.

Large-scale ecosystems, known as **biomes**, spread across continents and have types of plants and animals that are unique to them. For example, polar bears are unique to the Arctic tundra and orang-utans are unique to the tropical rainforest. Biomes cover a wide area and are identified by their climate, soils, plants and animal species. Each of these factors is reliant upon all the others. This is known as **interdependence** (Figure 1). Climate has the greatest influence over vegetation and soil within an ecosystem. During a period of low rainfall, less vegetation will grow, meaning that there is less food for some animals. Increasingly, however, ecosystems are being changed by human activity.

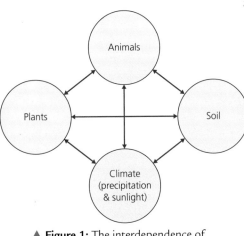

▲ **Figure 1:** The interdependence of ecosystems

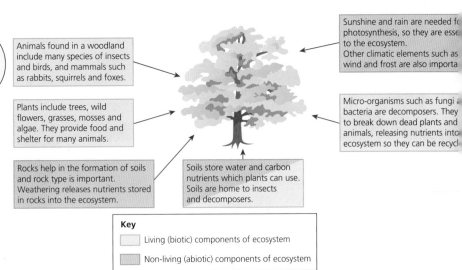

Animals found in a woodland include many species of insects and birds, and mammals such as rabbits, squirrels and foxes.

Plants include trees, wild flowers, grasses, mosses and algae. They provide food and shelter for many animals.

Rocks help in the formation of soils and rock type is important. Weathering releases nutrients stored in rocks into the ecosystem.

Soils store water and carbon nutrients which plants can use. Soils are home to insects and decomposers.

Sunshine and rain are needed fo photosynthesis, so they are esse to the ecosystem. Other climatic elements such as wind and frost are also importa

Micro-organisms such as fungi a bacteria are decomposers. They to break down dead plants and animals, releasing nutrients into ecosystem so they can be recycl

Key

☐ Living (biotic) components of ecosystem

☐ Non-living (abiotic) components of ecosystem

▲ **Figure 2:** The biotic and abiotic components of an ecosystem

Where in the world are the major biomes?

Climate and latitude are important factors which contribute to the location of the world's major biomes, which broadly match the world's climate zones (see Chapter 1, pages 4–5). The world contains eight major biomes. Each biome has its own climate characteristics which create distinct environments for a range of plants and animals to survive.

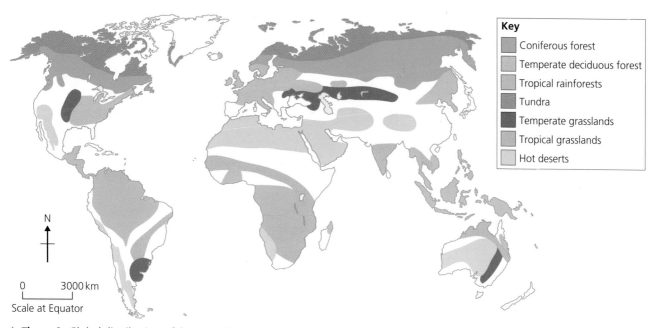

Key
- Coniferous forest
- Temperate deciduous forest
- Tropical rainforests
- Tundra
- Temperate grasslands
- Tropical grasslands
- Hot deserts

N

0   3000 km
Scale at Equator

▲ **Figure 3:** Global distribution of the major biomes

Figure 4 shows the distribution of biomes according to temperature. **Temperate** simply means a region characterised by milder temperature; they are neither hot nor cold regions.

Temperature	World ecosystem
Tropical	1. Tropical rainforests
	2. Tropical grasslands
	3. Hot deserts
Warm temperate	4. Mediterranean
Cool temperate	5. Temperate deciduous forest
	6. Temperate grasslands
Cold	7. Coniferous forest
	8. Tundra

▲ **Figure 4:** Classification of world ecosystems

Activities

1. Research the places in the world that contain the ecosystems listed in Figure 4.
2. Describe the global distribution of two contrasting ecosystems using Figure 3 and an atlas to help you.

From pole to pole: how do the two polar regions vary?

How does their location vary?

Arctic: located in the north polar ocean, including several larger islands such as Greenland and various other countries including Russia and Canada.

Antarctica: a continent that covers the South Pole region. It is covered by an immense ice shelf.

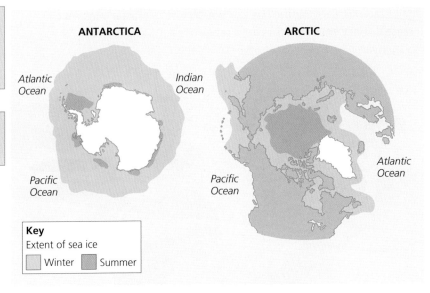

▲ **Figure 5:** The polar regions – Arctic and Antarctica

What is the climate like in the polar regions?

The climate of both polar regions consists of long, cold winters and short, cool summers. They are covered by snow and ice throughout the year, though the extent of this ice varies with the seasons. Antarctica is covered by an ice sheet 2.8 miles thick in some places. Temperatures rarely rise above freezing in these high-latitude regions. This is largely due to the low angle of the Sun in the sky. Due to the tilt of the Earth, the polar regions spend half of the year in darkness and half of the year in daylight. Polar regions tend to be dry, receiving as little as 250 mm of rainfall per year. This is because the descending air is unable to pick up moisture to form clouds and snowfall.

The Arctic is much warmer than Antarctica. The North Pole winter temperatures vary from −46 °C to −26 °C whereas the South Pole temperatures range from −62 °C to −55 °C. But why is there such a difference in temperature?

- The sea in the Arctic does not fall below −2 °C, which means that the whole Arctic region stays warmer than Antarctica.
- The weather in the Arctic travels south and relatively warm weather from the south travels north into the Arctic region. This is known as the Gulf Stream.
- All of the weather in Antarctica is kept within the continent due to the **circumpolar winds** and currents travelling around the coastline.
- Antarctica has an average height of 2300 metres, making it the highest of all the continents in the world. Temperature falls as altitude increases. In fact, with every 100 metres in altitude, the temperature falls by 1°C.

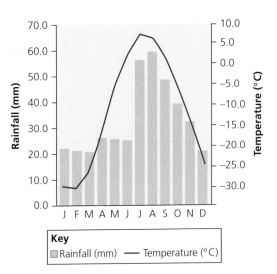

▲ **Figure 6:** Climate graph for Iqaluit in Canada

What flora and fauna are found in the polar regions?

The polar region to the north is characterised by what can grow in the **tundra**. This is a vast area of 11.5 million km² that consists of permafrost, which means that the ground is permanently frozen. Consequently, it is a treeless area. There are, however, low shrubs, reaching a height of around 2 metres, along with mosses, grasses and alpine-like flowering plants. There are approximately 1700 species of plant living in the tundra. Land mammals include polar bears, wolves, foxes and reindeer and sea mammals include walruses and whales. As the Arctic is part of a land mass, some animals are able to migrate southwards during the winter months.

Plant life in Antarctica is much less plentiful due to only about one per cent of the continent being ice free. There are some exposed rocks on which the hardiest of plants can grow. There are around 100 species of moss and 300–400 species of lichen. Both the Arctic and Antarctica have very productive seas due to large volumes of phytoplankton. Many animals that feed in the sea come onto land for part or most of the time, including large numbers of penguin species such as gentoo, emperor and Adélie. Likewise, fur seals, Weddell seals and elephant seals live in Antarctica.

▲ **Figure 7:** A killer whale hunting a seal in the Antarctic

Activities

1. Draw a climate graph for Vostok, Antarctica, using the data below (see Chapter 1, Figure 11 on page 5 for an example).

	Jan	Feb	Mar	Apr	May	Jun	July	Aug	Sept	Oct	Nov	Dec
Average temperature (°C)	−32	−44	−58	−65	−66	−65	−67	−68	−66	−57	−43	−32
Rainfall (mm)	0.1	0.0	0.7	0.5	0.4	0.5	0.6	0.7	0.3	0.2	0.1	0.0

2. Compare the climate graph for Iqaluit, Canada (Figure 6) with your graph for Vostok, Antarctica.
3. Explain why Antarctica is a colder polar region than the Arctic.

Tropical rainforests are found in:

- South America in the Amazon River basin
- Africa (Zaire basin, small area in West Africa and eastern Madagascar)
- Southeast Asia
- New Guinea
- Queensland in Australia
- west coast of India.

What are the characteristics of tropical rainforests?

Where are they located?

Tropical rainforests are found within the Tropics of Cancer and Capricorn (23.5° north and south of the Equator).

Rainforests now cover less than six per cent of the Earth's land surface, though this figure was once much higher. Despite this small area, it is thought that the tropical rainforests contain 50 per cent of all plant and animal species.

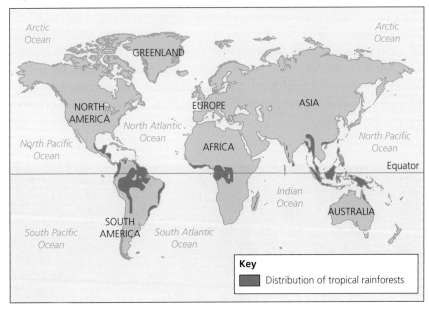

▲ **Figure 8:** Locations of tropical rainforests

Tropical rainforests are being destroyed at an alarming rate, with trees cut down on a large scale. This is known as **deforestation** (see Chapter 7, page 108).

What is the climate like?

Temperatures in the tropical rainforest are high and remain constant throughout the year because the Sun is always high in the sky. It is a hot and wet climate. There are no seasons like you would find in the temperate forest (see page 101). In fact, the mean monthly temperatures only vary by 2°C from 26°C to 28°C. Each day has a reliable 12 hours of daylight and 12 hours of darkness.

Annual rainfall totals are very high; often over 2000 mm. A heavy, thundery downpour can be expected most afternoons in the rainforest. This is because of the meeting of trade winds at the ITCZ where warm, moist air is forced to rise rapidly, cool and condense to form frequent rain. Due to the large amounts of moisture in the air from both rainfall and transpiration from the dense vegetation, the atmosphere is very humid and sticky. This can make it a rather unbearable climate for even the most intrepid of explorers.

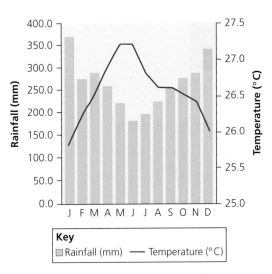

▲ **Figure 9:** Climate graph for Sibu, Malaysia

What flora and fauna are found in tropical rainforests?

The climate creates the perfect environment for a wide variety of species to survive. The growing season is constant throughout the year as the climate does not vary. Fifteen million plant and animal species have been identified successfully and many more have yet to be discovered.

Vegetation consists mainly of trees. In Amazonia, there may be as many as 300 species of tree in any one km², including mahogany, ebony and rosewood. There are distinct layers to the vegetation of the tropical rainforest, as shown in Figure 10.

- The tallest trees are known as **emergents** and can reach as high as 50 metres. Below this are three layers that compete for sunlight.
- The **canopy** is the next layer below the emergent layer and receives 70 per cent of the sunlight and 80 per cent of the rainfall. It is a continuous blanket of leaves. These trees are approximately 30 metres high.
- The next layer is the **under canopy**, consisting of trees growing up to 20 metres.
- The **shrub layer** is the lowest layer where only small trees and shrubs that have adapted to living in the shade can survive. Less than five per cent of sunlight reaches the forest floor.

The tallest trees are supported by buttress roots (see Figure 11). These emerge over 3 metres above the ground level to give the tree support. Trunks are usually thin and branchless as they compete for space. Leaves are dark green and smooth and often have 'drip-tips' to shed excess water. Vine-like plants, called lianas, grow around and between tree trunks and can reach lengths of 200 metres. These vines help to connect layers of the rainforest for the many animals that live there.

The tropical rainforest is filled with beautiful colours and patterns. Most of the birds, animals and insects live in the canopy layer. Insects make up the largest single group of animals, ranging from camouflaged stick insects to vast colonies of ants. Other species found in the tropical rainforest include toucans, jaguars, monkeys, chameleons, frogs and snakes. The rainforests of Borneo are one of the last habitats of the orang-utan.

There is an abundance of amphibian species. The poison dart frog is brightly coloured to warn predators. It has poison on its back and, when touched, can kill almost instantly. A single poison dart frog has enough poison to kill ten full-grown men!

▲ **Figure 10:** Structure of the rainforest

▲ **Figure 11:** Buttress roots in the Amazon rainforest, Ecuador

Activities

1. In which of these locations would you **not** find tropical rainforests?
   A. Amazon River basin
   B. Southeast Asia
   C. Namibia in southern Africa
   D. Queensland, Australia
2. Describe, using examples, how plants have adapted to survive in the tropical rainforest.

- Rainforests have 170,000 of the world's 250,000 known plant species.
- More than 2000 different species of butterfly live in South America.
- Around 8000 different species of plant are found in Central Africa.

Why are coral reefs such a unique ecosystem?

Where are coral reefs found in the world?

Coral reefs are found within 30° north and south of the Equator in tropical and sub-tropical oceans. Locations include:

- the western Atlantic Ocean including Bermuda, the Bahamas, Belize, Florida and the Gulf of Mexico
- an Indian and Pacific Ocean region extending from the Red Sea and Persian Gulf through to the western coast of Panama
- some areas of the Gulf of California
- the Great Barrier Reef off the eastern coast of Australia. This is the largest reef at 1500 km long and covering an area of 284,300 km². It is broken up into 2900 different reefs.

In total, 109 countries in the world have coral reefs in their waters.

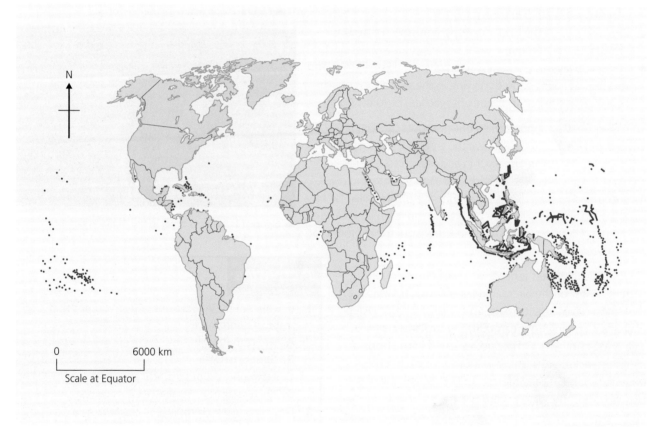

▲ **Figure 12:** Global distribution of coral reefs

What are the ideal environmental conditions for coral reefs to grow?

For coral to grow, there needs to be warm water all year around with a mean temperature of 18°C. The water also needs to be clear and shallow – no deeper than 30 metres. Beyond this, there is not enough sunlight for photosynthesis. Coral reefs are located on the seabed around the land, before the water depth increases. This is known as the **continental shelf**.

What flora and fauna are found in coral reefs?

Coral reefs are some of the most productive and diverse ecosystems on Earth. In fact, they are known as the 'rainforests of the oceans'. Less than one per cent (about the size of France) of the world's ocean surface is made up of coral reefs, yet it is estimated that they contain 25 per cent of all marine life. These species depend on the reef for food and shelter.

Coral reefs are made up of thousands of coral polyps which live together in reefs or colonies. Although coral may look like a plant, it is actually an animal related to the jellyfish. A single polyp is 2–3 cm in length and feeds on tiny organisms such as plankton. Each polyp is a small and simple organism consisting of a stomach topped with a mouth and tentacles. They can secrete calcium carbonate to make a mineral skeleton which helps to build the structure of the reef. Corals take a long time to grow, averaging between 0.5 cm and 2 cm per year.

There is a relatively small range of plant life in coral reefs. The algae on the coral produce energy through photosynthesis, giving the coral its vibrant range of colours. Sea grasses such as turtle grass and manatee grass are commonly found in the Caribbean Sea. Unlike algae, sea grasses are flowering plants. They provide shelter and a habitat for reef animals such as the young of lobsters and provide food for herbivores such as reef fish.

Some estimates suggest that there are up to two million species living in coral reefs and 4000 species of fish alone. Some species include:

- parrot fish – feed directly on polyps, tearing coral to get to them
- starfish – produce digestive juices that they squirt into the polyps; they then suck out the middle like a soup
- clams – settle on the coral bed and filter plankton from seawater
- eels – live within the coral, pouncing on small fish
- molluscs, worms, crustaceans and sponges
- larger mammals such as dugongs, which are related to elephants; they consume large quantities of sea grass.

Activities

1. Annotate a world map with the main locations of coral reefs in the world. Add the lines of latitude.
2. Describe the distribution shown on your map.
3. What is a polyp?
4. Suggest how **two** species have adapted to survive in the coral reef.
5. Why are coral reefs often compared to tropical rainforests?

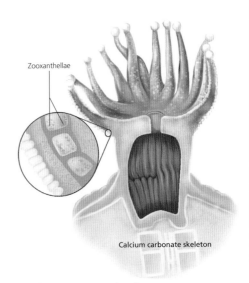

Zooxanthellae

Calcium carbonate skeleton

▲ **Figure 13:** A coral polyp

▼ **Figure 14:** Coral sea, Queensland in Australia

What is a grassland?

A grassland is a region where the annual average precipitation is high enough to cause grass to grow. In some areas, there might also be occasional small trees and shrubs.

What are the characteristics of tropical grasslands?

Where are they located?

Tropical grasslands, also known as savannah, are located between the latitudes of 5° and 30° north and south of the Equator, within central parts of continents. This includes:

● most of central Africa surrounding the Congo Basin
● parts of Venezuela
● the Brazilian highlands
● Mexico
● northern Australia.

What is the climate of the tropical grasslands?

The savannah region ranges from the fringes of the rainforest to the beginnings of the desert ecosystem. Consequently, the climate can range from tropical wet to tropical dry. Temperatures are high throughout the year. Cloud cover is limited for most of the year, allowing for daily temperatures of 25°C. The main characteristic of the climate in tropical grasslands is that there are two seasons: a longer dry season and a shorter wet season.

The annual range of temperatures is slightly larger than that of tropical rainforests as a result of the reduced angle of the Sun in the sky for part of the year. The wet, or rainy, season occurs when the Sun moves overhead, bringing with it the ITCZ (also known as the heat equator; see Chapter 1, Figure 28 on page 14). This is a belt of low pressure which brings bursts of heavy rainfall. In fact, 80 per cent of the annual rainfall occurs in the 4–5 months of the wet season. As the ITCZ moves away, the dry season begins. During the longer dry season, rainfall can be as low as 100 mm. Figure 16 shows how the ITCZ shifts to create the two seasons.

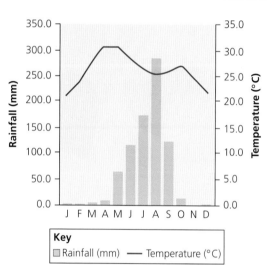

Key
▢ Rainfall (mm) ── Temperature (°C)

▲ **Figure 15:** Climate graph for Kano, Nigeria

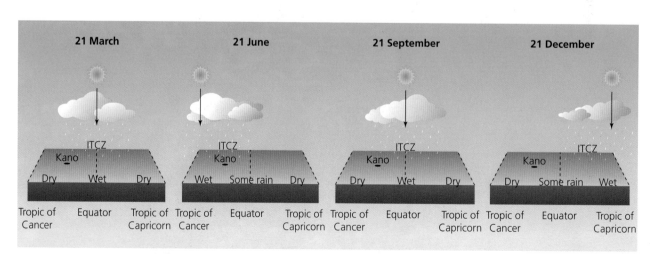

▲ **Figure 16:** The movement of the ITCZ, creating wet and dry seasons

What flora and fauna are found in tropical grasslands?

The length of the growing season depends on how long the rainy season lasts. With the summer rain, the grasses, such as the tall and spiky pampas grass, grow very quickly to over 3 metres in height. The baobab tree has adapted to the climate of the tropical grasslands by growing large swollen stems and a trunk with a diameter of 10 metres (see Figure 17). The root-like branches hold only a small number of leaves to reduce the loss of water vapour by a process called transpiration. The bark of baobab trees is thick to retain moisture and roots are long to tap into supplies of water deep within the ground. Many trees are also drought-resistant (xerophytic) or fire-resistant (pyrophytic) as a means of surviving the long dry season.

The savannah grasslands of Africa contain the world's greatest diversity of hoofed animals with over 40 different species. The grasslands are home to herds of plant-eating animals known as **herbivores**. Antelopes are very diverse, and include gazelles and impalas. Up to 16 grazing species can live in the same area of grassland, including elephants, giraffes, wildebeest, zebras and rhinos. African elephants are the largest mammals in the world. The **carnivores** (meat-eating animals) in this ecosystem stalk the herds; these include cats such as cheetahs, lions and leopards as well as dogs and hyenas.

▲ **Figure 17:** Baobab trees in Madagascar, Africa

Activities

1. How does the baobab tree survive in the tropical grasslands?
2. What is the difference between xerophytic and pyrophytic trees?
3. Using Figures 15 and 16, explain how the movement of the ITCZ affects the climate.

▲ **Figure 18:** Elephants at a waterhole in Etosha National Park, Namibia

What are the characteristics of temperate grasslands?

Where are they located?

Temperate grasslands lie in the centre of continents, between the latitudes of around 40–60° north of the Equator. The major temperate grasslands include the:

- plains of North America
- veldts of Africa
- pampas of South America
- steppes of Eurasia.

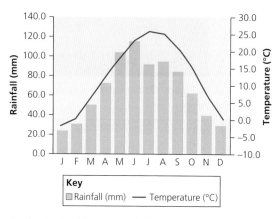

▲ **Figure 19:** Climate graph for Topeka, Kansas, USA

What is the climate of the temperate grasslands?

The climate of the temperate grasslands is cooler than that of the savannah. It is an ecosystem of extremes. Summers are very hot and winters are very cold. Summer temperatures can reach over 38°C and winter temperatures can plummet as low as −40°C. Average rainfall varies from 250 mm to 750 mm. Around 75 per cent of this rainfall occurs during the summer growing season. Snow acts as a reservoir of moisture to help the start of the summer growing season as it melts. The summer months can bring periods of drought and the occasional fire which helps to maintain the grasslands.

What flora and fauna are found in temperate grasslands?

The length of the growing season depends on the temperature. Vegetation does not grow as rapidly or as tall as that of the tropical grasslands. Trees and shrubs struggle to grow, but some trees, such as willow and oak, grow along river valleys where more water is available. Tussock grasses reach heights of 2 m and are found in clumps on the landscapes. Grasses, such as buffalo and feather grass, grow more evenly across the land, up to around 50 cm in height. Flowers including sunflowers and wild indigos can grow among the grasses.

The grasses provide a good habitat for burrowing animals such as gophers and rabbits and large herbivores such as kangaroos, bison and antelopes. Bison are typically found in the prairies of North America (Figure 20). The carnivores in temperate grasslands include coyotes and wolves as well as large birds such as eagles and hawks.

Activity

1. Copy and complete the following table by summarising the key characteristics of tropical and temperate grasslands.

	Tropical grasslands	Temperate grasslands
Location		
Temperature		
Rainfall		
Flora		
Fauna		

▲ **Figure 20:** American bison grazing in South Dakota, USA

What are the characteristics of the temperate forest ecosystem?

Where are temperate forests found?

Temperate forests are found between 40° and 60° north and south of the equator. Temperate refers to the temperature; it gets neither too hot nor too cold. It means 'not to extremes'. Temperate forest covers a wide range of forest types and their native flora and fauna, but the forests are mostly made up of deciduous or evergreen trees (see Figure 21). It is also possible to find temperate rainforests and temperate coniferous (needle-like leaves) forests in the world.

	Deciduous	Evergreen
Temperature	Moist, warm summers and frosty winters	Mild, nearly frost-free winters
Rainfall	Reliably high, year-round rainfall	Lower, more unreliable rainfall
Locations	Northern hemisphere including eastern North America, eastern Asia and western Europe (including the British Isles)	New Zealand, parts of South America, eastern Australia, southern China, Korea and Japan

▲ **Figure 21:** Comparisons between different types of temperate forest

What is the climate like in temperate forests?

Due to the tilt of the Earth, the Sun's rays hit different parts of the planet more directly at different times of the year. This has created four seasons of equal length: winter, spring, summer and autumn. This is where temperate forests thrive. Summers are warm and winters are mild. Rainfall ranges from 750 mm to 1500 mm and the average annual temperature is 10°C. An insulating layer of cloud cover helps to keep the temperature mostly above freezing. Precipitation falls throughout the year. Snow is common in mountainous areas during the winter, but is unlikely to settle at lower levels.

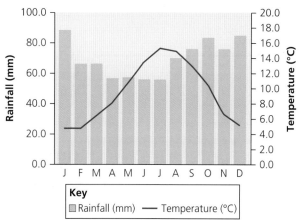

Key
Rainfall (mm) —— Temperature (°C)

▲ **Figure 22:** Climate graph for Kilkenny, Ireland

The temperate forest ecosystem has the second highest rainfall after tropical rainforests. This is largely due to their location at the meeting point of the Ferrell and polar cells. The warm tropical air is forced to rise over the denser, cold polar air. This creates an area of low pressure and subsequent rainfall (see Chapter 1, pages 2–3).

▼ **Figure 23:** Red deer under an oak tree in Richmond Park, England

▲ **Figure 24:** Black bear in western Montana, USA

Activities

1. Describe the climate of the temperate deciduous forest.
2. Draw an annotated diagram similar to Figure 10 to show the layers of the temperate forest.

What flora and fauna are found in temperate forests?

There are relatively few tree species when compared with the rainforest. Trees have a growing season of 6–8 months and may grow only 50 cm per year. Deciduous trees shed their leaves during the winter season. Leaves turn a spectacular range of reds, oranges and yellows during the autumn before they fall to the ground. In Britain, oak trees can reach heights of 30–40 metres. A single oak tree can produce 90,000 acorns in one year. Elm, beech, sycamore and chestnut trees grow less tall and have broad, thin leaves. Beneath this canopy is a lower shrub layer, known as the understorey. Trees and shrubs here vary in height from 5 metres for hawthorns to 20 metres for ash and birch trees. Unlike the rainforest, branches of the higher trees are more open and allow enough sunlight through to enable smaller trees to grow. The forest floor is often covered with brambles, grass, bracken and thorns.

Animals must adapt to cope with the colder winters and warmer summer months. Some animals migrate to warmer places and others hibernate to escape the cold. The types of fauna often depend on the region of the world. Many species are native to certain places, so they may only be found there. For example, Australia's temperate forests contain marsupial species such as koalas and opossums which are not found anywhere else in the world.

Black bears are found in the temperate forests of North America. They have adapted well to the conditions here. They have a heavy coat made of many layers of fur and build up a five-inch layer of fat before hibernating for the winter. Black bears also have long claws to climb trees and are **omnivores**. This means that they eat can plants and animals.

In the northern hemisphere, squirrels are widespread. Owls and pigeons are found in almost all temperate forests as are an abundance of other bird species. In Britain, rabbits, deer, mice and foxes are commonly found animal species.

What are the characteristics of the hot deserts?

Where are deserts found?

Deserts cover one-fifth of the Earth's land surface. They are located between 5° and 30° north and south of the Equator, around the Tropic of Cancer and the Tropic of Capricorn. They are usually found on the west coast of continents. The extensive Sahara and the Arabian desert cover the African and Asian land mass, respectively. The Sahara covers a staggering land area of 9 million km²; that is the same size as 37 UKs!

What is the climate like in hot deserts?

Due to their location near the tropics, deserts experience a fairly high number of daylight hours ranging from 14 hours in the summer to 10 hours in the winter. During the day, temperatures can reach 36°C, with extremes of 50°C recorded. At night, however, temperatures plummet to well below freezing. During the day, high levels of input from the Sun raise the temperatures. Bare rock and sand will also heat up. The lack of clouds in the sky means that the heat from the day escapes readily into the atmosphere during the night, causing temperatures to fall dramatically to −12°C or lower.

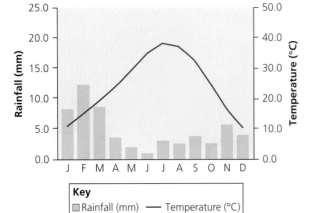

▲ **Figure 25:** Climate graph for Death Valley, California, USA

Annual precipitation is around 40 mm and extremely unreliable. In Death Valley in California, rain may fall only once every 2–3 years. The baked ground makes infiltration, the process where water passes through the surface of the ground, very limited. As a result, the water sits on the surface and evaporates rapidly in the heat of the day.

What flora and fauna are found in hot deserts?

In desert climates, vegetation needs to be resistant to the lack of moisture and intense heat. Most plants are **xerophytic**, meaning that they have adapted to an environment with very little water. Cacti and yucca plants are found in the driest and hottest places. Where the rainfall is slightly higher, thin grasses grow. Where bushes grow, they are far apart to avoid competition for water.

Cacti absorb large amounts of water during the rare periods of rain. They have thick, spiky, waxy leaves to reduce the loss of water through transpiration and to prevent animals from trying to eat them. Roots of xerophytes do one of two things. They are either very long, like those of the acacia tree with roots exceeding 15 metres to tap into groundwater supplies, or they are near the ground's surface and spread over a large area to take advantage of any rain that falls.

When a storm occurs, the desert bursts into life. Plant seeds then lie dormant for many months or years, awaiting the next downpour.

The lack of food in the form of plants makes it difficult for deserts to support many animal species. The desert ecosystem is very fragile as animals do not have alternative food sources which may be available in other ecosystems. Many animals are small and nocturnal, meaning that they only come out at night. With the exception of camels, animals would not be able to survive in hot sun so are likely to burrow into the sand during the heat of the day.

Animals have adapted considerably to survive in the desert.

- Meerkats, which live in the harsh land of the Kalahari Desert in southern Africa, occupy complex underground tunnel systems. They have adapted to the limited food sources by feeding on scorpions, whose venom they are immune to. They also eat lizards and small rodents.
- Camels have humps on their backs that store fat and water. They also have thick hair on their ears, long eyelashes for keeping out the sand and wide feet that act like snowshoes.
- Sidewinder rattlesnakes are found in the Mojave Desert in southwest USA and the Namib Desert in southern Africa. Their unusual sideways motion helps them to keep moving in shifting sands and ensures that only two parts of their body are touching the hot ground at any one time.

Activities

1. Suggest two reasons to explain why the temperature varies so much during a day in the desert.
2. For either flora or fauna, explain how species have adapted to survive in the hostile desert climate.

→ Take it further

3. Choose one major desert in the world. Create a fact file, or a class presentation, about your chosen desert. Create three to five of your own enquiry questions to guide your research.

▶ **Figure 26:** Cacti in the Sonoran Desert, Tucson, Arizona, USA

CHAPTER

7

Why should tropical rainforests matter to us?

What are the distinctive characteristics of the tropical rainforest?

What biodiversity exists in tropical rainforests?

→ In this section you will:

→ learn about the distinctive characteristics (climate, nutrient cycle, water cycle and soil profile) in the tropical rainforest ecosystem

→ understand how climate, soil, water, plants, animals and human activity in tropical rainforests are interdependent.

▲ **Figure 1:** Mist evaporating off the rainforest-covered highlands of Malaysia

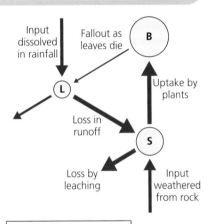

Key
○ Store of nutrients
→ Transfer of nutrients
B Biomass
L Litter
S Soil

▲ **Figure 2:** Nutrient cycle in the tropical rainforest ecosystem

Climate

The climate of the tropical rainforest is hot and wet with a reliable input of rainfall, often in excess of 2000 mm per year (see Chapter 6, page 94). The daily temperatures do not vary significantly and average between 26° and 28°C. However, the climate in the rainforest can vary at a much smaller scale, with the conditions in the canopy being very different from the conditions at the forest floor. For example, the Sun's rays can reach through some layers of the rainforest, but not others. These small-scale climatic conditions are known as a microclimate.

Nutrient cycle

Nutrient cycling is rapid in the rainforest. Figure 1 show the relationship between biomass, soil and litter. The size of the circles indicates the amount of nutrients held in each store.

● The forest floor is hot and damp, which enables dead leaves to decompose quickly. This explains the small circle for the leaf litter. This decomposition can occur within three to four months in the rainforest. In the UK, it can take two years or more for leaves to decompose.

● As organic material, such as leaves, decays and is recycled so quickly by the nutrient-hungry plants and trees, few nutrients ever reach the soil. The circle for the soil is even smaller than that for the litter. This is why many trees have their roots close to the surface or even above the surface of the ground; they are poised to take advantage of any nutrients available.

● The greatest store of nutrients is in the biomass – the living plants and animals.

Water cycle

Rainforests produce their own rainfall. As the rainforest heats up during the morning, the water evaporates into the atmosphere and forms clouds to make the rainfall for the next day. This is called **convectional rainfall**. Water is lost through pores in leaves and then evaporated by heat in a process known as **evapotranspiration**. The roots of plants take up some moisture, but much of the water is evaporated from the canopy later. It is the canopy which also intercepts most of the rainfall (see Figure 3).

The removal of trees by exploitative practices means that there is less moisture in the atmosphere and rainfall declines. This can sometimes lead to drought as we saw in Chapter 1, page 14.

Activities

1. Represent Figures 2 and 3 as flow diagrams.

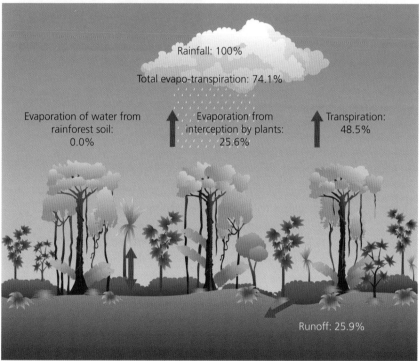

Rainfall: 100%

Total evapo-transpiration: 74.1%

Evaporation of water from rainforest soil: 0.0%

Evaporation from interception by plants: 25.6%

Transpiration: 48.5%

Runoff: 25.9%

▲ **Figure 3:** Water cycle in the tropical rainforest ecosystem

Soil profile

Soils in tropical rainforests are called latosols. Despite the vast amount of plant life supported in the rainforest, the soils are generally shallow and lack minerals. The fertility of the soil is only sustained by the rapid replacement of the nutrients from dead leaves. The humus, or decomposed, layer is very thin. Minerals such as calcium and magnesium are leached quickly through the soil due to high amounts of rainwater. The top layers of the soil are red in colour because of high concentrations of aluminium oxide and iron oxide. There is rapid chemical weathering throughout the profile, particularly of the original rock on which the soil has formed. This is layer is known as the parent rock.

Ferralitic soil (latosol)

HEAT

RAIN

Rapid recycling of nutrients

Intense chemical weathering

Red clay layer due to iron and aluminium compounds

Rapid leaching of dissolved materials

Clays decompose

Parent rock

Precipitation exceeds evapo-transpiration

Thick leaf litter layer

Very thin humus layer as litter is rapidly incorporated into the soil and decomposes

Greyish/red colour soil which is slightly acidic

Rapid leaching washes nutrients down and out of the soil

Soil depth can reach 30 metres

▲ **Figure 4:** Latosol profile

Indigenous peoples

Tropical rainforests are home to 50 million native, or indigenous, peoples. These people depend on their surroundings for food, shelter and medicines. In fact, their knowledge of medicinal plants used to treat illnesses is unrivalled. The people of the rainforest are often known as hunter–gatherers as they hunt animals and fish in the forest and gather wild fruits and nuts to eat. The Amazon supports the largest number of remaining native people, although many have been affected by the modern world. Most Amerindians now grow crops like bananas and use western goods such as pots, pans and utensils. They are also likely to make regular trips to towns and cities to visit markets for trade.

For centuries, indigenous farmers have practised a sustainable system called shifting cultivation. This involves having small agricultural gardens which have been cleared of trees and burnt. The ash released from the burning of the land adds minerals to the soil, making it more fertile. Crops are then planted on the land for 2–3 years or until all of the nutrients have been used. The farmers then move, or shift, to a new patch of land to cultivate.

▲ **Figure 5:** The Penan people of Borneo harvest the pith from the sago palm using a woven mat to collect starch

Interdependence in the rainforest ecosystem

Each part of the tropical rainforest ecosystem relies on every other part for its survival. The interdependent relationship between soil, climate, water, plants, animals and humans means that any small changes in human activity or the environment can have dramatic effects on the ecosystem. For example, the nutrient cycle relies on minerals from precipitation and the soil relies on the forest cover to intercept rainfall to prevent severe leaching of minerals.

Figure 6 shows the main components of the tropical rainforest ecosystem: climate (rain and sunshine), soil, vegetation (trees and plants) and animals. The important point is that that all these things are interdependent. They rely on one another and live in a sort of balance. The arrows show how they interact to create this interdependence. The diagram also shows people. It is possible for native people (indigenous tribes) to live as part of, and in harmony with, the ecosystem. Equally, people can badly upset the ecosystem's balance.

Activities

1. What examples of interdependence are there in the tropical rainforest ecosystem? Consider the relationships between soil, climate, water, plants, animals and people.

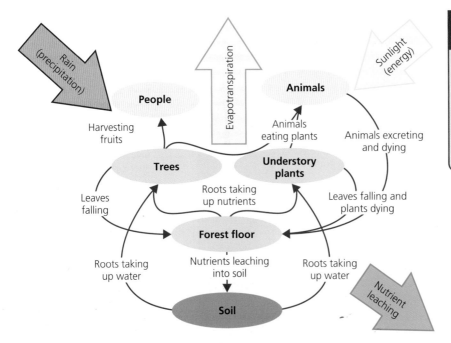

▲ **Figure 6:** Components of the tropical rainforest ecosystem

Why are the tropical rainforests being 'exploited' and how can this be managed sustainably?

What valuable goods and services are provided by tropical rainforests?

- The **goods** provided by an ecosystem are the physical products and items that can be used by people.
- The term **services**, on the other hand, refers to the unique role, or job, that the ecosystem plays in its environment.
- Goods are often locally produced, whereas the service role that an ecosystem plays can often have a global effect.

Goods

Without realising it, we rely on the tropical rainforests for our most basic needs; we are all connected to it in some way.

Goods	Some examples and/or uses
Fruit and vegetables	Passion fruit, cane sugar, bananas (Figure 8), citrus fruits, avocados
Nuts	Brazil nuts and cashews
Oils	Palm, coconut (used in sun tan lotion and candles), rosewood and ylang-ylang (used in perfumes)
Flavourings	Vanilla, cocoa, coffee, tea
Fibres	Rattan and bamboo furniture, rugs and mattresses
Wood	Teak, mahogany, rosewood
Gums and resins	Golf balls are covered in a gum called gutta-percha; chicle latex is used in chewing gum; paint products
Rubber	Products such as car tyres and shower mats from rubber tapping (Figure 9)
Medicines	Curare, used as a muscle relaxant in surgery; quinine, used in anti-malaria treatment; 70% of the plants that have proven anti-cancer properties are only found in tropical rainforests

▲ **Figure 7:** Some of the goods provided by rainforests

Why are tropical rainforests being 'exploited' and how can this be managed sustainably?

→ In this section you will:

→ learn about the valuable goods and services that can be found within tropical rainforests

→ investigate how human activity, including logging, agriculture, mineral extraction and tourism, has impacted on tropical rainforests

→ look at how the tropical rainforest in Crocker Range Biosphere Reserve has been managed sustainably.

▲ **Figure 8:** A banana plantation in Columbia

▲ **Figure 9:** Rubber tapping at a plantation in a Sumatran tropical rainforest in Indonesia

Services

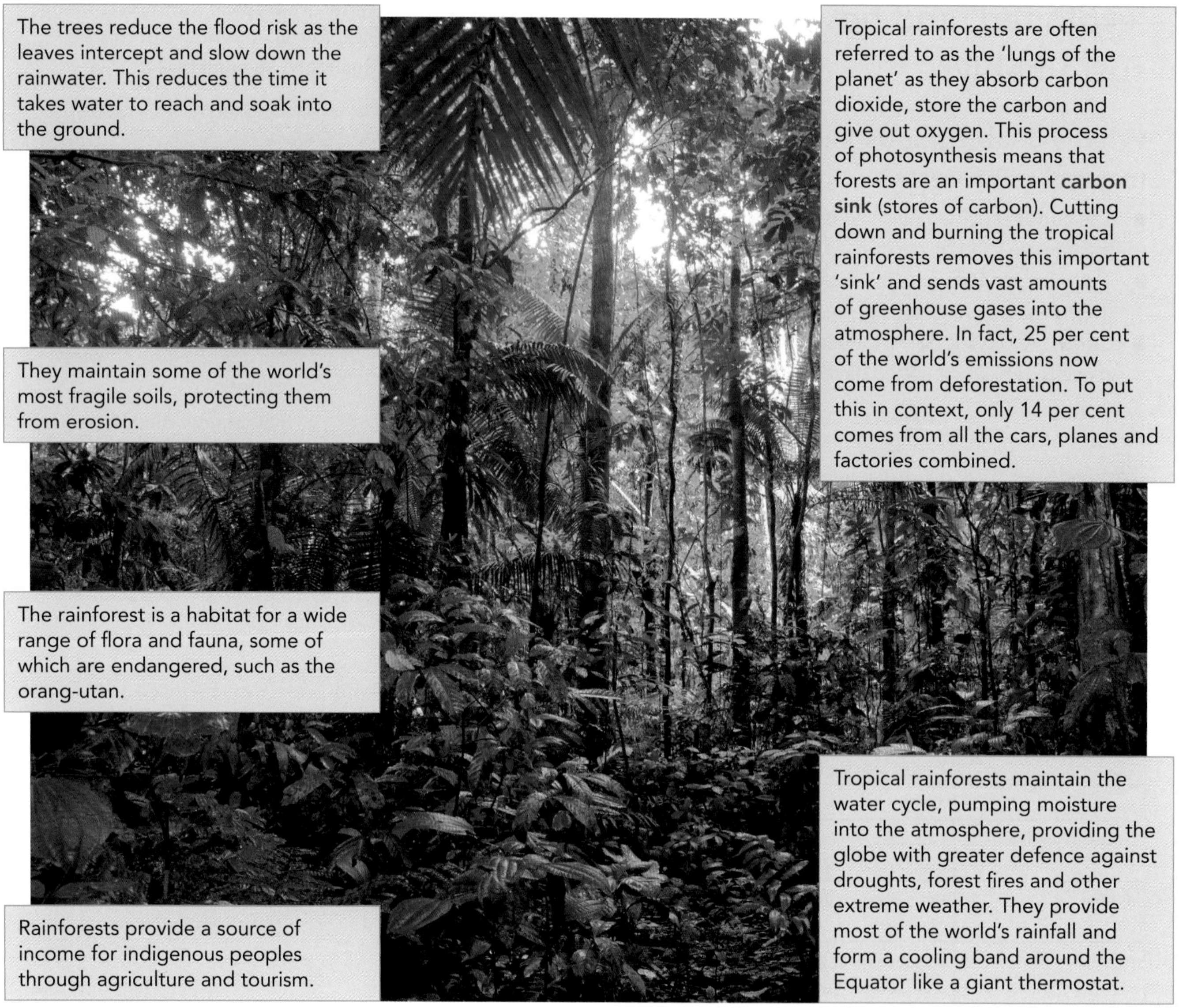

The trees reduce the flood risk as the leaves intercept and slow down the rainwater. This reduces the time it takes water to reach and soak into the ground.

Tropical rainforests are often referred to as the 'lungs of the planet' as they absorb carbon dioxide, store the carbon and give out oxygen. This process of photosynthesis means that forests are an important **carbon sink** (stores of carbon). Cutting down and burning the tropical rainforests removes this important 'sink' and sends vast amounts of greenhouse gases into the atmosphere. In fact, 25 per cent of the world's emissions now come from deforestation. To put this in context, only 14 per cent comes from all the cars, planes and factories combined.

They maintain some of the world's most fragile soils, protecting them from erosion.

The rainforest is a habitat for a wide range of flora and fauna, some of which are endangered, such as the orang-utan.

Tropical rainforests maintain the water cycle, pumping moisture into the atmosphere, providing the globe with greater defence against droughts, forest fires and other extreme weather. They provide most of the world's rainfall and form a cooling band around the Equator like a giant thermostat.

Rainforests provide a source of income for indigenous peoples through agriculture and tourism.

▲ **Figure 10:** Tropical rainforests perform a range of vital services to help to regulate the environment

Activities

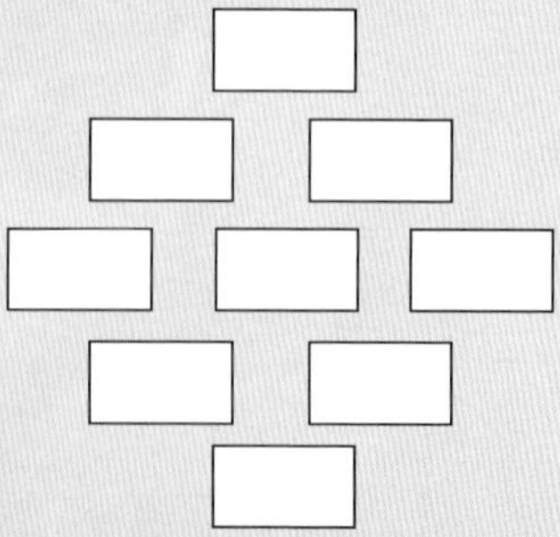

1. This activity is called Diamond 9.
   a. In pairs, write the name of nine specific goods (e.g. mahogany and coconut oil) that are found in tropical rainforests on nine separate sticky notes.
   b. Move them into the shape of a diamond. Put the 'good' that you think is the most important at position number 1 at the top of your diamond. Now move down to the second and third most important 'good'. The least important will be number 9 and will form the bottom of your diamond.
   c. Swap seats with someone from another pair. Explain your decisions to one another.
   d. When you return to your partner, do you want to move any of the 'goods'? Discuss your choices.
2. Which is the most important: goods or services?

How have humans 'exploited' tropical rainforests around the world?

This is a geographical enquiry to determine which stakeholder is most to blame for the destruction of the world's tropical rainforests.

Tropical rainforests cover seven per cent of the total land area in the world but contain 50 per cent of all plant and animal species. They provide vital goods and services on a global scale. However, tropical rainforests are being exploited at an alarming rate (see Figure 11). Countries with significant rates of **deforestation** include Brazil, Indonesia, Thailand, the Democratic Republic of Congo and other parts of Africa. Deforestation is the permanent removal of forests to enable the land to be used for something else. Currently, 31.5 million acres are being deforested every year; that equates to one acre per second! But who is to blame?

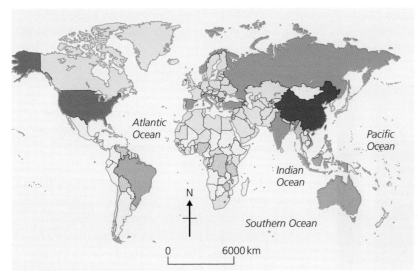

Key
2005–10, '000 ha/year net loss
More than 500
250–500
50–250
Small change (gain or loss)
Less than 50
Net gain
50–250
250–500
Hot deserts

▲ Figure 11: Net changes in forest area globally

Logging

Logging is the most widely reported cause of deforestation in the rainforest. Timber is harvested to create commercial items such as furniture, paper, doors and household utensils. About half of that wood is used for fuelwood. Many logging companies would argue that they fell the trees that they want selectively. However, in the process of cutting down one tree, many more are damaged. Furthermore, new road networks criss-cross the rainforest to enable companies to gain access to the trees they want.

In Indonesia, the logging and burning of land has been rapid. Indonesia consists of 17,000 islands between the Indian and Pacific Oceans. It has one-tenth of the remaining rainforests in the world, but is destroying them at a faster rate than any other country. The Indonesian government has licensed much of the rainforest for logging as a means of growing the country's economy; its greatest asset is its trees. Two million hectares of Indonesian rainforest are disappearing every year, and it is estimated that illegal logging has been responsible for the loss of 10 million hectares of forest. As we have already seen, the clearing of trees and burning of the land releases carbon into the atmosphere. Indonesia accounts for eight per cent of global carbon emissions, yet it barely covers one per cent of the Earth's land.

In contrast, reports suggest that illegal logging has decreased by 50–75 per cent across Cameroon, Indonesia and the Brazilian Amazon over the last decade. There is still, however, a long way to go before logging practices are brought under control.

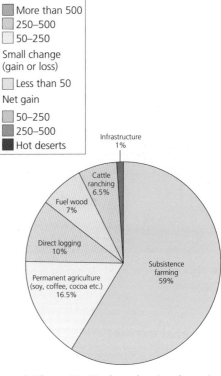

Infrastructure 1%
Cattle ranching 6.5%
Fuel wood 7%
Direct logging 10%
Permanent agriculture (soy, coffee, cocoa etc.) 16.5%
Subsistence farming 59%

▲ Figure 12: Pie chart showing the main causes of deforestation

▲ Figure 13: Logging trucks carry timber through the Amazon rainforest

Agriculture

Cattle ranching

An increase in the number of ranches in the northern regions of the Amazon basin has been fuelled by the construction of new industrial slaughterhouses. In these areas, cattle now outnumber people by ten to one. Around 80 per cent of Brazil's deforested areas are used for cattle ranching, making it the largest commercial cattle field in the world. Cattle ranching in the Amazon rainforest is responsible for 340 million tonnes of carbon every year and takes up 8.4 million hectares of land. Costa Rica, Honduras and El Salvador all have extensive cattle ranches, due to their proximity to the main market – the USA.

Cattle ranching has become very popular due to the fact that it is relatively low risk and low maintenance in comparison with cash crops such as palm oil. It is not as vulnerable to global price changes or climatic and environmental changes. Due to the American demand for beef, farmers make a good return. The consequences for the environment include river siltation and soil erosion due to large areas of exposed land.

▲ **Figure 14:** A palm oil plantation in northern Sumatra, Indonesia

Palm oil plantations

Palm oil is one of the most profitable **cash crops** for developing countries, grown for its commercial value. It is found in about half of all the products sold in supermarkets, from margarines and cakes to shampoos and cosmetics. Palm oil is also used to create fuel. This is known as **biofuel**. Indonesia has the world's largest palm oil plantation, providing employment for three million people. Before a plantation can be created, the area needs to be cleared of trees. This is done by a process known as **slash and burn** where the trees are cut down and burnt. The ash from the burnt trees provides short-term nourishment for the soil. However, once the palm oil has been harvested, the land is useless, making it a very destructive practice.

Mineral extraction

Gold, copper, diamonds and other precious metals and gemstones are found in rainforests around the world. Areas are also being surveyed for their oil and gas reserves. Peru in South America is the world's top producer of silver and second producer of zinc. The money countries make through their mineral wealth gives funds for **infrastructure** projects, such as electricity and roads, in developing regions. However, the environmental problems that mining creates can be devastating for local communities. They can experience soil and water contamination, particularly downstream of a mine, due to toxic run-off into rivers. People also need to be displaced from their land to enable roads to be built to allow access for large machinery and the transport of products.

▲ **Figure 15:** Gold mining in Guyana, South America

Tourism

Unsustainable **mass tourism** results in the building of hotels in vulnerable areas and can have a negative impact on the relationship between local communities and the government. Tourism can also drive the construction of roads to allow better access. In Indonesia, tourism has had an unforeseen consequence for indigenous ape communities; as tourists have offered them their food, the apes have become exposed to human diseases.

Dam building and hydroelectric power

Dam building is common along rivers such as the Amazon in South America and the Mekong in Laos and Malaysia. As a result of dams, thousands of people are forced from their land and large swathes of rainforest are flooded upstream of the dam. The dams are used to generate hydroelectric power to support other human activities that create more deforestation, such as large-scale logging. This was the case in the Malaysia state of Sarawak in Borneo, where more than 12 dams have been planned. The problems that dams create for indigenous peoples include disruption to the natural river system. As a result of silt being held back by the dam, fewer nutrients are supplied to land downstream for the small-scale agricultural practices of the local people.

Road construction

Pristine rainforest wilderness is being destroyed by massive road-building projects. It is argued that these large-scale projects are vital to help the poorest communities to gain a better standard of living, as the deforestation makes more land available for housing and urbanisation. In reality, however, most roads are built to make mines and hydroelectric dams possible in some of the remotest places in the world.

An early major road-building project was the construction of the Trans-Amazonian Highway, linking Belem in the Amazon rainforest with the capital city of Brazil, Brasilia. It began with a very thin cut through the rainforest but the road had an unforeseen consequence; as the trees were logged either side of the road, a 400-km-wide expanse of forest destruction was left in its wake.

Similarly, a road-building project in the Congo rainforest has led to 50,000 km of roads being constructed. Although this is a legal, national project, it has resulted in many more kilometres of illegal roads branching from the main road and has opened up the rainforest to illegal logging practices.

▼ **Figure 16:** A Chinese bulldozer driver cuts a path through the Congo forest for a major new tarmac road

Case study: attempts to sustainably manage an area of tropical rainforest

How is the tropical rainforest within Crocker Range Biosphere Reserve in Borneo being managed sustainably?

In 2014, the largest protected area of Sabah on the island of Borneo in Malaysia was designated as a UNESCO (United Nations Educational, Scientific and Cultural Organisation) Biosphere Reserve. This is a local, small-scale example of ecosystem management.

What is a biosphere reserve?

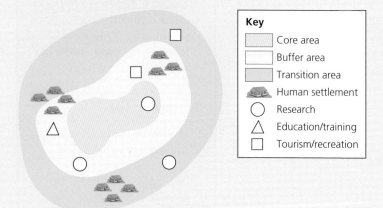

▲ **Figure 17:** Model of a typical biosphere reserve

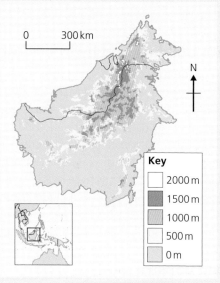

▲ **Figure 19:** Topography map of Borneo

Where is Crocker Range Biosphere Reserve?

The reserve stretches 120 km north and south and 40 km east and west, covering an area of 350,585 hectares. Crocker Range has a variety of tropical rainforest plants, ranging from lowland forest below 300 metres to cloud forest higher than 1500 metres, making it a unique ecosystem. The highest temperature is 32°C and the lowest is 20°C; annual rainfall is 3000 mm.

How 'valuable' is the Crocker Range?

Crocker Range is home to endangered species such as the orang-utan and the clouded leopard (Figure 20). The clouded leopard is **endemic** to the islands of Borneo and Sumatra and there are thought to be fewer than 10,000 left in the wild. Endemic means that the plant or animal can only be found in a small region or country in the world. This makes them very vulnerable to environmental changes and human activity.

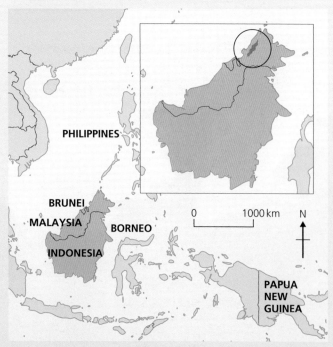

▲ **Figure 18:** Location of Crocker Range Biosphere Reserve in Malaysia

▲ **Figure 20:** A clouded leopard

How are different areas of the reserve being managed?

The biosphere reserve follows a typical concept, as shown in Figure 16.

- There is a core area of three legally protected forest reserves. This area is covered by natural vegetation and is strictly for long-term research projects, environmental education and tourism (Figure 21). It is estimated that the population in this zone is only around 200 people. These people might be engaged in small-scale agriculture such as the farming of coconuts and fruit.

- There are six permanent plots measuring 50 miles by 10 miles that are for ecological monitoring. They contain more than 300 plant species (for example, the native *Rafflesia pricei* plant in Figure 22), 101 mammals, 259 bird species and 47 reptiles.

- In the buffer and transition zones, approximately 400 communities as well as palm oil and rubber plantations are being observed carefully. The buffer zone itself contains 52 villages. Hunting activities are still a part of cultural traditions, including the hunting of wild pigs, squirrels and birds.

▲ **Figure 21:** A tourist crossing a river in the Crocker Range, Sabah

Activities

1. What is a biosphere reserve?
2. Describe the location of Crocker Range Biosphere Reserve.
3. Sketch the model of a typical biosphere reserve. Annotate your model with the key features of the Crocker Range Biosphere Reserve.

→ Take it further

4. In the same region as CRBR is Kambalu Park, which is a UNESCO World Heritage Site, designated in 2000. Research Kambalu Park and find it how it is being sustainably managed.
5. Research other examples of the sustainable management of tropical rainforests from elsewhere in the world. Include strategies such as ecotourism, community programmes and sustainable forestry.

▲ **Figure 22:** The flower of the endemic plant *Rafflesia pricei*

CHAPTER 8

Is there more to polar environments than ice?

What is it like in Antarctica and the Arctic?

What is it like in Antarctica and the Arctic?

➜ In this section you will:

- ➜ learn about the distinctive characteristics of Antarctica and the Arctic
- ➜ study the basic characteristics of the climate in these areas
- ➜ recognise features of the landscape and the seas that connect and surround them
- ➜ consider the differences in flora and fauna in the two polar regions
- ➜ explore the interdependence of factors including climate, soil, water, plants, animals and human activity.

Antarctica

Antarctica is bordered by the Antarctic Circle, which lies at 66° 33.5′ south of the Equator (see Chapter 6, Figure 5, page 92). South of the Antarctic Circle, the days lengthen in the summer and shorten to nothing in the winter months; periods of daylight and darkness stretch to six months at the poles. The 'summer' and 'winter' referred to are the southern hemisphere seasons.

Antarctica is a large land mass classed as a continent, which covers an area of over 13 million km². This is 60 times the size of the UK and is larger than the whole of Europe. The land is covered in ice, some of which is several kilometres deep. The mountains rise up to almost 5000 m high. The highest peak, Mount Vinson, is at 4982 m and was only climbed for the first time in 1966. Antarctica is the highest of all continents, with an average height of 1800 m. In fact, visitors to the South Pole are provided with tablets to combat altitude sickness. It is also the driest continent, receiving less than 3 cm of precipitation a year. It is considered, technically, to be a desert. In addition to the ice sheets and glaciers, there are also many ice shelves, the largest being the Ross Shelf and the Ronne Shelf. These extend out over the sea but are connected to the mainland. Several of the smaller ice shelves have broken up in recent years and there are fears over the state of some of the larger ones.

A mountainous peninsula extends out from the main body of the continent towards South America. It is on here that many of the scientific bases are located. This area also provides a habitat for many penguin species. The peninsula extends beyond the Antarctic Circle and is the part of the continent most visited by tourists.

Antarctica actually doubles in size during the winter months as sea ice grows out from the coast, extending the area that is available for animals such as penguins to nest and for seals to hunt beneath. This sea ice is relatively thin compared with that on land, but is still a barrier to shipping, sinking the ships of explorers like Sir Ernest Shackleton and, more recently, the *MS Explorer*, a cruise ship which sank in 2007 while carrying passengers.

Some parts of Antarctica are more remote from the coastline and their elevation and albedo have provided the most extreme temperatures recorded on the planet.

▲ **Figure 1:** The Antarctic landscape

Arctic

The Arctic is bordered by the Arctic Circle, which lies at 66° 33.5' north of the Equator. On this line, there is one day each year when the Sun never rises (the winter solstice) and one when it never sets (the summer solstice). North of the Arctic Circle, the days lengthen in the summer and shorten to nothing in the winter months; periods of daylight and darkness stretch to six months at the poles.

The Arctic has a vast ocean at its centre, surrounded by a number of countries which lie wholly or partly within the Arctic Circle. The term 'Arctic 8' is used to refer to the countries which form the **circumpolar** region and are part of the Arctic Council. They are: Russia, Canada, USA (Alaska), Norway, Sweden, Finland, Iceland and Denmark (Greenland and the Faroe Islands).

The land masses surrounding the ocean vary from dramatic mountains, to frozen plains and archipelagos such as Svalbard. Greenland's ice sheet is a major landmass, but there are also huge islands in Canada's northern territories. Much of the land is permafrost, where the ground is permanently frozen to a great depth. Snow covers the land, but may thaw in the summer months. Some define the Arctic as the area north of the tree line, where there is insufficient liquid water to allow trees to continue to grow. Google 'Arctic' or 'Antarctica' and the images that you are presented with will be of ice and snow. However, there are times of the year when the snow and ice melt. You will see the Arctic described as a wilderness, and also as a frontier, but for around 5 million people it is also called 'home'.

▲ **Figure 2:** The Arctic landscape; a glacier in Svalbard

	J	F	M	A	M	J	J	A	S	O	N	D
Iqaluit, Nunavut												
Temperature (°C)	−26	−27	−24	−15	−5	3	7	6	2	−5	−13	−22
Precipitation (mm)	22	19	21	28	29	36	58	62	52	43	32	20
Longyearbyen, Svalbard												
Temperature (°C)	−14	−15	−13	−11	−4	−3	6	5	1	−5	−9	−12
Precipitation (mm)	16	20	21	12	9	11	16	28	26	17	19	18
Amundsen-Scott Base, Antarctica												
Temperature (°C)	−28	−41	−54	−57	−57	−58	−60	−60	−59	−51	−38	−28
Precipitation (mm)	0	0	0	0	0	0	0	0	0	0	0	0
McMurdo Base, Antarctica												
Temperature (°C)	−3	−10	−18	−21	−22	−23	−26	−26	−25	−19	−10	−0.3
Precipitation (mm)	15	21	24	18	24	25	16	11	12	10	10	16

▲ **Figure 3:** Climate data for four polar locations

What is the difference between the Arctic and Antarctica?

Factor	Arctic	Notes	Antarctica
Climate	Polar climate with a large range between the winter and summer. Some snow falls as precipitation, varying across the region, with more near the coasts and on higher ground. The area is technically a desert, as it has very low precipitation totals. Average temperatures vary, with winters averaging around −34°C and summers between 2°C and 12°C, depending on the location. Air originating here is very cold and very dry. Winds blow strongly, with few features and no vegetation to slow them down.	The Arctic and Antarctic are at the extreme latitudes of the world and have a polar climate. This means that they have extreme temperatures, strong winds and low precipitation. Antarctica is more extreme in terms of temperature. Air descends here as part of the global circulation in the atmosphere. Antarctica is also surrounded by a cold circumpolar current, whereas the Arctic receives heat from currents such as the Mid-Atlantic drift.	Polar climate, with extremes of temperature made worse by altitude, albedo and cold katabatic winds which flow downhill. Coldest temperature ever recorded at Vostok base: −89.2°C. Winds flow from the centre of the continent towards the coast, keeping the air very dry. Very little precipitation, particularly inland. Strong winds blow lying snow around and cause dangerous whiteout conditions. Very little cloud as air is descending here. High pressure dominates. The area is technically a desert, as it has very low precipitation totals, with just wind-blown snow. Antarctica is the windiest continent.
Features of the land and sea	Large areas are made up of permafrost (ground which has remained frozen for several years). When the top few centimetres of this ground thaws in the summer, it produces a landscape with many depressions which fill with lakes. Marshland and boggy ground cover large areas. The soil flows when it thaws out and is not stable. There are dramatic mountains, such as Thor Peak on Baffin Island, and fjords, such as those fringing the coast of Greenland. Sea ice develops through the winter months, leading to pack ice as well as icebergs and other types of ice. Glaciers calve icebergs at their snouts where they enter the sea. (The Ilulissat Glacier in Greenland featured in the film *Chasing Ice*). One of the largest ice caps outside of Antarctica covers the higher ground of Greenland.	One difference between the ice in the Arctic and that in the Antarctic is what lies beneath it. Remove a few centimetres of ice in Antarctica and you expose more ice beneath. In the Arctic, however, you will reveal the ground or the sea. The albedo of these surfaces changes the way that the ground absorbs heat.	Antarctica is divided into two main areas and ice sheets – East Antarctica and West Antarctica – by the Transantarctic Mountains that stretch for 3500 kilometres across the continent. They rise to a height of almost 5000 m and include active volcanoes (e.g. Mount Erebus). Around 99% of the continent is covered with ice; the rest is bare, weathered rock. The peninsula extends for around 1000 km towards South America. A series of ice shelves connected to the land holds back glaciers and other ice which would otherwise flow into the sea. The largest of these shelves are the Ross Shelf and the Ronne Shelf. Smaller ice shelves are home to penguin rookeries. Ice sheets cover the mountains apart from a few peaks which stick up through the ice as nunataks, for example Ulvetanna in Queen Maud Land, Eastern Antarctica.
Flora and fauna	Animals and plants have adapted to sub-zero conditions and the absence of liquid water. The southern fringes of the Arctic have taiga, large expanses of coniferous forests, but these disappear with distance north along a line called the tree line. Plants in the tundra (the vegetation type that grows on permafrost) are adapted to dry conditions. Species like dwarf willow and lichens cling to the ground surface to avoid being damaged by the strong winds sweeping across the area. Some have natural 'antifreeze' inside them. Marine creatures include whales (such as the narwhal), seals, sea lions and walruses. Smaller creatures: midges and other insects swarm during the summer months in the boggy tundra areas.	The Arctic has been explored for hundreds of years and inhabited for thousands. By contrast, the first people to see Antarctica did so only a few hundred years ago. There are still no permanent residents in Antarctica, but an estimated 5 million people live and work north of the Arctic Circle. There are differences in the biodiversity that one will find in the two polar regions as a result of the wider variety of landscapes and less extreme temperatures in the Arctic. The depth of freshly fallen snow creates an extra habitat for small mammals (which are absent from Antarctica). Sled dogs are not allowed on Antarctica as a result of the Antarctic Treaty's environmental protection.	Antarctica is too extreme for plants to grow. There are two grasses which are found in a few places, otherwise only algae and lichens can survive. Penguins nest on the ice shelves, and the Emperor penguin over-winters, but many other species migrate north to avoid the extremes of cold during that time. Marine creatures, including penguins, must avoid the extremes of temperature in the interior, so most of the biodiversity is to be found at sea or around the coast.

▲ **Figure 4:** The differences between the Arctic and Antarctica

Tip

It is a good idea to use the word 'geographic' when referring to the actual point at 90°N or S, as there are also the magnetic poles. Make sure that you are clear on what the main similarities and differences are between the two polar regions; do not mention polar bears when talking about Antarctica or put penguins at the North Pole!

When using weather data, make sure that you use the appropriate units, and try to vary your vocabulary away from the obvious 'cold' as this is a relative term. Compare temperatures to freezing point and also consider the seasonal variation. Remember which hemisphere you are referring to when doing this.

Fieldwork ideas

It is unlikely that you will be fortunate enough to visit the polar regions, but you can make a virtual visit using Google Earth Pro™ (free to download). This app provides high-quality images of some areas of the regions and allows you to visualise the landscape. Small areas, such as Scott's Hut and the Arctic city of Iqaluit, have also been visited by StreetView™ cameras.

▲ **Figure 5:** Map of the Arctic

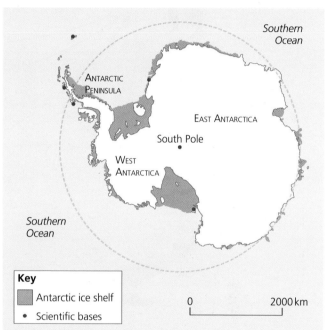

▲ **Figure 6:** Map of Antarctica

Activities

1. Look at Figure 6. Can you identify the following?
   a. three Antarctic ice shelves
   b. five scientific bases in Antarctica
   c. the area of Antarctica which lies outside the Antarctic circle
2. Chapters 4 and 5 explored the idea of landscape and how it was formed from a number of processes.
   a. Which of those geomorphological processes are evident in the Arctic? Which occur more quickly here?
   b. What additional processes occur as a result of the climate and landscape that are found here?
3. Draw a Venn diagram like the one shown here. Add ten descriptions to the Venn diagram, so that they are located in the Arctic, the Antarctic or both, depending on which they relate to. Here are three you can start with:
   • An ice-covered continent surrounded by an ocean
   • Has no permanent inhabitants
   • Sea ice forms in the winter months and melts back during the summer

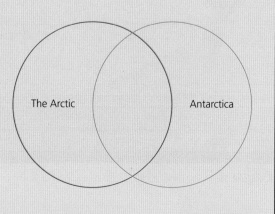

What is the interdependence of climate, soil, water, plants, animals and human activity in the polar regions?

In the polar regions, as with any ecosystem, the available energy is a key factor in the biodiversity of the area. Energy needs to move through the food chain in a **trophic cascade**, as animals consume plants or each other. At each stage energy is lost, so animals further up the food chain need large quantities of food to survive. The absence of available food and heat energy creates problems for Antarctic wildlife and plants in several ways.

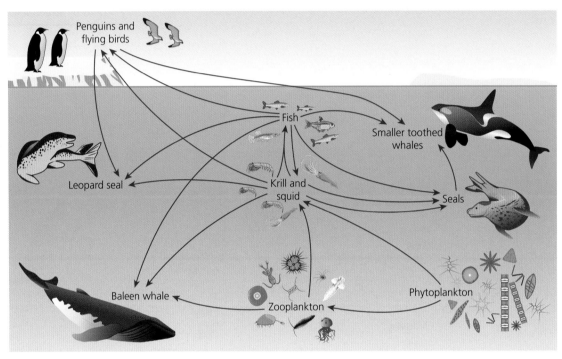

▲ **Figure 7:** A typical Antarctic food web

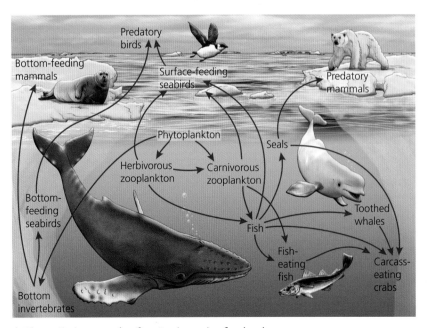

▲ **Figure 8:** An example of an Arctic marine food web

One major factor is the absence of water in liquid form, which has limited the growth of vegetation in the Arctic. In Antarctica, the least biodiverse area on the planet, there are no trees, shrubs or soil. The Antarctic Peninsula has a few areas of Antarctic hair grass and pearlwort, which flower, but the extreme dehydration and low temperatures mean that other parts of the continent are limited to moss, liverworts and lichens. There are no land animals, other than penguin colonies. A few animals live on the ice shelves around the continent, which is where many of the penguins have their rookeries, and the outer islands have seal and sea lion populations.

As with all food chains, the energy of the Sun lies at the start of the energy cascade. As a result of the absence of plants to capture this energy, the main food chains in Antarctica occur in the oceans. Here, tiny phytoplankton provide the food for krill, a shrimp-like creature which sustains many marine animals, including whales. The British Antarctic Survey released a set of stamps in 2014 showing a typical Antarctic food web.

Arctic biodiversity is less than many other parts of the world, but still shows greater diversity than Antarctica. The food web in the Arctic is more diverse as there are more plants, a wider variety of terrestrial animals and marine organisms. The animal that people perhaps associate most with this area is *Ursus maritimus* – the polar bear. This solitary animal ranges over a huge area and the decline in sea ice coverage has caused it major problems. It can swim, but it is being forced to do this more often, which uses more of its energy.

Strong winds strip moisture from plants and so Arctic plants tend to be dwarf, clinging to the ground. They reduce their moisture loss by having small leaves.

The extra depth of snow provides cover for small mammals such as lemmings and marmots. These are hunted by Arctic fox or owls which range over the tundra. Reindeer (also called caribou) are found on the southern fringes of the region and are usually associated with local nomadic groups.

How and why are polar ecosystems changing?

Changes due to climate change

It is important to remember here that the polar regions are said to be 'the canary in the coalmine' for global warming. They are our warning system that things are changing as the impacts are felt greatest here, in lands made from ice. In recent years, a number of scientific reports have outlined the rate of warming and fears have been expressed in particular about the stability of the great ice sheets in Greenland and the two huge areas which cloak the Antarctic mountains in several kilometres of ice. If these were to melt, there would be a catastrophic rise in sea level which would threaten some of the major cities that are explored in Chapters 9 and 10.

One of the changes that has taken place in recent decades has been the thawing of sea ice in the Arctic Ocean. In March 2015, this reached its lowest winter maximum on record. As ice thins, it becomes easier for it to melt away completely, leaving winds able to create waves where previously there were none. These waves are breaking against coastlines which have not experienced this before and which are made of permafrost – ground that is frozen to depth. In some parts of the Arctic, land which has been frozen for centuries is thawing out. The upper 'active' layer of permafrost is sensitive to changes in temperature. The thawing of ground ice results in a loss of stability, flooding and problems for transport and other infrastructure, and also releases huge quantities of methane: a greenhouse gas.

Activities

1. Compare the food webs and relationships that exist in the Antarctic with those in the Arctic, as shown in Figures 7 and 8. Use the following headings for your discussions:
   - biodiversity
   - difficulty of surviving in polar regions
   - possible threats to some of this diversity.
2. What impacts will changing climate have on some of these relationships?

→ Take it further

3. Research the ways that polar bear behaviour is changing as a result of changes to their habitats. Find out about the Canadian town of Churchill and its relationship with these animals.
4. What impacts will thawing of the permafrost have both locally and globally?

Active layer
Freezes and unfreezes

Permafrost
Soil frozen for two or more years

Talik
Unfrozen ground in permafrost areas

▲ **Figure 9:** Permafrost soil layers

Impacts of human activity

Indigenous people

▲ **Figure 10:** Inuit hunting for fish in a river in the early 1900s

People have lived in the Arctic for thousands of years. A wide range of indigenous (circumpolar) peoples, including groups called Inuit (Figure 10), Yupik, Chukchi, Nenets, Sami and Aleuts, live in specific areas. Greenland, for example, has the Kalaallit.

Some groups are nomadic, following large herds of reindeer; others are more sedentary and hunt marine animals. All of the groups are characterised by their resilience and ability to survive by adapting their diet, making full use of the available resources and learning to cope in the extreme (for us) conditions. Their culture, clothing and oral histories are connected with the land and the climate.

Early Arctic explorers encountered indigenous groups on their travels, sometimes trading with them, occasionally relying on them for help. Exploitation of the resources found in the Arctic soon followed, with ships catching large numbers of whales for the raw materials they provide. Inevitably, the land and resources which had 'belonged' to many indigenous groups through their presence on the land for centuries was taken, sometimes by force.

During the Cold War, military resources were installed in the area. These included the Distant Early Warning (DEW) detection network designed to warn of Russian nuclear missiles. Alaska's proximity to Russia gave it a great deal of strategic importance. The creation of the new Canadian territory of Nunavut in 1999 was a step towards returning control of land and resources to the local indigenous people.

Scientific research

Scientific research is a relatively new process compared with exploration. Captain Scott's expeditions at the start of the twentieth century were partly scientific, but today's scientists make use of the polar regions' particular environment for their research: the clean atmosphere helps astronomers, meteorites are found more easily here, and the geology and subsurface lakes provide important information. A key aspect of polar science is the reconstruction of past climates from gases trapped in the ice. These are extracted by drilling deep into it (see page 44).

There are still no permanent residents on the Antarctic continent, which has a population of just a few hundred during the long winter period. Some scientists and support workers have lived there through multiple 'seasons', but all leave temporarily. It costs up to $1 million a year to keep a scientist at the Antarctic. This money has to be sustained through grants and there is a priority for research that is the most 'valuable'. Scientists have to undergo medical and psychological testing before being accepted, as the remoteness and extreme conditions place a lot of stress on those involved.

Mineral exploitation: riches beneath the ice

Mineral exploitation is a fairly recent threat to the Arctic's ecosystems and landscape. Oil was first discovered in the Arctic in the 1960s, with the large Prudhoe Bay field in northern Alaska. The difficulties posed by the terrain, including high mountains, rivers which swell during the spring thaw and active earthquake zones, had to be overcome when considering how to transport the oil safely. The Alyeska pipeline was an expensive and controversial project, but once completed in 1977 it carried oil 800 miles from Prudhoe Bay to the nearest port. Despite the efforts to transport the oil safely by pipeline, the next link in the transport chain (oil tankers) proved vulnerable, with the *Exxon Valdez* oil spill in 1989 reinforcing the fragility of ecosystems in the Arctic. More than 25 years on, legal battles still continue over who should pay for the clean-up of oil which travelled more than 600 miles from the ship after it struck a rock.

Whaling in Antarctic waters

Many countries were once involved in the whaling industry in the Southern Ocean. South Georgia was a whaling station and still bears the scars of the industry around the port of Grytviken. At one time, there were thousands of whales killed here every year, but not any more. There has been a moratorium (ban) on whaling in the sea around Antarctica for around 30 years. This is overseen by the IWC (International Whaling Commission).

One country which continues to hunt whales in the sea around Antarctica is Japan. This has led to direct action by environmental groups such as Greenpeace in the past. Japan claims that it is catching whales for scientific purposes, although in 2014, the International Court of Justice declared that this was just a cover for commercial hunting. Japan planned to catch around 300 minke whales in 2015, although they no longer hunt humpback and fin whales. Norway and Iceland are two more countries which continue to hunt whales in other sea areas.

With whale numbers declining, the difficulties that these countries have had in catching their 'quota' of whales gives an indication of the problems facing these animals. Some people suggest that the seas around Antarctica should be a sanctuary for marine creatures, in the same way that the continent is protected from exploitation by the Antarctic Treaty (see pages 127–128).

Fishing the Arctic

Arctic waters provide around 70 per cent of the world's white fish catch. High latitudes support a rich biological diversity, and the industry supports coastal communities. The Barents Sea holds the last of the world's major cod stocks. It also attracts illegal fishing, as there are difficulties policing the waters and regulating activity over such a huge area. The Bering Sea and the Sea of Okhotsk also hold large stocks of cod and pollock, which are popular with consumers.

Melting sea ice is opening up areas of the Arctic that were previously inaccessible, and may tempt a larger fleet into these waters, where they would catch fish that might otherwise have been consumed by local wildlife. There is an area within the central Arctic Ocean known as the 'doughnut hole' which is outside any country's jurisdiction. It will be important not to follow the example of Newfoundland and Labrador, who overfished the available resource leading to the collapse of fish stocks. Other Arctic resources have also been overexploited.

Further links to sustainable food security are given in Chapter 16 on page 268.

◀ **Figure 11:** Sign in a Norfolk chip shop telling customers where their fish was sourced: the Barents Sea in the Arctic

Activity

1. Investigate the challenges that face scientists operating at the South Pole, particularly those who stay there over the winter months, when they are cut off from the rest of the world. What are the medical and psychological tests they have to take?

Who owns the Arctic?

The Arctic is currently 'heating up' as a result of its importance for geopolitical reasons. Several countries, including Russia, Canada and even Denmark, have 'claimed' areas of the Arctic, based on their geographical location, geology or historical claims. The Russians planted a flag at the North Pole (on the sea bed beneath it) in 2007 as a symbolic act. Should the Arctic belong to anyone?

▼ **Figure 12:** A former whaling station at Grytviken, South Georgia

Is tourism in Polar regions sustainable?

Polar regions are growing in popularity for tourism, with more companies operating all the time. They are remote places, which only the relatively wealthy can afford to visit. These are expensive locations for companies to operate in and so specialist equipment and logistical support are required. Some of the travel companies market these destinations by declaring that the holiday could be a 'last chance to see' such environments. It is, perhaps, ironic that by visiting these destinations, tourists are arguably hastening their loss through the greenhouse gases emitted by the flights they have to take to get there and the pollution of the oceans by the cruise ships they take to get close to the glaciers, fjords or wildlife habitats.

Antarctica, in particular, is not a cheap place to visit. Logistically, it requires an effort to travel the long distances involved and travel insurance can run into hundreds of pounds per week. The sinking of the cruise ship *MS Explorer* in 2007 was a reminder of the dangers.

Visitors may board a ship to the Antarctic Peninsula via the port of Ushuaia, Argentina, or they may fly to a location like Union Glacier. Smaller numbers travel from Port Stanley in the Falkland Islands, New Zealand and even South Africa. The Arctic is more accessible to tourists. Popular routes include cruises around the archipelago of Spitsbergen, the fjords of Greenland (which can also be visited on a day trip from Keflavik airport in Reykjavik, Iceland) and the NW Canadian/Alaskan coastline. The Hurtigruten company operates cruises along the Norwegian coastline (www.hurtigruten.co.uk).

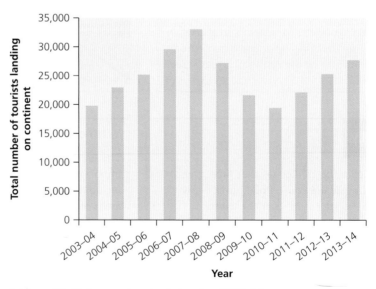

▲ **Figure 13:** Visitor numbers to Antarctica, 2003–14

Antarctica's tourist season lasts for just a few months of the year, during the Antarctic summer. Even in these months (November to March), bad weather can cause problems and clear conditions cannot be guaranteed.

No vaccinations are required to visit Antarctica.

Ships have to be 'bio-secure' and visitors are not permitted to eat, drink or urinate while on shore.

Tourist ships have to negotiate pack ice, which grows out from the coast, in order to get close to he places where penguins nest or to the historic huts (see page 125).

In December and January, penguin chicks hatch and can be viewed in the breeding grounds. There is a tourist code which asks visitors to stay at least 5 metres away from them.

During the later part of the season, much of the wildlife may already have left for the open sea, so the prime weeks cost a great deal more.

A post office is manned for part of each year at Port Lockroy. Letters and postcards can be sent and souvenirs purchased from the most southerly shop in the world.

There are limits on how many people can visit the shore at any one time, which means smaller ships are preferred, but these are more expensive. Visits tend to be for a short period only.

Popular places to visit include emperor penguin colonies, the Dry Valleys and Cape Royds. Watching seals and whales is also very popular.

Bad weather can cause flights to be cancelled.

Tourists need to respect the fragility of the environment by following visitor guidelines adopted under the Antarctic Treaty.

▲ **Figure 14:** Key facts about tourism in Antarctica

Case study: How are humans seeking a sustainable solution for polar environments?

→ In this section you will:

→ examine small-scale sustainable tourism at Union Glacier, Antarctica

→ look into small-scale conservation in Antarctica by the NZ and UK Antarctic Heritage Trust

→ study global sustainable management attempts in Antarctica through the Antarctic Treaty System

→ study global sustainable management attempts in the Arctic through global actions.

Small-scale sustainable tourism at Union Glacier, Antarctica

Union Glacier is a logistics hub, operated by Adventure Network International (ANI). Union Glacier itself is a large expanse of ice in the Ellsworth Range, which is part of the Transantarctic Mountains. The camp is near to a natural blue-ice runway, which can be used to land the large Ilyushin cargo planes which bring equipment for expeditions and scientific support. Each year, an advance crew arrives to prepare the camp for the four months

of the 'summer season', erecting tents and preparing other buildings and equipment. They lay fuel depots for field teams and welcome a small number of visitors who explore the local area and take part in a range of activities, which include:

- walking or trekking – a low-impact activity
- climbing, including a chance to climb Mount Vinson
- visiting penguin colonies; visitors must stay at least 5 m away from wildlife, be limited to groups of 20 and follow specific approach routes to the colony
- walking in the footsteps of Amundsen up the Axel Heiberg glacier.

Visiting Union Glacier is expensive and guidelines are given to tourists about how they should behave with respect to the environment. These are based on Antarctic Treaty protocols. The continent has been bio-secured to reduce the risk of contamination. Some equipment is powered by solar panels to reduce the use of diesel. All waste is carefully contained and removed at the end of the season. It is said that the continent needs advocates to ensure its future and each visitor will go home with stories of this fragile place.

▲ **Figure 15:** The Union Glacier camp

Case study: How are humans seeking a sustainable solution for polar environments?

Small-scale conservation in Antarctica

In 1908, Sir Ernest Shackleton built a pre-fabricated hut at Cape Royds to stay over winter as part of his *Nimrod* expedition. During this expedition, he was able to travel further south than had been possible before and a party of explorers succeeded in climbing Mount Erebus. In 1911, Captain Robert Falcon Scott built a similar hut, on Cape Evans, as part of his ill-fated attempt to reach the South Pole. This hut still houses around 8000 items (see Figure 17).

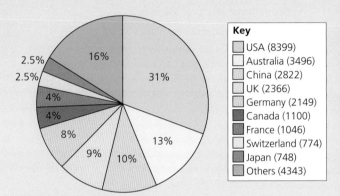

Key
- USA (8399)
- Australia (3496)
- China (2822)
- UK (2366)
- Germany (2149)
- Canada (1100)
- France (1046)
- Switzerland (774)
- Japan (748)
- Others (4343)

▲ **Figure 16:** Tourist visits to Antarctica, 2013–14

The huts have survived for over a century, despite being subjected to extremes of wind and temperature every year since then. They are in need of constant maintenance and this is carried out by the NZ Antarctic Heritage Trust, which raises funds to pay for the work by such means as the sale of merchandise. These buildings are a reminder of the heroic age of exploration. For many people, these small outposts of human endeavour are as important as the landscape in which they stand. The trust aims to keep the legacy of the explorers alive by preserving these fragile huts.

The UK Antarctic Heritage Trust helps to conserve other historic buildings on the Antarctic Peninsula. These date from the establishment of Port Lockroy during the Second World War, through to the early 1990s, and a connection to the early scientific bases established in Antarctica, and their living and working conditions. While they do not have the historic connections of those used by Scott and Shackleton, their presence is a reminder that people have visited and worked on this continent, and that it is not completely unspoilt.

▲ **Figure 17:** The interior of Shackleton's hut

Activities

1. Figure 16 shows the nationalities of tourists visiting Antarctica during the 2013–14 season.
   a. From which country did most tourists who visited Antarctica in 2013–14 come?
   b. What percentage of tourists came from named European countries?
   c. What reasons can you think of for the large numbers of visitors from the top three countries?
2. Which aspects of a tourist visit to the polar regions do you think would have the greatest impact on:
   a. the landscape
   b. the flora and fauna?

➜ Take it further

3. Some people would argue that no polar tourism is sustainable, as the distance and expense needed to travel to the poles is considerable. What are your views on this? Should there be a limit placed on the number of visitors to these regions?

Weblinks

The huts were photographed by Google as part of their Cultural Institute project and you can take a virtual look inside them here:
https://antarctic-heritage-trust.culturalspot.org/home

Case study: How are humans seeking a sustainable solution for polar environments?

Halley VI Research Station – built for the future

The Halley VI Research Station, a British scientific base, has been built with the future in mind. It focuses on studying atmospheric science and meteorology. Previous bases were built into the ice but, when the ice shelf moved, they were damaged. The new design of the base means that the whole thing can be moved if there is a problem in the future: it is built as a series of eight modules on hydraulic skis, which can be towed to a new location.

All research stations have to operate in a way that minimises their impact on the environment. Strict guidelines relating to the Antarctic Treaty, which is explored in more detail in the next section, must be followed by all staff and visitors. They include rules on waste disposal and the way that the base operates to reduce its environmental impact.

In December 2015, it was reported that the base may have to be moved already, as a large crack up to half a mile wide and codenamed Chasm 1, is opening up in the ice shelf. This may mean there is a calving event, in which the piece of ice with the base located on it breaks away from the mainland. The plan is for this to be a long-term British presence on the continent.

Halley VI factfile

→ Latitude 75°35′0″S, Longitude 26°39′36″W

→ Opened: 2013 (although there has been a base on the site since 1956)

→ Location: Brunt Ice Shelf, Caird Coast

→ Scientists working there: around 70 staff in the summer, 16 in winter

→ Work carried out: releasing weather balloons, atmospheric laboratory, aurora observations – this was where the existence of the hole in the ozone layer was first identified.

To find out more about the Halley VI base, visit: www.bas.ac.uk/polar-operations/sites-and-facilities/facility/halley/ where you can also find out more about the work of the British Antarctic Survey.

▲ **Figure 18:** The Halley VI Research Station

Case study: How are humans seeking a sustainable solution for polar environments?

Global sustainable management attempts in Antarctica through the Antarctic Treaty System

The Antarctic Treaty grew out of the International Geophysical Year of 1957–1958 and came into force in June 1961. Twelve countries originally signed the Treaty; by 2016 an additional 41 nations had acceded the Treaty, bringing the total number of Parties to 53. Every year the original twelve Parties to the Treaty, as well as those Parties that demonstrate interest in Antarctica by conducting substantial research activity there – together called the Consultative Parties – assemble for the Antarctic Treaty Meeting to take decisions and measures to improve the Treaty. Among these developments, the Protocol on Environmental Protection was signed in 1991 and entered into force in 1998.

Antarctica is one of the few places on Earth where there has never been any war and where the environment enjoys a great deal of protection. The Treaty and the Protocol were designed to ensure that this remained the case. The Protocol designates the whole area of Antarctica – all of the area south of the 60° S line of latitude – as a natural reserve, dedicated to peace and science.

Objectives of the Treaty and the Protocol

The principal objectives of the Treaty and the Protocol are:

➜ to demilitarise Antarctica; no military operations are allowed

➜ to set aside disputes over territorial sovereignty (although claims have been made by several countries for particular sectors of the continent, see Figure 20)

➜ to establish it as a nuclear-free zone; no testing or radioactive waste disposal is allowed

➜ to guarantee freedom for scientific investigation and research (several new scientific bases have been built in recent years) including meteorological data and hydrographic charting

➜ to promote scientific co-operation; scientific observations and results from Antarctica are exchanged and made freely available

➜ to promote logistical co-operation and communications to aid the safety of all on the continent

➜ to protect the Antarctic environment and the intrinsic values of Antarctica, including its wilderness and aesthetic values

➜ to ban any activity relating to mineral resources

➜ to ensure that any visits, including those by tourists, comply with the Treaty and the Protocol

➜ to preserve historic sites (such as the huts of Scott and Shackleton mentioned on page 125).

▲ **Figure 19:** The Antarctic Treaty logo

The protocol sets forth basic principles to all human activities in Antarctica as it:

- bans all commercial mining and resource extraction
- requires an environmental assessment of the impact of all activities before they can happen
- requires the conservation of Antarctic fauna and flora
- encourages minimisation of waste production and sets out rules for managing waste, including sewage
- prevents marine pollution
- designates environmentally protected areas.

The treaty remains in force indefinitely. Two further agreements have been added to the original treaty. These are the Convention for the Conservation of Antarctic Seals (CCAS, signed on 1972), and the Convention on the Conservation of Antarctic Marine Living Resources (CCAMLR, agreed in 1980).

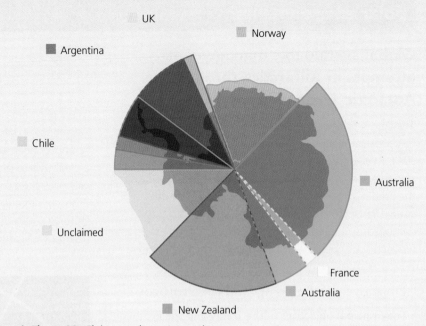

▲ **Figure 20:** Claims made on Antarctica

Strict controls on non-native species were introduced as part of the environment protocol and one consequence of this was the removal of sledge dogs. When explorers such as Amundsen and Shackleton arrived, they brought dogs with them and scientists used to have them for companionship and to pull sledges. All dogs were removed from Antarctica in 1994 as it was thought they might potentially spread disease to seals or attack native wildlife.

The treaty has stayed in place for over 50 years now and Antarctica has benefited from the stability it has provided.

Activities

1. Take each of the areas of the Antarctic Treaty and condense it into a phrase which has no more than five words. This will help you to remember these key points when it comes to the exam.
2. All tourists (and the companies they travel with) have to comply with the treaty, which means they have to take precautions to reduce the impact they will have on the continent before they arrive. Do some research to find out what these preparations involve.
3. Why are the Antarctic claims shaped as they are (like sectors of a pie chart)?

Take it further

4. Why are some areas claimed by one nation whereas one sector remains unclaimed?
5. What is the significance of the particular sections claimed by Australia and France?
6. Discussion point: Is there a need for an Arctic treaty?

Case study: How are humans seeking a sustainable solution for polar environments?

Global sustainable management attempts in the Arctic through global actions

Each of the following events and agreements was aimed at reducing the overall impact of global actions, particularly greenhouse gas emissions. The Arctic is one of the areas of the world which is seeing its climate change most rapidly and many global meetings have representatives from the Inuit council.

Activity

Monitor the BBC and other news media sites during your course to keep up to date with the latest news on climate change and the way that it might be affecting polar regions.

Earth Summits

A number of gatherings to discuss global issues, called Earth Summits, have been held in recent years. The first was held in Rio de Janeiro, Brazil, in 1992. A second Earth Summit called **Rio+20** was held in 2012 to review progress and set new goals. These were aimed at discussing the impact of human activity and setting targets for reducing future impacts.

▲ **Figure 21:** The logo of the Rio+20 Earth Summit

Agenda 21

Agenda 21 is an action plan of the United Nations. It relates to sustainable development and was a product of the Rio Earth Summit of 1992. Although non-binding, it has led to some changes in the way that countries approach sustainable development and acted as a 'blueprint' for how countries might attempt to reduce their ecological footprint. Around 178 countries signed the agreement. One outcome from Agenda 21 was the most commonly used definition of sustainability, developed by Gro Harlem Brundtland, and still widely used.

Kyoto Protocol

The Kyoto Protocol is an international treaty which was signed in Japan in 1997 to extend the 1992 United Nations Framework convention on climate change. It commits those countries that signed it to reduce greenhouse gas emissions. Levels of carbon dioxide have risen steadily since the first measurements emerged in the late 1950s, shown on a famous graph called the Keeling curve. In late 2014, carbon dioxide levels in the atmosphere broke through the 400 ppm (parts per million) level for the first time since the measurements were taken. The protocol ran out in 2012 and negotiations continued to develop further targets. An important thing to remember is that the rate of warming appears to be faster at the poles than elsewhere. Temperatures are rising and the loss of sea ice is a particular issue. One benefit of this is the opening up of the Northern Sea Route for ships to pass through the Arctic Ocean in the summer months.

Practice questions

1. Study Figure A showing a hot desert climate graph. Describe the yearly temperature and rainfall patterns. **[2 marks]**

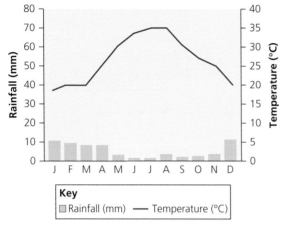

▲ **Figure A**

2. Explain why ecosystems are considered to be 'interdependent'. **[4 marks]**
3. Compare two canopies of the tropical rainforest with the forest floor. **[4 marks]**
4. State two species of animal found in coral reefs. **[2 marks]**
5. Describe the climate of tropical grasslands. **[3 marks]**
6. Explain how a named plant or animal has adapted to survive in the hot desert. **[3 marks]**
7. What is the term for the process by which water is lost from the pores in leaves and evaporated by heat?
   a) Convectional rainfall
   b) Condensation
   c) Evapotranspiration
   d) Microclimate **[1 mark]**
8. Which **two** statements below best explain why the nutrient cycle of tropical rainforests is rapid?
   a) Heavy rainfall washes away dead plant material.
   b) Nutrients are in high demand from the fast-growing plants.
   c) The forest floor conditions allow for the quick decomposition of dead plant material.
   d) There is great biodiversity in tropical rainforests. **[1 mark]**

9. Describe how tropical rainforests provide valuable services. **[4 marks]**
10. Evaluate the environmental impact of hunter-gatherers in the rainforest. **[6 marks]**
11. Describe the impacts of logging on the rainforest environment. **[4 marks]**
12. To what extent could road construction in tropical rainforest regions such as the Amazon bring economic benefits? **[5 marks]**
13. Using a named example, explain how rainforests could be managed on a local or regional scale. **[6 marks]**
14. Identify three distinctive characteristics of Polar environments that would apply to both the Arctic and Antarctica. **[3 marks]**
15. Suggest at least three ways that the Polar regions are different to each other. **[3 marks]**
16. What is meant by the term 'albedo'? **[2 marks]**
17. a) Explain, with the aid of a labelled diagram, why the Polar regions are so cold. **[4 marks]**
    b) What impact do these cold temperatures have on the biodiversity of Polar regions? **[3 marks]**
18. Suggest two unsustainable practices that are prevented under the Antarctic Treaty. **[4 marks]**
19. Look at this newspaper headline:

Antarctica concerns grow as tourism numbers rise

a) Why are there concerns? What problems can be caused by tourism? **[4 marks]**
b) Why do some people say that tourism in the Antarctic should continue to be allowed? **[3 marks]**
20. List three important objectives of the Antarctic Treaty. **[3 marks]**
21. Discuss the reasons why Antarctica matters to people living in the UK. **[4 marks]**

TOPIC 5

Urban Futures

Chapter 9: Why do more than half the world's population live in urban areas?

By the end of this chapter, you will know the answers to these key questions:

→ How is the global pattern of urbanisation changing?

→ What does rapid urbanisation mean for cities?

Chapter 10: What are the challenges and opportunities for cities today?

By the end of this chapter, you will know the answers to these key questions:

→ Case study: What is life like for people in Leeds, England?

→ Case study: What is life like for people in Rosario, Argentina?

→ How can cities become more sustainable?

London: a world city and the first to reach a population of one million.

CHAPTER 9

Why do more than half the world's population live in urban areas?

Why are cities important?

'We shall solve the city by leaving the city. Get the people into the countryside, get them into communities where a man knows his neighbours.'

Henry Ford, 1924

Manufacturing hubs in Shenzhen, Dongguan and Guangzhou are connected through the global supply web to other cities around the world. All cities are interdependent.

'In 2050, for every 100 of our future children born, 57 will open their eyes in Asia and 22 in Africa, and mostly in cities.'

Laurence Smith, 2011

'Being human is itself difficult, and therefore all kinds of settlements (except dream cities) have problems. Big cities have difficulties in abundance, because they have people in abundance.'

Jane Jacobs, 1961

Ancient cities stored as many resources as possible within their walls in granaries and rainwater cisterns, in case of sieges. Modern cities draw on a wide area to provide the resources they consume on a daily basis and are therefore vulnerable in different ways. Energy is a particular requirement and it may be that we will see blackouts of the kind that have hit the USA a few times in recent decades, sparking chaos.

The urban economy must continue to grow, in order to support the growing number of urban residents and the services they require. Urban residents earn more than rural workers and every new urban resident is a new urban consumer, buying electronics made in other cities.

The word paradise originally meant a walled garden or park. Open spaces are vital to the health of cities and their inhabitants.

- Places like Central Park, which attracts around 25 million visitors a year, are protected from any development, despite the huge value that the land has.
- In Beijing, one popular space is Houhai Lake, which is even used during the winter when it freezes over.
- London's parks were originally designed as places for the Royal family to go hunting.
- *Paris plage* is an artificial beach which is created annually along the banks of the River Seine.

Singapore is a city which has been referred to as a 'technopolis' as its growth has been managed and the city is technologically advanced, culturally vibrant and has a high quality of life for residents.

In the 1927 film *Metropolis* (Figure 1), Fritz Lang portrayed a futuristic mega-city where workers toiled in underground factories, while the rich enjoyed their lifestyle in skyscrapers above ground. All cities depend on an army of often unseen workers who keep the infrastructure working and service the city's needs.

133

Chapter 9 Why do more than half the world's population live in urban areas?

'Urbanisation is not about simply increasing the number of urban residents or expanding the area of cities. More importantly, it's about a complete change from rural to urban style in terms of industry structure, employment, living environment and social security'

Li Keqiang, Chinese Premier, 2012

Human capital, more than physical infrastructure, explains which cities succeed. People move to skilled areas because of higher incomes. The expertise and knowledge that a city's population brings helps cities become more productive. Some technologies, such as automation in factories, have decreased the need for unskilled labour, but the need to develop new technologies drives a demand for the brightest graduates.

A city can be seen as a place that people move through as well as to. When new arrivals move to a city, and gain the skills needed for them to move to their next stage, the city is succeeding. If people arrive poor and stay poor, then the city is failing them and it will start to decline.

Many US cities are built around the car. It could be said that the car helped the city to grow. The average car commute in 2006 lasted 24 minutes; the equivalent journey using public transport took 48 minutes. Convenience drives a lot of what people choose to do. Fuel costs could slow down car use, but it takes a lot for people to abandon their cars. Cars take up space on the roads and also when parked.

Consumer cities attract rich as well as poor. People are prepared to pay a premium for the benefits of living there. This leads to inequality within cities, and not everyone can share in this wealth, or access these experiences.

'Curitiba is not a paradise. We have all the problems that most Latin American cities have. We have slums. We have the same difficulties, but the big difference is the respect given by people due to the quality of the services which are provided.'

Jaime Lerner, Mayor of Curitiba, Brazil

▲ **Figure 1:** A still from the 1927 film *Metropolis*

Activity

Carry out some research to find five more quotes or thoughts on the importance of cities and what happens as they grow.

How is the global pattern of urbanisation changing?

➜ In this section you will:

➜ consider the definition of a city

➜ look at how urban growth rates vary in parts of the world with contrasting levels of development

➜ gain an understanding of the characteristics of world cities and megacities and their changing distribution since 1950.

How is the global pattern of urbanisation changing?

In 2007, the UN announced that for the first time more than 50 per cent of the world's population lived in **urban** areas. The number of urban dwellers rises by an estimated 180,000 every day. By 2050, 75 per cent of the world's population could live in towns and cities.

Urbanisation is an increase in the amount of people living in urban areas, such as towns or cities, compared with those living in rural areas, such as the countryside. This could be because of **migration** from rural to urban areas, or a natural increase if there is a high birth rate and low death rate within these urban areas (**internal growth**). The world is more urbanised than ever – a trend which will continue.

What is a city?

Figure 2 shows that cities are nearer the top of the settlement hierarchy. Settlements move up through the hierarchy as more people live in them; they develop more **functions** and provide more **services** as a consequence. The hierarchy starts at the bottom with isolated dwellings and farms where single families live, moving through hamlets, villages, towns and cities to **conurbations**. A conurbation is made up of a major city and its suburban areas, housing tens of millions of people and performing a large number of functions. An example of a conurbation is the Pearl River Delta area in China (Figure 3). These can then merge with other cities to form sprawling **urban belts**, such as the Taiheiyō Belt which follows the *shinkansen* (bullet train) routes on the main Japanese island of Honshu. It runs for over 700 miles and houses around half of the country's total population.

The actual point which determines when a settlement passes the threshold from town to city varies from country to country. In Sweden, a population of around 50,000 is needed for a settlement to be called a city. In contrast, the Welsh city of St David's had a population of less than 2000 at the 2011 census. .

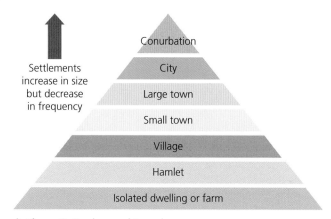

Settlements increase in size but decrease in frequency

Conurbation
City
Large town
Small town
Village
Hamlet
Isolated dwelling or farm

▲ **Figure 2:** Settlement hierarchy

▲ **Figure 3:** The Pearl River Delta, China; an example of a conurbation

135

Chapter 9 Why do more than half the world's population live in urban areas?

City locations

The first cities to flourish were found along major river valleys which allowed residents to settle and feed themselves. The first real cities are thought to have started after the Stone Age, around 10,000 years BP, in what is now Iraq, followed by cities in the Mediterranean. Agriculture was at the heart of the development of early settlements, as hunter–gatherers stopped their nomadic lifestyle. Specialist occupations and trades served the population.

Major city growth took place during the development of the Greek and Roman empires. More recently, one of the greatest stimuli for growth was the Industrial Revolution of the late eighteenth century. The growth of colonial powers, and the British Empire, led to more international trade, which boosted the importance of port cities such as Liverpool and Southampton. Today's major cities grow for similar reasons. Industrial development and raw materials still draw people to the major cities, but there are other factors now, such as global outsourcing and cities planned for a specific purpose such as Canberra and Brasilia.

Why is water an important factor for settlements?

Water is still an important site factor, providing communication and opportunities for trade, along with water supply and waste disposal. Many of the world's major cities are situated on a major river, sometimes close to its mouth, such as Rio de Janeiro. They are often built on the flat land created by the river, which sometimes floods the same area. The major floods that occurred in Brisbane, Australia, in 2011 were a reminder that many of the world's major cities may be vulnerable to sea level rise because of their location. Many cities were originally located on islands, for the added benefit of defence, even though they may have grown beyond those original locations and this factor is no longer relevant, for example New York and Paris.

Activities

1. Study Figure 2.
   a. Where does the settlement where you live sit on the settlement hierarchy?
   b. What do you think led to it being settled in the first place?
   c. What have been the major phases of growth in its history?

→ Take it further

2. Access the most recent census results to find out what the population of your home settlement is. What else can you discover from the census data? Use a tool such as http://datashine.org.uk/ and enter your postcode to find out more about the settlement you live in.
3. Produce an annotated map of your chosen settlement, adding details of the site, functions and nearby resources that may have contributed to its current status on the hierarchy.

▲ **Figure 4:** The Burj-al-Arab hotel, Dubai, located on the southeast coast of the Persian Gulf

What is the global pattern of urban growth?

The pattern of growth in urban areas has not been the same across the world. Cities in Europe and North America reached the peak of their growth in the 1950s or earlier. The most sustained period of urban growth in these **advanced countries (ACs)** took place during the Industrial Revolution of the late 1700s and early 1800s. Increase in population, driven by the 'baby boom' and the building of new houses, led to urban sprawl and the growth of the 'suburbs'. London and Paris were the first 'millionaire' cities (those with a population of more than 1 million people), but they have long since slipped down the league tables of the world's largest. Urbanisation is currently much more rapid in **emerging and developing countries (EDCs)** and **low-income developing countries (LIDCs)**. Cities in Asia and Africa have now overtaken these earlier cities in Europe and North America in terms of population size. EDCs and LIDCs tend to have towns and cities with youthful populations, as the younger people in the rural areas move to urban areas to get jobs. As many of the people are of child-bearing age, there is a high birth rate in these areas, which leads to a rapid natural growth. This trend will continue to cause growth for decades to come.

Growth in Chinese cities is driven by the huge **rural–urban migration** caused by the economic development of these urban areas and the demand for a large workforce. Almost 200 million people moved to urban areas in East Asia between 2000 and 2010. Measurement of this change is important, as managing new growth requires reasonable accuracy in the number of people involved. Infrastructure development has to keep pace with the growing population. Cities in China have grown despite the adoption of the 'one-child' policy. This policy was in place for 35 years and was only dropped by the government in 2015.

In cities such as Lagos in Nigeria the rate of growth has been particularly rapid. In the 1950s, the city had a population of around 300,000 people. Today, it is Africa's second largest city (after Cairo) with an estimated population of around 18 million people.

Most ACs have populations that are more than 70 per cent urban, but LIDCs have more potential for growth, with around two million people a week moving into cities in Africa and Asia. About 40 per cent of Africans lived in cities in 2015, but this is expected to rise to well over 50 per cent by 2050.

> ### Classification of countries
>
> For more information on the classification and distribution of ACs, EDCs and LIDCs, look at Chapter 11, page 169.

▼ **Figure 5:** Urban growth per hour

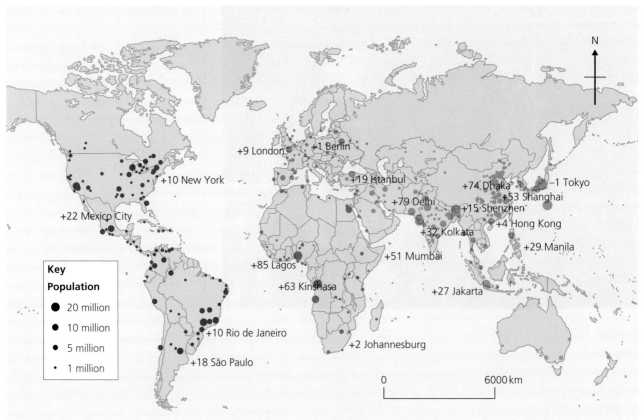

Key
Population
- 20 million
- 10 million
- 5 million
- 1 million

+9 London +1 Berlin +19 Istanbul +74 Dhaka −1 Tokyo
+10 New York +79 Delhi +53 Shanghai
+22 Mexico City +15 Shenzhen +4 Hong Kong
+32 Kolkata +29 Manila
+85 Lagos +51 Mumbai
+63 Kinshasa +27 Jakarta
+10 Rio de Janeiro +2 Johannesburg
+18 São Paulo

0   6000 km

137

Chapter 9 Why do more than half the world's population live in urban areas?

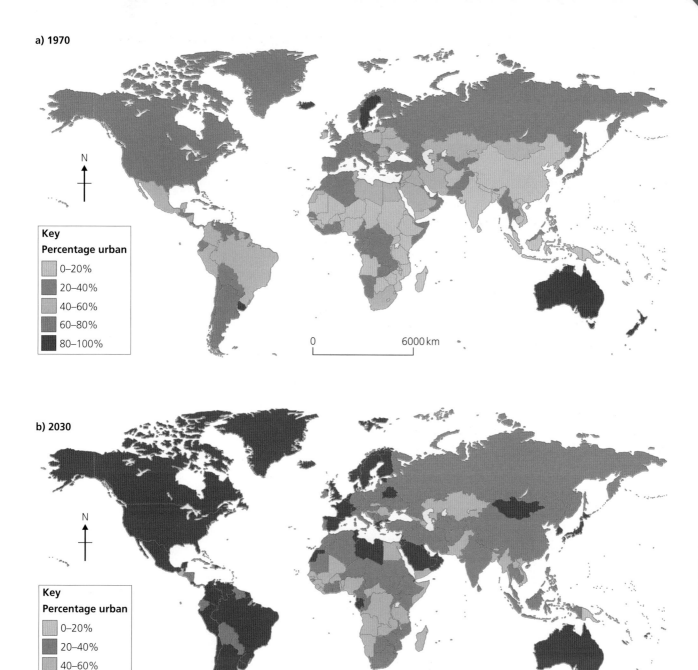

a) 1970

Key
Percentage urban
- 0–20%
- 20–40%
- 40–60%
- 60–80%
- 80–100%

0   6000 km

b) 2030

Key
Percentage urban
- 0–20%
- 20–40%
- 40–60%
- 60–80%
- 80–100%

0   6000 km

▲ **Figure 6:** How urban areas across the world are changing. These maps compare the percentage urban population of countries for 1970 (a) and 2030 (b)

Activities

1. Compare the percentage urbanisation shown in Figure 6 and how it has changed in:
   a. the Americas
   b. Africa
   c. South East Asia
2. Which parts of the world have undergone the greatest change in urbanisation over time?

Cities, megacities and world cities and their changing distribution since 1950

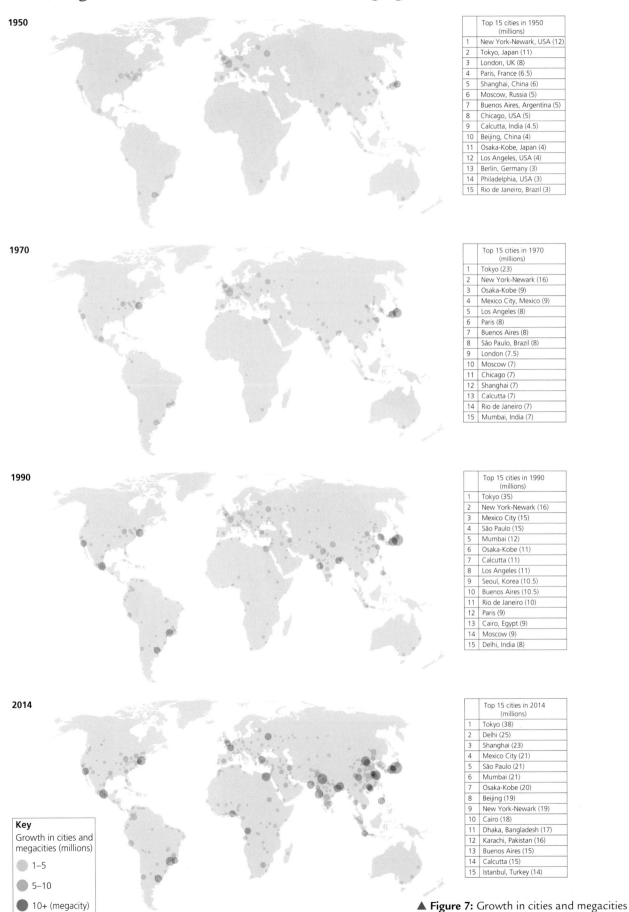

1950

	Top 15 cities in 1950 (millions)
1	New York-Newark, USA (12)
2	Tokyo, Japan (11)
3	London, UK (8)
4	Paris, France (6.5)
5	Shanghai, China (6)
6	Moscow, Russia (5)
7	Buenos Aires, Argentina (5)
8	Chicago, USA (5)
9	Calcutta, India (4.5)
10	Beijing, China (4)
11	Osaka-Kobe, Japan (4)
12	Los Angeles, USA (4)
13	Berlin, Germany (3)
14	Philadelphia, USA (3)
15	Rio de Janeiro, Brazil (3)

1970

	Top 15 cities in 1970 (millions)
1	Tokyo (23)
2	New York-Newark (16)
3	Osaka-Kobe (9)
4	Mexico City, Mexico (9)
5	Los Angeles (8)
6	Paris (8)
7	Buenos Aires (8)
8	São Paulo, Brazil (8)
9	London (7.5)
10	Moscow (7)
11	Chicago (7)
12	Shanghai (7)
13	Calcutta (7)
14	Rio de Janeiro (7)
15	Mumbai, India (7)

1990

	Top 15 cities in 1990 (millions)
1	Tokyo (35)
2	New York-Newark (16)
3	Mexico City (15)
4	São Paulo (15)
5	Mumbai (12)
6	Osaka-Kobe (11)
7	Calcutta (11)
8	Los Angeles (11)
9	Seoul, Korea (10.5)
10	Buenos Aires (10.5)
11	Rio de Janeiro (10)
12	Paris (9)
13	Cairo, Egypt (9)
14	Moscow (9)
15	Delhi, India (8)

2014

	Top 15 cities in 2014 (millions)
1	Tokyo (38)
2	Delhi (25)
3	Shanghai (23)
4	Mexico City (21)
5	São Paulo (21)
6	Mumbai (21)
7	Osaka-Kobe (20)
8	Beijing (19)
9	New York-Newark (19)
10	Cairo (18)
11	Dhaka, Bangladesh (17)
12	Karachi, Pakistan (16)
13	Buenos Aires (15)
14	Calcutta (15)
15	Istanbul, Turkey (14)

Key

Growth in cities and megacities (millions)

- 1–5
- 5–10
- 10+ (megacity)

▲ **Figure 7:** Growth in cities and megacities

139

Chapter 9 Why do more than half the world's population live in urban areas?

What are the characteristics of megacities?

In early 2015, a World Bank report suggested that the Pearl River Delta area of China (see Figure 3 on page 134) had overtaken Tokyo as the world's largest urban area, both in terms of area and total population. It is thought to house over 40 million people. Cities of such size would have been unheard of in the past, but are now becoming increasingly the norm.

The rapid rate of growth which has taken place in ACs (and more recently in LIDCs) has led to the creation of a number of cities with a population over ten million. Cities with a population of this size are called **megacities**. These are often, but not exclusively, capital cities. In 1950 there were only two megacities, but there are now thought to be over 30 and the number is growing. This is a dramatic rate of growth in just 65 years and the number continues to grow. Some of the most recent megacities have developed as a result of industrialisation and outward investment from ACs and are found in Africa and Southeast Asia. Although the number of megacities is growing, they still only house five per cent of the world's population at present. Some cities now have populations of over 20 million people, and these are continuing to grow, drawing in surrounding populations as well as growing internally.

Why are megacities important?

> The risks relating to megacities
>
> *'Megacities are major global risk areas. Due to highest concentration of people and extreme dynamics, they are particularly prone to supply crises, social disorganisation, political conflicts and natural disasters. Their vulnerability can be high.'*

As cities grow, their demographic pattern changes. People who move in are often of working age or younger, and are looking to support their families and offer them better life chances. Greater financial stability often gives couples the confidence to raise larger families, increasing the rate of growth still further, even without a rapid rate of immigration.

Many urban areas also get denser as they grow. This could potentially bring environmental benefits in the longer term, as people are concentrated in a small area rather than causing urban sprawl.

Year	Number of megacities
1950	2
1975	3
2007	19
2025	27 (estimated)

▲ **Figure 8:** The growth in number of megacities (population over 10 million)

It is important to plan for growth, or the urban form that develops in the early stages of a city's development tends to persist for decades.

Singapore is an example of a city that was planned carefully, initially under the leadership of Lee Kuan Yew, to cope with future development. Infrastructure was considered at the beginning as part of the planning process and there were long-term plans for its growth. During Mr Lee's time as prime minister, the city grew from a small settlement on a marshy island to a global hub for trade and a popular stopover destination for international travellers.

The megacity can offer some of the benefits of 'economies of scale' so that the impact of people is concentrated in one area, rather than sprawling over a larger area. There can also be a better 'civic identity' with the city, which fosters pride, rather than resentment at those in charge. Megacities may be more stable, and offer better public services, but internal divisions need to be tackled. The 'spread cities' of the USA are not a good model for this, as they involve too much internal movement, which is inefficient. Solar energy generation, recycled materials and careful integration of technology could help these cities become more efficient.

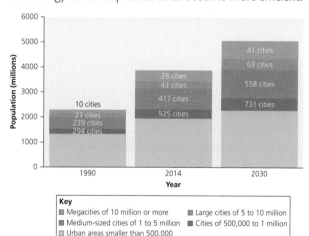

▲ **Figure 9:** Urban population growth is propelled by the growth of cities of all sizes

Activities

1. Study Figure 7.
   a. Identify the locations of the largest cities in each year.
   b. Describe the major changes that have taken place in the locations of the largest cities.
   c. What is likely to happen in the future?
2. Explain why there was a decline in the growth of cities in the ACs during the period from 1950 to 2014.
3. In which parts of the world are cities growing the fastest? Research one of the cities on Figure 5 to explore the reasons for its rapid growth.

▲ **Figure 10:** Shipping docks in Singapore, a world city

What is a world city?

A **world city** (also known as a global or alpha city) is one which is considered to be an important hub in the global economic system. As with many urban definitions, there is some variation as to what qualifies a city to become a 'world city', but they tend to have some or all of the characteristics detailed in the following box.

Characteristics of world cities

- Headquarters of multinational companies based in the city
- A centre for innovation in business
- A centre for media and communications: broadcasting and technology
- Integration into the global economy
- A major centre for manufacturing
- Important port facilities capable of handling bulk carriers
- Financial services: home of an important stock exchange or major banks
- Regional importance compared with other cities
- Highly rated universities, often specialising in research, which links to a high quality of healthcare provision
- Cultural opportunities including opera and ballet as well as cinema and live music

World cities are found in all continents. There are clusters in North America and western Europe. Figure 11 shows those cities which are generally thought of as being world cities.

▼ **Figure 11:** World cities

141

Chapter 9 Why do more than half the world's population live in urban areas?

▲ **Figure 12:** Canary Wharf, the financial district in London, a world city

Although it is not a megacity, London is a world city. Its status as a world city comes from its financial importance with the London Stock Exchange, the scientific research from its many universities, the cultural importance of the city's theatres and the commercial power of the many companies located there. It also has iconic buildings which are familiar to people all over the world, some of them relatively new. Decisions made here influence people around the world. For many overseas visitors it is the only part of the UK which they visit, so comes to 'represent' the UK to them.

World cities need to continue to grow if they are to keep their status; they also face competition from other cities hope to be classed as 'world cities' in their place. The nature of this growth needs to be managed if the cities are to remain competitive.

👣 Fieldwork ideas

For those learning in a rural location, it is worth investigating the possibility of immersing yourself in a busy city, so that you can remember what it was like when discussing cities during this part of the course.

Activities

1. What are the main differences between a megacity and a world city?
2. Create a table to show the strengths and opportunities provided by megacities for the people who inhabit them.
3. Explore the megacities that already exist using this interactive map: www.megacities.uni-koeln.de/documentation. Do they have any common characteristics?

→ Take it further

4. Look at Figure 11. Using the list of characteristics of world cities, suggest why at least three of these cities have been given world city status. You may want to use www.urbanobservatory.org to help with this activity.
5. Do you think it is possible for a world city to lose its status? What factors might lead to this happening?

✝ Geographical skills

One of the issues that face large cities is air quality. This is seen by the World Health Organization (WHO) as one of the greatest global threats to health, and large cities are the worst culprits.

Investigate the air quality around the world using the Plume Labs map: https://air.plumelabs.com

In which country is air quality particularly bad?

What does rapid urbanisation mean for cities?

→ In this section you will:

→ investigate the causes and consequences of rapid urbanisation in LIDCs, including the push and pull factors of rural–urban migration and internal growth

→ investigate the causes and consequences of different urban trends in ACs, including suburbanisation, counter-urbanisation and re-urbanisation.

What does rapid urbanisation mean for cities?

What are the causes of rapid urbanisation in LIDCs?

The rate of growth of LIDC cities is now the fastest in the world. The highest population growth rate is in the continent of Africa; urban populations there are expected to triple in size by 2050. There is still less than 40 per cent urban population in Africa, with plenty of potential to grow further. Cities such as Yamoussoukro, Côte d'Ivoire, may grow by over 40 per cent in the next five years.

City dwellers are predicted to double in number by 2050, rising to over 6 billion people, which will lead to further urban sprawl or increased density of occupation. There has been particular growth in the Pearl River Delta in China, including cities such as Shenzhen and Guangzhou. Some cities have specialised in manufacturing particular products, and this has drawn people into them from surrounding rural areas, looking to improve their quality of life.

Urbanisation is driven by:

- **rural–urban migration** – people being drawn from the rural areas to live in cities
- **internal growth** – when people who have moved into the cities have lots of children.

Rural–urban migration

The factors which draw people to cities are referred to as **pull factors**. These work in combination with **push factors** which tend to drive people away from rural areas.

Push factors

- Opportunities for employment other than agricultural work are limited and wages in rural areas are at poverty levels in many countries.
- Rural areas often have fewer services (including access to education and healthcare) and poorer infrastructure.

Pull factors

- There are more opportunities for employment than in rural areas and wages are often better.
- There are often better healthcare systems and schools in urban areas.
- There is the draw of stories which may filter back from people who left the village and who are now apparently doing better in the city.
- Cities become transport hubs, with road, rail, canal and air networks meeting there or passing through them. This encourages new arrivals to travel there and in turn this creates benefits for industrial location, drawing in a workforce from the surrounding area.
- Prestige comes from a city location, which drives up the cost of property and office space through demand.

Internal growth

Once people arrive in cities and find employment and housing, they will tend to have children. This increase in population due to higher birth rates is called internal growth and it can result in a rapid rate of population growth, particularly in LIDCs where cities have a large youthful population. By contrast, many cities in ACs are facing ageing populations and declining numbers.

It is not just cities and megacities that are experiencing an increase in population. Towns great and small are seeing rapid growth in many parts of the world. Are LIDCs going to repeat the pattern of the United States, where rural areas are often neglected as a consequence?

143

Chapter 9 Why do more than half the world's population live in urban areas?

Jing-Jin-Ji

The Chinese government is currently pushing forward a plan to develop a city region centred on Beijing which may eventually house 130 million people. It is known as Jing-Jin-Ji. The idea is that integrating existing urban areas into one supercity may lead to further innovation and environmental protection. The settlement could spread over 80,000 square miles and would require significant investment in transport, including high-speed rail, as well as services such as schools and hospitals. This is an extreme example of the planning decisions that are needed to cope with the increase in urban growth.

▲ **Figure 13:** Jing-Jin-Ji, a planned supercity which will connect Beijing, Tianjin, and Hebei

What are the consequences of rapid urban growth in LIDCs?

LIDC towns and cities are facing rapid rates of growth and may not always be able to cope with it very well. Investment needs to continue or the growth may slow. Infrastructure issues such as traffic congestion, poor air quality and inadequate housing may begin to restrict further economic growth.

In Africa, the last two decades have seen cities growing at their fastest ever rate. Urbanisation has not always resulted in improvements in the quality of life for those who live there, although the perception that leads them to move to the cities is that they will improve their life chances. As slums have grown, air quality has deteriorated and some cities are facing severe water shortages.

Infrastructure improvements such as paved highways and new bridges, sometimes as a result of World Bank funding, have enabled easier access to some LIDC cities. New arrivals to the city have some key priorities. They need to find somewhere to live and secure employment or a source of income. They have food, water and sanitation needs and their children will require education. The whole family may need healthcare. For some new arrivals, most of these needs are only partially met and their situation is precarious.

Informal growth of cities

Cities often grow in a planned way, but many cities, particularly those in LIDCs, attract people in such large numbers that the city's infrastructure cannot keep pace with that of the arrivals. Available land, even that which is unsuitable for development, is soon used, expanding along transport routes such as main roads and railways. This informal growth is characterised by the absence of services, particularly sanitation and healthcare, high population densities and criminal activities. Many people are employed in the **informal sector**, where they do not pay tax and have no legal working rights, for example working for cash on a building site or as a domestic cleaner. These jobs may be less reliable than formal employment.

Urban trends

The United Nation's Department of Economic and Social Affairs publishes a regular report on urban trends. The 2015 edition features a wealth of data, statistics and analysis of recent global urban trends. A PDF of the report can be downloaded from: http://esa.un.org/unpd/wup/Highlights/WUP2014-Highlights.pdf.

Lagos: a better life for new arrivals?

Lagos is a port which lies on the coast of Nigeria, guarding a swampy lagoon. The city flourished during the slave trade. More recently, Lagos has experienced a rapid population increase with numbers growing by 3.4 million people between 2000 and 2010. As a consequence, the city has effectively run out of room and now extends along bridges, leading to traffic congestion and sprawls up to 15 miles inland. The lack of space is not slowing growth; in fact the city is expected to double in size in the next 10 years. Lagos is Nigeria's most important city, and is the economic centre for West Africa, but many people live in one of hundreds of slum areas.

Many residents live without access to electricity or sanitation, and are threatened by flooding and disease; human waste flows through people's homes when it rains. Outbreaks of typhoid, yellow fever and the virus H5N1, among others, have occurred. Rates of HIV/AIDS infection are high. Life expectancy has dropped below 50. Near catastrophe was averted when a traveller infected with Ebola arrived in the city in late 2014, but the disease was contained. Many residents are also affected by corruption and the need to pay bribes to officials, and crime rates are high. There has been investment in high-profile developments such as a sport stadium and convention centre, but most residents don't benefit from this investment.

One particular area attracting attention is the slum area called Makoko. Unlike many slums which are built on land which has been left unused for some reason, Makoko extends out over the water, with buildings on stilts over a lagoon that is polluted and full of rubbish. The marshy ground used to swallow houses built of materials such as breeze blocks. It has been given the ironic nickname 'the Venice of Africa', but it is not a romantic place.

The area has become a floating city, extending out to the point where the water gets too deep. Canoes

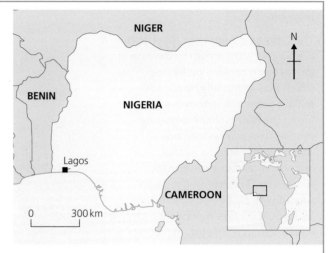

▲ **Figure 14:** Location map of Lagos

called *okos* transport residents around and act as floating shops for food, domestic fuel and also drinking water. It is thought that as many as 250,000 people may be living in the area. The slum at Makoko has not appeared overnight; it has been growing for at least one hundred years. Smoke from fires used for cooking and heating hangs over the houses.

In 2006, the World Bank identified nine of Lagos' largest slums for upgrading. These included Makoko. A loan of US$200 million will be used to help improve drainage and the management of solid waste.

In July 2012, the authorities removed many dwellings in Makoko to try to slow down its growth. Machetes and chainsaws were used to cut through the piles, however many people are still living in boats and refusing to leave as they have nowhere to go to. A fire in 2013 also destroyed many houses. There are some interesting plans in place to redevelop the area. Some involve communities of floating homes along with a floating school. However, it is unlikely that slum dwellers could afford these homes.

▲ **Figure 15:** Floating homes in Makoko lagoon, Lagos

145

Chapter 9 Why do more than half the world's population live in urban areas?

What is informal housing?

Informal housing is built on land which does not belong to those who are building it. This is often land which may not be suitable for the purpose: river beds which may fill with water after rains, land close to industrial activity which may be bad for people's health, or land on steep and unstable slopes. These properties are sometimes affected by landslides and flooding.

Children may have to leave education and go to work to support their families. This may include informal work such as street trading. There have been some projects focusing on improving the lives of young people as a way of leading new growth and reducing the numbers being drawn into criminal activity. In areas of informal housing, infrastructure is poor and there are problems with the reliability of electricity supplied and other utilities. Over time, areas are improved and self-help communities develop.

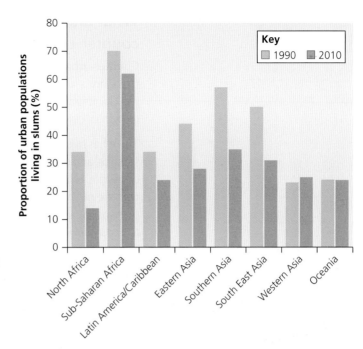

▲ **Figure 16:** Proportion of urban populations living in slums (%)

What are the causes and consequences of different urban trends in advanced countries?

There are a number of changes which take place in cities over time, including suburbanisation, counter-urbanisation and re-urbanisation.

What are the causes and consequences of suburbanisation?

Suburbanisation is the spread of cities outwards and the development of new residential areas. These areas are connected back to the city centre, but are distanced physically from it. Traditionally, they lie beyond the industrial and commercial activity of the city and the inner city housing which serviced that. Houston, Texas, for example has sprawled outwards in all directions, unconfined by a physical barrier. A million new residents have found a home in the hundreds of square miles of sprawl that surround the city. One driving factor is sun-belt migration: the search for a warmer climate by an ageing, affluent population. The city is now mostly made up of what could be called 'subdivisions': areas of housing and associated services which have been added over time.

Suburbanisation has enabled more people to benefit from living in a particular city, even though in reality they may be separated from it by miles of sprawl and face long commutes on crowded highways to reach their place of employment. Cities such as this also place large demands on resources, particularly water. Another consequence is poor air quality caused by the large number of vehicles on the roads.

Tip

The long-term sustainability of the urban growth described in this chapter is subject to change over time. With any exam question, it is useful to remember that your own opinions matter. If you have been to a city, add in your own observations to back up what you are saying. It is also important to look at the positive sides of city life, rather than focusing on the problems. Use experiences from any urban fieldwork that you may have carried out as well.

What are the causes and consequences of counter-urbanisation?

Counter-urbanisation refers to the movement of people from urban areas (back) into rural areas, particularly where those people had originally moved to the city. It is against the established pattern of movement, which has driven the growth of cities for the last few decades.

There has been an increase in the movement of people out towards the suburbs, and a 'hollowing out' of the central areas. This leads to decentralisation of people, employment and services towards the edges of urban areas. People who are moving out are often looking for a more peaceful place to live and perhaps to raise a family. They believe that crime rates may be lower and the cost of living less than in the city. People are encouraged to do this by improvements in the speed of rail links. Counter-urbanisation extends the usual urbanisation process beyond the city area and into smaller urban centres which are usually within commuting distance of the main centre as a result.

What are the key drivers of counter-urbanisation?

The people who move out of cities tend to be those who can afford to: the most affluent and also the most mobile. They are often those with young children, who have a notion that the countryside may be a 'better place' to bring them up. They may be driven out by traffic congestion, the higher cost of living, crime (or the perception of crime), the poor air quality, which might impact on their health, the dream of a rural idyll, or the marketing of estate agents and property companies, fostered by media. Deprivation scores vary across cities, but there are often clusters where multiple problems occur.

These demographic changes may continue to alter the character of the rural fringes of large cities for some time to come, particularly when there is a major difference in the price of property. Some people 'downsize', which involves selling a property in London and enjoying the benefits of a smaller house in a new rural location. An ageing population also means that there are more people reaching retirement and searching for a peaceful place to live. The designation of land around major UK cities as **green belt** land means that building is restricted in these areas, so developers sometimes leap-frog these areas and produce a new ring of developments further out.

Another trend is the migration of offices due to high costs of office space in London. Business and science parks often seek out-of-town locations, so that their workers can have a better quality of life and costs of land purchase are reduced.

There are two key trends in this movement. The first is a movement of employees out to rural areas. In many ACs, new industries have developed which are free to locate where they choose. The growth in the number of people who can work from home has also fuelled a demand for high-speed broadband for rural areas (see Figure 17). Businesses are realising the benefits of home-working. Software can log activity, so staff can still be monitored during working hours. Broadband internet is vital for industries to develop in many ACs, and this has improved, as has the use of mobile devices to maintain connectivity through VOIP services such as Skype. This is partly through the work of campaign groups who try to persuade companies to invest in rural broadband.

Activities

1. Write either a paragraph in estate agent speak to try to 'sell' the benefits of city life compared to living in the countryside, or a paragraph describing the benefits of rural life.
2. Pair up and see who has the most compelling arguments for living in one area rather than the other.

▲ **Figure 17:** High–speed broadband – essential or luxury?

147

Chapter 9 Why do more than half the world's population live in urban areas?

The second trend has been for people to live in the rural areas, but continue to commute back into the city for work. This has placed pressure on suburban rail services which are seeing an increase in passenger numbers. Ticket prices are particularly high on these lines as people have no choice but to use them to travel to work.

What are the consequences of counter-urbanisation?

Counter-urbanisation results in 'dormitory villages', where many residents work in the city, but desire a more rural lifestyle. It has also led to changes in the character of villages which are just outside large urban areas. House prices in these locations have increased in recent years. Places such as Hemel Hempstead, for example, are benefiting from their relative proximity to London. Similarly, there has been a recent rise in property prices in Bury St Edmunds because of the access it offers to Cambridge via rail.

Not all of this change has been welcomed by longer-term residents, who fear that the character of these settlements is changing. Some areas are also changing as a result of gentrification: properties are bought and renovated by middle-class or wealthier people; this raises the profile of the area and causes property prices to rise. This can result in local people being priced out of the housing market.

What are the causes and consequences of re-urbanisation?

In 2015, London's population reached 8.6 million. This is the highest it has ever been and surpasses its previous peak in the 1950s. This surprised some people, but was a sign that people are returning to live in the city and particularly in the inner city areas.

In many cities in AC countries there have been government initiatives to counter some of the problems created by inner city decline. These have often targeted the more deprived areas in the city for additional investment to support the growth of industry which might otherwise struggle to attract investment. Firms are paid a premium for new jobs created in these areas and are given other incentives to locate there. The European Union (EU) has also offered a range of financial support through the years that the UK has been a member. This has included investment funds, support for new employment and support for infrastructure projects which draw in industry.

This redevelopment of inner urban areas creates new homes and jobs, which attracts people from outside of the area to move in. This process is called **re-urbanisation**. Many of the people who move into these areas are pleased with the new developments, as are visitors and local government, however there can be negative aspects if developments are not well planned. A lack of affordable housing can lead to expensive apartments ending up empty. Traffic congestion due to increased numbers of residents can also be a problem.

▲ **Figure 18:** Urban redevelopment in London

> ### 👣 Fieldwork ideas
>
> If your school is in an urban area, think about your journey to school and the changes that you may have noticed during your time at the school. Map the changes that have taken place, and keep an eye on local newspapers for proposed future plans.

> ### Activities
>
> Carry out research into a redevelopment of a rundown area in your local town or city. What are the positive and negative impacts of the development scheme?

CHAPTER

10

What are the challenges and opportunities for cities today?

This chapter focuses on two cities, Leeds and Rosario, and the context for their growth. Although they are located in different parts of the world (Figure 3), they have some similarities. This chapter compares the way that the two cities have developed, the challenges that they have faced and the opportunities they offer to their residents. Both are dynamic and both have undergone periods of change during their history.

People in cities are rarely self-sufficient as they rely on technology and commerce for food and water rather than growing and collecting what they need. Urban residents risk becoming separated from the natural world that still feeds them. If cities are to remain sustainable, they need to face up to a series of challenges and make the most of the opportunities that they provide for residents. They need to ensure that residents are provided with the basics of life and that they feel safe and secure.

Tip

In the study of geography, cities are often said to be places where there are problems. It is important to remember the *benefits* that cities bring for their residents and also the advantages of people living in high densities in cities rather than in lots of smaller settlements.

▲ **Figure 2:** Rosario lies on the Paraná Rive

▲ **Figure 1:** Leeds, England

149

Chapter 10 What are the challenges and opportunities for cities today?

How are cities changing?

Since around 2007, for the first time in history, we now have more people living in **urbanised** places than in rural areas (see Chapter 9). These urban places range from small towns to sprawling megacities. Cities are influenced and shaped by their physical location, but they are also shaped by the economic, social, political, cultural and personal processes that have helped to create the character of the region within which they are located. We will be looking at Leeds and Rosario and the challenges that they face. The chapter explores how these cities operate.

Tip

Personal experience is important in exam questions. Do not be afraid to connect what you are learning about cities with your own experiences of them from family visits or fieldwork.

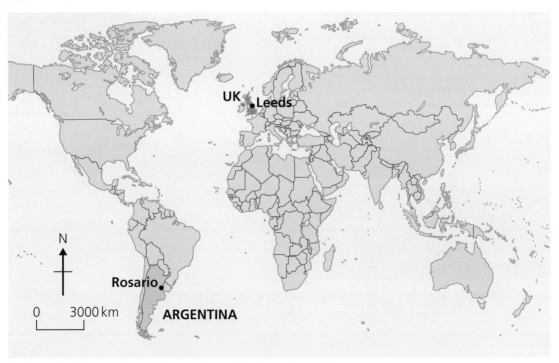

▲ **Figure 3:** Where in the world are the cities of Leeds and Rosario?

Case study: What is life like for people in a city?

What is life like for people in Leeds, England?

→ In this section you will:

- → look at the city's location and importance within its region, the country and the wider world

- → consider the patterns of national and international migration and how this is changing the growth and character of the city

- → explore the ways of life in the city, its culture, ethnicity, housing, leisure and consumption

- → investigate the contemporary challenges that affect life in Leeds.

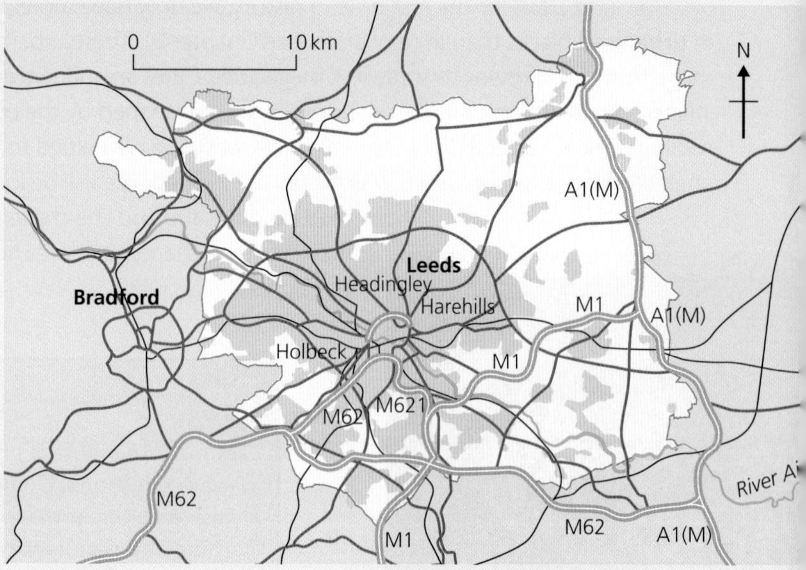

The first city we will explore is in the UK. It is a city which has a long history of industry, but has had to reinvent itself as the traditional employment base has declined.

What is the city's location and importance?

Leeds is the major city in West Yorkshire and lies at the heart of a conurbation which also includes cities such as Bradford and Huddersfield. It is the largest city in the Yorkshire and Humber region, which lies in the north of England.

It is the second largest metropolitan district in England behind Birmingham and covers an area of over 200 square miles in total.

The city's population is estimated at around 800,000 people, a rise of around 10 per cent in the last decade. This provides a large number of consumers as well as potential employees.

Leeds' economy has performed well in recent years and the city has not suffered as much as some nearby towns and cities, such as Hull and Bradford. It has succeeded in attracting investment and creating private-sector jobs.

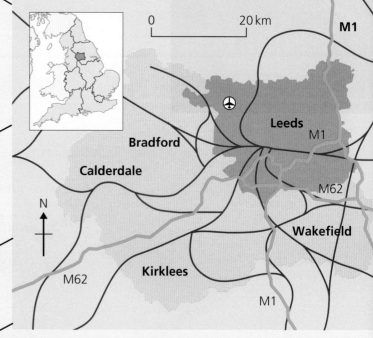

▲ **Figure 4:** Leeds metropolitan area

▲ **Figure 5:** Location map of Leeds

How did Leeds develop?

Leeds started out as a Saxon village, but grew quickly in medieval times, when many main roads that still exist today were named and set out. The early wealth of the city came from the wool industry. Wool from sheep grazing in Yorkshire and beyond was woven and dyed in the city. By the seventeenth century, the city was growing along the course of the River Aire, with markets and other trades moving in. Leeds was fought over during the English Civil War in 1643. As time passed, the textile industry was joined by pottery, brick making and various craft industries. The Leeds–Liverpool canal was completed in 1816, providing a route to and from the coast. The city grew to a population of 100,000 by 1850, at which time the railway arrived. The impressive Town Hall was built in 1858 (Figure 6).

▲ **Figure 6:** Leeds Town Hall

The city has a well-developed transport infrastructure and lies at the heart of a complex of motorways including the M1 (which connects it to London) and the M62 (a major east–west artery), along with major roads which connect it to other parts of the country. The city is well served by rail links, with a travel time to London of just over two hours. It has a canal and waterway network, as well as an international airport at Leeds–Bradford.

Leeds acts as a shopping destination for the north of England and also has several major universities and the associated research activity that goes with them.

Culturally, Leeds is a centre for the arts, with a number of galleries and music venues. The football team has not enjoyed success recently, but was previously one of the top teams in the country.

Internationally, Leeds has attracted interest through global connections between clothing firms and outsourced factories. There are good export links, with many of the firms operating within the city.

Year	Population
1801	94,421
1811	108,459
1821	137,476
1831	183,015
1841	222,189
1851	249,992
1861	311,197
1871	372,402
1881	433,607
1891	503,493
1901	552,479
1911	606,250
1921	625,854
1931	646,119
1941	668,667
1951	692,003
1961	715,260
1971	739,401
1981	696,732
1991	716,760
2001	715,404
2011	751,500

▲ **Figure 7:** Population growth in Leeds

What are the patterns of national and international migration in and out of the city?

Leeds has grown in size in recent years as a result of new arrivals into the city as well as natural increase from its existing population. Around 17 per cent of the city's population is from black and ethnic minority communities. The non-British population is higher than the average for the region. Those residents who are non-UK born tend to settle in the Gipton and Harehills wards of the city.

There was an influx of migrants, including 'new commonwealth' immigrants from the Caribbean, during the 1950s. Leeds claims to have the oldest Caribbean community in the UK, settling in areas like Harehills. The city has a West Indian carnival every year. Pakistan and India were also well represented at this time by a further influx.

Leeds has a large Irish community too, dating back to the early nineteenth century. The Irish settled in an area called 'the Bank' until the early twentieth century, when slum clearances forced the communities to disperse across the city. There was a second wave of Irish arrivals in the mid-twentieth century, when they mostly found work in labouring and manufacturing jobs, taking the numbers of Irish migrants to over 30,000.

After the Second World War, the city welcomed Polish, Ukrainian and Hungarian refugees and these also moved into inner-city Leeds. The extension of the EU in 2004 led to many new arrivals from countries such as Lithuania and Poland, although not in the same numbers as the previous arrivals. In 2013, the ONS estimated there were between 6000 and 9000 new long-term immigrants into the city, with net migration to the city of around 1700 in total.

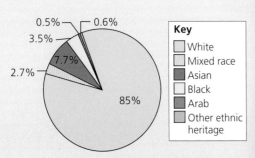

Key
- White
- Mixed race
- Asian
- Black
- Arab
- Other ethnic heritage

0.5% 0.6%
3.5%
7.7%
2.7%
85%

▲ **Figure 8:** Ethnic makeup of Leeds, 2011

▲ **Figure 9:** The Parkinson building, University of Leeds

153

Chapter 10 What are the challenges and opportunities for cities today?

What are the impacts of immigration on the character of the city?

The character of the city is diverse as a result of these different groups. One large group of people is the student population, which numbers over 30,000, along with over 7000 staff at the University of Leeds, one of two universities in the city. These young people produce a great demand for housing stock and they are important for the local economy. The city has responded by providing a wealth of entertainment and food options, particularly close to the university, which can be recognised by the famous Parkinson building (Figure 7). Around 18 per cent of the population of the city are aged 15 and under, compared with around 15 per cent for those aged over 65.

Leeds has a higher proportion of young people than the national average, which means that the city has as many people under 16 as it does over 60 years old. This creates a demand for services which are relevant for these age groups. Many of the retail and entertainment businesses in the city centre sell clothing and products for teenagers and young adults. There is a thriving café culture and lots of nightlife.

Leeds is a city which shows great diversity in its population, although around 89 per cent of the population were born in the UK. Between 1991 and 2011, the ethnic minority population in Leeds doubled in size, to reach 15 per cent of the total population. The largest groups within this were Pakistani and Indian. Some ethnic minority groups struggle to earn highly paid work. The Pakistani group also shows more clustering, with a preference for living in the same areas of Leeds.

Websites

For further statistical data, visit the Leeds Observatory website: www.westyorkshireobservatory. org/leeds.

Profiles of each of the wards within the city can be investigated at http://observatory.leeds.gov. uk/leedsprofiles and used for an activity exploring the city.

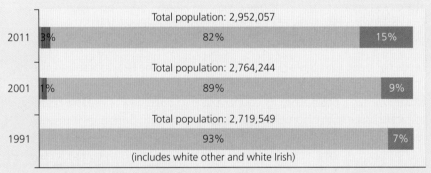

	Total population	White British	Non-white
2011	2,952,057	3% / 82%	15%
2001	2,764,244	1% / 89%	9%
1991	2,719,549	93%	7%

(includes white other and white Irish)

Key
■ White Irish ■ White other
□ White British ■ Non-white

▲ **Figure 10:** Ethnic diversity in the Leeds City region

▲ **Figure 11:** Cafe in Trinity Centre

▲ **Figure 12:** Queens Arcade

Activities

1. Leeds comes third in terms of economic importance compared to London and Manchester. What industries have contributed to its position in the table?
2. How can the city ensure that it doesn't slip down the table in the future?

▲ **Figure 13:** The Trinity Centre

	GVA, £ millions	GVA per head
Inner London	237,356	71,162
Greater Manchester South	38,645	25,950
Leeds	20,362	26,741
Greater Manchester North	17,620	14,375

* GVA measures the contribution to the economy of each individual producer, industry or sector in the UK

▲ **Figure 14:** Leeds' economic importance

What is life like for people in Leeds?

Leeds is very diverse with many different cultures, languages, faiths and races, and this is seen as one of the strengths of the city. There are, however, groups who may require additional support, such as help with the English language or with financial matters.

Leeds is already important for many industries, with companies such as the supermarket chain ASDA and the Danish food company ARLA having their headquarters there. There are also TV production companies and financial institutions. It has a well-developed digital infrastructure, which is attracting new businesses, as well as a rich industrial heritage. Many of the creative industries work from hubs, which are often based in old industrial buildings with attractive Victorian architecture. The supermarket founders Marks and Spencer opened their first penny arcade in Leeds in 1884, and grew from there to become a household name.

In 2014, the Tour de France cyclists lined up to start the first main stage of the famous race. Instead of France, they set out from Leeds, and were watched by millions of spectators lining the road and many more watching on television. This was part of a strategy by the Yorkshire tourism agency to raise the profile of the region. The city already attracts many visitors to its retail districts, such as the revamped Trinity Leeds mall (see Figure 13), but the Tour de France offered a chance for the city (and region) to sell itself on a global scale. Sport is also well represented in the city. Its football team and two rugby teams have enjoyed great success at the highest level. Leeds also has a cricket ground, which attracts test cricket, and is the 'home' of the county cricket team, Yorkshire.

The city sits close to the Yorkshire Dales and North York Moors National Park, and there are other Areas of Outstanding Natural Beauty (AONB) within a short distance of the city.

Leeds has been through a number of changes over the last decade and, like any city, is constantly evolving. New buildings are going up along the waterfront and in the canal basin. The city council plans to build new affordable housing to tackle some of the homelessness issues and bring in further investment. Redevelopment has already taken place on a large scale in some areas of the city, although not all of these developments currently have full occupancy. The city centre has changed dramatically over the last few decades. Taxi drivers in the city have to cope with regular changes to street patterns. Some businesses, such as nightclubs, even change their names at night or on different days of the week to provide a different experience for their young customers.

Major employers include the Leeds General Infirmary, which employs 7000 people, and local industries. The city makes a significant contribution to the country's economy. It sits at the heart of a city region which has an economy worth over £50 billion and a workforce of over 1.4 million. Figure 14 shows that Leeds is the third most important urban area in this respect.

155

Chapter 10 What are the challenges and opportunities for cities today?

What challenges does Leeds face?

Leeds faces a series of challenges, many of which are common to all AC cities. The city has introduced a strategy called 'Leeds 2030' in which it proposes 'to be the best city in the UK' by this date. This strategy targets the major issues facing many large cities such as:

- affordability of housing
- unemployment, particularly among young people
- social inequality, including deprivation and poverty facing young people.

Most city councils have strategies for dealing with these issues, with varying degrees of success.

The city faces some environmental challenges, which include the quality of water in the city's rivers. There is also environmental monitoring of the air quality.

Is Leeds a divided city?

One issue that faces all AC cities is **social inequality**: the division between the wealthier and poorer residents. These residents are not necessarily divided by long distances; some of the more prosperous areas are located very close to areas going through tough times. The wealthy areas of Leeds include Moseley Wood and Cookridge. Gipton and Harehills are among those areas which have not shared in Leeds' prosperity and deprivation is ingrained. Some of these have a history of housing migrant arrivals. In Holbeck, over 15 per cent of residents are on Jobseekers' Allowance and similar benefits in 2015, whereas in Weetwood the figure was just 0.2 per cent. There were also variations in child poverty, with a figure of 38 per cent for the Central Leeds constituency.

Leeds is recovering well from the financial crisis of 2008, but not all communities share equally in the city's prosperity. A 2015 report by Cities Outlook showed that over 20 per cent of children in Leeds were living in poverty, including **fuel poverty**, particularly in the Leeds Central constituency. According to the same report, Leeds has the third highest levels of inequality of any city in the UK.

 Edie
I can't recognise the city as it was when I was a young girl. A lot of the old buildings have gone and been replaced by modern ones.

 Ruth
The shopping in Leeds is great now. The new arcades mean I don't even need to worry about the weather.

 Dessy
The mix of people in Leeds has always been one of its strengths.

 Luke
I'm struggling to find somewhere affordable to live, and yet there are quite a few new flats sitting empty which are outside of many people's price range.

It takes me quite a long time to travel into work these days.

 Traci

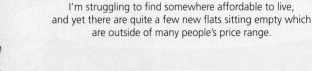
▲ **Figure 15:** What do residents think of Leeds as a city?

Definitions

Child poverty: in the UK child poverty is defined as living in a household with an income below 60 per cent of the national average (although this definition is under review).

Fuel poverty: a situation in which spending money to heat your home would take you below the official poverty line, or if you have required fuel costs that are above average.

Studying the problem?

There are large student areas to the north of the city centre which are not necessarily struggling financially, but have been affected by a process called 'studentification'. This means that the local community has been replaced by a student community. This is true of South Headingley and Hyde Park, where many rely on the private rented sector. This results in demographic imbalance, as well as rent and property price inflation. There will often be more pubs and takeaway restaurants in these areas, but the demand is seasonal, with quieter periods in the university holidays. Some work is provided, however, by the need for student property maintenance. Services such as schools are not needed to the level that one would expect. Crime levels in such areas can also be high, with offences ranging from theft of property to antisocial behaviour, such as noise.

▲ **Figure 16:** Leeds University

▲ **Figure 17:** Royal Armouries, Leeds

157

Chapter 10 What are the challenges and opportunities for cities today?

Pride in the community and the fabric of housing tends to be reduced in these areas, so there can be a problem with blight. There are also problems with car parking, from 'Gridlock Sunday' (when students return for the start of the new term) onwards, as students look for places to park their cars without charge. Any streets within reasonable walking distance of the university will fill with cars, causing resentment among residents. Despite this, the students bring millions of pounds into the local economy and the universities are major employers.

In the past, there has been a lot of development along the river and the Leeds–Liverpool Canal. The Royal Armouries area was an area of development, associated with the move of a national museum to the city. This has resulted in a number of new

▲ **Figure 18:** Anti-homeless spikes

housing developments along the canal, sometimes in regenerated warehouses and wharfs. Some larger retail and cultural developments such as Trinity, Eastgate and Leeds Arena have been likened to 'enormous hoovers' which suck up any available investment at the expense of local businesses. This threatens to remove some of the original 'soul' of the city. There have also been calls for a better mass transportation system in Leeds than at present. Fares are rising and there is a need for a well-developed tram system which could reach more areas of the city.

In general, cities are becoming more, rather than less, unequal. House prices, employment and the quality of services are all changing dramatically, but cities are not homogenous. These differences are reflected in the algorithms used by insurance companies to provide quotes for car and house insurance based on postcodes. Policies can vary by hundreds of pounds depending on location within a city, sometimes for places just a few hundred metres apart.

Another trend has been the rise in gated communities, where the rich hide behind walls and gated security. At the same time, 'anti-homeless spikes' discourage people from staying overnight near prestigious developments, and many public spaces are becoming private property.

Activities

1. Explore the website of Leeds City Council (www.leeds.gov.uk) to see what is planned for the future.
   a. i. If you were a young person living in Leeds, what do you think might persuade you to stay in the city?
      ii. What challenges do you think might persuade you to leave the city?
   b. Do the same activity but for a different group. Choose from:
      • a recently retired person
      • an unemployed person
      • a newly arrived refugee
      • an investor looking for a location for a new start-up company.

How can cities become more sustainable?

➔ **In this section you will:**

➔ investigate different initiatives to make Leeds more sustainable.

What lies in the future for Leeds?

One word that crops up in a lot of official documents is the word 'sustainable'. For a city to be sustainable, it needs to provide people with a good quality of life in a way that is:

● socially
● economically
● environmentally sustainable.

This means that the quality of life that people enjoy today needs to be protected for future generations, but in such a way that it does not risk the health of the city. This is a challenge for any city, requiring investment in technologies and the promotion of lifestyle changes. A focus on primary healthcare, investment in renewable technology and money spent on improving public transport would all help. Leeds City Council is focusing on these and many other areas.

HS2 and Leeds

In 2014, the government announced that it was considering extending the planned HS2 (High Speed railway line, which was due to finish in Birmingham) as far as Leeds, which already has a reasonably fast service to the capital. HS2 is planned to arrive in the city in 2032. Although this is a long way off, the city is already considering the potential benefits of being part of what the government has called the 'Northern powerhouse'. This refers to the government's plans to invest in the cities which lie in the north of England as part of a plan to reduce the dominance of London in the economy. It is feared that if London starts to lose investment, the country's economy could suffer unduly.

Leeds South Bank: a sustainable development?

Before the possible changes that HS2 might bring (which are some years away), there are major plans for an area called the South Bank of the city. This area is due to undergo the next major development in the city.

▼ **Figure 19:** High Speed rail plans for Northern England

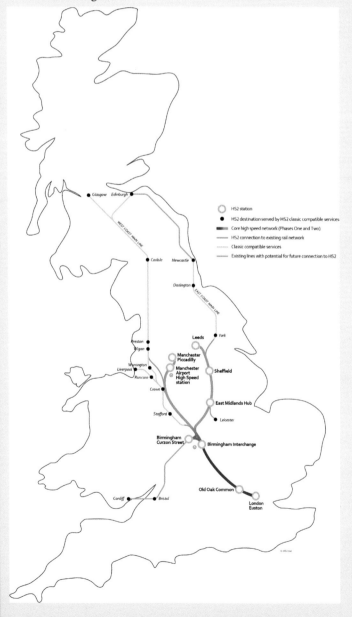

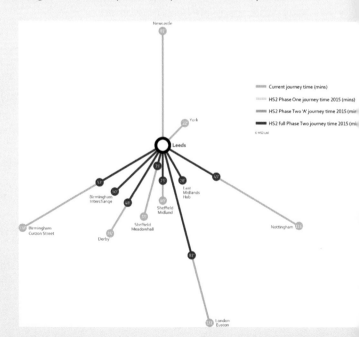

159

Chapter 10 What are the challenges and opportunities for cities today?

▲ **Figure 20:** Leeds South Bank development

Plans for the South Bank

→ A focus on infrastructure and investment, including a new HS2 station, which means that public transport is prioritised for residents

→ Retail, leisure, financial and professional services are supported

→ Incorporates previous developments at Royal Armouries

→ A cultural centre at the old Tetley brewery will support contemporary art

→ Educational improvements linked to Leeds City College, which will transform the former Alf Cooke Printworks into a vocational campus

→ Hub for new creative and digital industries

→ A new 3.5 hectare park and open space along the waterfront

→ Over 300,000 square metres of development land available

→ Creation of Holbeck Urban Village: digital technology and living spaces close to the waterfront, which have won awards for their improvements in economic, social and physical environment

→ Developments will include former mills and the Temple Works

→ New pedestrian and cycle bridges will connect new open spaces to improve connectivity

→ Clarence Dock will become Leeds Dock, hoping to build on success of similar developments in cities such as Liverpool and Birmingham, providing entertainment and restaurants alongside retail developments

→ Water taxi and shuttle-bus services will connect the area to the station, and reduce carbon emissions

Assessing sustainability

In order for a development to be sustainable, we might expect it to meet certain conditions.

→ **Social sustainability:** measures in place to improve the quality of life and the way that people who live in the area interact

→ **Economic sustainability:** providing employment and training for residents, so that they don't have to leave the area every day to travel to work elsewhere in the city

→ **Environmental sustainability:** development needs to offer buildings which are energy efficient, with an eye to renewable energy, low emissions from activities and protection of local habitats

Activities

1. Take a look at the planned development for the South Bank in the information box above.
   a. How sustainable are these developments? Consider the three elements of sustainability. Try to give each one an overall rating.
   b. What are the costs and benefits of developments like this for the city?

→ Take it further

2. List the adjectives used to describe the Leeds South Bank project. How does the language of documents like this match the reality of living in a city like Leeds?
3. Use a house price website such as Zoopla or Rightmove to compare prices for similar houses in different Leeds postcode areas.

Case study: What is life like for people in a city?

What is life like for people in Rosario, Argentina?

→ In this section you will:

→ look at the city's location and importance within its region, the country and the wider world

→ consider the patterns of national and international migration and how this is changing the growth and character of the city

→ explore the ways of life in the city, its culture, ethnicity, housing, leisure and consumption

→ investigate the contemporary challenges that affect life in Rosario.

▲ **Figure 21:** Location map for Rosario, Argentina

The second city we are going to explore is in South America. It shares many characteristics with Leeds, which is why it was selected, and is a comparable size within Argentina's hierarchy of major cities.

What is the city's location and importance?

Rosario is the largest city in the southern part of the Argentinian province of Santa Fe.

It is the third most populous city in Argentina after Buenos Aires (the capital city) and Cordoba. It has an estimated population of just over one million, based on information from the most recent census, and a population density of around 50 people per hectare. It is located around 300 km northwest of Buenos Aires and is a regional transport hub for a number of major roads, including the Aramburu Highway and the Highway Ernesto 'Che' Guevara, named after the city's most famous former resident. Rosario is also served by an international airport, called *Islas Malvinas*: the Argentinian name for the disputed territory of the Falkland Islands.

It lies on the Paraná River, which eventually flows into the Atlantic and is the second longest river in South America after the Amazon. The city is low lying; it is only around 40 m above sea level, which moderates its climate compared with other cities.

The city is made up of six districts, each of which has its own characteristics.

Rosario has rail, river and air transport links which have helped it develop as an important industrial centre within the region. The city's location on the *costanera*, the bank of the Paraná River which connects to the Plata Basin, places it on one of the largest and busiest waterways in the world and a major artery for communications throughout the region. The associated dockside development meant that it was a key point for the import and export of agricultural products. The fortunes of these industries have changed over the decades, but many remain profitable and the city is prosperous as a result. Its industrial importance means that it attracts investment.

161

Chapter 10 What are the challenges and opportunities for cities today?

How did Rosario develop?

Rosario was founded in the late seventeenth century when land was gifted to a soldier called Luis Romero de Pineda for services to the crown. A small settlement grew on his land, close to the River Paraná, as settlers drawn from across Santa Fe mixed with indigenous people. Livestock were farmed and the city developed through farming in the immediate area and trade.

In the late nineteenth century, the city became Argentina's first port to export goods and this drew in migrant workers. The importance of grain led to the city being called 'Argentina's Chicago', which developed alongside gang and Mafia activity after Italian migrants arrived.

Some industries fared less well and parts of the river bank became derelict with empty warehouses. These areas have recently started to undergo renovation as part of the redevelopments aimed at attracting tourism and further new investment. Around the year 2000, many of the city's chemical and steel plants had closed and unemployment was high. The city's fortunes have improved dramatically since that time.

The city's architecture, such as French renaissance buildings and the impressive Stock Exchange, are a sign of the city's wealth and importance over the last few centuries.

Alongside its port facilities, the city has developed as a milling and meat-packing centre for the region. A large complex run by Swift produces products such as corned beef for export. This has attracted people from across Argentina. In the last century, there have also been dramatic increases in the growth of soybeans, which are in demand for foodstuffs, vegetable oil and other products.

Patterns of national and international migration

- Rosario has attracted people from across Argentina. It is estimated that the country is second only to the USA in the number of immigrants it has received, and these have enriched the culture of cities such as Rosario.
- Arrivals included the Spanish in the sixteenth century and migrants from Europe in the nineteenth century. More recently, there has been an influx of migrants from other countries within South America and even from as far away as Korea, China and Taiwan.
- Italian immigration has been a key element in the growth of the city and has influenced hugely the culture (including the food) and the architecture. Italians formed the majority of immigrants into Rosario over the last century. One famous Italian Argentine is Jorge Mario Bergoglio, also known as Pope Francis.

The city has a relatively young demographic, as do many Argentinian cities given the country as a whole has a youthful population with a relatively high birth rate. There are, however, signs of some ageing across the city; this is part of a general trend with all cities.

✝ Geographical skills

A population pyramid is a type of graph which shows the number of people in a range of cohorts (age groups). It shows the population structure of a country and allows for long-term planning as the relative sizes of each cohort will reduce over time, unless there are significant changes in birth and death rate.

Tip

It is important that you don't fall into the trap of thinking that people living in cities like Rosario are less well off than those in Leeds or other cities in ACs. All cities provide benefits for their residents and not everyone can share in the wealth that they generate. Avoid seeing cities as places which only have problems; they also provide a range of opportunities for the people who live there and as these chapters have shown, they may well be our future salvation. Remember to be critical of images and text you may be shown out of context. What images of Rosario are presented if you carry out an image search online?

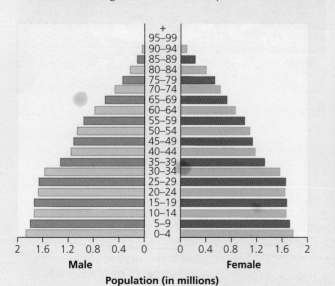

▲ **Figure 22:** A population pyramid for Argentina, 2009 (Source: Wikimedia.org)

What are the ways of life for people in Rosario?

A socialist city

Rosario has been described as the socialist and liberal hub of the country. It has a history of socialist activity. Ernesto (Che) Guevara, who later gained notoriety for his political involvement across South America, was born in the city. The city also has close links with the trade unions because of its industrial heritage.

▲ **Figure 23:** Che Guevara

Shopping in Rosario

Residents and visitors have good opportunities for shopping in *El Centro*: the central mall area. This is an area which has undergone investment and now attracts young people and families alike.

▲ **Figure 24:** El Centro, Rosario

The importance of meat

Argentina as a country has a close cultural connection to meat. It is an important part of the diet. In fact, Argentinians eat far more meat than other nations. There is a close link with the production of beef too. Cattle graze the large grassland areas called pampas and the gauchos, or 'cowboys', are still important. The *asado*, or grill, is an important feature of many restaurants, particularly in *La Florida* – the beach at the river's edge. Argentina is the third largest exporter of meat products.

▲ **Figure 25:** Argentina is famous for its meat

▲ **Figure 26:** The Argentinian flag

Raising the flag

The Argentinian flag was born in Rosario, created by Manuel Belgrano, and raised in the city for the first time. Rosario is therefore known as 'the cradle of the flag', and the impressive National Flag Memorial is sited on the bank of the Paraná.

What are the challenges facing Rosario?

Like any city of comparable size, Rosario has some issues that those in charge of the city have to deal with.

Unemployment

As recently as 2001 there were riots in the city, with high unemployment and economic problems leading to looting of supermarkets. There are still some crime problems facing the city, but there has been some improvement in the employment situation.

Crime

In some parts of the city, slum districts known locally as *villas miserias* are beset by high levels of poverty and crime. Drug use has grown among the city's population and spawned a violent drug war in some districts. Sicilian mobsters have been active in the city.

Criminals have allegedly infiltrated the police in the past and football in the city (and indeed in the country as a whole) is controlled by violent groups known as *barras bravas*. The two football teams in Rosario are Rosario Central and Newell's Old Boys. The city's reputation has been damaged by its association with crime.

Barrios are the neighbourhoods where people live.

Social inequality and divisions

Not everyone who lives in Rosario shares in the success of the city. There are many irregular settlements, or slums, which house over 100,000 people and occupy around 10 per cent of the space in the city.

Cities often grow in a planned way, but many (particularly in LIDCs) attract people in such large numbers that the city's infrastructure cannot keep pace with that of the arrivals. Available land, even that which is unsuitable for development, is soon used and settlements expand along transport routes such as main roads and railways. This informal growth is characterised by the absence of services, particularly sanitation and healthcare, high population densities, structural deficiencies and a low quality of life.

What is being done about these challenges?

Activities such as the Rosario Habitat Program are part of a wider regeneration of areas of Rosario. Regeneration can include one or more of the following options:

- complete replacement – demolition followed by rebuilding to meet the architectural styles of the present day and the ambition of the developers

The Rosario Habitat Program

The Rosario Habitat Program has been set up to reduce the inequalities in the city. The programme is led by the Public Housing Service, which has been in existence for over 80 years. Since it started in 2000, the scheme has helped over 5000 people to upgrade their houses. The programme involves comprehensive improvements, including:

- → new urban planning – new roads and basic infrastructure including sewerage, storm drains and community facilities
- → adding toilet facilities to houses
- → legal ownership rather than the previous uncertainty over the status of tenure
- → education programme for young people regarding risky behaviour
- → employment and income generation for residents; training and work experience for 16–25 year olds
- → money invested in social enterprises
- → targeted support for women in the community.

The project has achieved financial sustainability. It has generated over 150 construction and professional jobs, and trained almost 1000 people in business and entrepreneurial skills.

- regeneration – improvements to the fabric of the building, which might include changes internally or externally
- increasing height – the addition of new floors or replacing low-rise with high-rise development
- infill – additions to the area which may be out of keeping with the area they are slotted into.

One trend is the arrival of gated communities, known locally as *barrios privados* or *barrios cerrados*. These are designed to provide residents with a feeling of safety, with security guards and fences. Rosario has tried to limit these in order to keep the community spirit within the city and prevent the rich from becoming isolated from the poor. It is the first city in the country to have taken this step. Such gated communities are a common feature of other South American cities, where wealthy individuals often have a perception that they are at risk of crime. Footballer Lionel Messi was born in Rosario and he has a property in the area as his family has close ties with the city.

Empty land close to the city centre is prime development land and high-rise developments often locate in these places. In recent years, young people have returned to the city centres. These single and well-educated 'millennials' are joined in some cities by a large student population.

How can cities become more sustainable?

➜ **In this section you will:**

➜ investigate different initiatives to make Rosario more sustainable.

Does the city have a sustainable future?

Rosario has a plan to become more sustainable in its food production. Cities are hungry places and require a lot of resources each day. Food supply is one resource which needs careful thought, as cities are not naturally producers of food.

Rosario: a green city

One key development in Rosario has been the growth of **urban forestry** and agriculture. The city is gaining a reputation as a world leader in this aspect of urban design. Rosario promotes the development of urban forestry as a way of reducing the impacts of climate change within the city. This programme is called *Pro Huerta* (literally, Pro Garden).

Trees are planted among all new housing developments to reduce the ambient temperature in the area. Flood risk zones and peri-urban land have been planted up with food crops; this improves the diet of some low-income families, as well as providing them with some additional income from the sales of their produce. Community groups were given tools and seeds, and vacant land was turned over to the urban farmers some years ago. The production of food locally also reduces the need to transport crops into the city from nearby regions; this reduces CO_2. Local hotels and restaurants support this campaign by using these vegetables and fruits and promoting the value of local food and reduced food miles.

There are now over 800 community gardens in the city, supporting over 40,000 people. The city won a UN-Habitat award for its work in this area. Importantly, the majority of gardeners are women, who now earn income from their involvement, as well as gaining further skills. This is a scheme which other cities have also looked at copying, because of its many benefits.

▲ **Figure 27:** Trees within the city of Rosario

165

Chapter 10 What are the challenges and opportunities for cities today?

Sustainable tourism

Rosario, along with Argentina as a whole, is a growing tourist destination and attracts people from a wide area. The city is making the most of its many attractions and adding tourism as one of its functions and main sources of income. Rosario is also attracting those who wish to learn Spanish, with a growing range of colleges and courses for overseas students who can study in the city. The city has a range of physical attractions, including the waterfront and some of the buildings which have been built over the years.

Activities

1. Create a table with two columns headed 'Physical attractions' and 'Human attractions'. Put these tourist attractions into the correct column in the table.
   - The River Paraná and its *costanera*
   - The National Flag monument: *Monumento Nacional a La Bandera*
   - Tree-lined parks
   - Art galleries
   - Cafés and restaurants
   - The temperate climate, with warm summer temperatures
   - French renaissance architecture
   - A local cuisine based on meat, cooked on an *asado* (barbecue)
   - Paraná Gorge with its sandy beaches
   - Local musicians
   - Salsa and tango clubs for dancing
   - Nightclubs

→ Take it further

2. Visit the website for tourism in the city of Rosario (www.rosarioturismo.com/en/city/) and identify additional attractions that the city might have for visitors from within the country and overseas.

3. Find out more about the green cities scheme and the city farms in Rosario. What are the economic, social and environmental benefits of the scheme for Rosario and its inhabitants? The city's website has some useful additional information: www.rosario.gov.ar.

▲ **Figure 28:** Rosario Station

Activities

1. Compare the two cities featured in this chapter. They were selected as they are similar cities within their own country's context. They have a similar population size, have an industrial past, have attracted a range of migrants and are now planning for a sustainable future with present developments. Residents of both cities face challenges, but there are also those benefiting from the cities' relative economic strength.

   a. Identify some strengths and weaknesses of each of the two cities as regards:
      - cultural diversity
      - quality of housing
      - job opportunities for residents.

   b. Produce a brief report comparing the two cities, with some additional information from your own research so that you 'get to know' these cities even better. Research further images and read any current news stories. You can visit both cities virtually, using Google Street View for example.

Practice questions

1. Define the following terms:
   a) Urbanisation [1 mark]
   b) Megacity [1 mark]
   c) World city [1 mark]
2. Identify three typical city functions and, for each one, suggest a city that is well known for that function. [2 marks]
3. How has the global location of megacities changed since the 1950s? [3 marks]
4. Suggest some advantages and disadvantages of megacities for the people who live in them. [3 marks]
5. With reference to London, or another world city you have studied, explain why it has gained its status. [3 marks]
6. With reference to a city you have studied, outline the negative consequences of rapid urban growth in LIDCs. [5 marks]
7. How have some LIDC cities attempted to improve the quality of life for people who live in them. Evaluate the success of these schemes. [5 marks]
8. Define the term 'social inequality'. [1 mark]
9. Suggest how cities in advanced countries can be classed as divided cities as a result of **social inequality**, with reference to a named city. [4 marks]
10. Sustainability involves three elements. What are those three elements? [2 marks]
11. With reference to a city that you have studied, outline one scheme for improving the sustainability of a particular area. [4 marks]

Tip

As well as the main case studies, questions like questions 11 are common, testing a smaller element of the specification. Use pages 164–5 to help answer this particular question, but investigate whether there are other schemes closer to home that could provide an alternative example.

▲ **Figure A:** Leeds South Bank development

Dynamic Development

Chapter 11: Why are some countries richer than others?

By the end of this chapter, you will know the answers to these key questions:

→ What is development and how can it be measured?

→ What has led to uneven development?

Chapter 12: Are LIDCs likely to stay poor?

By the end of this chapter, you will know the answers to these key questions:

→ How has Ethiopia developed so far?

→ What global connections influence its development?

→ What development strategy is most appropriate?

A cityscape of New York. What factors influence wealth?

CHAPTER 11

Why are some countries richer than others?

Why are some countries richer than others?

→ In this section you will:

→ look at how 'development' can be defined and described

→ look at how global patterns of development can be classified into advanced countries (ACs), emerging developing countries (EDCs) and low-income developing countries (LIDCs)

→ study the social and economic measures that can be used to assess national development.

What is development and how can it be measured?

Development can be defined in various ways. For example:

'The act or process of change, evolution, maturity, progress' (dictionary.com)

'A state of growth or advancement' (Oxford Dictionary)

Everything develops over time: humans develop from tiny babies to adults, villages develop into small towns, seeds develop into forests, valleys develop into gorges. In general, development is seen as a positive process. The dictionary suggests its opposite counterpart is 'deterioration, disintegration'.

In a geographical sense, we think of development as being about improving people's lives. It is often associated with wealth but it is much more complicated than that. For example, you might consider human and environmental health as more important than wealth. The international economist Hans Rosling said, 'You move much faster if you are healthy first than if you are wealthy first'. Or perhaps being able to feel safe in your country and have a democratic, fair government with your human rights protected might be just as important as money. Figure 1 shows some of the many different features of development.

Development can happen on a small scale or a large scale, affecting either small groups of people or whole nations. It can be a slow process or more rapid. It is greatly influenced by the actions of humans and the decisions that influential people, governments or companies make.

▲ **Figure 1:** How can we describe development?

How are countries classified in terms of development?

The International Monetary Fund (IMF) classifies nations into three categories of development:

- **Advanced countries (ACs)**
- **Emerging developing countries (EDCs)**
- **Low-income developing countries (LIDCs).**

Countries are categorised according to wealth per person, trade and links with other nations. Only 16 per cent of world nations are classed as ACs, with 45 per cent as EDCs and 38 per cent as LIDCs (see Figure 2). However the pattern is not evenly spread.

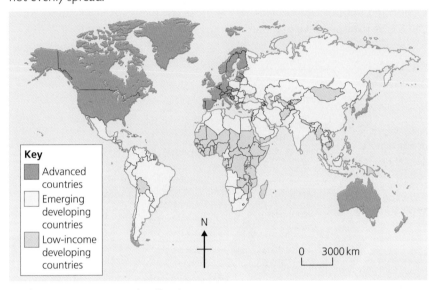

Key
- Advanced countries
- Emerging developing countries
- Low-income developing countries

N

0   3000 km

▲ **Figure 2:** IMF country classifications

LIDCs account for one-fifth of the whole world's population yet have a tiny fraction of the wealth, with people living on an income of just $370 to $2500 a year.

Advanced countries (ACs) share a number of important economic development characteristics including well-developed financial markets, high degrees of financial intermediation and diversified economic structures with rapidly growing service sectors. An example of an AC is the UK.

Emerging developing countries (EDCs) do not share all the economic development characteristics required to be advanced but are not eligible for the Poverty Reduction and Growth Trust. An example of an EDC is South Africa.

Low-income developing countries (LIDCs) are eligible for the Poverty Reduction and Growth Trust from the IMF. An example of an LIDC is Ethiopia.

Activities

1. Write your own definition for 'development'.
2. Where are the world's emerging developing countries located?
3. Name three low-income developing countries.
4. How are the countries in Figures 3 to 6 classified and what proof do you have?

▼ **Figure 3:** The Hoover Dam, United States

▼ **Figure 5:** Spain

▲ **Figure 4:** Morocco

▲ **Figure 6:** London, UK

How can development be measured?

Geographers find it useful to be able to measure how developed places are, and to compare them and see how they change over time. There are two main categories for measuring development: these are **social** (to do with people and society) and **economic** (to do with money) indicators.

Social measures of development

Social measures are to do with individual people and what it would be like for them living in that place. Sometimes social and economic indicators do not match: for example, some countries have excellent healthcare but a low income per person. Figure 7 illustrates some of the many social indicators we can use to measure development.

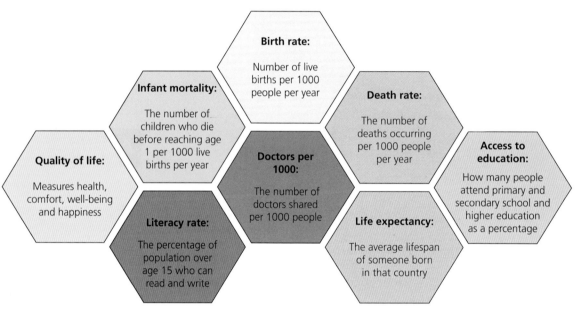

▲ **Figure 7:** Social development indicators

There are lots of other social indicators, including **population density** (the number of people per square km), the food intake per person, or access to technology such as mobile phones and the internet. These can be particularly useful since they rely upon other infrastructure to be in place. For example, having a high proportion of the population with a mobile phone relies upon access to electricity, signal pylons, service engineers, satellite access, disposable income, etc., so it is an interlinked indicator.

Economic measures of development

Economic measures tend to focus upon money and the features of a country's economy, such as employment and trade. These indicators are entwined with social measures, since without money it would be impossible to improve features like healthcare and education. Traditionally countries were evaluated and classified as more or less developed based upon the economic value of the **gross domestic product (GDP)** (the yearly value of goods and services produced within the country). It is now considered more accurate to combine multiple sources of information such as those in Figure 8.

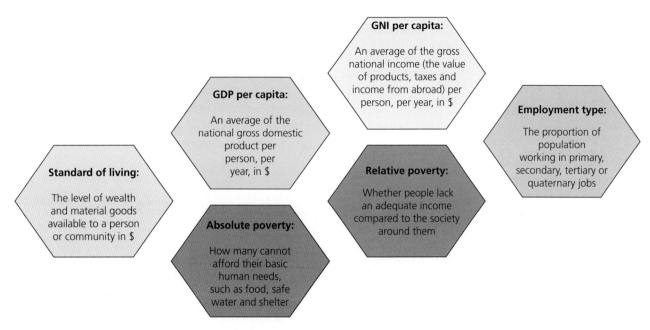

▲ **Figure 8:** Socio-economic indicators of development

Absolute poverty and relative poverty

Poverty is not always a clear-cut term; there are two forms. You might be considered to be in a state of **relative poverty** if you are living in an area where those around you have more wealth than you so that you cannot maintain the same lifestyle as them, even though you might have enough money to live. In the modern UK, 13 million people are living in relative poverty; 4 million of these are children (source: Joseph Rowntree Foundation). **Absolute poverty** measures your ability to meet your basic human needs of minimal food, water, safe shelter, sanitation, health and education. Someone living in absolute poverty may spend over 30 minutes a day walking to collect water or drinking from streams. They generally live on less than $1 a day.

Employment type

As a country becomes more developed, employment structure will change. This is illustrated graphically in Figure 9.

The changes can be seen as useful indicators of development because they show how society changes; modern workers prefer tertiary jobs that have improved conditions and pay. This model is useful when geographers wish to classify a country.

United Nations

The United Nations also assesses development by considering the value of infrastructure (roads, buildings, machinery, etc.), 'human capital' (the skills and health of the people) and 'natural capital' (resources such as forests, fuel and water). Considering more varied criteria produces a more detailed picture of a country.

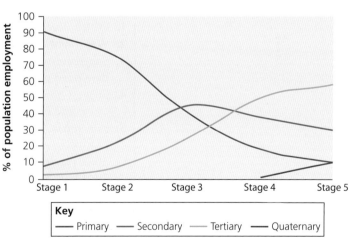

▲ **Figure 9:** Employment structure changes over time compared with the Rostow model (see pages 184–185)

Human development index (HDI)

A final useful indicator is the **human development index (HDI)** which measures life expectancy, education and income per capita to give countries a ranking and a score from 0 to 1 (with 1 being the highest). For example, Norway has an HDI of 0.944 whereas the Democratic Republic of Congo has an HDI of just 0.344. It is important to consider *why* these variations happen and what other influences there can be upon development other than just wealth.

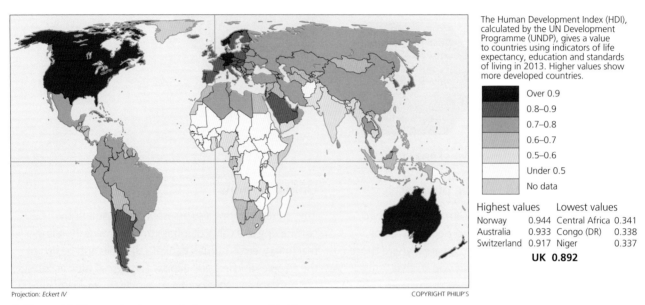

The Human Development Index (HDI), calculated by the UN Development Programme (UNDP), gives a value to countries using indicators of life expectancy, education and standards of living in 2013. Higher values show more developed countries.

	Over 0.9
	0.8–0.9
	0.7–0.8
	0.6–0.7
	0.5–0.6
	Under 0.5
	No data

Highest values		Lowest values	
Norway	0.944	Central Africa	0.341
Australia	0.933	Congo (DR)	0.338
Switzerland	0.917	Niger	0.337
	UK 0.892		

Projection: *Eckert IV*   COPYRIGHT PHILIP'S

▲ **Figure 10:** Human development index patterns worldwide

Activities

1. Which development indicator do you think is most useful? Why?
2. Why might a country such as the UK have a low birth rate?
3. Suggest a range of factors that might lead to high death rates in less developed places.
4. Suggest how access to education might be able to influence other social and economic measures.
5. Why might $GNI *per capita* be more useful than gross domestic product?
6. Study Figure 9 on page 171. Describe how the trend changes from Stage 1 to Stage 5.
7. Why might the proportion of people working in tertiary jobs have increased over time?
8. Which parts of the world have the lowest HDI rates? Why might this be?

Is development evenly distributed across the world?

Now that we understand development and how it is measured, it is useful to compare the development of nations across the world.

Figures 11a and 11b are distorted proportional maps that show the wealth of nations and GNI per capita, respectively. Countries are represented as either larger or smaller than their actual area dependent upon wealth. For example, Japan is much larger than usual because it has a high national wealth and a high income per person. On the other hand, while Figure 11a shows that China's national wealth is large, Figure 11b shows that the GNI per capita is very low.

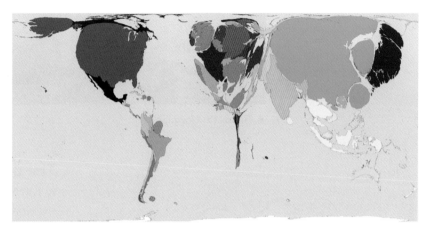

▲ **Figure 11a:** A proportional map showing the wealth of nations

Activities

1. Describe the pattern of wealth given in figure 11b.

✝ Geographical skills

When analysing maps, begin with the overall pattern and then focus on specific places using direction and specific place names or regions (continent, country, cities, tropics, etc.). Practise this by comparing Figures 11a and 11b.

▲ **Figure 11b:** A proportional map showing $GNI per capita across the world. How does it compare with Figure 11a?

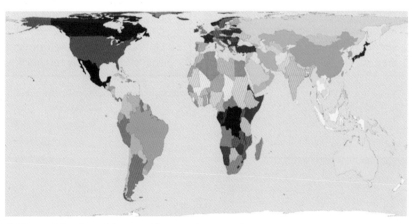

▲ **Figure 11c:** A world map with normal proportions

Just 62 people (53 men and nine women) own as much wealth as the poorest half of the world.

One per cent of the world own more wealth than the rest of us combined.

Number of people whose wealth is equal to that of poorest half of world

Year	Number of people
2010	388
2011	177
2012	159
2013	92
2014	80
2015	62

▲ **Figure 12:** Unequal world

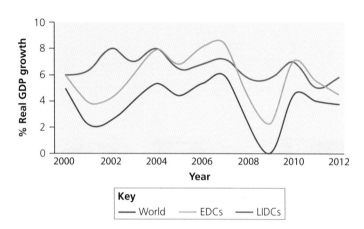

▲ **Figure 13:** How has wealth grown in different parts of the world?

The development gap

According to Oxfam (Figure 12), over half of all of the world's wealth was owned by just one per cent of the population. In fact, the top 62 billionaires own more wealth than the poorest half of the world ($1.76 trillion)!

Over time, according to Rostow's model (see pages 184–185), nations should become more developed and move out of the LIDC group. Figure 13 shows that the growth of wealth has been highest in LIDCs and EDCs since 2000, even during the global recession. However, in the last 50 years, only nine countries have graduated to the emerging economies category. So what is holding development back?

Activities

1. Study Figure 13. Describe the trend for EDCs compared with the world.

→ Take it further

2. Use the internet to find updated statistics for at least two contrasting countries. Try using The CIA World Factbook and the website of the United Nations Development Programme. How has the situation changed since this textbook was written?

Did you know?

It would cost $10 billion to provide clean water for everyone in the world, yet in Europe we spend $11 billion each year on ice cream.

What factors have led to uneven development?

National development is a long, slow process. It is influenced by a variety of factors that can either increase or hold back the speed of change. These factors can be caused by humans or nature.

Physical factors affecting development

Figure 14 shows a selection of natural (physical) factors that influence development. These are features that are present, or not present, in an area that are perhaps uncontrollable.

What has led to uneven development?

→ In this section you will:

→ gain an understanding of how the physical and human features of places can influence development

→ explore the factors that can make it difficult to break out from poverty

→ consider how we can visualise the uneven development of the world.

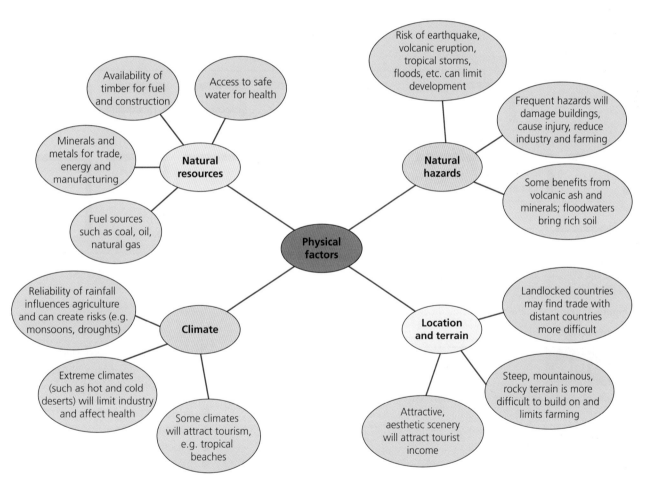

▲ **Figure 14:** Physical factors affecting development

Did you know?

Every baby born in an LIDC already owes a debt of $482.

Fourteen children die every minute from poverty, preventable disease and malnutrition.

Human factors affecting development

Humans have been shaping and moulding their environment since they first appeared in order to make living conditions comfortable and to find ways to improve their lives. We manipulate natural environments in order to extract the resources we need for fuel, for construction and for industry. However, this can lead to damage. Sometimes this manipulation crosses national borders, like when TNCs work in multiple countries or when resources are imported from elsewhere. The UK relies heavily on imports of raw materials and foodstuffs. In the past, this was made easier due to trade links by sea and through the colonies. However these links are not always beneficial to all concerned; colonies have often suffered and host nations are sometimes exploited by TNCs.

A selection of human factors can be seen in Figure 15. They are often interlinked: for example, politics links to trade, healthcare, culture and even technology. Historical influences can be felt for centuries, for good or bad.

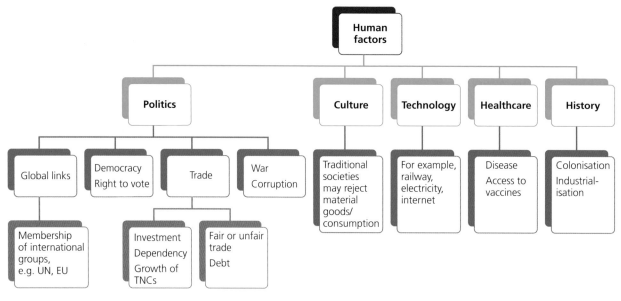

▲ **Figure 15:** Human factors influencing development

Activities

1. Which factor do you think will have the most influence on development? Why?
2. How can political stability have an influence on national wealth?
3. Norway has an HDI of 0.944 compared with 0.33 for Niger. Which specific factors will have had an influence on these different countries?
4. What advantages and disadvantages has the UK had that could explain how it became an advanced country?
5. How might trans-national companies help to improve national development?

→ Take it further

6. Choose one country in the world and find its HDI and $GDP/GNI per capita. Research the country and suggest which factors, physical and human, have most influenced its development, and why.

Think back to the world map shown in Figure 2, page 169. Many of the LIDCs are located in areas that could:

- be subject to extreme climates
- lack safe water
- experience natural hazards
- have an unstable political system
- be in conflict zones
- be former colonies.

Additionally LIDCs are more vulnerable to shocks such as climate change, disease and natural disasters since their economies are less varied and they often depend upon international investment (such as from TNCs).

What are the barriers to breaking away from poverty?

As seen in the previous chapter, there are many factors that influence development. Many nations in the world suffer from poverty, with over 3 billion people living on less than $2.50 a day. Figure 16 describes some of the factors that can make it hard to break out from this deprivation.

▼ **Figure 16:** Factors that make it difficult for countries to break out of poverty

Debt	Many LIDCs face huge national debts as a result of borrowing from other nations and international organisations to help with infrastructure or recover from a disaster. However, just like getting a credit card or loan, this borrowing comes at a cost and interest rates are high. Some nations will never be able to repay their debt and have to keep borrowing from others in order to make payments. Debt causes dependency whereby nations are trapped in a **spiral of decline**. Some debt is a legacy of colonialism, or unfair loans, or sometimes even from aid that was given with strings attached (bilateral aid). The Jubilee 2000 initiative suggested that 'third world debt' be cancelled, so that nations could restart their economies and take part in the world economy. If a government is in debt, it will not be able to invest in education and healthcare, which makes it impossible to then leave poverty behind.	**Example** Nepal had to spend $210 million on debt payments in 2015
Trade	In order to break out of poverty, trade is the key. A nation needs an income and this will involve importing goods that are needed while exporting goods and services to be sold abroad. The **balance of trade** needs to be positive, with more exports than imports (see Figure 19). In reality, however, trade is often unfair, with richer countries and TNCs taking a higher profit than LIDCs. For example, for a clothing TNC, the bulk of the profit stays in the AC where the headquarters is, while the EDCs and LIDCs that provide materials and labour get less. Nations can become dependent upon TNCs and their investment, which means local industry will not flourish and workers may be exploited.	**Example** Coca Cola in India
Political unrest	Many countries in poverty have unstable or undemocratic governments. This can lead to chaos and confusion, particularly over how to spend government funds and where to invest. Corruption can also be a problem, with money not being spent on the community. Since education is a key way to solve poverty, if governments do not focus efforts on improving school provision, this cannot happen. Similarly, conflicts such as civil war, terrorism and tribal disputes use valuable resources and distract governments from developing infrastructure. Stable nations are able to trade more easily.	**Example** Somalia: civil war and instability
Health	If a country is going to become wealthy, it needs to be healthy. LIDCs suffer disproportionately from illnesses and diseases that are preventable and treatable, such as diarrhoea, malaria and malnutrition. Lack of safe drinking water and inadequate food leads to many health problems, which in turn means people cannot work and therefore cannot access better food or healthcare. It is a cycle of decline (Figure 18).	**Example** Afghanistan, where only 13% of the population have readily accessible clean drinking water

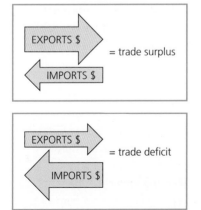

▲ **Figure 17:** The balance of trade

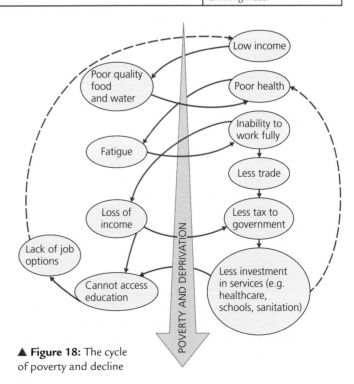

▲ **Figure 18:** The cycle of poverty and decline

How can countries break out of poverty?

There are various schemes that can be employed to help reduce poverty. These may be short term or long term and can be categorised into either **top-down** or **bottom-up** strategies (Figure 19).

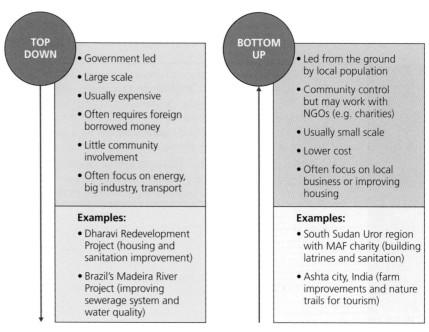

TOP DOWN
- Government led
- Large scale
- Usually expensive
- Often requires foreign borrowed money
- Little community involvement
- Often focus on energy, big industry, transport

Examples:
- Dharavi Redevelopment Project (housing and sanitation improvement)
- Brazil's Madeira River Project (improving sewerage system and water quality)

BOTTOM UP
- Led from the ground by local population
- Community control but may work with NGOs (e.g. charities)
- Usually small scale
- Lower cost
- Often focus on local business or improving housing

Examples:
- South Sudan Uror region with MAF charity (building latrines and sanitation)
- Ashta city, India (farm improvements and nature trails for tourism)

▲ **Figure 19:** Top-down and bottom-up strategies to help reduce poverty

How can trade help nations break out of poverty?

Many countries try to control trade by introducing tariffs to manage prices and quotas to manage the amount of goods being imported and exported. If a country participates in **free trade** then the movement of goods is not controlled and more profit can be made by trading with different places. **Fair trade** may also be introduced to ensure that producers receive a guaranteed fair wage for what they make.

Countries may group together to form **trading blocs** in order to improve their trade. Examples include the European Union or the nations of OPEC. Trade is often unfair for developing countries as they may be excluded by these blocs, but if nations can group together then trade will improve.

What about aid?

Aid is when a country, organisation or individual gives resources to another country. These resources could be money, products, training or technology and may be delivered on a short-term or long-term basis. Short-term aid helps in an emergency, such as a disaster, and usually involves food, shelter, search and rescue, bottled water, clothing, etc. Long-term aid is **sustainable** if it brings benefit to the economy, society and the environment. For example, digging wells for water is more sustainable than bottled water; planting seeds and building irrigation schemes for local farmers is more sustainable than offering bags of food.

Aid may be given in different ways, as shown in Figure 20.

Two successful examples of sustainable aid are Goat Aid and Water Aid. In these schemes, local communities take control of resources, such as a pair of goats or a well, and then use them to bring long-term benefits. Goat Aid involves giving a pair of goats to a community, particularly to young girls, in order for them to breed the goats and use their milk to produce surplus for sale. The proceeds from the sale of the milk can be reinvested in more goats or fertiliser or clothing, or to pay for school.

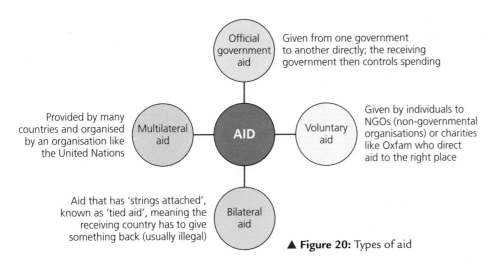

▲ **Figure 20:** Types of aid

How governments try to influence development: China's South–North Water Transfer Project – poverty breaker or problem maker?

China has the world's largest population, and the second highest national GDP, yet there are huge regional differences in terms of wealth, access to healthcare and access to resources. One of the most contested resources is access to safe water. This is a particular problem due to industrialisation and urbanisation in recent years which has led to water **over-extraction** (taking too much) from groundwater reserves in order to supply water to China's ever-growing cities, industrial zones and the northern agricultural regions. As a result, and in part due to climate change influencing weather patterns, there is a lack of water for major areas such as Beijing, and droughts and water pollution are common. The government decided to introduce a 'top-down', large-scale water supply strategy in order to help development for the country overall by improving water access, energy production, transport and trade.

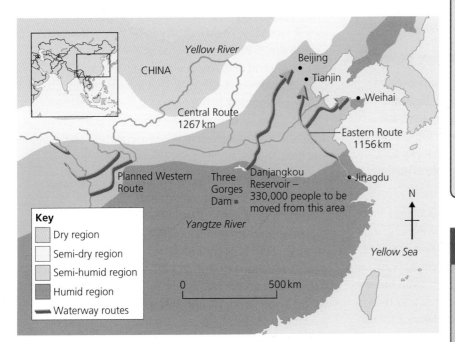

▲ **Figure 21:** The location of China's South–North Water Transfer Project

Activities

1. What do you think is the main factor preventing the escape from poverty? Why?

2. How might debt influence the level of poverty in a nation?

3. Compare the advantages and disadvantages of top-down versus bottom-up development strategies. Which do you think is best and why?

4. Look at Figure 18 on page 177, which shows the cycle of poverty. How might aid help to stop this cycle?

5. What are the problems associated with bilateral aid?

6. Why might Goat Aid be considered sustainable?

→ Take it further

7. Research an example of a top-down, bottom-up or aid scheme that has been used in a particular country. Decide how sustainable this method is and explain why and how it impacts different stakeholders.

Tip

When explaining the sustainability of a scheme, give examples to show how something brings benefit to all three strands: social, economic and environmental.

▲ **Figure 22:** China's Water Transfer Scheme

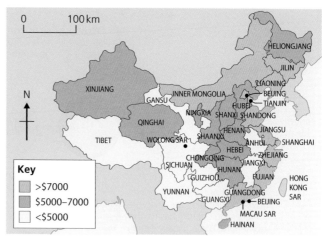

▲ **Figure 23:** China's regional inequality

What is the South–North Water Transfer Project?

The project is the largest of its kind and was first imagined in 1952. After a lengthy planning process, construction began in 2002 and is due for completion (in various stages) in 2050. The plan is to divert 44.8 billion cubic metres (cumecs) of water per year from the south to the northern areas of China. The four main rivers – Yangtze, Yellow River, Huaihe and Haihe – are being linked together, and will have their flows managed in order to provide water to populations and industry in the north. Each province in China is required to create a water supply company to oversee the administration of water in their area and to control the flows being sent from south to north. The scheme includes the creation of hydroelectric power pumping stations, flood control, water quality improvements and canals.

How is this project aiming to reduce poverty?

China is a nation of contrasts, and the most populated nation on Earth. Despite having the world's biggest economy and a well-respected education system, the average income per person remains low at $7594 per year. Within this there are regional differences. For example, coastal areas have a higher income than inland rural areas (as seen in Figure 23).

The average income per person in coastal Jiangsu province reaches over $13,400 per year, whereas in inland rural Guizhou province it is just $4200. There is an east–west divide in the country whereby the coastal east, with its heavy industry, Special Economic Zones and major cities such as Beijing, is developing more rapidly than inland and western parts. For a country famous for its

manufacturing and highly skilled electronics production, it is perhaps surprising that 39 per cent of citizens still work in agriculture (a primary employment). This proportion is higher than that of advanced countries. Most of these are in the south, with heavy industry towards the north and along the coast (where it is easier to trade from). The very west is inhospitable desert and mountain ranges making it difficult to cultivate or construct. So poverty is still a problem in China, and this scheme aims to reduce this.

The South–North Water Transfer Project aims to decrease poverty by improving water access to northern zones which currently experience drought and sandstorms. This would enable industry and agriculture to be more productive, relying less on groundwater stores (which would reduce water pollution) and therefore saving money and improving individual income through more jobs. It would also help industry to be 'drought-proof'. During the 2010 severe drought, economic damage to agriculture and failed hydroelectric power cost China over $3.5 billion in losses as well as industry having to reduce production. In the northeast, farmers lost half their income. With the transfer scheme in place, this is avoidable and can preserve economic activity and increase income per person.

Furthermore, the diverted waterways already in place have required new pumping stations which are able to produce hydroelectric power as water rushes through – therefore producing more energy, saving costs and improving the quality of life. The later stages of the project (due to start in 2020) will see water diverted to the west across the mountainous Tibetan Plateau which would boost economic growth and provide for the growing population here.

▲ **Figure 24:** China's need for water

desperately needed the 50 million cumecs of water sent in August. By preserving groundwater here, it was suggested that sandstorm severity was reduced as well.

However, the scheme is controversial. Over 330,000 people were required to leave their homes in order for construction to take place. Drought in the south is now beginning to occur as water is diverted. Some reservoirs are dropping. And since the population keeps growing, and since industry requires more and more water, some say this scheme will never be enough.

Lastly it is hoped that the scheme will improve water quality. It is estimated that 11 per cent of cancers of the digestive system were influenced by polluted drinking water. This particularly affects rural populations who have been drinking water containing toxins that exceed World Health Organization standards. In fact only 43 per cent of freshwater in China was considered fit for consumption in 2009. This problem was concentrated in the arid north which had only 20 per cent of the natural water reserves but had to supply 45 per cent of the national population. So, as part of the scheme, over $80 million has been spent by the government on projects to reduce water pollution and clean up industrial sewage, which will bring health benefits.

What have been the impacts so far?

When the project was launched, it was estimated that it would cost $62 billion, yet by 2015, more than $79 billion had already been spent (twice the cost of the controversial Three Gorges Dam project).

The project has been largely funded by the central and local governments, but also through over $20 billion in loans. One of the reasons for introducing the scheme was to reduce the impact of annual droughts and provide secure water (see Figure 24) since more than half of China's rivers had vanished between 1990 and 2010.

So far, the completed line to Beijing has provided safe water to major industry and the capital's population of over 21 million people, and the eastern line has successfully delivered water to northern coastal areas to replenish ground stores. The western line is still in planning. During the 2014 drought, diverted waters were sent as emergency relief to cities such as Pingdingshan which

Activities

1. Study the map in Figure 21, page 179. Describe the pattern of how China's climate varies.
2. Why does this transfer scheme need to happen? Explain at least three specific reasons.
3. Describe how having a lack of access to safe water can link to poverty.
4. Turn the facts of this example into an infographic or word cloud to revise from.
5. Use the internet to update the information from this page. How much progress has the project made to date? What are the impacts now?
6. How much water do you use each day? In China, each person uses an average of 75 litres per day. Compare this with your own use per day, week and year.

→ Take it further

7. This is a decision-making exercise. Imagine you are an engineer in China. You have to make a decision whether to support the water transfer project or not. Research the issue to find out about the social, economic and environmental impacts (positive and negative) of the project. Consider different viewpoints. Make a decision on whether to support the scheme or not. Debate your ideas with others.

CHAPTER

12

Are LIDCs likely to stay poor?

Ethiopia: from 'Cradle of Humankind' to modern nation

Ethiopia has been called the 'Cradle of Humankind', with evidence of the earliest known modern human bones found in the southwest at Omo. It is a nation of contrasts. Landlocked and surrounded by five other countries (see Figure 1), it is the tenth largest African nation by area and the second largest by population size after Nigeria. The landscape varies dramatically from the Western Highlands to the Eastern Lowlands, from areas of dense vegetation to desert, and from relative wealth to perpetual famine and poverty.

What is the level of development now?

Ethiopia is categorised as an LIDC and in 2015 had a GNI per capita of just $505, compared with a world average of $10,858 and a UK GNI per capita of $40,967. Figure 2 shows how the level of wealth per person has changed over recent years. Compared with other Sub-Saharan nations, Ethiopia is significantly less wealthy per person and is also below the average level for other LIDCs across the world. This may be due to the large population of over 94 million, making Ethiopia the thirteenth most populous nation in the world. In comparison, the population of the UK is 64 million.

How has an LIDC developed so far?

→ In this section you will:

- → consider what has influenced development in Ethiopia so far
- → study how developed Ethiopia has become, linking to the Rostow model
- → learn about which Millennium Development Goals have been achieved.

Ethiopia factfile

- Population: 94 million
- Land area: 1.1 million km2

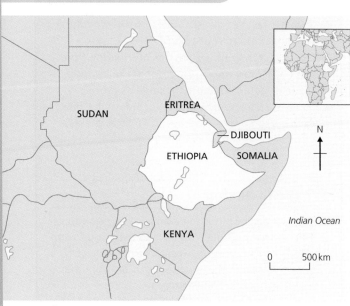

▲ **Figure 1:** Location map for Ethiopia

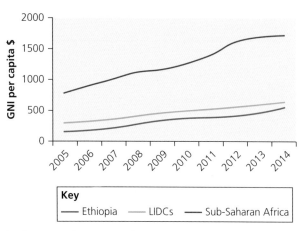

▲ **Figure 2:** Ethiopia's wealth over time

Key
— Ethiopia — LIDCs — Sub-Saharan Africa

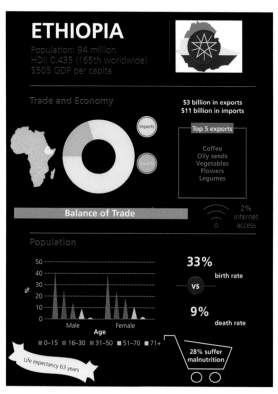

▲ **Figure 3:** Ethiopia in numbers

The high birth rate and a slowly falling death rate means that natural increase is occurring and the population is growing by 2.6 per cent per year. As healthcare improves, life expectancy is gradually increasing and death rates decline, which means the population will continue to grow.

Due to a history of famine, drought, poor healthcare, disease, poverty and conflict, Ethiopia has one of the lowest levels of development in the world with an HDI of 0.435 and although life expectancy is increasing, at 63 years it is still lower than the world average of 72.

▲ **Figure 4:** Subsistence agriculture dominates (source: Darren Thompson)

Economically, the country is reliant on agriculture with 89 per cent of all exports and 80 per cent of all jobs. As you can see from Figure 3, the balance of trade is in deficit with more imports than exports at present. The landscape is largely rural (see Figure 4) and large-scale agriculture has only recently begun to develop.

▲ **Figure 5:** Old meets new in Ethiopia (source: Darren Thompson)

Vision for the future

Ethiopia's government vision is, 'To become a country where democratic rule, good governance and social justice reign with the involvement and free will of its peoples; and once free of poverty to become a middle-income economy.'

Activities

1. Look at Figure 1. How many times could the land area of the UK (244,000 km²) fit into Ethiopia?
2. The total world population is 7.3 billion. What percentage of the world's population does Ethiopia have compared with the UK?
3. Study Figures 4 and 5. Describe the living conditions and any indicators of development you can see.
4. What is 'natural increase' and why is it occurring in Ethiopia?

5. Analyse Figure 2. Describe what is happening to GNI per capita in Ethiopia compared with other places using evidence from the graph.
6. What is the internet access in Figure 3? Why might this be?

→ Take it further

7. Use the information on these pages and further research to explain why Ethiopia is classed as an LIDC rather than an EDC.

Modelling development

It can be useful to think of development as a process that occurs over time. In 1960 an American economist named Rostow created a model to show the stages that countries are likely to pass through on their way to being more developed. There are various development models but Rostow suggested that all countries have the potential to break out of the cycle of poverty and develop through five linear stages and ultimately reach what he called 'economic maturity'. This can be considered similar to the way in which a child develops into an adult. The model has been criticised for being too simplistic and perhaps outdated. However, it can provide a useful guide, as seen in Figure 6.

There are five stages of progression shown in the model and outlined in Figure 7.

According to the Rostow model, as countries become more mature employment patterns change from mainly **primary** to **secondary**, then **tertiary** and finally some **quaternary** jobs. This links to improving levels of technology, education and social aspiration as the population moves away from working the land to working in more comfortable and better-paid conditions. However, this model does rely on countries starting from the same point and having similar access to resources before 'take off'. Many countries might actually skip stages and progress more rapidly.

More people are employed in primary jobs such as agriculture in LIDCs, with such countries typically in Stage 1 or 2 of the Rostow model. ACs use considerably more energy and spend more years in education, reflecting that such nations are in Stage 4 or 5 of the Rostow model.

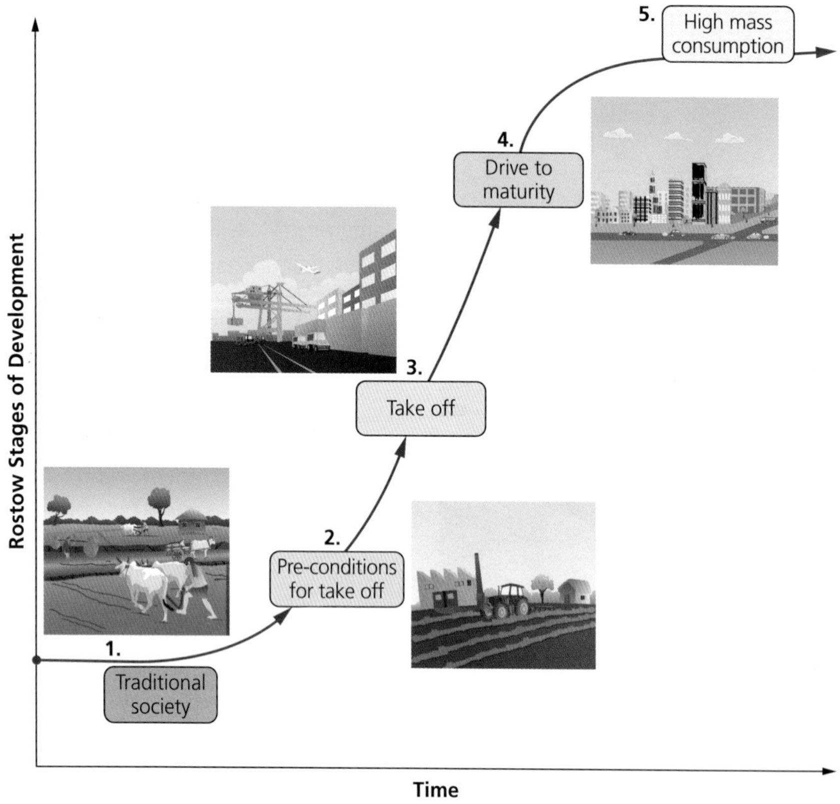

▲ **Figure 6:** Rostow's model of development

How can Rostow's model help determine Ethiopia's path of economic development?

With a negative balance of trade, meaning that Ethiopia imports more than it exports (see Chapter 11, Figure 17, page 177), and with primary employment dominating the population, it could appear that Ethiopia is in Stage 1 of the Rostow model. However, government spending has led to improvements in healthcare and education and with the arrival of Trans-National Companies (TNCs) and improving infrastructure, it seems Stage 2 is more appropriate. Figure 5 on page 183 shows that while traditional practices such as nomadic livestock farming and water collection still happen, these are now being modified by newer technologies to improve efficiency and quality of life. So the Pre-conditions for Take off are emerging.

Activities

1. If development means 'change', it might have varying consequences. Draw a mindmap or table to suggest the positive and negative consequences of development on people and place.
2. Draw a flow chart or diagram of your own to explain how a country can develop through the stages of the Rostow model.

3. Using information in this chapter, explain which stage you think Ethiopia is now.

→ **Take it further**

4. Research a trans-national company (TNC) such as BP or Nestlé and find out where it is based around the world. At what stage of the Rostow model are these places?

Stage 1: Traditional society

This is what we might have expected in the UK before the Industrial Revolution. Economies are based upon **subsistence** which relies on collecting natural resources to meet an individual's basic needs for survival, with very little extra for trade. **Primary** industries, such as farming, mining and logging, dominate employment. Agriculture is the most important industry, with the most employment; you cannot become developed without first having secure access to food and water. Farming here is mostly small-scale and labour intensive. It often involves shifting cultivation (where farmers move regularly), 'slash and burn' techniques and nomadic lifestyles. During Stage 1, the economy is very vulnerable to uncontrollable influences such as the weather, disease, war, pests, famine, etc.

Stage 2: Pre-conditions for take off

By this stage, people are beginning to have surplus produce that they can trade, and **infrastructure** (particularly roads and communications) has improved so that trade is easier. Agriculture still dominates but now becomes more commercial and large scale, using machinery and fewer workers. Because productivity increases, resources can be processed more efficiently and some more profit is made. This leads to investment and an increase in wealth. **Secondary** industries such as manufacturing start to take off, particularly in textiles and processing raw materials extracted by primary workers. Governments start to encourage **trans-national companies (TNCs)** to invest; for example, an international clothing company may set up factories here. As a result, the economy begins to experience **globalisation**: countries become interconnected by trade and culture with other places.

Stage 3: Take off

During this stage, secondary manufacturing dominates the economy as **industrialisation** occurs and more factories are built and machinery is introduced. The increase in wealth means that governments can invest in social schemes like education and health, as well as general infrastructure. TNCs often dominate the economy, which can lead to dependency as the country relies upon these international companies to provide investment and jobs. This may lead to problems such as workers being exploited, or environmental damage. As workers increasingly switch from primary to secondary jobs, this leads to rural–urban migration and **urbanisation** as towns and cities grow. There might be some inequality of wealth; a rural–urban divide can exist between places that have more wealth and services and those which do not. Increasingly the nation becomes more modernised with new airports, roads, railways, public services, education and healthcare as well as access to electricity and the internet. This continues to encourage international investment and can lead to a 'spiral of prosperity', or the **multiplier effect**, whereby investment leads to wealth, which leads to more investment, etc.

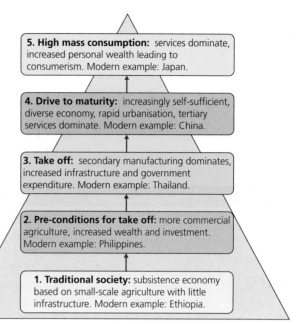

▲ **Figure 7:** Development is a progression

Stage 4: Drive to maturity

The country is becoming more self-sufficient as the economy diversifies and does not have to rely upon foreign investment so much. A snowballing of government investment leads to rapid urbanisation and a depopulation of rural areas. This can cause issues of urban congestion and rural decline. As education and aspirations improve, employment changes again so that more are involved in **tertiary** 'service' jobs, such as customer care, sales, nursing, teaching, IT support, etc. Very few people now work in primary jobs, as resources can often be imported cheaply from somewhere else. Universities and easy school access mean that high-tech industry and the beginnings of **quaternary** jobs (such as research and development) start to appear.

Stage 5: High mass consumption

This is seen as the ultimate point to reach. Tertiary service jobs now dominate the economy and secondary manufacturing shifts to smaller factories with less environmental impact. As the population becomes wealthier, **consumption** (buying or using resources) increasingly focuses on high-value goods such as cars, electronics, leisure activities, designer goods, etc.

What have been the influences upon Ethiopia's development?

Ethiopia has been influenced by a wide range of physical and human factors, including climate and landscape, politics and history.

The political, technological and social influences upon development

Date	What was happening?
Pre-1935	Ethiopia was once known as Abyssinia and was one of only two African countries (with Liberia) that avoided European control in the colonial era.
1935–41	During the build up to the Second World War, Italy colonised Ethiopia and had control from 1935 until 1941, when rebels and British troops claimed back independence.
1941–74	Although the Italians had invested in highways, rail and power, the nation was set back after the Second World War, due to the conflict and the loss of life and instability that followed. Years of unrest, coupled with drought and famine and the growth of Communism, led to a successful military coup in 1974. The Soviet Union (now known as Russia) and Cuba financed this rebellion, and the military evicted the government, leading to many arrests, banishments and deaths.
1974–87	At least 1.4 million people died in the civil war and the Derg government remained in power until 1987. The monarchy was abolished and the land was declared a new republic state. The period 1977–78 became known as the Ethiopian 'Red Terror'. During this time, the government grabbed tracts of land and evicted owners, leading to migration, refugees and economic decline. There were up to 50,000 people killed during the Derg era; a further 1.5 million were forcibly relocated.
1984–85	The Derg government pursued a strict policy on agriculture, but productivity declined. From the mid-1980s onwards Ethiopia suffered severe drought and eventual famine. The 1984–85 famine (the inspiration for the original Live Aid 'Do they know it's Christmas?' charity song) killed a million people in just one year due to drought and high food prices. International agencies became involved and over $2000 million in food aid was delivered from NGOs. Ethiopia has remained food deficient since this time, made worse by continued population growth.
1991–2001	With the collapse of the Soviet Union, and the international spotlight on famine, support from other nations helped to stabilise the nation and remove Derg control and from 1991 it became the Federal Democratic Republic. The new government allowed free trade, lifted price controls and provided farmers with cheaper access to imported fertilisers and machinery without paying tax.
2001 to now	Following the events of 11 September 2001 and the Middle East conflicts, the USA gave more support to Ethiopia and agricultural production and the economy have been rising gradually since then. The Growth and Transformation Plan, following on from the Millennium Development Goals, is the government's ambitious plan to end poverty. Since 2012, new training programmes and investment have enabled farmers to learn new skills (such as mixing crop types with beans to help soils stay fertile) and increase yields. The government is stable, although there are some claims that free speech is limited, but more trust is now being shared with local authorities and the people themselves.

▲ **Figure 8:** A timeline of recent Ethiopian history. Which influences are political, social and technological?

Tip

Physical, political and social influences are interlinked. Try to make links between multiple factors, for example, between rainfall and farming and politics.

The physical influences upon development

Ethiopia is divided into different physical zones, which experience a range of different terrains and climates. Figure 9 shows how the country can be simplified into three zones: Western Highlands, Central Zone and Eastern Lowlands.

Climate and relief both exert an influence on how successful agriculture can be, and since access to safe drinking water and food are essential in order to improve a nation's health and wealth, this is a key factor influencing Ethiopia's development.

One of the key issues with climate is the unpredictable and unreliable nature of rainfall (Figure 8). Ethiopia is close to the Equator, yet due to the relief and to winds, temperatures can vary wildly (lowland desert areas can reach up to 60°C) and the monsoon season can often fail. This makes agriculture very difficult to manage.

In many places, inaccessibility, water shortages and infestations of disease-carrying insects such as mosquitoes and tsetse flies prevent the use of potentially valuable land. As a result, agriculture has remained subsistence level until recently. Eastern areas particularly suffer from drought when rainfall is limited and unreliable, and this has led to farmers over-farming or over-grazing the remaining land, leading to soil erosion and desertification (where areas become dry and desert-like; a problem which is a cycle of decline).

Ironically for a nation suffering repeated drought and famine, Ethiopia is one of the world's main producers of food; but food for export, not for locals. In recent years, the more productive land has been bought up by nations such as Saudi Arabia who import food from Ethiopia and are setting up their own farms, leading to Ethiopian farmers losing out.

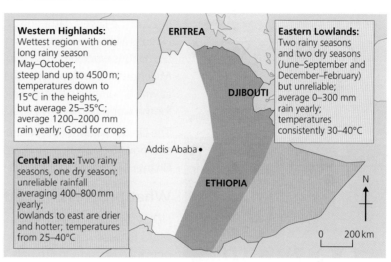

Western Highlands: Wettest region with one long rainy season May–October; steep land up to 4500 m; temperatures down to 15°C in the heights, but average 25–35°C; average 1200–2000 mm rain yearly; Good for crops

Eastern Lowlands: Two rainy seasons and two dry seasons (June–September and December–February) but unreliable; average 0–300 mm rain yearly; temperatures consistently 30–40°C

Central area: Two rainy seasons, one dry season; unreliable rainfall averaging 400–800 mm yearly; lowlands to east are drier and hotter; temperatures from 25–40°C

ERITREA · DJIBOUTI · Addis Ababa · ETHIOPIA · N · 0 200 km

▲ **Figure 9:** Ethiopia has a varied physical environment

Activities

1. Draw up a table that compares physical, political, technological and social influences upon Ethiopia's development.
2. Which influence do you think is the most significant? Why? How does it link to other factors?
3. What is malaria and how can it affect people?
4. Why is it important for a nation to have access to food and water in order to become developed?
5. Describe why desertification can be such a devastating problem.

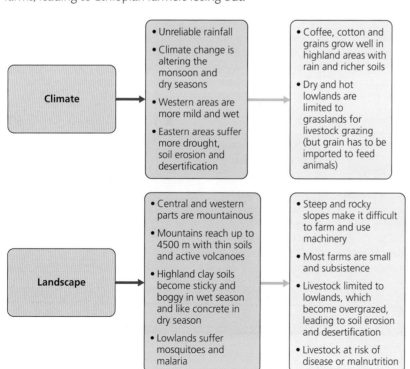

Climate
- Unreliable rainfall
- Climate change is altering the monsoon and dry seasons
- Western areas are more mild and wet
- Eastern areas suffer more drought, soil erosion and desertification

- Coffee, cotton and grains grow well in highland areas with rain and richer soils
- Dry and hot lowlands are limited to grasslands for livestock grazing (but grain has to be imported to feed animals)

Landscape
- Central and western parts are mountainous
- Mountains reach up to 4500 m with thin soils and active volcanoes
- Highland clay soils become sticky and boggy in wet season and like concrete in dry season
- Lowlands suffer mosquitoes and malaria

- Steep and rocky slopes make it difficult to farm and use machinery
- Most farms are small and subsistence
- Livestock limited to lowlands, which become overgrazed, leading to soil erosion and desertification
- Livestock at risk of disease or malnutrition

◀ **Figure 10:** Climate and relief influence development

▲ **Figure 11:** Millennium Development Goals

How far have the Millennium Development Goals been met?

What are the Millennium Development Goals?

In 2000, the largest gathering of world leaders in history met at the United Nations Millennium Summit and committed to a set of targets that would see nations work in partnership to reduce extreme poverty. These became the **Millennium Development Goals (MDGs)** with a deadline of the end of 2015, at which point new targets for the **Sustainable Development Goals** were set for the world to meet by 2030.

The United Nations (UN) claims the MDGs have produced the most successful anti-poverty movement in history towards meeting Article 55 of the UN Charter. Eight aspirational goals were set, as shown in Figure 12.

What progress has Ethiopia made?

LIDCs, such as Ethiopia, have made good progress towards meeting the MDG targets – particularly for reducing child mortality and increasing primary education. In Ethiopia, massive government investment has seen improvements in infrastructure, health and education.

Ethiopia is on track to meet three targets: provision of primary education, reducing child mortality and improving maternal health. Although agriculture has been improved, and poverty has begun to reduce, **malnutrition** is still a problem. People do not receive the correct calories, protein, vitamins and minerals to remain healthy. A National Nutrition Strategy focuses on providing

---

MDG 1: Poverty and hunger
- Population living in poverty has dropped to 29% from 49% in 2000
- Unemployment still high but poverty should halve by end of 2015
- 40% of children are malnourished
- 28% of the population are food insecure or lacking essential nutrients ✗

MDG 2: Primary education
- On track to meet this goal
- 96% of children now enrol in primary school (up from just 50% in 1990)
- Literacy rate is low at 36%, showing quality of provision is not effective
- More males than females in school; very few females in secondary education ✔

MDG 3: Gender equality
- Representation by women in government has risen to 22% (from 2% in 2000)
- Education gap is closing now 93% of girls in primary school (was 43% in 2000)
- Unemployment higher for women and women still in traditional roles (e.g. water carrying) ✗

MDG 4: Child mortality
- Infant mortality reduced from 97/1000 to 45/1000 since 1990
- Malaria still accounts for 20% of deaths, diarrhoea another 20%
- 65% of children receive vaccinations
- Rural–urban divides (rural areas lag behind) ✔

MDG 5: Maternal health
- Maternal mortality dropped 23% due to better before and after care
- 55% of women now receive access to contraception
- Still some social stigma around family planning
- Fewer forced pregnancies and average age of mothers is increasing ✔

MDG 6: Combat disease
- HIV/AIDS pandemic has stabilised and new cases have declined, but still 1.1 million adults living with HIV
- Malaria was leading cause of death but now 100% of population can access a malaria net
- 89% of population live within 10 km of a doctor but every doctor is shared by 3333 people ✗

MDG 7: Environmental sustainability
- Hydroelectric power has risen to 41% of energy
- Access to safe drinking water has risen to 69% (but waterborne disease still common)
- Urban areas have improved more rapidly
- Soil erosion and desertification due to drought and over-farming ✗

MDG 8: Global partnerships
- Food/other aid contributes 30–50% of total external assistance
- Still receiving $1500–2000 million in Official Development Assistance aid per year
- National debt is 21% of total GDP but has declined massively since peak of 155% GDP in 1995 ✗

✗ = not likely to meet goal   ✔ = goal should be met

▲ **Figure 12:** Ethiopia's MDG progress in 2015

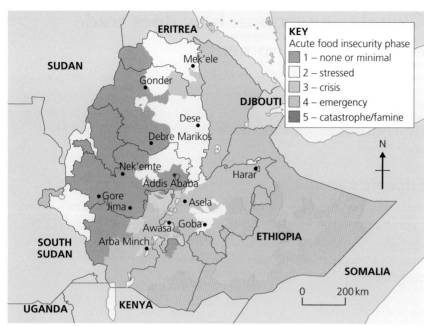

KEY
Acute food insecurity phase
1 – none or minimal
2 – stressed
3 – crisis
4 – emergency
5 – catastrophe/famine

▲ **Figure 13:** Food insecurity is still common in Ethiopia

▲ **Figure 14:** Vast improvements have been made in transport infrastructure, often by Chinese investment (source: Darren Thompson)

vitamins and food aid, but 40 per cent of children are still malnourished. Famine is a big problem (Figure 13) and clean drinking water is also difficult to find.

Ethiopia's economy has improved at an average of 11 per cent per year, which means fewer people now live in poverty, but high unemployment remains and wealth is not equally spread. A national Education Development Plan has ensured that 96 per cent of children enrol in primary school (rising from 50 per cent in 1990), however quality varies and the adult literacy rate is still just 36 per cent. Malnutrition also links to success at school.

Child mortality has been reduced successfully following investment in maternal health and child health, and now 65 per cent of children receive vaccinations for preventable illnesses. Diarrhoea and malaria are still the biggest killers each year, but the HIV/AIDS pandemic has stabilised since new treatment centres and education were established.

Environmental sustainability has not been met, although access to safe water has improved. Basic sanitation is still low and slums remain. The government has invested billions in transport infrastructure and energy supplies (see Figure 14) which has improved travel times and reduced soil erosion and pollution.

Ethiopia still relies on foreign support, particularly food aid and official development assistance for infrastructure, services, water supply and population control.

What are the future priorities?

The government was aiming for a GNI per capita of $698 by the end of 2015, and for poverty to reduce to 22 per cent of the population with 98 per cent having access to clean water. Food security is important to achieving this aim, and irrigation schemes are being expanded to help this.

Activities

1. Which of the Millennium Development Goals is the most important for improving Ethiopia's development? Why?
2. Study Figure 12. By how much has national debt decreased? Why is this important to development?
3. Why is it important to improve gender equality?
4. Diarrhoea is preventable, so why are 20 per cent of deaths still due to this?
5. Analyse Figure 13. Describe the pattern of food security.
6. Study the two photos in Figure 14. What difference will road quality make to the standard of living?
7. How far have the Millennium Development Goals been met in Ethiopia?

→ **Take it further**

8. Think back to Figure 9 earlier. Compare it with Figure 13. Make an overlay map that compares food security and the climate, then analyse it to describe why some places are more food secure by linking to climate and relief.

What global connections influence development?

→ **In this section you will:**

→ explore what sort of trade Ethiopia carries out and the influence of this

→ learn about how trans-national companies impact on Ethiopia

→ investigate the impact of aid and debt relief on development.

Global connections: how does trade influence development?

In order to be established in Stage 2 of the Rostow model, and then move into Stage 3, Ethiopia needs to ensure the economy is growing. Currently Ethiopia has a *trade deficit* since exports value $3 billion but imports value $11 billion. This means debt remains, and there is less government income to support development.

Ethiopia's economy

Figure 15 shows the major Ethiopian exports. As a Stage 1–2 country, it is not surprising that 80 per cent of exports and 46 per cent of the national GDP is from agriculture. Ethiopia is one of the world's largest producers of food and flowers, although this economy is vulnerable to climate change and global price changes.

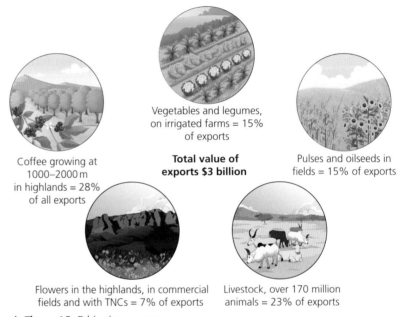

Vegetables and legumes, on irrigated farms = 15% of exports

Coffee growing at 1000–2000 m in highlands = 28% of all exports

Total value of exports $3 billion

Pulses and oilseeds in fields = 15% of exports

Flowers in the highlands, in commercial fields and with TNCs = 7% of exports

Livestock, over 170 million animals = 23% of exports

▲ **Figure 15:** Ethiopian exports

The economy has been growing at an average of eleven per cent (see Figure 16), which is considerably faster than the rest of the world. At the same time, per person income has grown from a GNI per capita of $203 in 1990 to $505 in 2015. This means that fewer people now live in poverty.

Figure 17 shows that Ethiopia has links with other nations, which relates to target 8 of the Millennium Development Goals. The increase in international trade is evidence that the government and the economy are becoming more stable. Interestingly, the imports shown in Figure 18 include the products expected for a developing nation, with refined petroleum (needed for manufacturing industries particularly) and construction materials, showing an investment in improving infrastructure and building quality.

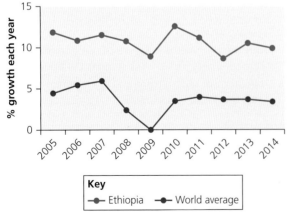

Key
—●— Ethiopia   —●— World average

▲ **Figure 16:** GDP annual growth %

Future economic growth

For Ethiopia to continue to develop, other sources of income other than primary industry are required. Secondary manufacturing is taking off, and TNCs are being encouraged to invest. A country in Stage 3–4 of the Rostow model would have more employment in tertiary jobs, such as customer service and leisure, and recently the tourism and travel trade has begun to take off in Ethiopia.

There are over 2.5 million workers involved in tertiary service jobs in tourism, contributing four times as much to the national economy in just ten years. In a land full of adventure, mountains, desert, volcanoes and historical sites (including nine World Heritage Sites), there is plenty of potential for tourism to take off and numbers have been growing. There is still a lack of hotels and services for tourists, but investment is increasing. Simien Lodge is the highest hotel in Africa and was built by a British entrepreneur.

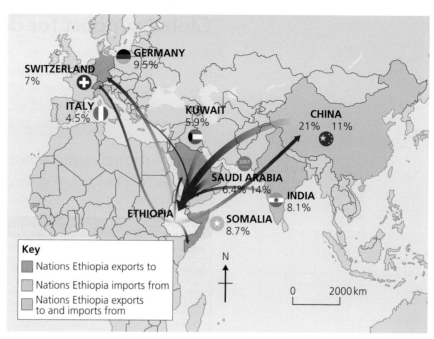

▲ **Figure 17:** Ethiopia's trading partners

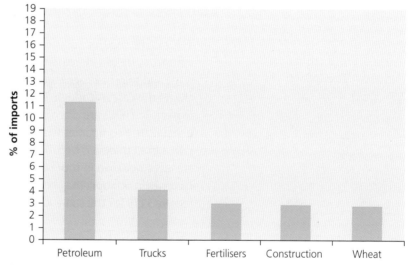

▲ **Figure 18:** Ethiopia's top five imports

Activities

1. Why is trade important to aiding development?
2. What is a 'trade deficit'?
3. Analyse Figure 16. Compare Ethiopia's trend against the rest of the world.
4. What might be the cause of the dips in growth shown in Figure 16?
5. Describe the pattern of countries which Ethiopia trades with.

→ Take it further

6. Find out about tourism in Ethiopia, particularly eco-tourism.

Global support for development

Ethiopia has increasingly strong global links, as seen through trade and through politics. As part of the UN strategy, there is also global support from other nations to assist Ethiopia and other LIDCs to meet their development goals. Support can be from one government to another, from organisations such as the UN, from NGOs and charities, or from businesses.

Trans-national companies: help or harm?

A range of TNCs have begun operating in Ethiopia, in primary, secondary and some tertiary industries.

Company	What do they do in Ethiopia?
Hilton Hotels	Leisure and recreation services, hotel creation
Siemens	Manufacturing of telecommunications, electrical items, medical technology
General Electric (G:E)	Aviation manufacturing, delivering rail links
Afriflora	Flower growing – the world's largest producer of fair trade roses
Dow Chemicals	Manufacturing chemicals, plastics and agricultural products
H&M	Textiles manufacturing, university education in textiles

▲ **Figure 19:** TNC investment in Ethiopia

TNCs can bring both advantages and disadvantages. Investment in hotel infrastructure can increase tourism. Workers in hotels are often paid a fair wage and may have access to the facilities out of hours. However this is not always the case. Although TNCs bring employment and therefore income, workers in LIDCs are often paid a low salary and working conditions can be difficult. The companies wish to make a profit and the reason they locate to LIDCs like Ethiopia is because regulations on wages and working conditions are less strict than in more developed locations. For example, workers in factories in Ethiopia may get $50 a month while workers in an EDC might receive $175 for the same job.

Did you know?

The highest mountain in Ethiopia is Ras Dashen at 4550 m. How many stairs in school would you have to climb to reach this height?

▲ **Figure 20:** Tourism is a growing economy in Ethiopia (source: Darren Thompson)

What about aid?

Ethiopia has benefited from international development support through aid and debt relief. Five million people receive food aid each year. Charities such as Oxfam, Farm Africa and Mission Aviation Fellowship (MAF) have been working to support Ethiopians for over 30 years. In fact aid from MAF was so successful that it led to the local creation of Abyssinian Flight Services, which has now taken on the responsibility of flying aid to those in need, as a sustainable aid example.

Oxfam has operated to provide 'Goat Aid' in Ethiopia, which is a particularly sustainable form of aid especially when targeted at young women. The 'Girl Effect' is the idea that if young girls can be supported to receive education, income, status and security then they will be able to avoid potential issues such as early/forced marriage, prostitution, unplanned pregnancies, disease and poverty, and can then be equal members of society. This, in turn, improves development. Providing a pair of goats through Goat Aid to young girls can encourage this Girl Effect and so support equality and reduce birth rates.

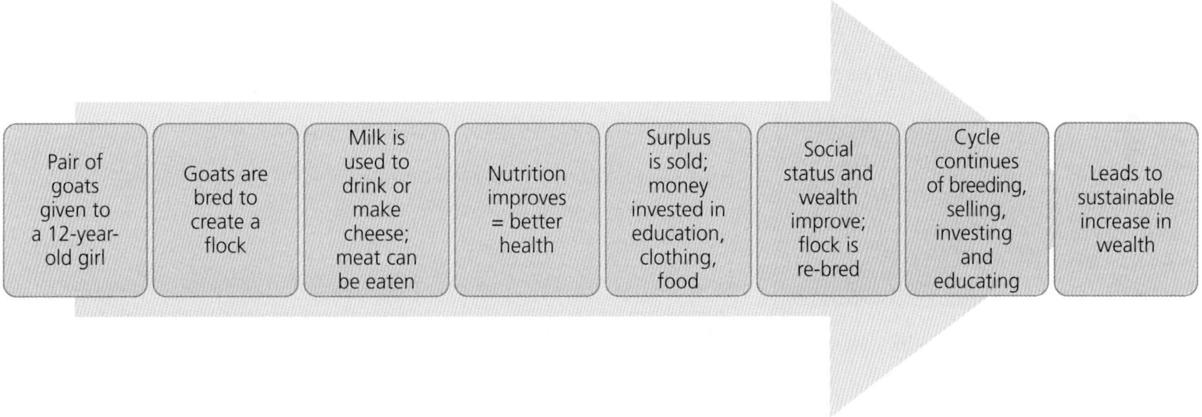

▲ **Figure 21:** Sustainable Goat Aid

Support from the international community meant that in 2006 Ethiopia benefited from debt relief. In 1995, the national economy was in debt by 155 per cent ($10 billion). As a result of debt relief, however, by 2012 the debt had declined to 21 per cent of the national economy ($7 billion). These debt payment savings meant that the government could invest more in local services. However, Ethiopia does still depend upon international aid of over $550 million each year.

Activities

1. Draw up a table that compares the advantages and disadvantages of TNCs for the host country.
2. How can the growth of tourism be beneficial for national development?
3. Why is it important for Ethiopia to have received debt relief?
4. Describe the benefits of aid. Think back to the previous chapter.
5. Why is it important to invest in young girls through aid?

→ **Take it further**

6. Create a flow chart or mindmap that explains how aid, debt relief and TNCs can bring benefit and also harm to countries like Ethiopia.

What development strategy is most appropriate?

➜ In this section you will:

➜ compare the impacts of a top-down development strategy with the impacts of a bottom-up development strategy.

Which development strategy is most appropriate: bottom up or top down?

There are different approaches to improving development, as explained in Chapter 11. Ethiopia has received both nationally led top-down strategies and also locally led bottom-up strategies.

Bottom-up strategies

Bottom-up strategies are led by local populations and are sometimes known as 'self-help' schemes or 'grassroots' projects. They are likely to be supported in the early days by non-governmental organisations (NGOs), especially charities, until they can be self-sufficient. Bottom-up strategies are targeted on very specific small-scale needs, as chosen by the people, which are likely to have an immediate impact.

Figure 22 shows an example of a bottom-up strategy where locals created sanitation and water supply schemes through digging latrines and wells, developing irrigation and building water pumps. This scheme was all self-led with support from charity donations such as the Mission Aviation Fellowship which transported tools to remote locations.

Farm Africa has worked with communities to breed goats and chickens and create beehives in rural areas. Figure 23 shows wheat fields benefiting from education on the use of fertilisers and planting legumes between crops to keep soils fertile and rich in nitrogen. Communities then share this training and when the animals breed, the people will donate some of them to another community in order to bring benefit to others and spread development.

Another example of self-help includes the charity Abyssinian Flight Services, which now flies tools and aid to other places in Ethiopia that need them. The locals were trained up by the charity MAF and have now taken over the responsibilities themselves.

There are many examples of self-help schemes to improve farming, to improve slum quality, to create community banks and savings facilities, to reduce orphanages by placing children with families, and to develop community cohesion. All these schemes move development towards sustainability on a small scale.

▲ **Figure 22:** Self-help scheme creating basic sanitation (source: Darren Thompson)

▲ **Figure 23:** Self-help scheme supporting local farmers (source: Darren Thompson)

I was a labourer who could not feed my five children. Then I received three goats through Farm Africa. Working with the community, I bred the goats, and made sales, and then donated three goats of my own to another woman to help her.

▲ **Figure 24:** How Farm Africa has helped Gebre, an Ethiopian mother

Top-down strategies

The Ethiopian government has been investing 60 per cent of its national income into education, health and infrastructure in order to improve quality of life. The Growth and Transformation Plan aims to develop industry, expand services and boost the economy. It has succeeded in ensuring economic growth, and large-scale spending on infrastructure and transport has benefited many communities. Around $3.6 billion has been spent converting rural mud roads into asphalt roads, so reducing travel time and making it easier for people and industry.

There has been investment in energy provision including renewable energy (Figure 25). In Tigray state one huge wind turbine facility cost $200 million and although it does produce energy, hundreds of farmers were evicted in order to build there. Hydroelectric

▲ **Figure 25:** National investment in energy sources

power (HEP) systems have been constructed on the Omo River Valley under Chinese sponsorship in order to produce electricity for industry, however this led to 'land-grabbing', with local populations removed and vast areas flooded. The discovery of bones of our earliest ancestors at Lake Turkana, the world's largest desert lake, has given Ethiopia the title of the 'Cradle of Humankind'. The Omo HEP dams will dry up the lake and increase water pollution nearby.

So top-down schemes are larger in scale and bigger in impact. The potential costs can seem excessive, but the ultimate aim is to reduce poverty and increase economic development.

Sustainable development?

Sustainable development means that the needs of the present will be met (socially, economically and environmentally) while protecting the needs of the future. Resources cannot be exhausted and environments need to be protected. It is a balance.

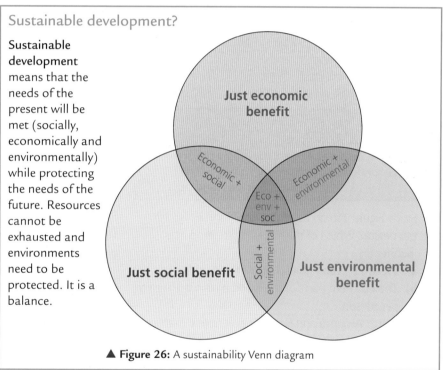

▲ **Figure 26:** A sustainability Venn diagram

Activities

1. What is the difference between a 'bottom-up' and a 'top-down' development strategy? Give an example to illustrate each strategy.
2. What are the limitations of 'bottom-up' strategies for development?
3. Which of the different strategies do you think will be most beneficial for long-term, sustainable development in Ethiopia?
4. Analyse the photographs on this spread. Describe how these strategies will improve quality of life.

5. Draw your own sustainability Venn diagram. Take one bottom-up and one top-down strategy and annotate your diagram to analyse how sustainable each option is.

→ Take it further

6. Choose one of the example strategies and find out what progress has been made. What other development strategies are being used in Ethiopia now?

Practice questions

1. Study the image in Figure 1 on page 168. Describe what is meant by 'development'. **[1 mark]**

2. Complete the following table. **[3 marks]**

Country classification	Example nation
Advanced countries (ACs)	
Emerging developing countries (EDCs)	
	Somalia

3. Study Figure 6 on page 184. The Rostow Model demonstrates how countries can develop over time from being traditional to becoming more developed. Describe what is meant by Stage 3 'take off'. **[4 marks]**

4. Name one social measure of development. Describe how it shows how developed a country is. **[3 marks]**

5. What is the difference between 'absolute poverty' and 'relative poverty'? **[2 marks]**

6. Study Figure 9 on page 171. Describe the trend for secondary employment over time. **[3 marks]**

Tip

A 'trend' means a pattern. So, describing this trend means describing the pattern from a graph. Use phrases such as 'rises rapidly', 'plateaus' and 'steady'.

7. Study Figure 11b on page 173, which shows wealth per person. Which of the following statements is incorrect?
   a) Wealth is evenly spread across the world.
   b) The northern parts of the world have more wealth per person.
   c) North America and Europe have more wealth per person.
   d) Africa has the least wealth per person. **[1 mark]**

8. How can physical factors, such as natural resources, affect how developed a place can become? **[3 marks]**

9. What is meant by 'debt'? **[1 mark]**

10. Why can bilateral aid, also known as 'tied aid', be a problem for the nation receiving it? **[3 marks]**

11. Sometimes nations employ different strategies to help reduce poverty. These can be classed as 'top-down' or 'bottom-up' strategies. Discuss the advantages and disadvantages of each type of strategy, and assess which type is likely to be most effective long term. **[8 marks]**

12. Study Figure 2 on page 182. How has Ethiopia's wealth changed over time? **[2 marks]**

13. Using Figures 9 and 10 on page 187, suggest how the natural physical conditions of a sub-Saharan nation like Ethiopia can lead to poverty. **[4 marks]**

14. What is meant by 'sustainable development goals'? **[1 mark]**

15. Study the following table of development factors in Ethiopia.

	2000	2010
Infant mortality	9.7 per 100	4.5 per 100
Under 5 mortality	16.7 per 100	10.1 per 100
Girls in primary school	53 per 100	93 per 100

   a) Which technique would be best for showing this information?
      i) Line graph
      ii) Radar graph
      iii) Pie chart **[1 mark]**
   b) Using the information from the table, describe the relationship between female education and childhood mortality. **[2 marks]**
   c) Give reasons to explain why childhood mortality decreases. **[3 marks]**

16. Study Figure 16 on page 190. What was Ethiopia's GDP annual growth in 2013? **[1 mark]**

17. What are trans-national companies? Give an example of one. **[2 marks]**

18. Evaluate the impact that a trans-national company can have on a location. Suggest some possible advantages and disadvantages for the host nation. **[4 marks]**

19. Describe how aid can bring benefit to an area. **[3 marks]**

20. Self-help schemes are often found in areas trying to escape poverty. Explain what is meant by 'self-help'. **[2 marks]**

21. With reference to a named LIDC example, describe how either a top-down strategy or bottom-up strategy has led to improvements in living conditions for the local population. **[6 marks]**

Tip

Case study questions rely on your ability to refer to place-specific facts. You should quote named places, companies, statistics, strategies, etc. to prove you know your case study. These are level marked, which means you can access full marks only by showing deep knowledge and understanding.

Chapter 13: **How is the UK changing in the 21st century?**

By the end of this chapter, you will know the answers to these key questions:

→ What does the UK look like in the 21st century?

→ How is the UK's population changing?

→ How is the UK economy changing?

→ Case study: why is Oxfordshire an ideal location for high-technology industries?

Chapter 14: **Is the UK losing its global significance?**

By the end of this chapter, you will know the answers to these key questions:

→ What is the UK's political role in the world?

→ Case study: what has been the UK's political role in stopping the conflict in Ukraine?

→ Case study: what has been the UK's political role in stopping the conflict in Somalia?

→ How is the UK's cultural influence changing?

→ Case study: how has food from different ethnic backgrounds contributed to life in the UK?

The Millenium Footbridge over the River Thames in London. How is the UK changing in the twenty-first century, and what is its political and cultural influence?

CHAPTER 13

How is the UK changing in the 21st century?

What does the UK look like in the 21st century?

→ In this section you will:

→ gain an overview of the geographical characteristics of the UK, including physical geography, rainfall patterns, population density and land use

→ explore the issues of water stress and housing shortages in the UK.

▲ **Figure 1:** Glencoe in the Grampian Mountains

▲ **Figure 2:** The Vale of York, with Middlesbrough in the distance

Can you locate your home town or school on Figure 3? Find the name of your nearest river. Where are your nearest hills or mountains?

What does the UK look like in the 21st century?

What are the physical characteristics of the British Isles?

Look at Figure 3. It shows the physical geography or **relief** of the British Isles. The map shows hills and mountains, lowlands and rivers.

Notice the following characteristics:

● Most mountains are located in the north and west, especially in Wales and Scotland. Figure 1 is a photograph of the Grampian Mountains in Scotland. It is a bleak and hostile environment with few roads and settlements. However, some consider it to be spectacularly beautiful and it attracts many visitors.

● Much of the south and east of the UK is relatively flat with a few hilly areas. Figure 2 is a photograph of the Vale of York. The gently rolling landscape is largely used for farming. This landscape, with its mostly flat land and moderate climate, is better suited for settlements, roads and railways and is more densely populated than the Grampian Mountains.

● There are a lot of rivers in the UK, most of which flow from the hills or mountains down to the sea. The longest river in the UK is the River Severn (354 km) which is just longer than the River Thames (346 km). The largest lake in the UK is Loch Neagh in Northern Ireland which has an area of 383 square km (roughly equivalent to 38,300 football pitches).

Activities

1. Use Figure 3 to answer the following questions.
   a. In which country of the UK are the Southern Uplands?
   b. What is the name of the highest peak in the Southern Uplands and what is its height above sea level?
   c. Ben Nevis in Scotland is the highest mountain in the UK. How high is it above sea level? In what mountain range is it located?
   d. What is the name of the large lake in Northern Ireland?
   e. The River Severn is the UK's longest river. For much of its course it flows close to the border of which two UK countries?
   f. What is the name of the mountain range in Wales?
   g. Dunkery Beacon is the highest peak on which of southwest England's moors?
   h. Mount Snowdon is the highest peak in Wales. True or false?
   i. There are several groups of islands off the coast of Scotland. To which group do Skye and Rhum belong?
   j. What is the name of the lowland vale that lies between the Pennine Hills and the North York Moors?

2. Do this activity as a class. Use Figure 3 to make up three questions of your own, similar to those in Question 1. Write them out on separate pieces of paper, fold them and place them in a container along with the questions from the rest of the class. Now take it in turns to select three questions each from the container and attempt to answer them.

3. Compare the Grampians (Figure 1) with the Vale of York (Figure 2). Refer to the physical landscape and the opportunities for human use.

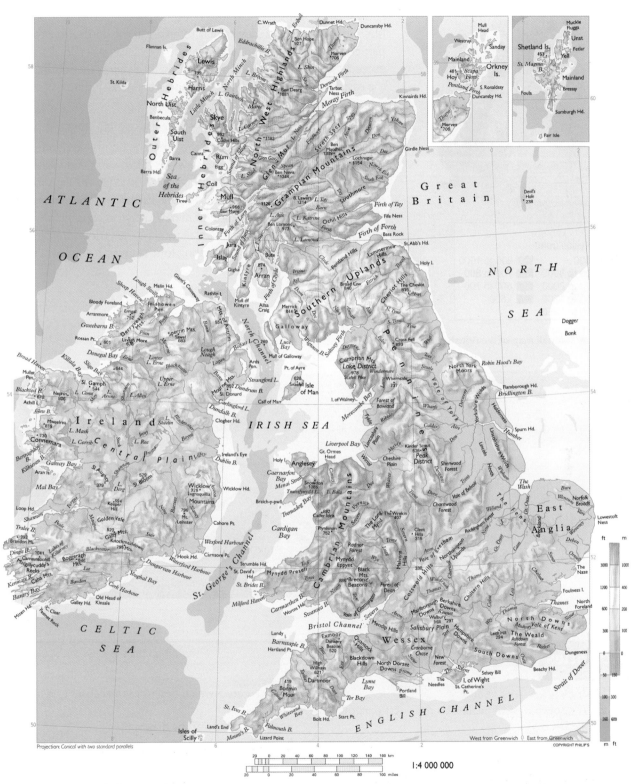

▲ **Figure 3:** The relief of the British Isles

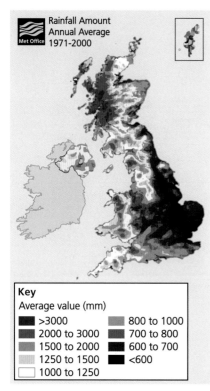

▲ **Figure 4:** Rainfall map of the British Isles

What are the rainfall patterns in the British Isles?

Look at Figure 4. It shows the distribution of precipitation in the British Isles. Notice that the highest rainfall totals are in the north and west, particularly over the mountains. Here the average annual rainfall totals exceed 2500 mm. The lowest precipitation totals are in the south and the east. Here the driest areas in East Anglia and Lincolnshire receive an average annual rainfall total of 500–625 mm.

The main reason for the variation of rainfall in the British Isles is the prevailing wind direction. Most of the time, the British Isles is affected by winds from the southwest. These winds bring warm and moist air from the Atlantic Ocean. On reaching the British Isles, the air is forced to rise up and over the mountains (Figure 5). This leads to cooling, condensation and the formation of rain clouds. This explains why the mountains receive the highest rainfall totals. When the air transfers to the east it is much drier, accounting for the lower rainfall totals in the rain shadow.

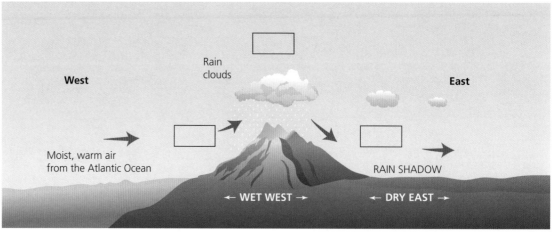

▲ **Figure 5:** The formation of relief rainfall

Activities

1. Study Figure 4. True or false?
   a. The south west of England is the driest part of the UK.
   b. The wettest part of the UK is north west Scotland.
   c. Some parts of south east England received less than 700 mm average annual rainfall.
   d. West is wet, east is dry.

2. Study Figure 5 which describes the causes of relief rainfall.
   a. Make a copy of the diagram.
   b. Write the following sentences in the correct boxes:
      • Air sinks to the east, warms and becomes drier
      • The air cools and condenses to form rain clouds
      • Warm, moist air is forced to rise up and over the mountains
   c. Why do the mountains in the west of the UK receive high rainfall totals?
   d. What is meant by the term 'rain shadow'?

Water stress in the UK

Water supply is an issue in the UK. This is because most rain falls in the west and north whereas the greatest demand for water – for domestic use, industry and agriculture – is in the south and east. Demand is in the south and east and supply is in the north and west.

The term **water stress** can be applied to those areas where water is in limited supply but where there is a large and growing demand for water. Look at Figure 6. It shows water stress in England. Notice that most of the areas with serious water stress are in the south and east, where the lowest rainfall totals occur and population densities are highest. In the future these areas may suffer from water shortages and even drought. There are a few possible solutions.

- Transfer water from the wetter west to the drier east. This could involve rivers, canals or pipelines.
- Construct new reservoirs in the east to capture and store water. This would be very expensive.
- Focus on water conservation by reducing leaks from pipes and encouraging people to use less water.

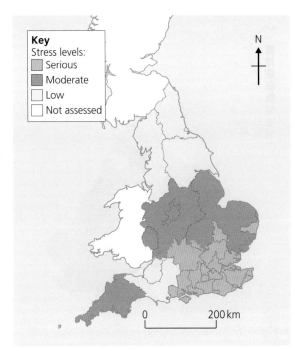

Key
Stress levels:
- Serious
- Moderate
- Low
- Not assessed

0   200 km

N

▲ **Figure 6:** Water stress in England

Activities

1. Study Figure 6.
   a. What is water stress?
   b. Describe the pattern of water stress in England.
   c. Suggest reasons for the location of 'serious' water stress in England.
2. This is a decision-making exercise.
   a. Work in pairs to consider the three options to reduce water stress in the southeast of England. Spend some time discussing and investigating the options. Look up some water conservation measures. Then copy and complete the following table.

Option	Advantages	Disadvantages
Transfer water from northwest to southeast		
Construct new reservoirs in the southeast		
Encourage water conservation		

   b. Which option(s) do you favour and why? Justify your decisions.

Tip

Remember that 'water stress' involves water quality as well as water quantity. Water stress can have huge environmental impacts on wildlife and natural ecosystems.

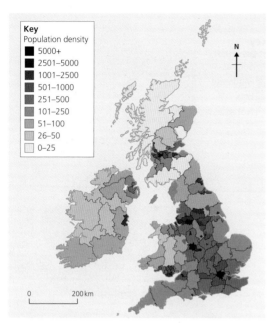

Figure 7: Population density in the British Isles, 2011 (key shows number of people per square kilometre)

Key
Population density
- 5000+
- 2501–5000
- 1001–2500
- 501–1000
- 251–500
- 101–250
- 51–100
- 26–50
- 0–25

◀ **Figure 8:** Low population density at Bwlch y Groes, West Wales

Flat land suitable for building

Fertile land suitable for farming

Plentiful supplies of water

Cities providing opportunities for work

Moderate climate

Extreme, hostile climate

Presence of raw materials for industrial development

Steep and mountainous landscape

Thin soils not well suited to farming

Remote with poor communications

Lack of natural resources

Extensive forests and woodlands

Figure 9: Factors affecting population density

Activities

1. Study Figure 9 which identifies some factors affecting population density. Sort the factors into two groups: high population density and low population density.
2. Study Figure 8. Why do you think this area of West Wales has a low population density?
3. Why do cities such as London (Figure 10) have very high population densities?

What is the population density of the British Isles?

Look at Figure 7. It shows the **population density** of the UK in 2011. You will notice that population density varies a great deal across the British Isles.

- **Low population density:** Much of northern Scotland has a low population density. This is because a large part of this region is mountainous and experiences a hostile climate. It is not an ideal location for human settlement and economic activity. There are also relatively low population densities in Ireland and Wales (Figure 8).
- **High population density:** The rest of the UK, with its gently rolling hills and moderate climate, is much better suited for settlement. The highest density of population stretches from northwest England to the southeast. This area developed as the UK's industrial heartland during the nineteenth century, attracting huge numbers of people to live and work here. Well served by transport routes, it remains the UK's most important economic region.
- **Very high population density:** With their high-rise housing blocks and modern housing estates, cities such as London (Figure 10) experience extremely high population densities. The attractions of employment, shops and entertainment encourage many people to live in urban areas.

Figure 10: High population density in central London

How is the land used in the UK?

In 2011 the Centre for Ecology and Hydrology released its latest land cover map of the UK (Figure 11). This information is gathered from satellite images and digital cartography and gives land cover information at a very detailed level for the whole of the UK. The vast majority of the UK is farmland.

Look at the urban (black) areas on the map. Can you spot your nearest town or city? Notice how the large urban areas are surrounded by the grey shading. This is the outward growth or sprawl of urban developments, particularly housing.

Digital mapping

Satellite image: an image of the whole or part of the Earth taken from space using satellites

Digital cartography: where a collection of data is compiled into a virtual image, for example a digital map with details of roads, such as Google Maps

The mountains of the UK, particularly in Scotland, tend to have rough pasture or heather moorland. Here the harsh climate and poor soils limit the growth of commercial crops and so sheep grazing is the main form of farming.

Broad-leaved woodland	
Coniferous woodland	
Arable farming and horticulture	
Improved grassland (livestock, such as dairy, beef and sheep)	
Rough grassland	
Heather moorlands	
Montane (mountain) habitats	
Suburban/rural development	
Urban	
Water (lakes, rivers)	

Over the higher land in Wales and Scotland, rough pasture dominates and this is mostly used for grazing sheep.

In the east and south of the UK, where the climate is warm, sunny and relatively dry, arable farmland dominates. Farms specialise in growing cereals such as wheat and barley, vegetables and root crops. Horticulture (fruit, salad vegetables and flowers) also takes place in this part of the UK on rich soils such as the Fens in East Anglia or in greenhouses.

To the west of the UK, grassland dominates. The mild and wet climate is ideal for grass, which forms rich pastures for dairying, beef cattle and sheep.

Coniferous woodland, often large plantations used for timber production, occupy tracts of northern England, Wales and Scotland. These are often on poor acidic soils in relatively mountainous, remote areas.

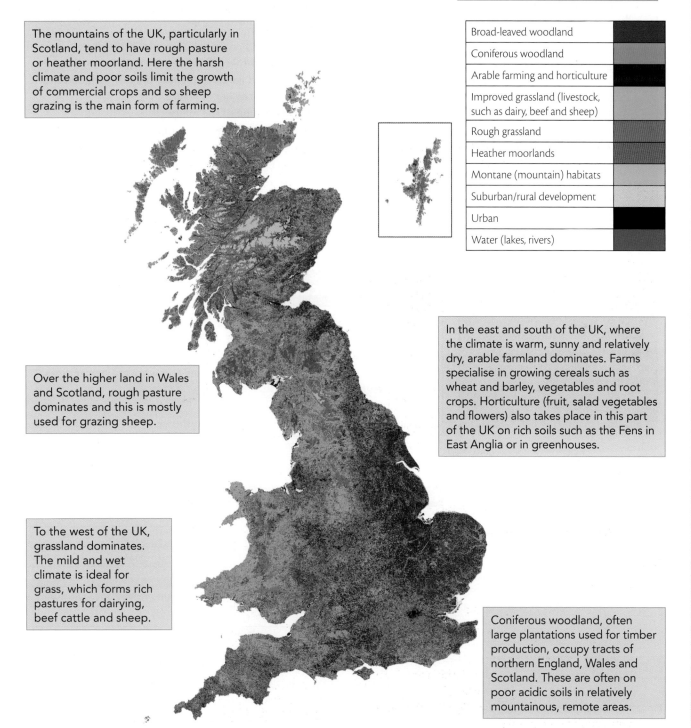

▲ **Figure 11:** Land cover in the UK, source: www.ceh.ac.uk/services/land-cover-map-2007

Activities

1. Study Figure 11 on page 203.
   a. Describe the pattern of 'Arable farming and horticulture'.
   b. Describe the pattern of 'Heather moorlands'.
   c. Suggest reasons why most of the improved grassland is located in the west of the UK?
   d. Is rough grassland only found in the mountainous parts of the UK?
   e. Compare the patterns of deciduous woodland and coniferous woodland.
2. Work in pairs to suggest why a land use map of the UK is important for future planning.

→ Take it further

3. Use to internet to find out about 'montane habitats' in the UK.
   a. Where are the montane habitats in the UK?
   b. What are the climatic conditions like?
   c. What plants and animals are found here?
4. Use the internet to obtain your own copy of the land cover map at www.ceh.ac.uk/services/land-cover-map-2007.
   a. Copy and paste the map into a Word document.
   b. Now add labels to identify the different colours listed in the key in Figure 11.
   c. Label some of the major cities in the UK.
   d. Label your home town or school.
   e. Label some of the major mountain areas.
   f. Use the internet to find some photos of the different types of land use to illustrate your work.

Tip

When studying the land use in the UK, consider the overall patterns of land use. Make specific references to regions in the UK and be prepared to give reasons for the patterns you have identified.

⊥ Geographical skills

Study Figure 12. It lists the percentages of different land uses in the UK.

- Use the data to produce a pie chart. Remember that you will need to multiply the percentages by 3.6 to convert to degrees.
- Use colours to show the different land uses and write the percentages in the segments or alongside.
- Don't forget to include a title.
- Now write a brief summary of the pattern shown by the pie chart.

Land use	Percentage
Grasses and rough grazing	52%
Arable/horticulture	20%
Urban land use	14%
Forest and woodland	12%
Inland water	1%
Other agricultural land	1%

▲ **Figure 12:** Land uses in the UK

Housing shortages in the UK

The UK is facing a shortage of housing. As the population increases and life expectancy rises, more and more people are seeking affordable housing. It has been estimated that up to 250,000 new homes need to be built each year to keep pace with demand. Currently just over 110,000 are being constructed annually.

The problem is most serious in London and the southeast. An estimated 160,000 new homes will be needed in the next five years in southern England. Some 15,000 new homes will be needed in London alone.

High-density flats or small houses are well suited to urban environments such as London, Birmingham and Manchester (Figure 13). These enable large numbers of people to be settled in a relatively small area of land.

A lot of new housing developments are, however, taking place on the edges of towns and cities (Figure 14). These developments can threaten the green belts: zones of countryside with strict planning controls surrounding most large towns and cities.

In 2014 the government announced plans to develop two 'garden cities': Ebbsfleet in Kent and Bicester in Oxfordshire. Some 15,000 new homes are planned for Ebbsfleet (Figure 15) and 13,000 new homes are planned for the outskirts of Bicester. The homes will create village communities with plenty of green space and opportunities for shopping, recreation and employment.

Garden cities, such as Welwyn Garden City and Letchworth Garden City, were first introduced in the 1920s to re-house people living in poor-quality houses in London. A further wave of new towns, including Milton Keynes, followed the Second World War when bomb damage wiped out many homes in London.

▲ **Figure 13:** New high-density housing development in North London

▲ **Figure 14:** New housing development in a Gloucestershire green belt

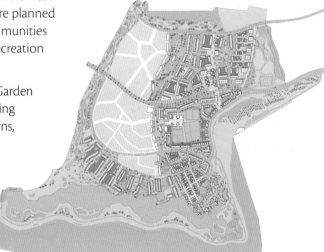

▶ **Figure 15:** New housing development in Ebbsfleet, Kent

Activities

1. Study Figures 13 and 14, showing two types of new housing.
   a. Compare the types of houses in the two photos.
   b. Why is high-density housing better suited to urban areas such as London?
   c. Why do many people wish to live in houses on the edges of towns and cities?
   d. Should protected areas of the countryside such as green belts be used for new housing developments?
2. Study Figure 15 which shows planned housing developments in Eastern Quarry New Town at Ebbsfleet, Kent. What are the attractions for young families of living in this new development?

→ Take it further

3. Use the internet to find out more about green belts.
   • Find a map that shows the location of green belts in the UK.
   • What is the purpose of green belts?
   • Why are green belts under threat today?
4. Make a study of the development of one of the new garden cities. Choose to study either Ebbsfleet or Bicester. Find out where your chosen garden city is located and what developments are planned. What are the advantages and disadvantages of the new housing developments?

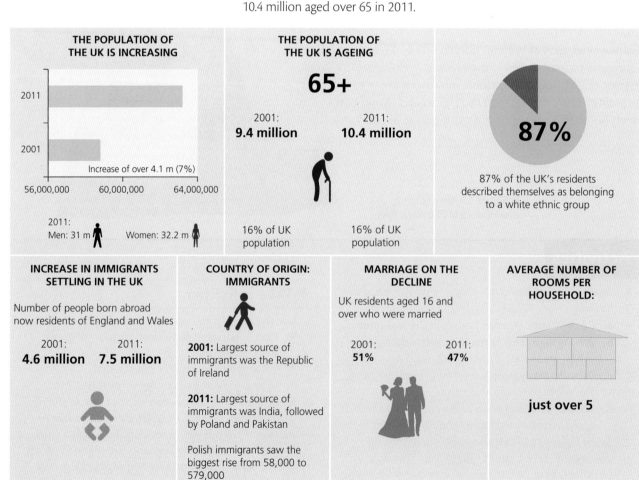

How is the UK's population changing?

→ **In this section you will:**

- → look at how population is measured
- → study the population structure of the UK
- → learn about the UK's changing population
- → look at the issue of ageing population in the UK
- → explore how the population has changed in Boston, Lincolnshire.

How is the UK's population changing?

How is population measured?

The population of a country is measured by a survey called a **census**. In most countries of the world, including the UK, a census is carried out every ten years. The most recent UK census took place on 27 March 2011.

The UK census, run separately by the Office for National Statistics (England and Wales), National Records of Scotland (Scotland) and the Northern Ireland Statistics and Research Agency (Northern Ireland), paints a picture of the nation and how we live. It provides a valuable snapshot of the population and its characteristics, helping the government to plan funding and public services for the future (Figure 16).

How has the UK's population changed since 2001?

The census of 2011 revealed some interesting trends in the UK's population since 2001. These are summarised in Figure 16.

- The overall population increased by over 4 million people to just over 63 million.
- Much of this growth was the result of in-migration, particularly from India, Poland and Pakistan.
- The most rapid increase of migrants was from Poland.
- Birth rate has increased slightly – this is partly due to the age profile of the new migrants arriving in the UK who are starting families.
- The number of elderly people in the UK rose by about 1 million people to 10.4 million aged over 65 in 2011.

▲ **Figure 16:** What did the 2011 UK census discover?

Look at Figure 17. Notice that the UK's population rose significantly from 2001, and particularly from 2004. While some of this growth can be explained by natural increase (births minus deaths) much of it reflects an increase in immigration, particularly in the first few years of the decade. During this time the UK offered enormous perceived opportunities (higher-paid jobs and opportunities for an improved quality of life) particularly to people living in countries of Eastern Europe that joined the EU in 2004, such as Poland.

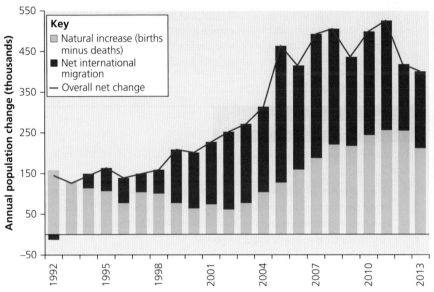

Tip

Be careful when interpreting divided (compound) bars. Measure the length of each colour separately and use the axis to work out the correct value. Double check that your total for all the separate sections is the same value as for the entire bar.

▲ **Figure 17:** The UK's changing population

UK area	Population (million)	Percentage
England and Wales	53	84
Scotland	5.3	8
Wales	3.1	5
Northern Ireland	1.8	3
TOTAL	63.2	100

▲ **Figure 18:** UK population, 2011

Activities

1. Study Figure 17.
   a. For 2005 estimate the proportions of the overall net change attributed to natural increase (births minus deaths) and net international migration.
   b. Suggest why there was a sudden rise in immigration from 2004 to 2005.
   c. Describe the trend for overall net change from 2001 to 2011.
   d. Describe and suggest possible reasons for the trends since 2011.
2. Use the data in Figure 18 to produce a pie chart to show the population of the countries of the UK.

Activities

→ Take it further

1. Study Figure 19. Use the internet to try to find out why there was a big increase in migration to the UK from Poland and Nigeria between 2001 and 2011.

2. Access the interactive ONS website at www.ons.gov.uk/ons/interactive/census-3-1---country-of-birth/index.html to discover the population structure for immigrants to the UK. Compare the population structures for Poland, Ireland and India. Find out which countries have younger profiles and which ones have older profiles.

✝ Geographical skills

Figure 19 shows the top ten countries for non-UK-born residents in 2001 and 2011.

1. Draw a series of parallel bars to represent the data. For each country, draw two bars side by side to show the numbers for 2001 and 2011. Use two different colours to shade each bar. Do this for each of the ten countries to give you 20 bars in total.

2. Which country experienced the greatest growth between 2001 and 2011?

3. Which other countries have shown a significant increase?

4. Which country has experienced a fall?

2011 rank	Country of birth	2001 census	2011 census
1	India	456,000	694,000
2	Poland	58,000	579,000
3	Pakistan	308,000	482,000
4	Republic of Ireland	473,000	407,000
5	Germany	244,000	274,000
6	Bangladesh	153,000	212,000
7	Nigeria	87,000	191,000
8	South Africa	132,000	191,000
9	United States	144,000	177,000
10	Jamaica	146,000	160,000

▲ **Figure 19:** Top ten countries for non-UK-born residents in England and Wales, 2001 and 2011

What is the population structure of the UK?

The structure of the UK's population can be shown using a graph called a **population pyramid** (Figure 20). Bars are drawn to represent each five-year age band. The length of each bar relates to the number of people of that age in the population.

Population pyramids can be used to see trends in the population, such as declining birth rates or increases in the number of elderly people. These trends provide useful information for the government in helping to plan for future education, housing, employment and healthcare.

Key	
Males	
■ 2011	— 2001

Key	
Females	
▢ 2011	— 2001

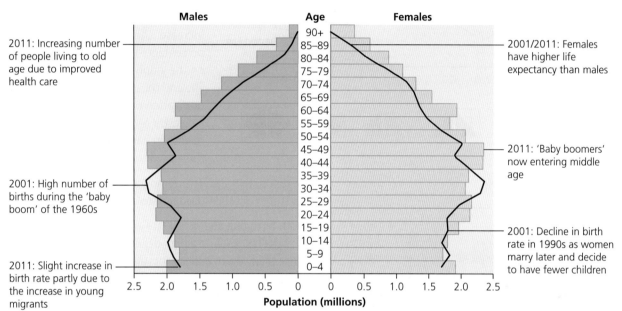

2011: Increasing number of people living to old age due to improved health care

2001: High number of births during the 'baby boom' of the 1960s

2011: Slight increase in birth rate partly due to the increase in young migrants

2001/2011: Females have higher life expectancy than males

2011: 'Baby boomers' now entering middle age

2001: Decline in birth rate in 1990s as women marry later and decide to have fewer children

▲ **Figure 20:** Population pyramid for the UK, 2001/2011

Activities

1. Study Figure 20.
   a. What is a population pyramid?
   b. Identify three changes that have taken place between 2001 and 2011.
   c. Do you think the government should plan for more primary school places? Why?
   d. Is the government right to be concerned about growing numbers of pensioners in the future?
   e. Is the death rate likely to increase in the near future? Why?
   f. Why might there be a shortage of labour in the UK in 2021?
2. Several thousand mostly young working people have migrated into the UK in the last ten years. What are the arguments in favour of, and against, allowing migration to continue? Use the internet to help you research this question and present your findings in the form of a table.

✝ Geographical skills

Study the information in Figure 21. This shows how the structure of the UK population has changed since 1911.

1. Draw divided (compound) bar graphs to show these changes.
2. Use three separate colours to shade each of the three age groups across all three bars.
3. Write a few sentences describing the changes in the UK's population structure from 1911 to 2011.

Age group	1911	2001	2011
0–14	30.8%	18.8%	17.6%
15–64	63.8%	65.4%	66.0%
65+	5.3%	15.9%	16.4%

▲ **Figure 21:** UK's population structure, 1911–2011

How has the UK's population changed?

Look at Figure 22. It is a graph called the **demographic transition model**. It shows changes in the population of the UK since 1700. Notice that there are three lines on the graph:

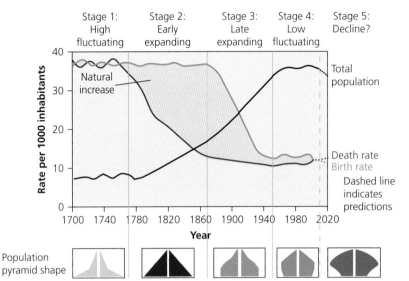

- **birth rate** – the number of live births per 1000 of the population per year
- **death rate** – the number of deaths per 1000 of the population per year
- **total population** – this is the total population of the country.

The difference between the birth rate and the death rate is called the **natural increase**. This is usually expressed as a percentage. The natural increase is shaded on the graph between the birth rate line and the death rate line. The total population of a country is the natural increase +/– migration. In the UK, migration has contributed quite a lot to the growth of the population.

▲ **Figure 22:** The UK demographic transition model

The demographic transition model can be divided into a number of stages.

Activities

1. a. Make a careful copy of Figure 22. Use separate colours to show the different parts of the graph.
    b. Add detailed labels to accounts for the trends.
2. Study Figures 20 and 22.
    a. Look closely at the UK's population pyramid. Suggest which stage of the demographic transition model it belongs to.
    b. Give reasons for your choice.
    c. How is recent migration to the UK affecting birth rates and total population growth?
    d. Do you agree that migration is helping to prevent the UK drifting into Stage 5 of the demographic transition model?

- **Stage 1:** Here, both birth rate and death rate are high. Disease and poor living standards in the UK result in a high death rate. Children support the family and because many die in infancy, lots are born to guarantee that a few will survive. The birth and death rates cancel each other out so the UK's total population does not grow much.
- **Stage 2:** Death rate drops as healthcare and standards of living improve. Improved diets due to food imports from countries such as the USA, Acts of Parliament restricting child labour and improvements to public services all helped to reduce death rates. As the birth rate is still high, the UK's total population starts to increase.
- **Stage 3:** Birth rate starts to decline. Infant mortality falls due to better healthcare (improved medicines and hospitals) so fewer children need to be born. Women are being educated and are choosing to have fewer children. The UK's population continues to grow but starts to slow down.
- **Stage 4:** Here both birth rate and death rate are low. The UK's society is now advanced with excellent healthcare and high standards of living. Women are following careers and choosing to have fewer children. Contraceptives are widely available and acceptable. Infant mortality rates are very low. People are living longer due to excellent healthcare in the UK. The total population levels off.
- **Stage 5:** In theory as the population ages, with large numbers of people reaching old age, the death rate starts to become higher than the birth rate. Children are expensive to look after and families are deciding to have fewer children. This stage has not been reached in the UK but has happened in some countries, such as Germany.

Only Stages 1 and 4 are sustainable, in that the total population remains fairly stable. Most countries strive to reach Stage 4 but do not wish to move into Stage 5!

Ageing population in the UK

What did the 2011 census reveal?

In 2011, 9.2 million people (16 per cent of the UK's population) were aged 65+. This is almost a million more people than in 2001. In England and Wales, of those people over 65 in 2011, only 10 per cent were still economically active. Over half described themselves as being in good health (Figure 23). Some 14 per cent of older people provide free healthcare to others in their households.

Look back to the UK's population pyramid in Figure 20. Notice that the number of people (length of bars) aged over 65 increased between 2001 and 2011. Just below this group are the people who were born just after the Second World War when there was an increase in births. Below them is a bulge of people in their 40s and 50s (the so-called 'baby boomers') who will be turning 65 in the next 10–20 years. The UK is gradually becoming a country with an **ageing population**.

▲ **Figure 23:** Most over-65s in the UK enjoy good health

An ageing population: challenges and opportunities

An ageing population does present many challenges. Elderly people have greater medical needs and the costs of looking after them will rise in the future. They will need increasing amounts of care to enable them to stay in their own homes (Figure 26, page 212). Their children – in middle age – will increasingly be responsible for their care.

However, an ageing population brings with it huge amounts of wisdom and compassion for others. Many older people give up their time to work as volunteers in the community and some continue to work in paid employment (Figure 27, page 212). Many newly retired people enjoy good health and have money to spend on travel, home improvements and hobbies such as gardening. Several businesses specialise in providing services for older people.

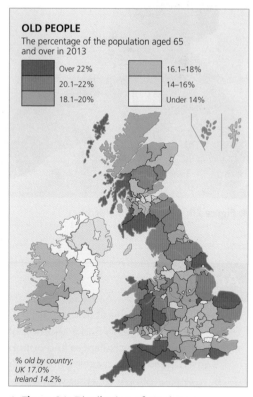

OLD PEOPLE
The percentage of the population aged 65 and over in 2013

Over 22%	16.1–18%
20.1–22%	14–16%
18.1–20%	Under 14%

% old by country;
UK 17.0%
Ireland 14.2%

▲ **Figure 24:** Distribution of pensioners in the UK

Activities

1. Study Figure 24 which illustrates the distribution of pensioners in the UK. It shows that elderly people are concentrated in certain parts of the UK.
   a. On a blank outline map of the UK, draw the high concentrations of elderly people (areas above 22 per cent).
   b. Use an atlas to locate and label some towns within these areas.
   c. Describe the distribution of the high concentrations of elderly people.
   d. Why do you think there are such high concentrations along the south coast of England?
   e. How might high concentrations of elderly people create challenges for local authorities?

Figure 25 summarises the causes, effects and responses to the UK's ageing population.

Causes	Effects	Responses
Large number of people born after the Second World War and through into the 1960s ('baby boomers') are now moving into old age	Healthcare costs are very high and will increase as the elderly require support services and expensive treatments	The government issued Pensioner Bonds in 2015 to encourage older people to save money for the future
Improved healthcare and new treatments, especially for diseases such as cancer and heart conditions, prolong life	Shortage of places in care homes, many of which are expensive	Pensioners receive support in the form of care, reduced transport costs and heating allowances (winter fuel payments); this is expensive for the government and may be withdrawn from wealthy pensioners in the future
Reductions in smoking, which caused a huge early death toll in the past	Many older people are looked after by their middle-aged children, often affecting their lives and their ability to remain in full-time employment	Retirement age, which used to be 65, is being phased out to encourage people to continue working
Greater awareness of the benefits of a good diet	Older people are valued employees as they have high standards and are reliable	State pension age is gradually being increased to 67
People living more active lives and benefiting from regular exercise	Older people act as volunteers in hospitals, advice centres, food banks, etc.	The government could encourage people to take out private health insurance to cut NHS costs
Many older people are reasonably well off financially so can afford a good standard of life	Many older people are keen to travel and to join clubs, societies, sports centres, etc.; this helps to boost the economy and provide jobs	Pro-natalist policies to encourage an increase in birth rate to balance the population structure; this could include cheaper child care, improved maternity and paternity leave and higher child benefit payments
		Allowing more immigration would also address the need for a larger young workforce and higher birth rate, but this is controversial

▲ **Figure 25:** The UK's ageing population – causes, effects and responses

▲ **Figure 26:** Caring for the elderly

▲ **Figure 27:** Working beyond retirement age

Activities

1. Work in pairs for this activity.
   a. Use the internet to find a selection of photos showing some challenges and opportunities associated with an ageing population in the UK.
   b. Use your photos together with some text boxes to produce a poster divided into two halves: challenges and opportunities.
2. Study Figure 25. Look back to the UK's population pyramid (Figure 20, page 209) and think about why the UK's population is ageing.

   a. What health and lifestyle changes are responsible for people living longer today than in the past?
   b. Choose one 'Effect' from Figure 25 and explain why an ageing population can cause **problems** for the country.
   c. Now choose another 'Effect' and explain why an ageing population can bring **benefits**.
   d. What 'Responses' are the government making to try to cut the costs of an ageing population?

How has the population changed in Boston, Lincolnshire?

Where is Boston?

Boston is a market town located in eastern England in the county of Lincolnshire (Figure 28). It has a population of about 65,000 people.

Britain's most Eastern European town

Look at Figure 29. Between 2001 and 2011, the population of Boston grew at a faster rate than for Lincolnshire as a whole. The main reason was the influx of immigrants from Eastern Europe. About one in ten people in the town come from the 'new' EU countries, such as Poland, Lithuania and Latvia. Back in 2001, there were just over 200 non-British people and they were from Germany.

In 2004 the EU was enlarged to include Eastern European countries whose people could freely migrate to other EU countries such as the UK. In 2008 Romania and Bulgaria joined the EU and migrants from these countries have recently arrived in Boston.

▲ **Figure 28:** Location of Boston, Lincolnshire

Area	2011 census population estimate	2001 census population figure	Change (persons)	Change (%)	Average annual change 2001–11 (%)
Boston	64,637	55,750	8,887	15.9%	1.6%
Lincolnshire	713,653	646,645	67,008	10.4%	1.0%
East Midlands	4,533,222	4,172,174	361,048	8.7%	0.9%
England	53,012,456	49,138,831	3,873,625	7.9%	0.8%

▲ **Figure 29:** Population changes, 2001–11

Why have migrants moved to Boston?

The migrants have chosen to move to Boston in search of jobs that are better paid than those at home. Most of the migrants are aged between 20 and 30. Look at Figure 30 to see how much this age group grew between 2001 and 2011.

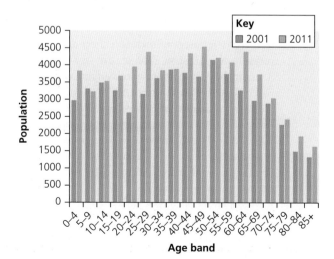

▲ **Figure 30:** Population structure of Boston, 2001–11

Activities

1. Study Figure 29.
   a. What was the increase in population in Boston between 2001 and 2011?
   b. Compare the percentage change in population (2001–11) between Boston and England as a whole.
   c. Use the internet to find population figures for your home town in 2001 and 2011. Work out the percentage increase to compare with Boston. To do this, calculate the difference in population between 2001 and 2011. Divide this value by the total population in 2001 and multiply by 100.
2. Study Figure 30.
   a. Describe the changes that took place in the 20–24 and 25–29 age groups between 2001 and 2011.
   b. Why do you think so many immigrants were in their 20s?
   c. Why do you think there was an increase in the 0–4 age group?
   d. What changes took place for people in their 60s?
   e. Suggest reasons for these changes.

Many of the immigrants have found work on nearby farms (Figure 31) or in fruit and vegetable processing factories where there is a demand for cheap labour. While the wages might be low by British standards, they are much higher than in Poland, enabling the workers to earn good money which they can send home to their families.

How have these changes affected Boston?

New shops specialising in Eastern European products have opened on the high street and some aspects of local culture have been introduced to the town (Figure 32). Many people welcome this ethnic diversity as it adds variety to the town. However, schools have had to cope with children whose first language is not English. With many younger migrants, there has been increased pressure on child-care services and healthcare. However, there have also been increased employment opportunities in shops and public services. The migrants work hard and pay their taxes.

▲ **Figure 31:** Immigrants working on a Lincolnshire farm near Boston

▲ **Figure 32:** A Polish shop in Boston

Activities

1. Study Figure 31.
   a. What are the men in the field doing?
   b. What time of year do you think this photo was taken? Why?
   c. What is the main purpose of the tractor?
   d. What are the advantages for the farmer of employing immigrants?
   e. How do the immigrants benefit from this work?

→ Take it further

2. Figure 32 is a photo of a Polish shop in Boston. Use the internet to find out more about Eastern European influences in Boston.

   a. Research an Eastern European shop or restaurant in Boston. (Make sure you type 'Lincolnshire' into your search engine otherwise you will get Boston in the USA!) 'U Ani' is a Polish restaurant in Boston and 'Nikos Restaurant' specialises in Lithuanian food. You can find both of these on Facebook. Find out what foods or other products are for sale. Produce a small information poster for your chosen shop or restaurant.

   b. Access a street view of Boston using www. bostontown.co.uk/index.php/street-view and take a virtual tour of parts of the town. See if you can find some examples of Eastern European shops and restaurants.

How is the UK economy changing?

The UK has one of the largest economies in the world. In the past, the UK economy was dominated by heavy manufacturing industry based on a rich resource base. Most industries were powered by coal mined from South Wales, the Midlands, northeast England and Scotland. Towns and cities grew up producing steel, ships and textiles (Figure 33). Ports such as London, Liverpool, Glasgow and Bristol developed as important hubs for imports and exports. The UK became the industrial powerhouse of the world.

In the last few decades of the twentieth century, heavy manufacturing industry based on coal declined. Due to competition from abroad and changes in technology, many of the UK's industries became outdated. Factories closed and many people lost their jobs. The UK's economy is now dominated by the service sector. This includes financial services (Figure 34), high-technology industries based on research, media and creative industries, and tourism.

There is still some manufacturing in the UK including cars, chemicals, light engineering and food processing. These modern industries are very efficient and can compete on the world market even though they employ fewer people than in the past.

Construction is also important in the UK. This includes housing, road building and major transport projects such as Crossrail (Figure 35, page 216), which will open in 2018 linking West and East London with Heathrow Airport.

How is the UK economy changing?

→ **In this section you will:**

→ study the major political and economic changes since 1997

→ investigate how employment sectors and working hours have changed since 1997

→ investigate the pattern of core UK economic hubs

→ explore the economic changes in Oxfordshire.

▲ **Figure 33:** Ship building on the River Clyde, Glasgow

Activities

1. Study Figure 33.
   a. Describe what is happening in the photo.
   b. Why are so many men employed to work in the shipyard?
   c. What effects would the closure of the shipyard have on the local community?
2. Study Figure 34.
   a. What is the evidence that Canary Wharf is a modern financial centre?
   b. Suggest why developers have built huge skyscrapers in this part of London.
   c. This area used to be part of London's docks. Why do you think the planners decided to keep many of the old dock basins when Canary Wharf was developed?

▲ **Figure 34:** Canary Wharf – London's modern financial centre

▲ **Figure 35:** Crossrail, linking West and East London

What have been the major political and economic changes since 1997?

Changes in the UK's economy have been driven by several factors. These include technological developments, world markets and government policies. Since 1997 the UK has experienced a Labour government (1997–2010), a Conservative/Liberal Democrat coalition government (2010–15) and, in 2015, a Conservative government came into power.

In 1997 the Labour Party led by Tony Blair returned to power after a gap of some 18 years. In the period to 2008, the economy grew steadily based on political decisions to keep taxes low and enable private companies to thrive.

- In 2008 the UK entered an economic recession caused by the global financial crisis. As the banking system started to collapse, the UK government had to step in to support UK banks and building societies.
- The recession caused unemployment to rise from 1.6 million in January 2008 to 2.5 million by October 2009.
- At the end of 2009, the UK came out of recession and the economy started to recover.
- In 2010 the Labour party lost the election and was replaced by a coalition government involving the Conservatives and Liberal Democrats.
- The new government introduced spending cuts to reduce the country's huge financial deficit.
- Strong growth of jobs in the private sector reduced unemployment to below 2.5 million in October 2013.

How have employment sectors changed since 2001?

Figures 36–38 show the different sectors of the UK economy and how these have changed since 2001.

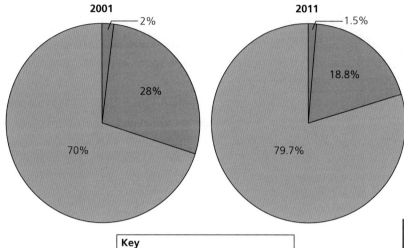

Key
- Agriculture
- Services
- Industry (including construction)

▲ **Figure 37:** Employment in different sectors of the UK economy, 2011

Sector	Percentage (GDP)
Agriculture	0.6%
Construction	6.4%
Production (manufacturing)	14.6%
Services	78.4%

▲ **Figure 36:** Economic importance of different sectors of the UK economy, 2014

Employment sector	Employment (thousands)		
	2001	**2013**	**% change, 2001–13**
Agriculture, forestry and fishing	388	368	−5%
Mining and quarrying	72	64	−10%
Manufacturing	3,519	2,420	−31%
Construction	1,955	2,019	3%
Accommodation and food services	1,756	1,976	13%
Professional, scientific and technical	1,713	2,621	53%
Education	2,217	2,723	23%
Arts, entertainment and recreation	752	890	18%
TOTAL	**28,580**	**30,677**	**7%**

▲ **Figure 38:** Workplace employment for selected industries in the UK

✝ Geographical skills

Study Figure 38 which shows employment data for selected employment sectors in the UK between 2001 and 2013.

1. Draw a bar graph to show the percentage change for 2001–13. To do this, draw a horizontal line to represent no change. For each employment sector draw a bar above (increase) or below (decrease) the horizontal line. Keep the vertical scales the same.

2. Use two different colours to shade the bars: one colour for increase and a different colour for decrease.

Activities

1. Figure 36 lists the economic importance of each industrial sector to the UK's economy.
   a. Present the information in the form of a pie chart.
   b. Use the internet to find a photograph to illustrate each of the sectors and stick them alongside your pie chart. Make sure you give each photo a caption.
2. a. What is 'construction'?
   b. Why do you think construction is a very important part of the UK economy today?

3. Study Figure 37. Describe the changes that have taken place in percentage employment between 2001 and 2011.
4. What evidence is there that service sector industries are growing at the fastest rates?

→ Take it further

5. Use the internet to find a selection of photographs that illustrate the service sector in the UK. Present your information in the form of a collage. Don't forget to caption each photo.

How have working hours changed since 2001?

Since 1988 working hours in the UK have been regulated by law. The maximum working week has been set at 48 hours. Every six hours workers are entitled to a 20-minute break. Night workers can work a maximum of 8 hours. The minimum paid holiday time is four weeks, or 28 days, a year.

In 2011 the average number of hours worked a week by full-time employees in the UK was 42.7. This is one of the highest figures in the EU, beaten only by Austria (43.7) and Greece (43.7).

Between 2001 and 2011 there were a number of changes in people's working hours. The number of hours worked by both men and women fell. Fathers worked fewer hours and worked less in the evening and at weekends. They now spend more time bringing up their children than in the past (Figure 39). However, during the ten-year period studied, the number of mothers in full-time work increased.

The average number of hours worked by men in full-time jobs fell from 46 hours to 44 hours a week.

The proportion of households with two full-time earners increased from 26 per cent to 29 per cent.

For women, average hours in full-time employment fell from 41 hours to 40 hours a week.

Fathers are working shorter hours: in 2001, 40 per cent of fathers worked 48 hours or more a week; by 2011 this had fallen to 31 per cent.

Only one in five families have a father who is the sole earner.

Fathers are also working less at weekends and in the evenings: in 2001, 67 per cent worked in the evenings, whereas in 2011 the figure had fallen to 50 per cent.

In 2011 mothers with a family were more likely to have full-time jobs than in 2001.

▲ **Figure 39:** Fathers now spend more time at home bringing up children

Activities

1. Why do you think fathers are working shorter hours?
2. Suggest reasons why more mothers have full-time jobs?
3. What are the advantages and disadvantages of both parents having full-time jobs?

What is the pattern of UK economic hubs?

In the past, the UK's economy was dominated by coal mining, heavy industry and manufacturing. Economic growth was generated by large regions, such as South Wales, northeast England, Yorkshire and Clydeside. Today, the pattern is much more complex, with the development of relatively small, more specialised centres of economic activity. These are called **economic hubs**.

Some economic hubs are whole cities, such as Cambridge and Oxford. These cities have developed high-technology, research-based industries due to their highly qualified graduate labour force. Elsewhere, economic hubs can be districts within cities, such as Canary Wharf in London, Salford in Manchester or the Titanic Quarter in Belfast. Throughout the country there are business and science parks located on the outskirts of towns and cities, often tapping into nearby universities. Figure 40 shows the location of some of the UK's economic hubs.

👣 Fieldwork ideas

A local economic hub could include a science or business park. To investigate change and assess its significance, primary data could be collected using questionnaires and land-use mapping. Old maps (secondary data) can be used to consider change over time. Future change can be ascertained by interviews or by using information on company websites. Information regarding the regional and economic significance may be obtained using secondary data sources, such as local government reports and internet research.

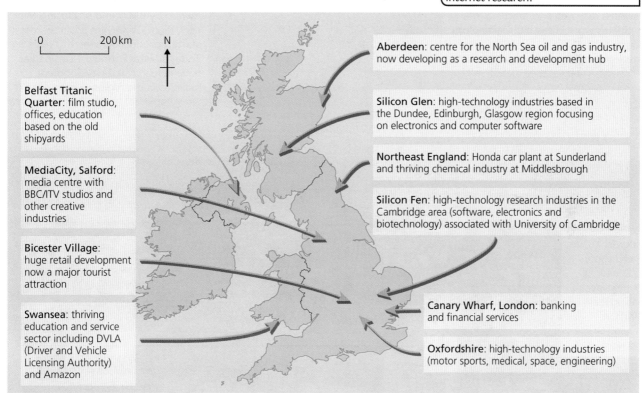

▲ **Figure 40:** A selection of the UK's economic hubs

Activities

1. Study Figure 40 which shows a selection of the UK's economic hubs.
   a. Which economic hubs specialise in high-technology industries?
   b. Which economic hub specialises in financial services?
   c. In which economic hub are there BBC and ITV studios?
   d. How is Aberdeen adapting its industries for the future?
   e. What economic activities are based at Swansea?

→ Take it further

2. Study Figure 40. Choose one economic hub to investigate. Produce an information poster about your chosen economic hub describing its location and its main industries. Try to discover why it has decided to focus on particular types of industry. Include photos and statistics.

Case study: How is the UK economy changing?

Case study of an economic hub: high-technology industries in Oxfordshire

Oxfordshire is one of the UK's most important locations for scientific and technological industries. Centred on the city of Oxford with its world-class universities, a cluster of high-technology industries has developed including high-performance engineering, space and medical research.

There are an estimated 1500 high-technology companies in the Oxford region varying in size from small start-ups to large multinationals, such as Unilever. These companies employ 43,000 people and contribute hugely to the local and national economy.

The rapid growth in Oxfordshire as a centre for the hi-tech industry has led to a number of changes and developments, both within the hub itself and more broadly affecting the region and the UK.

Changes to the economic hub

The number and range of companies has increased over the years, and science and research parks have physically expanded to accommodate this growth. This has resulted in new road networks as well as the construction of new buildings and services. Harwell Campus is planning several new developments including an innovation centre, new technical and office buildings, and facilities for leisure and

The University of Oxford and Oxford Brookes University provide first-class research and teaching. Many graduates work in the high-technology industries.

Oxford has a long tradition as a centre for the UK motor industry. Currently owned by BMW and producing Mini cars, Plant Cowley (as it is now known) started production over 100 years ago. Today several Formula 1 companies have research and development facilities in the region (Figure 42).

Oxfordshire has a rich history and beautiful countryside making it an attractive location to live and work.

Several large existing research organisations such as the UK Atomic Energy Authority and the Medical Research Council attract new companies to the area. The clustering of similar companies brings many benefits such as the sharing of ideas and new technologies.

Oxfordshire is well served by road and rail. It is just 40 miles from Heathrow Airport and 50 miles from London (Figure 42).

▲ **Figure 41:** Why is Oxfordshire an ideal location for high-technology industry?

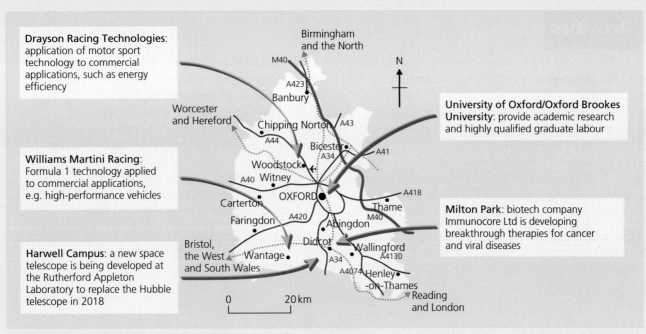

Drayson Racing Technologies: application of motor sport technology to commercial applications, such as energy efficiency

Williams Martini Racing: Formula 1 technology applied to commercial applications, e.g. high-performance vehicles

Harwell Campus: a new space telescope is being developed at the Rutherford Appleton Laboratory to replace the Hubble telescope in 2018

University of Oxford/Oxford Brookes University: provide academic research and highly qualified graduate labour

Milton Park: biotech company Immunocore Ltd is developing breakthrough therapies for cancer and viral diseases

▲ **Figure 42:** Oxfordshire: a science and technology economic hub

accommodation. From 2016, new developments will include a residential quarter, which may eventually result in the construction of 1400 new homes.

A report published in 2010 identified that about a third of the firms in the high-tech hub were at least 25 years old, yet some 40 per cent of companies had been dissolved. The rest of the companies had changed ownership. These mergers and acquisitions have particularly affected firms in the biotech sector. This high level of change illustrates the somewhat fragile state of scientific and technological companies, and the importance of balancing innovation and business. It also shows how knowledge-based industries have to be at the cutting edge if they are to survive and prosper.

Regional and national impact

The development of the high-tech industries in Oxfordshire has had both positive and negative impacts.

As employment has soared – much of this was in the early 2000s when employment in Oxfordshire's high-tech industries grew by 40 per cent compared with 18 per cent nationally – this has placed considerable demand on housing, infrastructure and services. House prices are extremely high in the area and many people on low incomes are unable to afford to buy. Commuting time is high in the Oxford region too, contributing to increased levels of air pollution.

However, on balance, the region has benefited enormously with vast amounts of money being spent in retailing,

restaurants and hotels. Many companies have global connections resulting in large numbers of people visiting the area from overseas. This brings revenue to the city and to the wider region.

Many support industries, both regional and national, have benefited from the development of Oxfordshire's high-tech industries, particularly in the creative, legal and financial sectors. Just imagine all the different industries supplying materials, knowledge and support services to the hundreds of high-tech companies in Oxfordshire! Consider the need for construction, maintenance and servicing. For example, employment in education in Oxfordshire has witnessed a dramatic growth, rising by 50 per cent from 1998–2008, providing jobs for teachers and lecturers as well as many in the service sector.

Nationally, the Oxfordshire high-tech companies bring a huge amount of prestige to the country, being associated with some of the most highly respected and innovative companies in the world in biotechnology, medicine and motorsports.

Oxford Instruments is one of the region's success stories. Specialising in the production of high-tech tools and instruments for industry and research, the company has developed from its humble beginnings in 1959 to become a global company with offices across the world employing over 1500 people. It has brought considerable wealth and success to the region and to the UK.

Activities

1. Study Figure 42 to answer the following questions.
   a. What types of industry are located in Oxfordshire's high-technology economic hub?
   b. On what major road are the Harwell Campus and Milton Park?
   c. Both the Harwell Campus and Milton Park are close to Didcot. Why is this a good location?
   d. Describe Oxfordshire's excellent transport connections with other parts of the UK and the world.
   e. Why are the universities in Oxford a huge advantage for the development of a high-technology economic hub?
   f. Why is a cluster of similar industries an advantage to companies involved in research?

2. Find out more about the recent developments and those proposed for the future at Harwell Campus by accessing their website at www.harwellcampus.com/uploads/pdf/07/10/akh-harwell-campus-growth-plans-8715.pdf

▲ **Figure 43:** Ordnance Survey map extract of the Harwell Campus, scale 1:25,000 © Crown copyright and/or database right. All rights reserved. License number 100036470

Activities

1. Study Figures 43 and 44, which show the Harwell Campus. Figure 43 is a map extract and Figure 44 is an aerial photo.

   a. In which direction is the photo looking?

   b. In what grid square is the building labelled X located?

   c. What is the number of the road at Y?

   d. Suggest why embankments have been constructed around parts of the Harwell Campus.

   e. Describe the layout and design of the Harwell Campus.

   f. Do you think the Harwell Campus is an attractive place to work? Why?

   g. What are the other advantages of this location for high-technology industries?

   h. A motor sport company wishes to move onto the Harwell Campus. They need a plot of land for buildings of about 500 m² and a further plot of land about the same size as a vehicle test track. Where would you suggest the company could be located and why?

→ Take it further

2. Use the internet to find out more about one of the companies in Oxfordshire's economic core. Find out what the company does and try to discover why Oxfordshire is a good location.

   - Williams Martini Racing: www.williamsf1.com/team
   - Drayson Racing Technologies: www.draysonracingtechnologies.com
   - European Space Agency Business Incubation Centre, Harwell: www.esa-bic.org.uk/default.aspx
   - Immunocore Ltd: www.immunocore.com

3. Find out more about the companies that have located on the Harwell Campus by accessing the website at http://harwellcampus.com. Click 'Our Vision'.

   a. How large is the site?

   b. How many organisations and people are based on the campus?

   c. Make a list of some of the organisations on the campus and identify what they do.

   d. Write about two recent breakthroughs or discoveries that have been made.

   e. What is the vision for the future?

▲ **Figure 44:** Aerial photo of the Harwell Campus

CHAPTER

14

Is the UK losing its global significance?

What is the UK's political role in the world?

What is the UK's political role in the world?

➔ In this section you will:

➔ explore the role of the UK in conflict zones, focusing on case studies of Ukraine and Somalia.

Tip

Make sure you learn the key terms and that you use them correctly. Examiners will credit your use of correct geographical terminology.

In the days of the British Empire, the UK had a major role in world affairs. This is no longer the case. However, the UK does have a part to play as a member of several global organisations such as the World Bank, the United Nations, NATO and the EU. While some involvement has involved military action, for example in Iraq and Afghanistan, the UK is mostly involved in non-military support and co-operation with other nations.

Important terms for this chapter:

● **Unilateral:** This is involvement by a single country. For example, the UK spends over £4 billion on foreign aid towards healthcare, education and disaster relief for countries across the world.
● **Multilateral:** This involves groups of countries working together. Examples include the United Nations, the World Bank and the European Union.
● **Refugees:** People who have been forced to move to a different country, often in fear of their lives.
● **Internally displaced people:** People forced from their homes but who resettle elsewhere within their country.

What is the role of the UK in conflict zones?

A **conflict zone** is an area (usually a country or part of a country) where two or more groups of people have a serious disagreement that results in economic, social or military aggression. Look at Figure 1. It shows the impacts of the recent civil war in Syria which has resulted in some 200,000 people being killed since 2011. Cities have been bombarded and thousands of refugees have fled to safety in parts of Europe, including the UK. The civil war in Syria is just one of many conflicts in the world. Can you think of any others?

◀ **Figure 1:** Damaged building in Homs, Syria

Country/territory	Conflict
Colombia	Armed violence involving the government and various guerrilla groups. Around 50,000 people have been killed. Many people have been forced to move.
Iraq	Following the US-led invasion in 2003 and recent civil unrest, some 400,000 people have fled the country and a further 1 million have been internally displaced. In 2013, hundreds were killed during uprisings.
Afghanistan	For several years, military forces from countries including the US, UK and France have been fighting a 'war on terror' in Afghanistan. In 2010 alone some 10,000 people were killed. Afghanistan is one of the poorest countries in the world.
Israel/Occupied Palestinian Territories	One of the longest-running disputes involves claims by Israelis and Palestinians over land in the eastern Mediterranean. Since 2000, over 8000 people have been killed.
Kashmir	This mountainous region has been at the centre of a long-running dispute involving Pakistan and India. Over 70,000 people have been killed.
Ukraine	Conflict between the largely Ukrainian west and Russian east reached a head in 2014 when Crimea was annexed by Russia.
South Sudan	In 2011, following Africa's longest-running civil war, South Sudan became the world's youngest nation. Violence between different groups has continued, with 10,000 people killed since 2013.
Somalia	With a repressive government, armed opposition groups and frequent droughts and famines, Somalia has experienced conflicts for several decades. Piracy and armed criminal gangs have brought death and terror to thousands of people. Over 1.5 million people have become refugees in other countries.
Myanmar (Burma)	Myanmar has been affected by civil war since the end of British rule in 1948. Conflicts between the government and ethnic minority groups have led to thousands of internally displaced people and human rights issues.

▲ **Figure 2:** Conflict zones across the world

Activities

1. Study Figure 1 which shows the war-torn city of Homs in Syria.
   a. Describe the impact of the conflict shown in the photo.
   b. Why do you think there are few people in the photo?
   c. Where do you think the people have gone?
   d. What are the challenges that lie ahead if this area is to be restored to become a vibrant community once more?
2. For this activity you will need a blank world outline showing the countries of the world. Use this world outline and the information from Figure 2 to produce a map showing the world's main conflict zones.
   a. Use an atlas to locate and shade the countries and territories listed in Figure 2. Add Syria, which is described on page 224.
   b. Use the information from Figure 2 to create a text box for each country. Write the country's name and give a brief description of the conflict.
   c. Use your own knowledge or the internet to find out about other countries that are currently experiencing conflict. Add them to your map and write a text box for each. A good site to use is www.insightonconflict.org/conflicts.

→ Take it further

3. Use Figure 2 or your own research to identify a conflict that is of interest to you. Don't choose Ukraine or Somalia as they are studied in this chapter.
   a. Consider the causes of your chosen conflict.
   b. What have been the impacts on the people, the economy and the environment?
   c. What is being done to reduce the conflict and what role is the UK playing?
   d. Do you think the conflict will continue into the future?
4. For your chosen country or territory, select some photos to illustrate the conflict and use annotations to identify the main issues.

Case study: What is the UK's political role in global conflict?

Ukraine

Where is Ukraine?

Ukraine is a country located in Eastern Europe, sandwiched between Russia in the east and Poland in the west. It is Europe's largest country and has a population of about 45 million people (about three-quarters of the UK).

The focus of the current conflict is in Crimea and elsewhere in eastern Ukraine.

▲ **Figure 3:** Conflict zones in Ukraine

- Crimea: This is a peninsula of land stretching out from southern Ukraine between the Black Sea and the Sea of Azov. It is separated from Russia by the narrow Kerch Strait (Figure 3). This geographically separate region has long historic links with Russia. Many of its people speak Russian rather than Ukrainian. Russia's Black Sea fleet is based in Sevastopol.
- Eastern Ukraine: Focused on the cities of Donetsk and Kharkiv, uprisings of pro-Russian separatists have resulted in hundreds of people being killed. Many thousands have been made homeless (Figure 4).

Why is there a conflict in Ukraine?

In 1991 the collection of states known as the Soviet Union broke up. Several new countries were formed including Ukraine. Ever since, there have been divisions in Ukraine between the west and the east of the country. In the west most people speak Ukrainian and consider themselves to be European. In the east most people are Russian speakers and are much more closely linked with Russia.

In 2014, Ukraine's pro-Russian president Viktor Yanukovych was driven out of office by violent protests in the capital Kiev. Russian-backed forces responded by taking control of the Crimean peninsula to support its many citizens living there (Figure 5). The territory voted in a referendum to join Russia, although this has not been recognised by countries in the West.

The conflict has since spread to include much of eastern Ukraine, where the Ukrainian government forces have been in military conflict with pro-Russian separatists. The West supports Ukraine and believes that Russia is supporting the uprising. Russia, for its part, denies any involvement.

▲ **Figure 4:** Houses in Donetsk damaged by artillery fire

What is the UK's involvement?

The UK has been involved in trying to stop the conflict in Ukraine. Most of the UK's influence has been expressed through international organisations of which it is a member, including the EU (European Union) and NATO (North Atlantic Treaty Organization).

● The UK government has condemned the Russian intervention in Ukraine and has repeatedly expressed its disapproval to Russia.
● The European Union and other Western countries have imposed sanctions (penalties) on Russia focusing on banking, energy and defence. There are travel bans on some Russian individuals and their assets (such as money in banks) have been frozen. Further sanctions may be imposed in the future.
● NATO condemned Russia's military intervention and stated that it was a breach of international law. NATO is planning to create a new 'spearhead' force which could be used to establish and maintain a ceasefire between the Ukrainian army and the pro-Russian separatists in eastern Ukraine. The UK has offered to contribute 1000 personnel to the new force.

▲ **Figure 5:** Russian-backed forces seize control of Crimea in 2014

What have been the impacts of the conflict?

Between April 2014 and January 2015 some 5000 people had been killed in the conflict. Many more have been injured or made homeless. The tensions with Ukraine and the rest of Western Europe have led to serious problems and shortages in Crimea (Figure 6).

Transport systems have been disrupted, with long delays for drivers wishing to cross into the Crimean peninsula.

Shoppers have faced shortages of food.

Mastercard and Visa have withdrawn from Crimea, preventing people from using credit and debit cards.

Power blackouts have been common, affecting mobile phone networks, heating and hot water supplies.

There are no train or bus links between Crimea and the rest of Ukraine.

Air and sea links have been badly affected, with just Russian carriers operating in Crimea.

◀ **Figure 6:** Problems in Crimea

Activities

1. Read through the Ukraine case study and answer the following questions.
   a. Why is there conflict in eastern Ukraine?
   b. Which groups of people have suffered as a result of the conflict?
   c. How have sanctions affected the people living in Crimea?
   d. In what ways has the UK been involved in trying to reduce the conflict?

→ Take it further

2. Do you think the conflict in Ukraine is likely to continue into the future? Use the internet to assess the situation now. Is there anything else that could or should be done to reduce the conflict?

Case study: What is the UK's political role in global conflict?

Somalia

Where is Somalia?

Look at Figure 7. It shows an location map of Somalia. Notice that Somalia is located in the far east of Africa. It is sometimes called the 'Horn of Africa' due to its shape.

- The northern part of Somalia is called Somaliland. It borders the Gulf of Aden. Much of this area is mountainous.
- The rest of Somalia borders the Indian Ocean. The land here is much flatter and most of it is dry semi-desert (Figure 9). This is an extremely hostile environment in which to live.
- Somalia has a population of 10.5 million people (about one-sixth that of the UK).

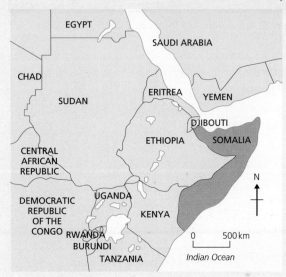

▲ **Figure 7:** Location map of Somalia

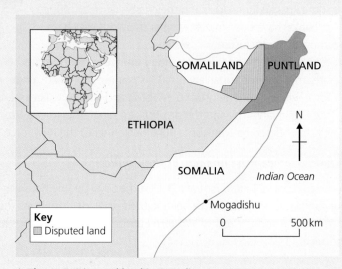

▲ **Figure 8:** Disputed land in Somalia

Why is there a conflict in Somalia?

Somalia was formed in 1960. Before then, the area was controlled by the UK and Italy. Disputes with its neighbours – Kenya, Djibouti and Ethiopia – soon broke out over land that was settled by Somali people.

In 1991 President Siad Barre was overthrown and the country was thrown into chaos. For two decades there was no government. Fighting between rival warlords ravaged the country. It was ill-equipped to deal with the droughts and famines of 1992 and 2010–12 that killed an estimated 500,000 people.

In 2012 an internationally backed government was installed and a degree of stability returned. The decades of conflict have left Somalia one of the poorest countries in the world.

Look at Figure 8. Somaliland has now proclaimed itself as a separate state and the region of Puntland runs its own affairs. Notice that there is a disputed territory in the north of Somalia between Somaliland and Puntland.

In recent years Somalia has been linked to Islamic terrorism and also to piracy, with several ships being attacked in the Indian Ocean and people and vessels held to ransom. Today Somalia is one of the most unstable places on Earth.

▲ **Figure 9:** People collecting firewood in Somalia's semi-desert

What is the UK's involvement?

- The UK is part of the United Nations (UN). Troops were sent to monitor a ceasefire in 1992 but finally withdrew in 1995 leaving the warlords to fight on.
- The UK's Department for International Development is working with the new Somali government to address shortages in food, employment and healthcare. Its healthcare programmes, such as the Joint Health and Nutrition Programme for Somalia, aim to save thousands of lives and to provide an essential package of health services. The UK government is also investing in programmes addressing the issues of piracy, terrorism and migration. The cost of these programmes is estimated to be some £500 million (2012–17).
- In 2013 the UK government announced that it would send a British military team to train troops and help combat human rights abuses. An additional £50 million was promised to support the region. Money was pledged to build up an anti-piracy naval force and to refurbish Mogadishu's central prison.
- Several UK charities such as Oxfam, Save the Children UK and Care International UK work in Somalia to reduce poverty and address issues of health and women's rights.

▲ **Figure 10:** Violence on the streets of Mogadishu

What have been the impacts of the conflict?

- An estimated 500,000 people died as a result of the famines of 1992 and 2010–12; tens of thousands of people fled to Kenya and Ethiopia in search of food.
- Every year thousands of Somalis attempt the perilous crossing of the Gulf of Aden to reach Yemen in search of security and a better life. Many die in their attempt.
- Many thousands have been displaced within Somalia. They live in overcrowded camps with poor access to food, water and sanitation (Figure 11).

▲ **Figure 11:** Many Somali people have been forced from their homes by the conflict and live in overcrowded camps

Activities

1. Use the information about Somalia, together with your own internet research, to construct an information poster. Include the following:
   - a map showing the location of Somalia in Africa; use Figure 8 to draw the different territories within Somalia and don't forget to include a scale
   - photos showing the Somalian environment and some aspects of the recent conflict; remember to caption or annotate your photos to describe what they show
   - text panels considering the causes and effects of the conflict
   - a text panel describing the involvement of the UK in trying to resolve the conflict and reduce its impacts.

→ Take it further

2. Several UK charities are working in Somalia to support local people who have been affected by the conflict. Find out what they are doing by accessing information on their websites. Here are three charities for you to consider.
   - Save the Children UK: www.savethechildren.org.uk/where-we-work/africa/somalia
   - Oxfam: www.oxfam.org/en/countries/somalia
   - Care International UK: www.careinternational.org.uk/where-we-work/somalia

How is the UK's cultural influence changing?

→ **In this section you will:**

→ learn about the UK's media exports and their global influence

→ explore the contribution of ethnic groups to the cultural life of the UK.

How is the UK's cultural influence changing?

The term **cultural** is used to describe the values and beliefs of a particular society or group of people. It's all about what makes a society special. Culture is often illustrated by writings, paintings or creativity in the form of fashion, architecture or music. In the UK we might consider paintings by great artists such as Turner and Constable to be part of our cultural heritage. Writers such as Shakespeare and Wordsworth, buildings like St Paul's Cathedral designed by Sir Christopher Wren, and bands such as The Beatles can all be considered to be part of the UK's culture (Figure 12).

Activity

1. Study Figure 12. Work in small groups to brainstorm aspects of the UK's culture. Consider what makes the UK special in terms of art, writing, music, fashion, film, food, architecture and buildings. Produce a poster in the form of a collage entitled 'The UK's Cultural Heritage'. Include photos and other illustrations taken from the internet, newspapers and magazines.

◀ **Figure 12:** Culture in the UK

What are the UK's media exports?

The creative or **media** industries include films, television programmes, books, magazines, music, plays and video games (Figure 13). The government estimates that the UK's creative industries are worth more than £63 billion a year, generating £70,000 every minute for the UK economy. They employ some 1.5 million people in the UK and account for £1 in every £10 of UK exports.

▲ **Figure 13:** The UK's media exports

What is the global influence of the UK's media exports?

- Since the London Design Festival started in 2003, over 80 cities around the world have started their own versions. This has stimulated home-grown creative designers and businesses, providing employment opportunities for many people.
- The UK architecture industry enjoys a global reputation for professionalism, integrity, design flair and delivery. UK architects are responsible for designing some of the world's leading sporting venues and facilities, such as the 2011 Cricket World Cup stadium in Pune, India.
- Approximately 100,000 students graduate annually in the UK in subjects such as architecture, design, music, fashion and digital media. Many are foreign students who return to their home countries to develop their own creative sectors.
- The UK is renowned for its production of computer games from *Tomb Raider* and *Harry Potter* to *Grand Theft Auto*. It has the largest games development sector in Europe, generating £2 billion in global sales each year. This creative output has stimulated the development of computer games in many other countries, such as the US, Japan and Asia. Serious Games International is a British games company that has recently opened offices in Singapore employing local people to develop its products for foreign markets.

> **Tip**
>
> You need to focus on how the UK's media exports has economic impacts around the world, for example by stimulating local industries.

▲ **Figure 14:** The German version of *The Office* is called *Stromberg*

▲ **Figure 15:** Peppa Pig

The story of Peppa Pig

One of the most successful UK media exports is *Peppa Pig* (Figure 15). Created by three friends in 2000, these five-minute cartoons featuring Peppa and her family and friends are now screened in more than 170 countries worldwide earning $US1 billion (£640 million). The character has been licensed by 600 companies worldwide, providing income and employment opportunities for thousands of people.

Peppa's pink smiling face has become a brand and can be seen on everything from sunglasses and crayons to wellington boots and tins of pasta! *Peppa Pig* is made by a team of 30 people at the Elf Factory in London.

The brand has recently broken into the extremely valuable US market which is eight times bigger than that of the UK. It could deliver merchandise sales of $1 billion in the first year alone through sales in US stores Toys 'R' Us and Walmart.

However, though popular, Peppa has sometimes been at the centre of controversy. In the first two series, her family did not wear seatbelts, and the show's heroine has been accused of encouraging children to behave badly by answering back and jumping in puddles. This has raised questions about the programme's suitability in some parts of the world!

Television programmes

One of the UK's most successful media exports is television programmes. In 2013–14 they accounted for over £1.28 billion a year of export earnings. The growth in international sales of UK television programmes has almost quadrupled since 2004. Among the most successful programmes to be exported in 2013/14 were *Atlantis*, *The Musketeers* and *Mr Selfridge*. Other popular exports include *Downton Abbey*, *Dr Who*, *Sherlock* and *Luther*.

The main markets are English-speaking countries such as the USA (47 per cent of the market), Australia and New Zealand. However, the Chinese market is now expanding rapidly, increasing by 40 per cent from the previous year to £17 million. Two of the most popular exports to China are *Sherlock* and *Downton Abbey*. There are other growing markets in South America, India and Scandinavia.

UK television programmes are popular abroad because of their originality and very high quality of production. Sales of programmes include the original broadcasts together with rights to remake (format) the programmes. Many programmes have been remade for a local audience. This provides opportunities for employment in the media sector involving both creative and technical work. *The Office*, for example, is shown in its original format in over 90 countries but has been licensed for remakes in eight countries including Chile. In Germany the programme has run for five seasons and a film was released in 2014.

Other successful television exports include:

- *Downton Abbey* which is broadcast in 250 countries including Russia, South Korea, Sweden and the Middle East and has a global audience of more than 160 million
- *Who Wants To Be a Millionaire*, Britain's most successful TV game show ever, with the format being exported to 107 countries including Indonesia, Algeria and Ecuador
- *Top Gear*, reportedly the most watched factual TV show in the world with a global audience of some 350 million people in 170 countries
- *The Great British Bake Off* which has been licensed by countries around the world including Austria, Ireland, Poland and Belgium
- *Come Dine With Me*, ITV's most successful export with local versions being made in 36 countries including India and Serbia
- *Undercover Boss*, a Channel 4 show which is broadcast throughout the world, with local formats being produced in 20 countries including the USA, Canada, Denmark and France
- *Broadchurch*, whose star David Tennant reprised his role as a detective in the US Fox remake, entitled *Gracepoint*.

Country	Sales 2013/14 (£m)	Percentage change, 2012–13/14
USA	523	+10%
Australia/ New Zealand	95	−10%
Canada	75	−5%
Sweden/Norway/ Denmark	68	+8%
France	37	+21%
Italy	35	+13%
Germany	31	+7%
China	17	+40%
Spain	16	−17%
Netherlands	16	+28%

▲ **Figure 16:** Top ten countries for exports of UK television programmes, 2013/14

Activities

1. Study Figure 16.
   a. Suggest reasons why sales of UK television programmes to the USA are so high.
   b. Why do you think China is experiencing a huge increase in sales?
   c. Suggest why costume dramas like *Downton Abbey* are so popular in China.
   d. Why do you think quiz programmes and reality programmes such as *The Great British Bake Off* are often remade rather than shown in their original form?
   e. The branding of products has become big business. Give some examples of how UK television programmes have become branded.
2. Select one of the UK television programmes referred to above. Conduct some research using the internet to discover more about its export to other countries. Which countries have bought the programme? What are the attractions of the programme for export?

✝ Geographical skills

Draw a flowline map to show the export of UK television programmes. A flowline map uses lines of different thickness to represent data. This way, some lines are thick and others thin. A flowline map is used to show movement from one place to another. It gives an instant impression of the differences in the data set. Figure 16 lists the top ten countries by sales of UK television programmes in 2013/14. To draw the flowline map follow the steps below.

- On an outline map of the world, use a colour to shade each of the countries listed in Figure 16.
- Use a different colour to shade the UK.
- Now use a pencil to draw arrows from the UK towards each of the countries listed in Figure 16. Use a single arrow for Australia/New Zealand and also for the Scandinavian countries Sweden, Norway and Denmark.
- You need to work out a scale to show the thickness of each arrow, for example, 10 mm = £100 million.
- Carefully draw an arrow from the UK to the USA.

- Now use your scale to draw a second line parallel to the first. To do this, use the scale and a ruler to mark a number of points (at least three) the exact distance away from the first line you have drawn. If you use a scale of 10 mm = £100 million, the distance between the lines will be 52 mm (£523 million).
- Join up the points and you should have a second line that is roughly parallel to the first. You now have a thick line and can draw an arrowhead pointing to the country of sales.
- Use a colour to shade your flowline.
- Repeat for the other countries but be careful. You may need to jiggle the flowlines on the map if certain areas become crowded. You just have to do your best to make the map look as accurate as you can.
- Complete the map by writing a title, naming the countries and writing a scale.

Depending on the size of your base map, you may need to tweak the suggested scale.

Figure 17: British actor Eddie Redmayne won the Oscar for best performance in 2015

Films

The UK film industry is a very important part of the UK's creative industries exports.

- In 2012, the UK film industry exported £1.3 billion worth of film services, of which £792 million came from royalties and £550 million from film production.
- Film exports were 71 per cent higher than those in 1995, when such data were first collected.
- In 2012, UK films achieved a 15 per cent share of the international box office, equivalent to over US$5.3 billion.
- The James Bond blockbuster *Skyfall* accounted for US$1.1 billion alone!
- In 2013, 66,000 people were employed in the UK film industry of whom 42,000 worked in film and video production. Employment is concentrated in London and the South East.
- The vast majority of companies directly involved with the UK film industry are small companies employing fewer than 10 people.

Most films produced today are international in terms of their funding, directing, acting and production so it is not always possible to identify a completely 'UK' film. The UK film industry enables the UK to show off its strengths in acting, scriptwriting, production, music and visual effects. For example, in 2014 the film *Gravity* won the Best Visual Effects Oscar for the London-based company Framestore.

Activities

1. Study Figure 18 which is a location map featured on the website of Pinewood Studios.
   a. Why is Pinewood an excellent location for an international film studio?
   b. Both Shepperton and Teddington are close to the River Thames. How might this location be an advantage for the film studios?
   c. Why do you think Soho has been identified on this map? You may need to use the internet to find the answer.
   d. Look at the aerial photo of Pinewood Studios in Figure 20. Suggest reasons why this is an excellent site for a film studio.
   e. Imagine that a film studio wished to locate in Central London. Suggest some advantages and disadvantages of choosing a site in the middle of London.

2. Study Figure 20. It shows some of the benefits to the UK economy of the British film industry. Draw a similar diagram to show how a local community might benefit from a film being set there, say in a country house, a village or an area of attractive countryside. Use the internet to find a central photo for your diagram.

→ Take it further

3. Use the internet to find out more about the work of the Oscar-winning company Framestore (www.framestore.com). Find out about the work that they do. What films have they been involved with? How do they support the UK economy by providing jobs? What other companies benefit by supplying Framestore with goods and services?

4. Do you think the government should continue to provide tax incentives to enable the UK to remain an attractive place for films to be made? Explain your answer.

Pinewood Studios

Pinewood Studios is a well-known British film company with its headquarters based in Buckinghamshire, just outside London (Figure 18). It has further studios elsewhere in the UK at Shepperton and Teddington, also in Canada and the Dominican Republic. Several box office hits have been made at Pinewood Studios including *Skyfall*, the *Harry Potter* series and the *Pirates of the Caribbean* films. The 2014 Oscar-winning film *Gravity* was also made at Pinewood Studios.

Pinewood Studios does not actually make films, instead concentrating on providing the sets and facilities for others to do so (Figure 19). The UK prides itself on offering first-class production services, diverse locations and outstanding acting talent. The government offers tax incentives to encourage outside investment into the UK.

Pinewood, along with other film studios in the UK, provides employment to thousands of people directly and tens of thousands of other people who supply goods and services (Figure 20). Sets have to be constructed and maintained, technical equipment needs operating, accommodation and hospitality need arranging and transport needs to be provided. Locations used for film making benefit hugely too. Hotels, restaurants and cafés provide accommodation and food and many local people benefit by offering support services.

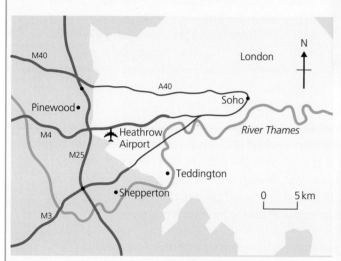

▲ **Figure 18:** Location of Pinewood Studios in the UK

▲ **Figure 19:** Modern set at Pinewood Studios

66,000 people employed directly by the British film industry

Construction workers and builders create and maintain sets

Global success of the film industry raises the status of the UK, encouraging tourism

Investment improves the quality of the local environment

Many small businesses and industries supply goods and materials to the film industry

Local services such as hotels, pubs and restaurants benefit by supplying accommodation, food and drink

Local services such as taxi drivers benefit from film companies making films in the UK

▲ **Figure 20:** Benefits to the UK economy of the British film industry

Case study: The contribution of ethnic groups to the cultural life of the UK through food

Contribution of ethnic groups to the cultural life of the UK

The UK is a multicultural country. It has a long tradition of welcoming migrants from all over the world. Take a walk in any large town or city and you will see evidence of the many ethnic groups that live and work together in the UK.

Look at Figure 21. It shows Green Street in the London borough of Newham. It is a multi-ethnic street with some 400 independent shops and market stalls owned and run by Indians, Pakistanis, Bangladeshis, Africans and Caribbeans.

Ethnic groups from all over the world have chosen to migrate to the UK, some in search of employment and others forced out from their homes by civil war or natural disasters. They have introduced aspects of their own cultures, such as music, food and fashion, and have contributed hugely to the economy and modern-day cultural landscape of the UK.

▲ **Figure 21:** Green Street, Newham: a multi-ethnic street in London

Tip

Make the most of your local town or city to provide you with examples of how different ethnic groups contribute to the cultural life of the UK.

'Today, the shop windows of Green Street are crammed with bright saris, bolts of shiny cloth and glittering high-carat gold jewellery. Indian music drifts through the air. Little squads of serious women shoppers halt to chat at street corners. Heels clatter in and out of stores decorated with posters for Asiana magazine.

On the pavement, you walk round battered cardboard boxes, marked "security checked": mangoes from Pakistan. The market stalls go big on the African and Caribbean trade: five different kinds of plantain, spinach-like callaloo and a mysterious Ugandan vegetable.'

Source: *The Guardian*, 30 August 2006

Ethnic food in the UK

While roast dinners may still be the most popular food in the UK, many people choose to enjoy a range of foods from different ethnic backgrounds. Consider pizzas, spaghetti and pasta from Italy, chicken tikka masala from India, kebabs from the Middle East and spring rolls from China. When did you last have an Indian or Chinese meal? What did you eat?

The Balti Triangle, Birmingham

Birmingham is one of the most multicultural cities in the UK. Some 30 per cent of its population come from ethnic minority groups, mainly from Pakistan, India and the Caribbean. The ethnic food retail sector is very important in Birmingham and one of the best-known areas specialising in food is the so-called Balti Triangle in the south of the city. Here there is a cluster of some 50 restaurants serving balti dishes – combinations of meat and/or vegetables cooked with particular spices (Figure 22).

Balti was largely developed in Birmingham in the 1970s by people who had migrated from Kashmir, now a disputed region located within both Pakistan and India.

The Balti Triangle is an important tourist attraction. Apart from the restaurants, there are many shops offering cooking utensils, clothing such as saris and kaftans, jewellery and Asian arts and crafts (Figure 23).

▲ **Figure 22:** Cooking a traditional balti dish

▲ **Figure 23:** Shops in the Balti Triangle, Birmingham

Activities

1. Study Figure 21.
   a. What is the evidence that Green Street is a multicultural street?
   b. What are the advantages of living in a multicultural community such as Green Street?
   c. Is there a multicultural street in your local town or near to your school? Describe its characteristics. Does it have a range of shops and restaurants? Does it have a street market?

2. Study Figure 23 which shows a street in the Balti Triangle in Birmingham.
   a. Describe the different shops and try to identify what they are selling.
   b. One of the shops sells Halal food. What does 'Halal' mean?
   c. What do you think the first-floor rooms above the shops are used for?

→ Take it further

3. Make a detailed case study of Birmingham's Balti Triangle. Present your study as an information poster or Powerpoint presentation. You will find several sites on the internet, including one dedicated to the area at www.balti-birmingham.co.uk.
   ● Find out more about balti dishes and what makes them special.
   ● The migrants who developed balti came from Kashmir. Find a map to show the location of Kashmir.
   ● Can you find out why people migrated to the UK from Kashmir?
   ● Where is the Balti Triangle in Birmingham? Find a map to show its location in the city.
   ● What makes the Balti Triangle special? What other shops and services are offered in the area?
   ● Illustrate your study with some photos.

👣 Fieldwork ideas

Conduct a survey in your local town or shopping centre to investigate ethnic foods. Locate shops and restaurants that sell ethnic food and plot their location on a map. Take photos to annotate.

Practice questions

Figure 3 on page 199 shows the relief of the UK and Figure 7 on page 202 shows population density in the UK. Refer to both maps in answering questions 1 and 2.

1. Which statement about the relief of the UK is correct?
   a) Most highlands are in the south of the UK.
   b) There are no highlands in Scotland.
   c) Most lowlands are in the south and east of the UK.
   d) Most highlands are in Northern Ireland. **[1 mark]**

2. Which statement below correctly describes the pattern of population?
   a) Lowest population density is in the south of the UK.
   b) Lowest population density is in the highlands.
   c) Lowest population density is in England.
   d) Lowest population density is in the lowlands. **[1 mark]**

3. Water stress exists in the UK because most rain falls in the north and west but most demand is in the south and east. Assess the advantages and disadvantages of constructing new reservoirs in the southeast of the UK. **[4 marks]**

4. Explain the formation of relief rainfall. **[4 marks]**

5. The graph below shows UK house building from 1970–71 to 2010–11.

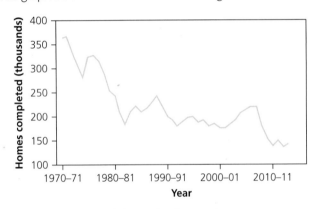

   a) Describe the trend shown by the graph. **[2 marks]**
   b) How many houses were built in 2007–08? **[1 mark]**
   c) In 2007 the government set a target of building 240,000 homes a year by 2016. Use evidence from the graph to suggest if this target seems likely to be achieved. **[4 marks]**

6. A student has population data grouped by age and sex for a country in Africa. Select the most appropriate form of data presentation to display this data.
   a) Pie chart   c) Bar graph
   b) Population pyramid   d) Line graph **[1 mark]**

7. Assess the UK government's responses to the challenges of an ageing population. **[6 marks]**

8. Figure 38 on page 217 shows employment in selected industries in the UK.
   a) Which employment sector showed the most growth (2001–13)? **[1 mark]**
   b) Suggest reasons why this sector grew so much. **[4 marks]**
   c) Assess why the UK manufacturing sector witnessed a significant decline in employment (2001–13). **[4 marks]**

9. Case study – an economic hub in the UK.
   Assess the importance of locational factors for a UK economic hub. **[6 marks]**

10. Case study – the UK's political role in one global conflict.
    Evaluate the success of the UK's involvement in one global conflict. **[6 marks]**

Tip

For multiple choice questions such as questions 1 and 2, work through the options eliminating those that are **incorrect**. You are more likely to choose the correct answer if you approach it like this.

Tip

Look at question 3. Make sure you consider both advantages and disadvantages equally.

Tip

For question 4, consider using an annotated diagram to support your answer.

Tip

For question 5a), describe the overall pattern using some data to support your points.

Tip

For question 7, consider a range of responses and comment on how useful and appropriate the responses have been.

Tip

Make the most of your case study knowledge by referring to specific information and using facts and figures where possible.

Resource Reliance

Chapter 15: Will we run out of natural resources?

By the end of this chapter, you will know the answers to this key question:

→ How has increasing demand for resources affected our planet?

Chapter 16: Can we feed nine billion people by 2050?

By the end of this chapter, you will know the answers to these key questions:

→ What does it mean to be food secure?

→ How can countries ensure their food security?

→ Case study: How is the UK trying to ensure its food security?

→ How sustainable are these strategies?

Refugees in the Shousha refugee camp in Tunisia, waiting for food distribution. How might our use of resources affect all of our futures?

CHAPTER

15

Will we run out of natural resources?

How has increasing demand for resources affected our planet?

➜ In this section you will:

- ➜ learn about what natural resources are
- ➜ consider how access to resources of food, energy and water has changed over time
- ➜ explore why the demand for resources has changed over time
- ➜ consider what the environmental impact is of the increasing demand for resources
- ➜ understand how mechanisation has affected the environment
- ➜ explore how humans modify ecosystems to meet demands for food, energy and water.

What is resource reliance?

Our planet is rich in resources and materials that are vital for promoting life. Since the very first humans walked the Earth, we have found ways to manipulate and use these resources to make our lives easier, healthier, more comfortable, and to make an income. Humans are now able to use technology to adapt to any environment in order to survive, but the result is that we are entirely dependent upon exploiting resources. We use more now because we can; infrastructure and technology empowers us to be more demanding.

How has access to resources changed over time?

World **consumption** (use) of resources has increased rapidly over time, whether for food, water or energy. Our ability to access resources has changed largely due to technological change. In the past, our access was limited by primitive tools: humans were restricted by how deep we could dig, how heavy the materials could be, how far we could transport them, and the technological processes required. Nowadays we can:

- grow foods that require less water
- irrigate fields from hundreds of miles away
- transport materials across the world
- dig deeper and in more difficult conditions than ever.

The resources of our planet have become more accessible and so we are able to exploit them more easily. As a result, humans are overusing many resources (see Figure 1) and as our population grows, technology improves and our desires increase; this is likely to continue.

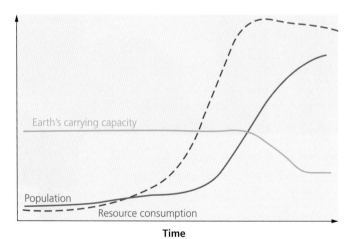

▲ **Figure 1:** Resource consumption exceeds Earth's ability to provide

Earth has a biological **carrying capacity** (a maximum number of species that can be supported) which depends upon population size, resource availability and demand. As technology improves, this carrying capacity can increase. For example, due to technology, humans can now:

- live in space-saving, high-density, high-rise buildings
- use processed foods and synthetic materials
- create genetically modified plants and animals to be more productive
- extract the most remote resources across the globe.

As a result our planet can support more human life.

However, this carrying capacity does have a limit and as population rises and our desires demand more resources, these resources will eventually run out. Consumption of resources is unequally distributed, with the developed world consuming about 75 per cent, despite having a smaller fraction of world population. But this pattern is changing as wealth increases in EDCs and LIDCs. If the entire world consumed resources at the same rate as a typical middle-class European, the Earth would only be able to support 3 billion people sustainably. If, however, we only consumed what we need for a healthy and comfortable lifestyle, this figure would rise to 30 billion people!

Why has demand for resources changed over time?

Increasing global population

One of the main reasons why demand for resources has increased over time is because global populations have increased.

- Until the 1800s world population was steadily below 1 billion.
- Then a gradual increase began, reaching 2 billion in 1927.
- In the twentieth century, the population explosion set in; it took just 84 years to reach 7 billion. In July 2015, the global population was estimated at 7.3 billion.
- We have an average growth now of a billion people every 12 years.

Clearly, more people means more demand for resources of food, water, energy, shelter, space, jobs and so on.

Increasing consumption

It is not just population size that is important. It is also our changing aspirations that drive demand for resources. As global income increases, so does demand for more varied food, bigger housing, more luxuries and more travelling. All of this relies on resources. It is our rapid consumption that damages our life-support system; it is not the actual number of people expanding that is the biggest issue. While both population and consumption are multiplying, it is *consumption* that multiplies fastest.

As shown in Figure 2, consumption of food, water, energy and natural resources spirals rapidly as population and income increase, while at the same time global resources decline, so that access of resources per person also declines.

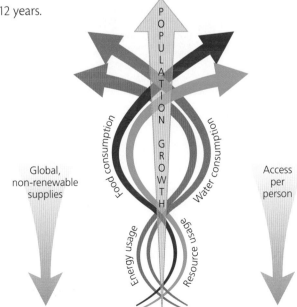

▲ **Figure 2:** The spiral of consumption

Changing technology and employment

Population growth and resource use is also driven by changing technology. Due to the Industrial Revolution in the late eighteenth and early nineteenth centuries, people earned more money through using machinery and new resources, and could therefore afford better food and live longer.

Over the twentieth and twenty-first centuries, global employment has changed with more people now working in secondary or tertiary jobs. A change in resources is, therefore, needed. New technology, such as electronics or robotics, means demand for new resources increases and with more mobile devices in the world than people, there is increased use of finite minerals. Global food and industrial manufacturing has had to increase in order to satisfy demand, which uses more resources.

As technology improves and populations grow, there is a need for people to access more remote locations (Figure 3). This increases access to resources, but also increases demand for construction materials or transportation, which accounts now for over 40 per cent of all energy used worldwide.

New technology such as **fracking** or **green energy** has increased our ability to use global resources more efficiently. The growth of the use of renewable resources can also help increase the carrying capacity to support bigger populations and bigger demand. However, raw materials are in decline. Non-renewable sources such as minerals, fossil fuels and metals cannot be replaced as quickly as they are consumed. With growth of EDCs worldwide and improving incomes in LIDCs along with population growth, there is a risk that resources will run out.

▲ **Figure 3:** Increased infrastructure to remote locations

Activities

1. Describe what is meant by the population explosion.
2. Explain why access per person to resources will decrease over time.
3. Study Figure 3. Suggest how an increase of infrastructure here might have an impact on natural resources.
4. How does industrialisation lead to increased resource use?
5. Suggest how new technologies might make access to resources easier in future.

→ Take it further

6. Think about the Millennium Development Goals (Chapter 12, page 188). How many nations have met Target 1?

Feeding the world: our increasing need

As global populations increase and incomes increase, there is a rapidly rising demand for food resources worldwide. Figure 4 shows an increase in food demand over time, with a link between global wealth and demand for food. By 2030 the world economy may have doubled and the population may have risen beyond 8 billion. Nations such as China and India that have a quarter of the world's population between them and steadily improving incomes will struggle to feed their populations adequately.

Figure 5 shows the pattern of world hunger and how it has changed over time, with the majority of undernourished people in Africa and Asia; this is in line with the highest population growth. There is currently enough food to feed the whole world, yet over 795 million people are still undernourished. Demand for food is rising while supply to the right places is not keeping pace, and food security is an issue (see Chapter 16).

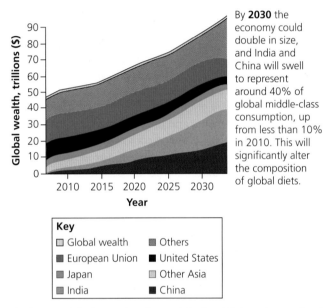

By **2030** the economy could double in size, and India and China will swell to represent around 40% of global middle-class consumption, up from less than 10% in 2010. This will significantly alter the composition of global diets.

Key
- ☐ Global wealth
- ◼ European Union
- ◼ Japan
- ◼ India
- ◼ Others
- ◼ United States
- ☐ Other Asia
- ◼ China

▲ **Figure 4:** The increasing demand for food links to increasing wealth

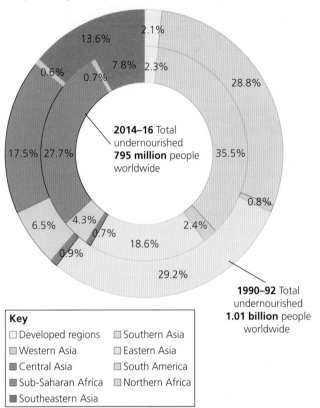

Key
- ☐ Developed regions
- ◼ Western Asia
- ◼ Central Asia
- ◼ Sub-Saharan Africa
- ◼ Southeastern Asia
- ◼ Southern Asia
- ☐ Eastern Asia
- ☐ South America
- ☐ Northern Africa

▲ **Figure 5:** Distribution of hunger in the world: proportion of undernourished people by region, 1990–92 and 2014–16

Activities

1. Study Figure 4. Describe the trend of global wealth over time.
2. Study Figure 5. Compare the patterns of data for 1990–92 and 2014–16. How has the pattern changed?
3. Why might the proportion of hungry people in southern Asia increase?

→ Take it further

4. Use the United Nations FAO website to find the most up-to-date statistics on world food. How has the pattern changed compared with Figure 5? Are the same places still hungry?
5. Where does the food you eat come from? Calculate your food miles and decide whether this is sustainable.

Why can we not meet modern demands for food?

There are various factors that contribute to challenging food security. These are explored in pages 244–245.

Population growth

- Since 1950 the world population has been in a state of exponential growth. It is projected we will reach 9 billion people by 2050. This means more mouths to feed.
- Currently one in seven people goes to sleep hungry and 25,000 people die from hunger-related disease every day.
- There is then more pressure on land to produce food, which can lead to over-use.
- If demand for food is high due to population rise, then prices can also rise – making it more difficult for those in poverty to feed themselves.
- In Africa and southern Asia, the price of food can take 55 per cent of your income; in Europe and North America it takes 22 per cent.

Climate change

- Climate change and global warming (see Chapter 3) involve cycles and seasons, which can affect farming.
- Global levels of precipitation are changing, and the influence of extreme weather like La Niña and El Niño is hard to predict (see Chapter 1). In 2015, El Niño caused monsoon rains to fail and Indonesia suffered massive grass and forest fires, while La Niña brought excessive rain to South America which damaged palm oil, wheat, coffee and sugar.
- Cases of floods or droughts are increasing, and regions that were once fertile either have to change their crops or go out of business.
- Temperature change influences what can grow; for example, the Champagne region in France is becoming too hot and arid to grow the required grapes, while southern England can now produce more wine than was possible before.
- Weather changes also influence how pests can spread.
- Unreliable rainfall forces more reliance on irrigation.

Land and water degradation

- Intensive farming practices can lead to soil exhaustion, with nutrients and fertility in decline; fields become less productive.
- Traditional fallow (rest) periods for fields have been lost due to increased demand, so soils cannot recover.
- Leaching of nutrients from soils can lead to the formation of toxic 'iron pans' and poison water.
- Over-fishing has led to fish stocks declining worldwide.
- Commercial shipping increases water pollution; over-fishing and the use of trawler nets can damage aquatic ecosystems and change food webs.
- Water degradation also reduces absorption of carbon dioxide, which contributes to global warming and loss of species.

Global water crisis

- The water levels of many nations such as China, Egypt, India and the USA have been in decline for decades due to over-extraction and poor river management. Water deficits will affect agriculture.
- Sub-Saharan Africa has the most water-stressed nations, with over 300 million people here at risk. These areas also rely on agriculture and export food globally.
- Constant irrigation of land in previously arid places (such as Chinese deserts and eastern Africa) has drained groundwater supplies, leading to desertification.

Politics

- Many nations in the world have surplus food 'mountains' while others starve. Ethiopia and other LIDCs are global food producers and yet go hungry.
- Governments and multinational companies can set prices, fix quotas and control trade for better or worse.
- Governments can choose to tax foods as 'luxuries' which makes it harder for people to afford them (like fruit juice and bottled water in the UK).
- Multinational farming companies can restrict small-scale farmers' incomes by buying the best land, irrigation and fertilisers.
- Governments could support farming better so that nations became less reliant on imports. In the UK, more and more farmers are quitting farming because their income is not protected, which means we rely on foreign imports instead of making the food ourselves.

Natural disasters

- Many of the world's prime agricultural regions, such as those in southern Asia and Africa, are also hazard zones either from natural tectonic and climatic risk or human-induced risk through conflict.
- Disasters damage critical infrastructure or reduce transportation.
- Agricultural income forms over 30 per cent of the national GDP in locations such as Ethiopia, Mali and Nepal and yet these regions are also at risk of earthquake, flood, storms or drought.
- In the last decade, an estimated US$30 billion of damages was due to hazards, of which 82 per cent was from floods or drought.
- An estimated 11 million livestock and 5 million fish were lost in 2003–13 due to hazards; this is enough to feed over a billion people.

Our changing diet

We want to eat more and have more variety. Our diet has changed to include more meat and more luxurious foods all year round. The increase in meat consumption means that more cereals and grains have to be produced to feed livestock. This also consumes more water.

Random fact!

Insects are one of the most efficient foods to eat. Around 80 per cent of a cricket can be eaten, compared with only 40 per cent of a cow or pig.

Agricultural diseases

- Weather changes influence how diseases and pests spread. Warm, wet conditions are ideal for breeding tsetse flies and spreading livestock disease. Excessive rain also causes fungal and bacterial diseases in plants.
- Temperature changes allow migration of pests, insects and bacteria to new locations.
- Many dramatic diseases have scarred agriculture; BSE ('mad cow disease'), for example, led to 4.5 million cows being destroyed in the UK and a ban on the sale of UK beef abroad. Bananas are at risk of extinction from the Panama fungus.
- With our reliance on a smaller number of species, and from a smaller number of places, we are at risk of sudden shocks if disease strikes.
- Each year, sixteen per cent of world crops are lost to disease, often in LIDC producer nations.

Fossil fuel reliance

- You may not think it, but fossil fuels play a big part in the food production system. Not only for transporting goods to consumers, but also as part of the growth of food.
- Chemical fertilisers, pesticides and herbicides are developed from fossil fuels; since we need to produce more food, this also means using more fossil fuels.
- Agriculture relies heavily on petroleum-based products, which then creates more CO_2 and can link to human-enhanced global warming. These products are also expensive.
- Small-scale subsistence farmers who cannot afford chemicals (which are increasingly needed as soils erode) cannot produce as much food or re-nourish soils, leading to more degradation.

Loss of biodiversity

- In the period between the 1930s and the 1960s, the developed world experienced the 'Green Revolution', with new technology and genetic engineering being introduced to improve agricultural productivity. The increase in GM (genetically modified) foods made it more common for farmers to use engineered or hybrid strains with the result that other strains went into decline.
- Biodiversity is declining, with many older species being lost each year. Around 90 per cent of the world's food is generated from just 15 plant and eight animal species. Of the roughly 300,000 edible plant species worldwide, we rely on just three (maize, wheat and rice).
- More than 90 per cent of crop varieties have been lost from farms, along with half of our domestic animals.
- Being increasingly reliant on a smaller number of species is risky; not only is there less balance to the ecosystem, but there is vulnerability to sudden shocks.

Land use changes

- Traditionally nations used to feed themselves, and primary industries like fishing and farming dominated. With industrialisation, land use has changed to accommodate more factories and new businesses. Growing populations also need housing, and the growth of tertiary and quaternary jobs has spread into rural areas. There has therefore been a loss of agricultural land as nations urbanise.
- Land which is left is then marginalised, facing over-cultivation, soil exhaustion and contamination.
- The price of quality agricultural land has risen sharply. In the UK, prices have risen more rapidly than London house prices. The most expensive land is in Dorset, with the least expensive in the Scottish Highlands. This price change is also due to scarcity; there is less land available, so prices rise.
- Land is now used for investment, new housing, transportation and industry. This places pressure on fragile ecosystems elsewhere to provide enough food on less land.

Tip

Making relational links between factors is a high-level skill. Identify and explain relationships between multiple factors to outline the challenge for food, water and energy consumption.

Activities

1. Which issue do you think is most to blame for why food demands are not met? Explain your choice.

A watery planet but not enough to drink?

Earth contains over a billion trillion litres of water. In fact, around 70 per cent of our planet is liquid, but very little of this is safe to drink. Most water on Earth is saline (salty) and the remaining fresh water is often trapped or inaccessible, locked in ice caps or deep underground in groundwater (Figure 6). Just 2.5 per cent of the world's water is fresh water and, of this, only a fraction is at the surface and usable. Nearly 2 million people die each year from a lack of safe drinking water.

Water is used in different forms:

- **blue water** is fresh water from rivers, lakes, seas and groundwater
- **green water** is from precipitation
- **grey water** is polluted or recycled water.

If the volume of polluted grey water increases, then it places more demand on blue water to refresh and clean our water systems. However, using recycled water (for example, for irrigating crops or watering gardens) helps to reduce stress on blue water sources.

We often think about water just in terms of its visible use for drinking and cooking, yet almost everything relies upon water at some point, from producing metal for cars, to generating electricity, to processing paper, etc. It is our hidden 'virtual use' of water that is difficult to judge.

> ### Fact
> Water-related diseases are still some of the world's biggest killers. One child dies every 17 seconds from diarrhoea caused by dirty drinking water.

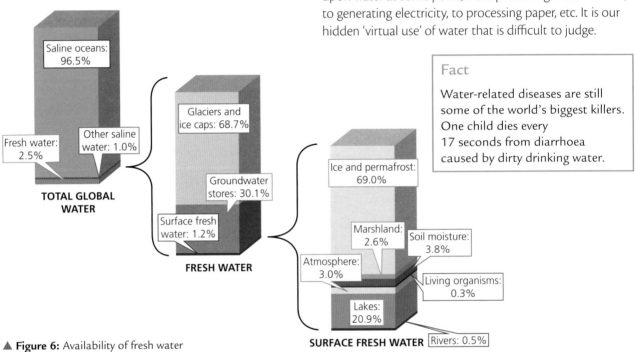

▲ **Figure 6:** Availability of fresh water

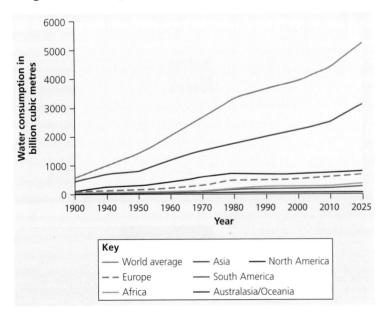

▲ **Figure 7a:** Water consumption worldwide, 1900–2025

Activities

1. Study Figure 6. Describe the different ways that water is stored on Earth.
2. Analyse Figure 7a. How has water use changed over time?
3. Describe the pattern shown in Figure 8. Which parts of the world have most water scarcity? Suggest reasons why.
4. How much more water does it take to produce meat than wheat? Calculate how much bread or meat you consume each week; then work out how much water this takes.
5. Look back at Chapter 12 and Ethiopia. Describe how economic water scarcity here can affect the country's ability to escape poverty.

Why can't we supply enough water to meet global needs?

Rising population

As with food consumption, water consumption increases over time and with population size. Fresh water demands have tripled in the last 50 years (Figure 7a) and this is largely due to population growth along with changing lifestyles and eating habits. Figure 7b shows the pattern of water use across the world; there is generally a link between high populations and water consumption. However, it is not just a matter of population size, since both India and China use less water than the USA, Brazil or Spain.

The global average water footprint per person is 1385 m³ per year (1 m³ = 1000 litres), which is about 3794 litres per day. Over half of this is used for oily crops, meat production or industrial processes.

Water consumption varies by region with the USA using over 7800 litres per capita per day, while China uses just 2900 litres.

Many LIDCs and EDCs have higher than average water footprints; for example Chad, in Africa, has the same consumption as Sweden. This is largely because they are major food producers so they need water for agriculture. However, their populations lack the water to meet basic needs for health and income, and suffer from **water scarcity** (see Figure 8).

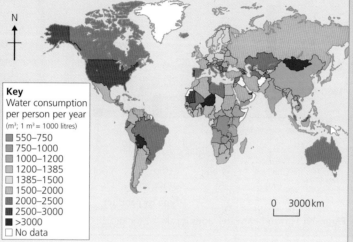

Key
Water consumption per person per year
(m³; 1 m³ = 1000 litres)
- 550–750
- 750–1000
- 1000–1200
- 1200–1385
- 1385–1500
- 1500–2000
- 2000–2500
- 2500–3000
- >3000
- No data

0 3000 km

▲ **Figure 7b:** Water consumption worldwide (per person, per year)

Industry and agriculture

Industrial change contributes to increasing use of water. Manufacturing and commerce all require water; as nations become more industrialised, they require more water. But agriculture is still the biggest user across the world, taking 70 per cent of all fresh water and up to 80 per cent of LIDC water supplies. Industry uses 20 per cent of all world water, with only 10 per cent used for domestic water supply.

Economic reasons

Much of Africa is unable to afford reliable access to quality fresh water, even though this is a basic human right and a Sustainable Development Goal (a set of goals produced by world leaders in 2015, see Chapter 12, page 188). The water received is often of a poor standard, and most is used for agriculture and industry rather than private use.

Lack of rainfall

Precipitation is not evenly spread across the world, and much water received is lost in evaporation and run-off. Many of our biggest food producers are in semi-arid or water-stressed regions. Of any precipitation in Africa, up to 80 per cent is evaporated, which means there is a lack of water per person for crops, drinking and soil replenishment.

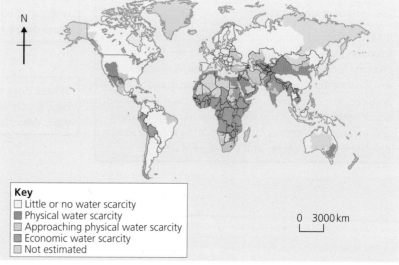

Key
- Little or no water scarcity
- Physical water scarcity
- Approaching physical water scarcity
- Economic water scarcity
- Not estimated

0 3000 km

▲ **Figure 8:** Many countries suffer from water scarcity

Use of water to produce food and goods

It may surprise you how much water is used for everyday processes (see Figure 9). Our changing diet has increased water use because of more demand for meat. You can save more water by not eating a kilogram of meat than you could by not showering for six months! The growth of coffee plants and the production of coffee to drink uses 120 billion m³ of water per year; this is 65 times as much water as flows out of the River Thames every year. So as our diet changes, and population and income grow, more people demand higher-value foods, and so our water use increases too.

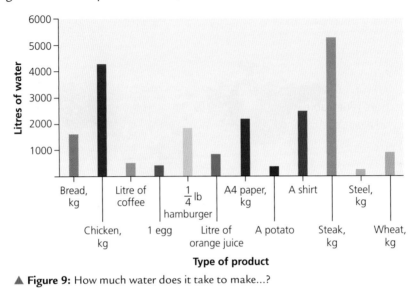

▲ **Figure 9:** How much water does it take to make...?

Climate change

Climate change and global warming have also been blamed for a lack of fresh water worldwide. The decline in mountain glaciers and the collapse of polar ice caps lead to excessive fresh water melt. This water then flows into the sea and becomes saline. Combined with a decrease in snowfall, this means glaciers are not being sustained and so fresh water supplies decline.

Generating electricity

It takes water to make electricity. Thermoelectric sources (such as coal, gas, nuclear) are the fastest growing users of fresh water worldwide. Any water which is wasted here is then contaminated and polluted, returning to the hydrological cycle as grey water or water that is unsafe to drink. As populations and income rise, and as industrialisation spreads, so does demand for energy and therefore water.

Did you know?

A typical British person uses 150 litres of water per day directly (for showers, drinking, etc.). This rises to 3400 litres per day when indirect use (for transport, food and other products and industrial processes) is also considered.

Websites

Use www.worldometers.info to see how much food, water and energy has been used this year. How many years do we have left of our resources?

Where does the food you eat come from? Calculate how much water you use directly each day and each year. What is your water footprint?

Running on empty: are we running out of energy?

We are using more energy supplies than ever before. North America, Europe and Asia lead the world in energy use.

Much of our energy comes from **fossil fuels** such as coal, gas and oil. These are formed from broken down plants and animals that died a very long time ago. They are **non-renewable**, which means there is a finite supply. Based on known reserves and our current use, we may run out of oil by 2055! We are beginning to use more **renewable** sources, which we can use again and again, such as solar radiation, wind power, hydropower (from waves, tides and rivers), geothermal heat and biomass (organic material such as wood or peat). However, we are still heavily reliant on non-renewable energy resources (see Figure 10).

Our use of coal, oil and natural gas is increasing fastest. Along with a growing population and increased industrial need, this is likely to rise still further. We still have plenty of coal left, however its use is restricted by pollution control measures with the aim of reducing the levels of greenhouse gases, CO_2 and SO_2, in the atmosphere. There needs to be more focus on renewable energy sources, not just because we are running out of options, but because we need to reduce water use and emissions.

How has demand for energy changed over time?

Global energy demands have increased in line with population growth. Energy is required to fuel our lifestyles, our industries and our food. The average energy consumption per person has increased 10 per cent since 2000. This demand is set to rise, particularly rapidly in EDCs and LICDs.

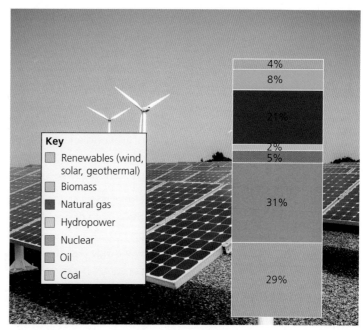

Key
- Renewables (wind, solar, geothermal)
- Biomass
- Natural gas
- Hydropower
- Nuclear
- Oil
- Coal

4%
8%
21%
2%
5%
31%
29%

▲ **Figure 10:** Types of energy used worldwide

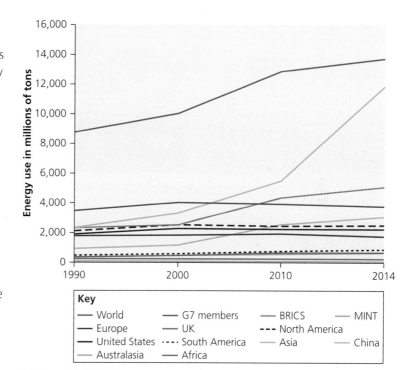

Key
— World — G7 members — BRICS — MINT
— Europe — UK --- North America
— United States ···· South America — Asia — China
— Australasia — Africa

▲ **Figure 11:** World energy consumption

Figure 11 shows how energy consumption has changed in different regions of the world over time. ACs have remained steady in their energy consumption, while Asian countries and the **BRICS** (Brazil, Russia, India, China and South Africa) have increased their use very rapidly due to their recent industrialisation. Generally, energy use increases with wealth. The highest consumption per person is in the USA, while the lowest is in Bangladesh. Europe consumes 23 per cent of the world's energy but has just ten per cent of the world's population.

Energy is used across the globe for electricity, transport, industrial manufacture and domestic heating. As more nations becomes industrialised, and as incomes increase, there is an ever-increasing demand for fuel for energy. At least 27 per cent of all energy generated each year is wasted and lost during production and transport. Use of renewable sources has begun to increase recently, but they still remain less efficient as energy sources than fossil fuels, and the systems can be very costly to set up. Hydroelectric power only accounts for six per cent of all world energy, despite Earth being a watery planet. Geothermal energy, which contributes 95 per cent of Iceland's heating and electricity, is only two per cent globally.

Use of energy in Asia has grown most rapidly in recent years, particularly with the growth of populations in China and India and with increased manufacturing, agriculture and infrastructure here. Asia has now become the biggest consumer worldwide (Figure 12). China has replaced the USA as the largest national consumer, however, per person, China still consumes less than the USA.

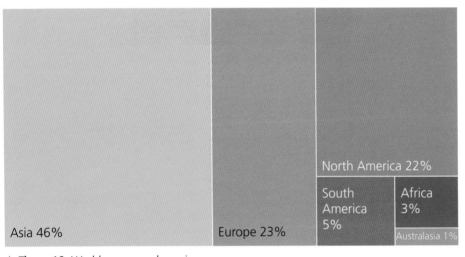

▲ **Figure 12:** World energy use by region per year

Energy is expensive: 15 per cent of the entire world's GDP is spent on energy sources. There are inequalities between nations that have reliable electricity and power and those that do not; there can even be variation within nations. The increase in energy demand leads to more use of fresh water, as seen earlier in the chapter, which is also increasingly expensive and environmentally difficult for developing nations.

Activities

1. Study Figure 10. What proportion of energy is based on fossil fuels?
2. Analyse Figure 11. Describe how energy consumption in Asia has changed over time. Compare this to the trend for China.
3. Suggest reasons why human energy use has increased most rapidly since 1950.
4. Suggest some of the potential impacts of increased energy use on the environment. Compare the impact of renewable and non-renewable fuels.
5. Energy consumption in ACs has declined in recent years. Suggest reasons why this might have occurred. Try researching 'Agenda 21', 'sustainable development' and 'energy efficiency'.

➜ Take it further

6. Research the BRICS and MINT nations. What do these nations have in common? How have they contributed to world energy demands? Try to link development data such as population growth and GDP per capita to energy use.

What is the impact on our planet of increasing demand for resources?

It is not possible to use natural resources for food, water and energy on such a large scale without there being a dramatic impact on ecosystems and environments. In order to feed, water and fuel a growing world, landscapes have been changed drastically. However, with improving technology this can be minimised and managed.

> ### Fact
>
> 1 Tw (Terawatt) is enough to power 10 billion light bulbs. The world uses 15 Tw per year.

The cost of feeding a growing population

Mechanisation of farming

Over time, farming practices have changed dramatically. Traditional subsistence agriculture that relied upon human and animal manual labour (through ploughing, weeding, sowing and watering) has become largely industrialised through changing technology (see Figure 13). This **mechanisation** has led to the introduction of large-scale farming and the use of tractors, combine harvesters, mechanical ploughs, motor vehicle transport (for importing materials like fertilisers and exporting goods) and even aircraft and satellite technology.

▲ **Figure 13:** How farming has changed

How are ecosystems and the environment affected?

Some of the implications of modern farming are shown in Figure 14.

- In order to house machinery and produce food on a large scale, farms have increased in size. This has led to the destruction of hedgerows, which affects the small mammals which live there and the food webs they are part of.
- Farming is now a year-round process with consumers wanting produce out of season. As a result, fields are not given time to recover. The traditional farming practice of 'fallowing' allowed fields to recover nutrients. This is no longer an option, particularly in LIDCs, and as a result soils become exhausted.
- The increase in use of chemical fertilisers and pesticides not only costs farmers but can also cause problems for local water supplies if **eutrophication** occurs where chemicals wash into water.

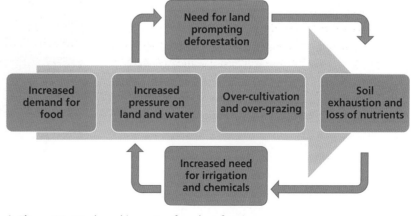

▲ **Figure 14:** Needs and impacts of modern farming

Deforestation

In many parts of the world, forests have been cleared to make the land available for other uses. This process, where trees are cut down without any intention of replacing them, is called **deforestation**. Trees can be cleared for mining (see page 254) or for the creation of new roads and transport links. In places such as South America and Asia, however, trees are often cut down to develop grazing land for livestock or for plantations where palm oil, sugar or wheat can be grown.

How are ecosystems and the environment affected?

One major consequence of deforestation is that the world loses the carbon storage of trees that helps to combat the rise in greenhouse gases (see page 51). Deforestation also influences local ecosystems in a number of other, more direct ways.

- Tree roots store water and nutrients and bind soils together.
  - The loss of trees leads to leaching of soils, increased surface run-off and soil erosion, all of which reduce agricultural productivity.
  - Tree loss increases the risk of floods and landslides.
- One deforestation practice called 'slash and burn' involves trees being cropped and then burnt to clear the land (see Chapter 7, page 108). In Indonesia, this process led to the world's largest ever wildfires in 2015 with over 5000 km² ablaze. More carbon dioxide was released during the burning than was emitted by the entire USA in a year! Indonesia has particularly high greenhouse gas emissions not because of industry or personal consumption, but because of agricultural practices and deforestation.
- There is also damage to local habitats and food chains.

Commercial fishing

Commercial fishing has increased throughout the twentieth and twenty-first centuries, with over 1 billion people relying on fish for their primary food source. Commercial fishing utilises large trawlers rather than small boats, with thermal sensors and digital imagery helping workers to identify where fish stocks are located.

How are ecosystems and the environment affected?

Commercial fishing techniques have led to over-fishing of popular species such as cod and the accidental death of other, unplanned species (such as dolphins caught by mistake in large nets meant for tuna, or coral reefs being

▲ **Figure 15:** Deforestation and wildfires in Indonesia

snagged by deep trawlers). The average fish catch has been declining for ten years; tuna and cod are particularly threatened. This means fishing boats have to travel further, as stocks migrate away. As a result, they use more diesel fuel, causing water pollution and an increase in the use of fossil fuels.

Meeting our thirst: how is water provided?

Fresh water supplies are limited and water extraction is increasing. The impact of irrigation for agriculture or water extraction for use in industry has seen many areas of the world become dry as groundwater stores deplete.

As stores deplete, this can lead to desertification where arid areas become even drier. This has been seen in places such as Lake Chad or the Aral Sea due to excessive water

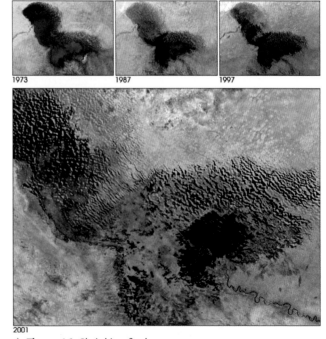

▲ **Figure 16:** Shrinking fresh water

extraction. Figure 16 shows the situation in Lake Chad, where the lake has shrunk due to climate change, over-grazing, deforestation and desertification. As with food consumption, the matter is a political and economic issue: populations need to be able to afford fresh water, but multinational companies or large-scale farms often dominate and price out local residents.

You might think that the solution is to use seawater; we have plenty of that. Unfortunately, the process of desalinating the seawater to remove the salt, leaving it pure enough to drink and use, is very expensive. It also creates lots of toxic brine which must then be removed; this in turn requires energy and water!

Since water supply is unequally spread across the world, one possible solution involves the transfer of water from a region where there is plenty to a region without. There are various examples of water transfer schemes throughout the globe, such as the Chinese South–North Water Transfer Project covered in Chapter 11. The UK is another region that has required water transfers. In 2012 southern England faced a severe drought after two dry winters. The incidence of drought in the UK is increasing, which leads to water shortages in high population areas in the south.

- One example of a successful UK water transfer scheme is the transfer from Norfolk's River Ely Ouse to the River Stour in Essex. This has been running since 1972 but was expanded in 2014 by enlarging the Abberton reservoir. Tunnels and pipes bring water to the reservoir from Norfolk's excess in order to supply 400 million litres of water per day to Essex, one of the driest counties in the UK and home to a high-density population.
- Similarly, the Elan Valley water transfer has been successfully supplying Birmingham with water from 100 miles away in Wales via the Craig Goch dam and reservoir. This provides 160 million litres of water per day. This scheme is to be expanded and may one day even supply the River Thames and London.

Currently around 40 per cent of all blue water abstraction in the UK is for domestic use, 40 per cent is for energy, 20 per cent is for industry and just one per cent is for agriculture (quite a different pattern to the world average seen on page 246). We spend £82 million a year on irrigation and water transport to industry.

How are ecosystems influenced by water provision schemes?

The transfer of water from one region to another does have a potential implication for local ecology since the chemistry of the water in each area is different.

- Water transfer can lead to nutrient imbalances which can affect aquatic plant and animal life.
- Sediment can accumulate within pipelines and against dams in reservoirs. This can result in a chemical imbalance leading to either excessive plant growth (as with eutrophication) or limited growth.
- These schemes rely heavily on the hard engineering of rivers through pipe networks and dams. This alters natural floods and can reduce water access for the donor area.
- River channels can silt up or have an increased saline content.
- The introduction of water to a new area can also spread non-native invasive species which can threaten the new ecosystem.

Did you know?

Each person on the planet uses on average over 8 tonnes of natural resources per year, or 22 kg per day.

Activities

1. Suggest how commercial agriculture and deforestation can impact the environment locally, regionally and internationally, both in the long term and the short term.
2. What is eutrophication? How can it affect ecosystems?
3. Why might environmentalists suggest that hedgerows be reintroduced to fields? What benefit could they bring?
4. Using Figure 16, describe how water supply in Lake Chad has changed over time. Suggest how this will affect local plants, animals and soils.
5. Consider water transfer schemes. Create a table to compare benefits and costs to the donor area and the receiving area. Are these schemes sustainable?

→ Take it further

6. Research and investigate one of the following water transfer schemes:
   - the Ely Ouse to Essex transfer scheme
   - the Elan Valley transfer scheme
   - the Severn–Thames transfer scheme.
   Describe and evaluate the positives and negatives of the scheme.

How are we meeting our energy needs?

Our planet still relies heavily on fossil fuels and non-renewable energy sources. The sourcing of these can cause damage to the environment locally and internationally. Technology is enabling humans to access more resources than ever before.

The impact of resource extraction: mining

Mining and drilling are the main methods for extracting fossil fuels (coal, natural gas and oil) and nuclear minerals from the surface or deep underground. The UK has a history of mining both on land and out to sea, for coal, gas and oil. However, we now import more fossil fuels than we produce and, as a result, mines across England and Wales have been abandoned. This has left chasm quarries in the landscape, toxic soils and abandoned buildings. It has also resulted in the social cost of high local unemployment. Figure 17 shows some of the visible impacts of mining.

▲ **Figure 17:** The environmental impact of mining

Impacts of coal mining

- Quarrying leaves a visual impact on the landscape with open pits and waste heaps of discarded material.
- Washing of coal during processing contaminates water and soil with sulphur and carbon which contribute to acid rain.
- Coal power stations require vast amounts of water.
- Mining results in deforestation, chemical leaching and fresh water pollution.
- Forests can be replanted after quarries are abandoned, but will be fragmented and may have poorer soils.
- Danger of landslips in highland areas due to soil erosion; increased local flood risk.
- Waste slurry heaps may contain mercury and lead; the removal of these chemicals is important to avoid spills.

Impacts of natural gas and oil drilling

- Natural gas produces the least carbon of all fossil fuels.
- Extraction of gas and oil from rock formations can lead to water pollution.
- Conventional mining of gas and oil involves pumping air and water into coal beds to bring oil and gas to the surface. This can sometimes be abrupt and major oil spills have been experienced (such as the BP Horizon spill in the Gulf of Mexico).
- Modern 'fracking' (hydraulic fracturing) processes pump a mixture of water, sand and chemicals under high pressure into deep shale rocks in order to split them apart and force gas or oil rapidly to the surface.
- Fracking uses less water than coal power stations, and emits fewer greenhouse gases, but there are concerns about groundwater supplies becoming toxic. The fracking fluid remains in the ground and could contaminate water and soil with bromide, diesel, methane, lead or hydrochloric acid. In 2012 over 1 trillion litres of toxic waste water from fracking processes had to be treated. Some also claim the process leads to seismic activity with 'microquakes'. As such it is controversial, although the UK ended a ban on fracking in 2012.
- In the USA, fracking is widespread and has increased the amount of fuel gained from fossil fuels and reduced the country's CO_2 emissions.

Impacts of nuclear power

- Nuclear power produces significantly less CO_2 than other thermal energy types, and only two per cent of the CO_2 of coal burning.
- Nuclear energy involves mining for radioactive isotopes such as caesium, strontium, uranium and plutonium. This involves quarrying and the associated issues of deforestation, soil erosion and leaching. However, isotopes are required in smaller quantities and so quarries can be smaller.
- Vast quantities of water must be used to process isotopes and cool nuclear reactors when making power. Although this can be sourced from seawater and recycled, it can become contaminated with radioactive materials and waste.

- There is widespread concern over nuclear safety, especially following the Chernobyl disaster in 1986 and the 2011 Fukushima disaster in Japan which followed a tsunami. If a meltdown occurs, landscapes can become irradiated and forced into exclusion zones for years. Leaching of waste into food chains means farmers have to destroy harvests and livestock to prevent human illness.
- The main problem is nuclear waste. Materials have to be stored in protective casks (cement, concrete or steel) for 50 years before being buried permanently underground or in the sea. Radioactive elements can still emit fatal levels of radiation for years after use. This 'half-life' can range from 30 years for some isotopes to 24,000 years for plutonium.

Impacts of renewable energy

Renewable energy sources also have an impact on the environment. Hydroelectric power uses vast quantities of water, and while much can be reused, the reservoirs can lead to excessive evaporation and silting. In the USA alone, 40 billion litres of water are lost each day from reservoirs. The dams and reservoirs require energy during their construction from concrete, and they can disrupt local ecology and affect life cycles. Flooding of landscapes to create reservoirs can be controversial: the Three Gorges Dam project in China has been blamed for landslides, water pollution, flash flooding and drought.

Geothermal energy has been harnessed in nations such as Iceland and the USA for many years. It is clean, renewable and produces minimal carbon dioxide. Although water is pumped underground to be heated, it does not become overly contaminated and can be recycled. Geothermal stations are very efficient as they can run all day long. Iceland produces so much

▲ **Figure 18:** Renewable energy in the Azores

energy that there are currently plans to transfer some by pipeline to the UK.

Activities

1. Explain how mining can have an impact on the local environment.
2. Study Figure 17. Describe the possible environmental implications of abandoned mining areas in the short and long term.

The impact of deforestation

Figures 19 and 20 shows how deforestation of tropical areas has increased over time. With 13 million hectares of forest deforested each year, less than 30 per cent of the world is now covered by trees.

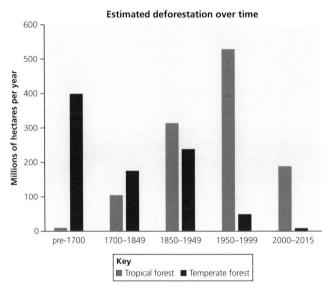

▲ **Figure 19:** Global deforestation

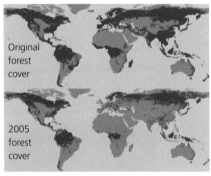

▲ **Figure 20:** Global deforestation

Deforestation for fuel (firewood), materials for construction or to use the land for farming (see page 109) has been practised for millennia. However, deforestation is increasing. Temperate forests in the northern hemisphere have been reduced to a bare minimum and now tropical forest destruction has led to only two per cent being left worldwide.

The impact of deforestation can lead to:

- habitat loss
- wildlife destruction
- soil erosion
- increased landslides or flood risk
- loss of nutrients.

Forests also act as carbon stores; their destruction releases this carbon back into the atmosphere where it contributes to global warming.

It is possible to use forests in a sustainable manner through replanting. Many companies now operate afforestation schemes to replant fast-growing trees. However, these do not produce the same natural forests and can still deplete habitats.

Fracking: fuel for thought

In the USA in 2015, 49 per cent of all gas and oil extracted was through fracking. The UK currently imports oil and gas from overseas, yet we have shale reserves across the country, such as in Yorkshire and the Mendips. The UK ban on fracking has ended and, in 2015, the government formally offered up licenses to allow companies to frack natural shale in areas inland. However, there are still many concerns from the public and there is an ongoing debate about safety. In Oklahoma, earthquakes increased by 100 times during fracking regimes. The UK does not have major seismic risks. It does, however, have an energy crisis (see Figure 21). Is fracking the answer?

	Population	Energy consumption	Energy production	Energy import	Total CO_2 emissions
	(millions)	(TWh)*	(TWh)	(TWh)	(TWh)
2010	62.2	2355	1730	705	484
2004	59.8	2718	2619	135	537
Change 2004–10	3.9%	−13.3%	−33.9%	+420%	−10.0%

* TWh = Terawatt hours; a measure of energy. 1 TWh is equal to 114 megawatts, enough energy to power a city of 200,000 people, or 90,000 homes, for an entire year.

▲ **Figure 21:** Energy in the UK

Activities

1. Study Figures 19 and 20. Describe how the pattern of woodland in the world has changed over time. Use data from the graph and the map in your answer.
2. Suggest reasons why tropical rainforest destruction has increased so rapidly.
3. Consider Figure 21 and describe how energy use in the UK has changed over time.

→ Take it further

4. Produce a Venn diagram to compare the social, economic and environmental implications of fracking. Is it a sustainable solution to the UK's energy crisis?

CHAPTER

16

Can we feed nine billion people by 2050?

What does it mean to be food secure?

→ **In this section you will:**

→ look at what is meant by food security and food insecurity

→ explore the different factors that influence food security

→ study the world patterns of access to food and how they are illustrated

→ look at the relationship between population and food supply.

What does it mean to be food secure?

What is food security?

'When all people at all times have physical and economic access to sufficient, safe and nutritious food to meet their dietary needs and food preferences for an active and healthy life.'

The World Food Summit of 1996

What does it mean to be food insecure?

How long has it been since you last ate? It was probably no more than a few hours and your next meal will only be a few hours away. For many people in the world that is not the case. They are victims of 'food insecurity'. This means they are unsure as to when they might next eat, or they know that it will be a struggle to source the food they need and may have to spend most of the day finding and preparing their next meal.

There are estimated to be over 800 million people who go hungry every day and this number is rising. Significant numbers of people across the world do not have enough food resources, while others consume more than their fair share of food.

For the poorest people in the least developed countries, diets are basic and repetitive. They also lack the range of nutrients that are essential for child health. Without food security, children may not receive enough **calories** in the crucial first eighteen months of life. As a result, they may face a lifetime of poor health, restricted growth and a reduced life expectancy.

However, food insecurity is not just an LIDC problem. More and more people in the UK are becoming reliant on food banks. Diets in ACs can also be unhealthy due to high levels of salt, sugar and fat being consumed. Although some people eat a poor diet through choice, others find that it is too expensive to buy 'healthy' food and they may see the junk food as a cheaper, more affordable option. People in ACs may also be uneducated about food nutrition and what constitutes a healthy diet. There is a great deal of advertising and promotion of unhealthy junk food and processed food and so many people in ACs are not getting the nutrients needed for a healthy life. This is explored in more depth on page 264.

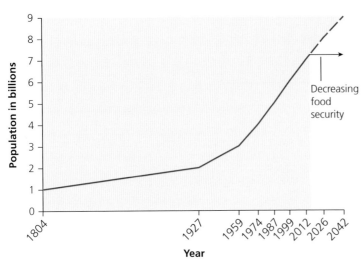

▲ **Figure 1:** World population, 1804–2042

What factors influence food security?

The factors that influence food security are also explored in Chapter 15, pages 243–5. These include physical and human factors.

Population growth	Global population has increased dramatically since 1950 (see Figure 1), and although the 'population explosion' has now slowed down, it is projected that the world population will reach 9 billion by 2050.
	Population growth is highest in LIDCs, where there is a high birth rate due to infant mortality.
Water insecurity	There is a rapidly decreasing global supply of fresh water, which is used for irrigation. In some countries, the groundwater supplies are drained, leading to desertification.
Climate and climate change	Drought, changing rainfall patterns and flooding can all damage food crops, producing short-term supply issues.
	Some scientists believe that rainfall may become unreliable and more extreme in years to come. For example, the US state of California is currently undergoing a dramatic period of drought, which has persisted for some years.
	Droughts have plagued many parts of East Africa for decades, triggering large-scale aid efforts.
Length of growing seasons	If demand for food is higher, there is more pressure on land to produce food, which can lead to over-use.
Soil	Desertification is reducing the amount of land that has soil fertile enough for people to farm on.
	Intensive farming can lead to soil exhaustion, so fields are less productive.
Diseases	Diseases threaten livestock. In 2001, for example, an outbreak of foot and mouth disease in the UK led to over 10 million sheep and cattle being killed in order to stop the spread of the disease.
Pests, insects and bacteria	Pests and insects are becoming more immune to insecticides and blighting crops.
	Changes in weather allow pests, insects and bacteria to thrive and migrate to new locations.

▲ **Figure 2:** Physical factors that influence food security

Food consumption and changing diets	According to expert predictions, a 70 per cent increase in food consumption is expected in the next few decades. This will be partly the result of the increase in global population, but will be boosted by an expected increase in average calorie consumption.
	Diets are changing globally and there is greater consumption of meat in countries like China and India which have not previously eaten it in large quantities. This increase will result in the need to double the production of poultry and other meat around the world.
	The world's average daily calorie availability is predicted to rise to over 3000 kcal per person per day. However, will this be enough to keep pace with the rising number of mouths there are to feed?
Politics and trade	Countries that are food secure are not necessarily those which produce most of their own food. Some of these countries rely extensively on imports. However, maintaining this food security requires effort. Although there are well-established connections between countries, these can be upset by changes in commercial decisions, cultural changes such as diets, the availability of subsidies if they are used in particular ways, and the political stability of countries.
	Foods are traded as commodities. This means that prices are based on future production, so there are problems if crops are damaged by unforeseen events.
	Increasing demand also increases prices. A growing taste for chocolate in China, for example, has seen a rise in the price of cocoa.
Rising global food prices	There are also problems when food prices rise suddenly. This problem is called **food price volatility** and is illustrated in the example of tortilla prices on page 260.

▲ **Figure 3:** Human factors that influence food security

Rising food prices: tortilla uncertainty

In 2006, tens of thousands of people marched through Mexico City to protest about a 25 per cent increase in the price of tortillas. Mexico imports large amounts of corn from the US but, around this time, demand was growing for the corn crop to be used to make bio-ethanol rather than eaten. The percentage of US corn production used for bio-ethanol went from 10 per cent to 40 per cent in just four years. Mexico's food import bill went from $2.6 billion (1990) to $18.4 billion (2010). Corn tortillas are a staple part of the Mexican diet, particularly among the poor, but are also used as animal feed, leading to shortages and price spikes. The average Mexican family spends a quarter of its income on food, but this increased dramatically. Panic buying of corn during 2007 led to further unrest. It is thought that during 2011, over half of Mexicans experienced some periods of food insecurity.

An Action Aid report in 2012 suggested that Mexico needed to invest in small-scale agriculture, develop its farming infrastructure and negotiate with the USA to lessen the impact of food imports on food prices.

In 2008, the growing global food crisis led to riots in over 30 countries. In 2014, the Food and Agriculture Organization (FAO) reported that 37 countries required external assistance for food.

Activities

1. Define the term food security.
2. Look at the list of factors in Figure 4.
   a. List the human factors.
   b. List the physical factors.
   c. Describe the impact that each of the factors will have on food security.

→ Take it further

3. Carry out some research on the impact that two or more of the factors in Figure 4 have had on the food security of a specific country.
4. What evidence can you find of growing food insecurity around the world?
5. Can you identify any further factors that affect food security?

▲ **Figure 4:** Factors that affect food security

What are the world patterns of access to food and how are they illustrated?

The World Hunger Index

The **World Hunger Index (WHI)**, or Global Hunger Index (GHI), was devised as a way of examining progress towards the Millennium Development Goal (MDG) of food security and solving hunger. MDG number 1 was to 'Eradicate extreme poverty and hunger' (see Chapter 12, page 188).

The WHI uses a range of indicators to examine 'hidden hunger', including undernourishment, the proportion of underweight children and the rate of child mortality. Each country is given a score from zero (no hunger) to 100. Higher scores are not good.

Average daily calorie consumption

One way to look at world food consumption is to map the calories per person that are consumed on average for each country (Figure 6). This can give an indication of the global distribution of available food and food inequality.

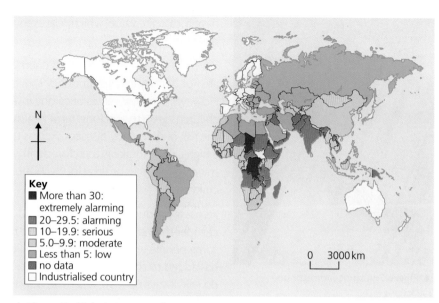

▲ **Figure 5:** Global Hunger Index scores, 2011

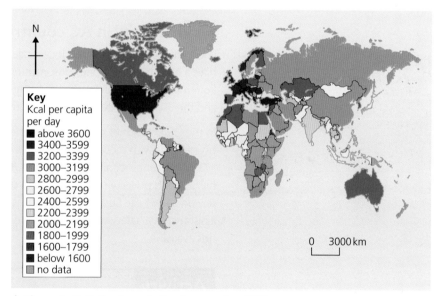

▲ **Figure 6:** Daily food supply (kcal) per capita, 2009

Activities

1. Look at Figure 5.
   a. Which parts of the world have the highest scores on the Global Hunger Index? Are these the places you expected to score badly?
   b. How could higher scores be improved?
2. Look at Figure 6.
   a. What is the connection between this map and the one in Figure 5?
   b. Identify three countries and write a short description of what the two maps tell you about them.
3. Which of the maps do you find the most useful in identifying those countries which might be at risk from food security problems both now and in the future?

▲ **Figure 7:** Calorie indicator on packaging

What are calories?

Calories are one of the ways in which food consumption is measured. Foods have a 'calorific value' which relates to the energy that they provide as they are digested.

We need to remember that this energy may come from fats and sugars which are not healthy in large amounts, so a high number is not necessarily better. However, very low values of calorie intake over a long time can certainly restrict children's growth and long-term health, and adults on low-calorie diets run the risk of deficiency diseases. Access to a healthy diet rather than just having a high calorie intake is therefore an important consideration as vitamins and minerals found in healthy foods support bone and brain development in children.

As mass-produced and well-marketed processed foods are often seen as cheaper than the healthier alternative of cooking meals from scratch, there are some people who feel that eating healthily is too expensive. This perception has added to the rising rates of obesity in countries across the EU. Consumers do not always take the health advice that is provided on packaging and in the media, such as portion size, guidelines for amounts of calories to be consumed and the advice to have five daily portions of fruit and vegetables.

Food security in AC countries

Food security also varies on a local scale. Even in those countries which currently have a high average calorie consumption, there are people struggling with food. Four million people are classed as being in **food poverty** in the UK, for example, and the use of food banks has risen in the last decade (see page 266).

In the USA the child poverty rate – the percentage of children living in households with incomes below 50 per cent of the national median average – is 23.1 per cent. According to a 2013 UNICEF report, only Romania has a higher child poverty rate. In the USA, these young people and their families rely on SNAP: the Supplemental Nutrition Assistance Programme. This welfare assistance is a 'safety net' and there are many areas of the world where this is not available.

Activity

1. Explore 'Who grows what' with this interesting interactive map: www.selborne.nl/foodmap/whogrows.php. Which country are you most connected with through the foods that you eat?

What is the relationship between population and food supply?

Malthus and Boserup: food for thought?

Two people who considered the relationship between population and food supply, and created influential ideas and theories about it, were the Reverend Thomas Malthus and a Danish economist called Ester Boserup.

In 1798, Reverend Malthus predicted that the rate of global population growth would inevitably produce a population larger than could be fed, as the number of people was growing faster than the world's ability to produce food. He proposed that this would lead to a catastrophe, involving famine and war. Malthus had views on population control which shaped his writing, but the idea of resources being finite is something that is important to consider. People have suggested that he was writing well before modern technology, which makes land more productive, along with contraception, improvements in healthcare and a dramatic reduction in fertility rate in many parts of the world, which reduces the rate of population growth.

Boserup, writing in the 1960s, was more optimistic, perhaps, when she talked about 'necessity being the mother of invention'. When we approach the point of resource depletion, she argued that we would respond by technological advances which would increase food productivity. There would also tend to be a response among the population to reduce their overall consumption, which would 'buy' enough time for a solution to be developed. The area of land currently in food production is the highest it has ever been.

Some people suggest that Malthus may still be proved right over 200 years later, as there may be a limit to the extent to which we can continue to boost productivity without causing damage to the natural systems which sustain agriculture.

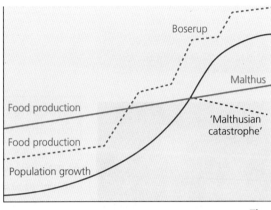

▲ **Figure 8:** The theories of Malthus and Boserup on food production compared to population growth

Activities

1. Do you most agree with the ideas of Malthus or Boserup?
2. Discuss: can technology always be relied upon to provide an answer?

Food in China

Countries vary in the amount of food that they produce. China is the world's largest producer of food by calories, and also by the value of food produced, with rice representing a third of that. It is also the largest producer of a number of other foodstuffs including wheat, onions, garlic, cabbage, potatoes, carrots, grapes and watermelons.

China has been through a number of periods when large numbers of people have died from famine. Between 1958 and 1962 an estimated 30 million people starved to death, because of a combination of drought, poor weather and Communist Party policies prohibiting farm ownership. During the 'Three Bitter Years', as they were called, food production stalled as farm workers were directed to concentrate on the production of iron and steel. Peasant farmers were ordered to kill wild birds which were eating seeds, but vermin numbers rose as a consequence. Fertile topsoil was buried and ruined with stones by an ill-judged recommendation to plough much deeper than usual.

China currently has an estimated population of 1.3 billion. Feeding so many people would be a challenge for any country. China has to look to sustain a high level of food production at a time when it has also been prioritising industrial growth and manufacturing. This has led to water stress and environmental issues. Grand projects such as the Three Gorges Dam have been undertaken, leading to the forced movement of millions of people.

One risk for the stability of global food supply is the sheer scale of China's population and its demands for resources. If Chinese people change their diet and start asking for new food, the demand will soon outstrip global supply of those items.

How can countries ensure their food security?

→ **In this section you will:**

→ look at the strategies for increasing food security

→ consider food security in the UK.

How can countries ensure their food security?

Strategies for increasing food security

▲ **Figure 9a:** Diets that are high in calories can often be unhealthy

▲ **Figure 9b:** Asparagus – a seasonal food

Reducing overeating and obesity

The number of people classed as obese is increasing in many countries around the world, regardless of their level of development. Obesity occurs when people are overweight and have high body fat. The body mass index (BMI) is sometimes used to help diagnose this; people with values of over 30 are considered to be obese.

Health campaigns which encourage people to eat less and take more care of their weight could result in less food being consumed and wasted. Better food habits could also lead to a lower demand for red meat and less exploitation of declining fish stocks in the sea. Obesity is a consequence of globalisation and increased affluence (wealth). In Dubai, the fast pace of life has led to a proliferation of fast-food restaurant chains.

There are some imaginative strategies being tried to reduce people's weight.

In 2008, Japan introduced the 'metabo' law which sets maximum sizes for the nation's waistline. New Zealand's immigration guidelines mean that those without a healthy BMI are denied entry to the country.

Medical assistance is also available. The AspireAssist device can be surgically implanted and works by removing food from the stomach before the calories it contains can be absorbed.

Reduce food losses and food waste

This is an essential area to tackle. Estimates vary, but it is thought that between a third and a half of all the food that is produced is never consumed. There are many points during the cycle from field to fork where food may be lost or damaged; some during its growing, some during the processing of it. Some waste is due to people confusing use-by and sell-by dates on food packaging. Portion control in the home and elsewhere can reduce the level of food being wasted.

Supermarkets apply strict criteria to the food which they will purchase and these result in further waste, as food that is perfectly edible does not necessarily make it to the shelves. This is sometimes based on size, so fruit that is undersized is left to rot, or imperfections on the surface. Recent campaigns have encouraged consumers to ignore how food looks, but concentrate on how it tastes.

Tackling conflict

Farming involves an investment in time and a large workforce or sophisticated machinery. Where the farming workforce is engaged in conflict, either by choice or conscription, and crops are damaged during fighting, food productivity declines. Farm workers may be killed or injured or flee the area as refugees. The land may be polluted by chemicals or otherwise damaged along with valuable infrastructure for irrigation. In Somalia, thousands of farmers have abandoned their land for these reasons, along with unsustainable taxes that were imposed on farmers by members of al-Shabaab militant groups in the area. Rapid resolution of conflict can lead to farming being re-established.

Improve forecasting of possible extreme events

Crops can be damaged by extreme weather events. Some of these can be predicted. Soft fruit farmers in ACs take steps to protect against frosts, with air-stirring fans, local heating sources and fleece covering. Local-scale forecasts are difficult to obtain in many parts of the world, although mobile phones could improve the quality of communication.

Drought in 2014 in countries such as Brazil, the USA and Australia affected the global commodity market, increasing the price of coffee, cocoa, wheat and other grains. In 2011, drought in the Black Sea area led to crop failure and panic buying in the Middle East and North Africa. In Turkey, warm weather in early 2014 caused apricots to develop earlier than usual and bad frosts then damaged the crop. Almost three-quarters of the world's hazelnuts are grown on slopes near Turkey's Black Sea coast; hail storms and frost destroyed the flowers on hazelnut trees at a critical time. Damage to the hazelnut crop affects confectionery companies in particular. A quarter of the world's hazelnut supply goes into making a well-known cocoa and hazelnut spread.

A Christian Aid project in Kenya provided small farmers with short- and medium-term forecasts for rainfall, which led to better choices of crops and reduced food losses.

Reducing soil erosion and desertification

There are fears that the world's soils are reaching a crisis point; their fertility and structure are declining due to poor management. Areas are losing huge amounts of topsoil as it is blown or washed away. A centimetre of soil takes thousands of years to develop. Strategies include mulches, wind breaks, bunds made from stones to trap surface run-off and inter-cropping so that the soil is not left bare after the main harvest. Over time, areas which lose their soil dry out and become more like deserts, in a process called desertification (see page 187).

Decreasing reliance on other countries

Many large multinational companies have taken steps to increase their involvement in different parts of the production chain and thus decrease their reliance on other countries. This has meant buying up suppliers, shipping companies or land in other parts of the world. This process is called **vertical integration**. China, along with other countries, has taken steps towards ensuring its food by buying up large tracts of land in Africa and cultivating it with cash crops for export back home. This may provide jobs for local farmers, but they do not always benefit from this relationship. This process is called **land grabbing**, although the amounts of land, and crops, involved are disputed. It is part of a wider Chinese involvement on the continent.

Food production within countries needs to be promoted, although there are often limits to how much this can be increased. There may be other pressures on the available land and much farmland has already undergone substantial change over the last 50 years to increase production.

Look at a typical basket of food from the family supermarket shop. Which countries are you reliant on for your own food security? What is the relationship between the UK and those countries? Investigate the companies that are producing that food and their relationships with those countries too. You may be surprised and even shocked at what you discover.

Tip

You will need to become familiar with the methods that might be used to close a 'food gap' between what is produced now and what will be needed by mid-century. This gap needs to be closed in ways that both improve the lives of farmers, but also reduce the impact of agriculture on the environment. Make sure that you can name at least four.

Case study: How can countries ensure their food security?

Food security in the UK

The UK has a population of 60 million people and currently enjoys a high level of food security. The UK's food strategy is overseen by DEFRA (the Department for Environment, Food and Rural Affairs). In June 2014 it recommended that the UK should plan ahead to mitigate the impact of changing climate and global demand for food, to ensure its future food security. It made recommendations for what could be done. It recognised that the many decisions made by millions of individual consumers every day cumulatively determine how the UK sources its food.

For any government, feeding its population has to be a top priority. This can be a balance between crops grown within the country and imports of food from other countries. It is not uncommon to have a situation in which a country both exports and imports the same food products.

How is the UK trying to ensure its food security at a national scale?

In 2013, 23 countries were involved in supplying the UK with the majority of its food. Around half of the total requirements were met from within the UK itself, meaning that the UK is not self-sufficient in many foods. In this same year, the average UK household wasted £470 worth of food, reflecting a relatively high supply of food compared with consumption.

Roughly 68 per cent of foods that we *can* produce in the UK *are* actually produced here, although that figure has been declining steadily. Fruit and vegetables are among the products that have been most affected by a decrease in self-sufficiency because of their year-round (rather than seasonal) availability for consumers.

▲ **Figure 10:** A stall at Sheffield Market

There are close ties with the European Union (EU) for many food imports, so the UK's relationship with the EU is important.

The DEFRA report suggests a strategy of **sustainable intensification**. This means increasing the global food supply while minimising negative environmental consequences.

The longer-term success of measures that have been taken is not yet known, but different small-scale strategies have been used in the UK to help increase its food security.

How successful have attempts to achieve food security at a local scale been?

Past attempts to achieve food security include the Green Revolution of the 1960s, discussed on page 269. At a local scale, present strategies include food banks, allotments and urban gardens.

Food banks

Food banks are stores of food that people can access on request or by referral from an agency such as the Citizens Advice Bureau. Food is donated by schools, churches, businesses and individuals and held in a central location. Certain foods are required – generally essentials which are non-perishable. Volunteers check and sort the food and pack it into boxes. People in need of emergency food are identified

Summary of DEFRA report recommendations on food security

→ Encourage consumers to support British farmers

→ Better long-term weather forecasts to prepare for extreme events

→ Sustainable intensification: producing more food

→ Explore alternatives to importing soybeans for animal food

→ Research how to reduce carbon emissions from agricultural production

→ Provide additional funding for agricultural technology, for example controlled traffic farming using GPS and selective harvesting to reduce food waste

→ Explore public attitudes and EU barriers to further use of GM technology

→ Encourage new farms and try to recruit more farmers

by doctors, health visitors and social workers and given a voucher. This entitles them to three days' worth of food, along with further advice and support. They also provide 'Baby basics' for new mothers and extra items at Christmas.

A DEFRA report in 2014 gave a figure of 4 million people in food poverty in the UK. Such people may need the help of a food bank if faced with a sudden loss of income or change in circumstances. In April 2015 it was revealed by the Trussell Trust, the biggest provider of this sort of emergency food aid which oversees 400 food banks across the UK, that the number of people relying on food banks had passed *one million*. This was despite record employment and reflected the relatively high price of food compared with incomes. Politicians have said that food banks should never become a permanent part of society in the twenty-first century, but they may be around for a while to come as food security varies within the UK.

▲ **Figure 11:** More than 1 million people were relying on food banks in the UK in 2015

Allotments

These are growing in popularity in the UK. Rising food prices have led to long waiting lists in some council areas for these subsidised plots of land, on which families can grow food crops. The Landshare website (**www.landshare.net**) connects people who have spare land with those who would like to grow food in an area. Locally sourced food reduces food miles to a minimum, promotes healthy outdoor activity, improves community cohesion and provides a positive use of open space.

Urban gardens

These are larger, more formal, projects where individuals or small co-operatives work together to grow food and promote healthy eating (see page 270). In the UK, the Incredible Edible Todmorden scheme has been particularly successful. This West Yorkshire town has planted crops on roundabouts, road verges, herb gardens, orchards and raised beds outside colleges and other local businesses.

▲ **Figure 12:** The Incredible Edible Todmorden scheme

Activities

1. Explore the statistics on food bank use shared by the Trussell Trust in their press release: www.trusselltrust.org/2015/04/22/foodbank-use-tops-one-million-for-first-time-says-trussell-trust
   a. What was the percentage growth in the use of food banks in the period 2014–15?
   b. What are the main reasons given for people being referred to food banks?

➔ Take it further

2. Where is the nearest food bank to your school? If possible, get in touch to see how many people it supports. Why not do a food collection and donation from your school to support those in food poverty in your local area? Without you realising it, there may well be some pupils at your school whose families use the food bank.

👣 Fieldwork ideas

- Depending on your location, you may be able to organise a trip to a farm to look at food production. Farms which welcome visitors are listed here: www.visitmyfarm.org.
- You may also be able to link up with local supermarkets. The Co-operative works in some parts of the country to offer visits.

▲ **Figure 13:** Cod and chips – a sustainable species and appropriately caught?

▲ **Figure 14:** The Fairtrade Foundation logo

How sustainable are strategies to protect food security?

In the same way as fast food might satisfy our immediate cravings, some possible strategies for ensuring food security may actually only result in a short-term improvement. Is the longer-term view of Malthus going to occur regardless of what is done more locally? Is global co-ordination of food supply possible? There is a need to ensure the **sustainability** of whatever measures are put in place. As mentioned in Chapter 15, this requires measures that are taken to be environmentally, economically and socially viable in the longer term.

Ethical consumerism

It is difficult to enter a supermarket without being tempted by food which has been cleverly marketed, and part of this marketing is now related to the way that the food has been produced. A 2015 DEFRA report suggested that UK consumers should be encouraged to purchase British products to support farmers and also to increase their consideration of the impact of their food choices on their health. Consumers are increasingly aware of the ethical background of the food they consume. Some labelling campaigns have been very successful. The Marine Stewardship Council (MSC) publishes handy guides to enable customers to choose sustainable fish, something which is not straightforward as it depends on how and where the fish was caught as well as the species.

Fairtrade

Fairtrade is a global movement which describes itself as 'a movement for change'. It started in 1988, producing coffee from Mexico for Dutch supermarkets. There are now over 1.4 million farmers and workers involved in over 1100 producer organisations in over 70 countries including Mexico, Mali, India and Papua New Guinea. Fairtrade fortnight raises awareness of the goods that are produced. Farmers get paid a higher price than they would traditionally get for their crops. The Fairtrade logo has become more common, and some of the major chocolate brands are now made with Fairtrade cocoa. Some supermarkets only stock Fairtrade bananas.

There are also extensions of the scheme where entire towns, such as Wells-next-the-Sea in Norfolk, are labelled as 'Fairtrade Towns' by promoting products in local businesses and schools.

A significant aspect of the Fairtrade scheme is the **social premium** which is paid to local producers who are often organised into **co-operatives**. The fair price encourages farmers to share their best produce and to improve it, and the social premium funds improvements for communities, including water supply, improved infrastructure or improvements in education for producers' children.

Supermarkets in the UK and elsewhere now stock a range of Fairtrade products, which have diversified beyond food. Similar schemes such as the Rainforest Alliance, with their 'Follow the Frog' campaign, have also drawn the attention of consumers to the methods used to produce the food that they eat.

Methods of food production

The sustainability of any method of food production is reliant on it continuing to produce a good yield without it damaging the long-term health of the soil or resulting in depletion of local groundwater.

Monoculture is the method of cultivation for many cash crops, using a plantation system. This requires large inputs of fertilisers and pesticides, as there is a risk that any pest or disease could decimate the entire crop.

As we have already seen, some methods of production cannot claim to be sustainable.

● Water tables can be lowered by indiscriminate abstraction of water for irrigation. Chemicals may also leach down into the groundwater and contaminate the drinking water supply if there is no regulation to prevent their use in large quantities.

● The way that pesticides and herbicides are applied sometimes risks workers' health, but they may fear to speak out and risk losing their job. Suppliers will be inspected from time to time, but the standards of production are not as high in some parts of the world as in others.

Technological developments: past and present

GM stands for genetically modified. This is something that has been done to some extent with most of the plants and animals that we are familiar with. Domesticated animals have been bred for generations to produce more meat or more milk or to grow faster. **GM foods** have had specific changes introduced into their DNA using genetic engineering, which is different from conventional breeding.

Specially bred, high-yielding varieties of crops (HYVs) are the result of efforts to genetically modify crops so that they are disease or drought resistant. This has become more 'scientific' and the genetic material is now manipulated in a laboratory. There has been a focus on key cash crops such as soybean, maize, oilseed rape and cotton seed. One example of this is the modification of crops to enable them to be resistant to aphids (insect pests).

Green Revolution

One large-scale attempt to introduce these HYVs more widely was called the **Green Revolution** and took place in the 1960s. Seeds, advice and some equipment were introduced to farmers in LIDCs. The seeds included an HYV called 'miracle rice', which produced yields ten times higher than those of traditional rice, but which required fertilisers and irrigation. In the Philippines, a new variety of rice called IR8 was distributed to farmers. This also required fertilisers and pesticides to reach its potential yields.

The Green Revolution was not seen as a long-term success. Farmers couldn't afford the increased investment that was required to see the increases in yields, and were not necessarily covering the extra costs of fertilisers and pesticides. Health problems emerged, and the use of machinery in some locations meant that people lost their traditional employment. Increased production also resulted in lower prices for food, which meant that small-scale farmers were paid less than before for the food they produced. Diesel pumps were provided to some farmers to help with irrigation, but these used up the groundwater faster than ever before and wells ran dry. When the pumps later ran out of diesel or broke down, farmers couldn't afford to repair them or buy fuel.

One new concept is the creation of vertical farms which use **hydroponics**: a system where plants such as salads grow in nutrient-rich water or gels rather than soil. They can be organised in vertical 'walls' of food and stacked in close proximity with artificial light and heating to promote growth. Food could theoretically be grown indoors, underground or in unused buildings.

Organic methods

Where crops are grown without any chemicals, and where livestock are not fed with animal feeds which contain any artificial additives, the food can be described as organic. The Soil Association's organic logo identifies food produced in this way.

Intensive farming

This involves high levels of input (machinery, seeds, chemical support, technology and research) to ensure high levels of output from each hectare of land. Yields have risen for many crops as a result of intensive methods of production.

Activity

1. Explore the idea of vertical farming and other options for producing food in urban areas. Could increased urbanisation be one solution to our food security problems: if people crowd into cities, does this leave more land available for food production?

What are some 'bottom-up' approaches to food security?

Many of the examples we have looked at so far have been 'top-down' approaches. However, some initiatives start small with 'grassroots' projects in city neighbourhoods, or a group of people with an idea, rather than being organised with large budgets by central government. Indeed, as we have seen, some large-scale efforts are not successful because they don't take local conditions into account.

Urban gardens

Cities are not completely covered by concrete and tarmac. They all have substantial amounts of private and public open green space, which may be used for food production. Informal and unsanctioned use of this space has occurred. So-called 'guerrilla gardeners' have taken over vacant lots in cities such as New York and 'seed bombed' them so that they are covered with flowers.

Urban gardens (also called city gardens or community gardens) are larger, more formal projects where individuals or small co-operatives work together to grow food and promote healthy eating. A large part of many cities could potentially be used in this way. The Brooklyn Grange project in New York is a one-acre farm in the heart of the city. In 2010, a layer of soil was laid on the roof of an office block, crops were planted and beehives installed. Food grown on the farm is sold to local restaurants and farmers' markets. Community events are held and local schoolchildren help on the farm and learn about food production.

Permaculture

Permaculture is derived from the term 'permanent agriculture' and refers to the way that the crops are planted, and the soils are managed, so that they can be used indefinitely. Those using this method of crop management will typically operate a small-scale farm. They will take great care over soil health and the way that nutrients are maintained within the area being used for food production. Many of the principles are taken from the way that natural systems operate without human interference.

The co-founder of the movement, David Holmgren, gave his name to the twelve principles, which include:

- use and value diversity
- catch and store energy
- use and value renewable resources and services
- use edges and value the marginal
- produce no waste
- use small and slow solutions.

In practice this means planting nitrogen-fixing plants instead of using fertilisers, planting a range of crops, including perennials, and growing out from a small area rather than starting with a large area under cultivation.

▲ **Figure 15:** An urban garden in Queens, New York

'Goat cycle'

The UK-based charity Oxfam's Unwrapped scheme offers people the chance to choose a 'gift' of a goat. A goat gift from Oxfam costs £25. The donation supports their Livelihoods projects, which include giving out livestock such as goats to communities in the developing world, as well as activities like business and agricultural training for farmers. The goats that Oxfam distribute are vaccinated and locally sourced. Goats can provide their owners with manure and milk, and can give birth to other goats over time, which can be sold. This means that agriculture is supported as well as the family that receives the goat. As a goat can continue to provide milk, manure and other baby goats over time, it is a sustainable gift. It is also a fairly hardy animal that can survive in most locations. Oxfam only provides livestock where keeping them is a traditional or essential part of people's way of life. They don't introduce the practice of animal husbandry, release animals into the wild or import animals.

Some criticism of such schemes suggests that animals are being provided in areas that are already suffering from water shortages and desertification, which will add to the demands for water. They also suggest that the scheme is designed to ease the conscience of people in the UK rather than being truly helpful in the long term. Andrew Tyler of Animal Aid has said that: 'All farmed animals require proper nourishment, large quantities of water, shelter from extremes of weather and veterinary care. Such resources are in critically short supply in much of Africa.'

Oxfam are clear that the provision of livestock is always part of a larger sustainable livelihoods programme, and they are concerned with long-term environmental sustainability because it is an essential requirement for human development and well-being – especially relevant to poor people, whose lives and livelihoods are more closely linked with the natural environment. Local staff, partners and local communities have detailed knowledge of the grazing patterns and feeding practice needed to decide if and where animals should be provided. Communities are also supported in adopting environmentally friendly farming practices to help them use land and water resources more efficiently, protect and even restore natural resources.

▲ **Figure 16:** The Oxfam Unwrapped scheme

Food security in the media

This chapter has provided a wealth of information on the nature of food, but this is an issue which continues to feature prominently in the media. Keep an eye out for news stories relating to food throughout the course. Some suggested websites are listed below:

- World Resources Institute report: www.wri.org/sites/default/files/wri13_report_4c_wrr_online.pdf
- National Geographic's FOOD feature has a wealth of information on global food supply: http://food.nationalgeographic.com
- The Landshare project: www.landshare.net
- Fairtrade Foundation: www.fairtrade.org.uk
- Trussell Trust website, with an interactive map showing the locations of foodbanks: www.trusselltrust.org/foodbank-projects
- DEFRA committee reports for July 2014 and January 2015, which are really useful and accessible documents: www.parliament.uk/business/committees/committees-a-z/commons-select/environment-food-and-rural-affairs-committee/news/food-security-report-substantive

Activities

1. Look closely at the contents of your next weekly shop for ethical and environmental labelling. What words are used on the packaging and what do you think they are intended to make you think about the food in terms of:
   a. how healthy it is
   b. how its production affected the environment?
2. What impact can permaculture have on food security if it encourages small-scale and slow farming when what is needed is large additional quantities of food?
3. Explore the opportunities for urban gardening in the area near your school. You could go on a fieldtrip in the immediate vicinity of the school and map possible places where food could be grown.

Practice questions

1. What are 'natural resources'? **[1 mark]**

2. Choose the correct definition for 'carrying capacity'.
   a) How far a heavy resource can be carried by hand.
   b) The maximum number of species a location can support.
   c) How big a population can become.
   d) How long a natural resource will last for. **[1 mark]**

3. Study Figure 2 on page 241. Suggest reasons why population growth has led to resources becoming exhausted. **[3 marks]**

4. Study Figure 5 on page 243. Describe the trend: how does the number of undernourished people vary between 1990 and 2014? **[4 marks]**

5. a) State one reason why we are not meeting modern demands for food. **[1 mark]**
   b) Explain why this reason makes it difficult to have enough food. **[2 marks]**

6. Study Figure 7a on page 246. Describe the trend for world water consumption over time. **[2 marks]**

7. What are 'renewable' energy sources? Why are they considered more sustainable? **[4 marks]**

8. Complete the following table. **[4 marks]**

Method	Positive consequences	Negative consequences
Mechanisation of farming		
Deforestation		Loss of habitats and soil erosion
Commercial fishing	Over 1 billion people rely on fish for their main food source	

9. There are various different methods for producing energy. Choose two of the following methods, and evaluate their advantages and disadvantages. *Nuclear power, natural gas, coal mining, oil drilling, geothermal energy, hydro-electric power.* **[8 marks]**

10. Study Figures 19 and 20 on page 256. Describe how deforestation in tropical forests has changed between 1700 and 2015. Refer to data from the graph and map. **[4 marks]**

11. Define the term 'food security'. **[1 mark]**

12. With reference to physical and human factors, explain why food security is a growing issue for many countries, both LIDCs and ACs. **[4 marks]**

13. How is the World Hunger Index calculated? **[2 marks]**

14. With reference to a country that you have studied, outline the problems that it faced when trying to feed its population both now and in the past. **[4 marks]**

15. a) How is food waste related to the issue of food security? **[2 marks]**
    b) Outline the attempts being made by the UK to reduce food waste on a national and more local scale. **[4 marks]**

16. Evaluate the methods that are being suggested by the government of one AC country to ensure its future food security. **[6 marks]**

17. Outline how two of these approaches can contribute to food security:
    a) Urban gardens
    b) Permaculture
    c) Fairtrade
    d) The 'goat cycle' **[4 marks]**

Tip

Question 4 is complicated as there is more than one type of information in the graph. You need to compare how the total numbers of undernourished people changes over time, but you also need to comment on how the proportions of people changes in different areas over time, using data as evidence to prove your point to get the 4 marks. You may want to use the acronym PEEL: Point–Evidence–Explain–Link.

Fieldwork and Geographical Exploration

PART

3

Chapter 17: Geography fieldwork

By the end of this chapter, you will know the answers to these key questions:

→ What is fieldwork?

→ What is the geographical enquiry process?

→ How do you decide on an enquiry question?

→ What fieldwork techniques and methods can be used?

→ How can you use secondary sources?

→ How can you present and analyse your findings?

→ What are the health and safety issues?

→ How do you reach conclusions and evaluate your work?

Chapter 18: Geographical exploration

→ Typhoon Haiyan: What short-term and long-term aid is needed to help the population of Guiuan in the Philippines?

CHAPTER

17

Geography fieldwork

What is fieldwork?

> **Fieldwork:** the experience of understanding and applying specific geographical knowledge, understanding and skills to a particular and real out-of-classroom context.

Fieldwork is an essential part of your GCSE studies. It gives you an opportunity to compare what you have learnt in your lessons to what geography is like in the real world. It will also help you to remember the geographical content you need to learn for your exams, as it is easier to visualise coastal and river landscapes and processes if you have walked alongside them.

The OCR GCSE Geography B specification gives a prominent position to fieldwork and it is embedded throughout the content. As you read through this textbook, you will have noticed that there are fieldwork ideas alongside the main content of the chapters. This may give you some ideas about what types of question you might want to investigate as part of your fieldwork.

You will be doing fieldwork on at least two separate occasions in contrasting locations. One will be in a physical geography context and the other will be in a human geography context. You will be examined on your physical geography fieldwork in Paper 1 and your human geography fieldwork in Paper 2. You will be asked questions based on fieldwork in an unfamiliar context (for example, looking at the way a student has presented their fieldwork results), as well as questions about your own fieldwork experience (for example, evaluating the techniques you used to collect your fieldwork data).

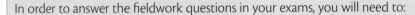

In order to answer the fieldwork questions in your exams, you will need to:

- understand the geographical enquiry process
- decide on an enquiry question or hypothesis
- collect data on your field trip using a range of fieldwork techniques and methods
- write up your findings by:
  - presenting the data you have collected in various ways, such as drawing maps, graphs and diagrams
  - analysing the data you have collected using your geographical knowledge
  - drawing conclusions and summaries
  - reflecting on your fieldwork investigation, including looking at the limitations of data-gathering methods and any conclusions you have drawn.

▲ **Figure 1:** Fieldwork is an essential part of your studies

What is the geographical enquiry process?

Figure 2 shows the process of geographical enquiry.

How does this relate to your fieldwork?

- **Step 1 Ask questions:** identify an issue and decide on an enquiry question; for example, you may decide to compare the quality of life in an inner suburb of your local town with an outer suburb.
- **Step 2 Gather information:** you will need **primary data** from your field trip and **secondary data** collected by other people, for example from sources on the internet.
- **Step 3 Select the best information:** analyse your findings by looking at the data you have collected and explaining what the information means.
- **Step 4 Produce your work:** write up your report in a suitable format including appropriate graphical techniques.
- **Step 5 Evaluate:** evaluate your findings, identifying any issues, for example problems with data collection or limitations of data collected.

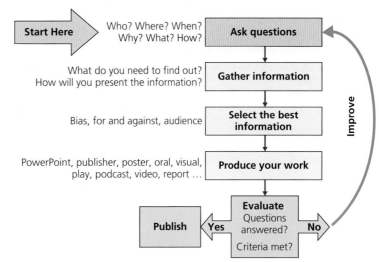

▲ **Figure 2:** The process of geographical enquiry

How do you decide on an enquiry question?

Each piece of fieldwork will be based on an enquiry question which will help you decide what data to collect and how to focus your fieldwork visit.

What issues are suitable for physical geography fieldwork?

Physical fieldwork involves the study of physical features and the processes that have led to their formation. For example, you might choose to study wave energy and its impact on longshore drift by looking at the arrangement of pebbles on a beach and their height either side of groynes. Some common areas to explore are listed below.

- **Hydrology:** rivers and fluvial environments; explorations of flood management and changes to drainage basins, including the perception of flood risk to residents
- **Coasts:** processes acting to change the coastline and the management of these processes which may involve hard or soft engineering methods
- **Upland glacial landscapes:** mountain landscapes which show evidence of past glacial activity and how they are currently being used
- **Ecosystems:** these could include coastal areas such as sand dunes or salt marshes, or woodlands or other habitats associated with particular environments; some of these may act as an additional amenity for people or be affected by changes in land use

▲ **Figure 3:** Local issues can make good fieldwork topics

What issues are suitable for human geography fieldwork?

Human fieldwork involves the study of urban environments or processes which involve human interaction. As humans are not as 'reliable' as physical processes, there needs to be an element of flexibility in the planning. While tide times are predicted months in advance, it is impossible to guarantee that people with a full range of ages and genders will be standing around waiting to be questioned in a location you have selected.

Human fieldwork options will vary depending on the location of your school. Common areas to explore are listed below.

- **Urban areas:** looking at urban land use and structure, social inequality or changes that have taken place in recent times; this can include processes such as gentrification, urban redevelopment and rebranding
- **Tourism:** impact of large numbers of visitors on the nature of a place; while a large volume of tourists may change the character of a place, they may also provide economic stability for local residents
- **Industrial change:** how has employment changed in an area over time; the relative balance of primary, secondary and tertiary opportunities
- **Environmental impacts:** the impacts of human activities on land, air or water quality

What fieldwork techniques and methods can be used?

Ways of collecting primary data include:

- measurements that you make using a variety of equipment
- images, such as photos you take or sketches you draw
- maps or diagrams you complete while you are outside
- responses to questions you ask people through questionnaires or interviews.

There are two main types of primary data that students may collect on fieldwork: quantitative and qualitative.

Tip

Refer to data as plural: data are, rather than data is.

▲ **Figure 4:** Students carrying out fieldwork in a river landscape

Quantitative data refer to numbers. These could be the sizes of pebbles on a beach, number of cars in a car park or footfall past a shoe shop. Numbers can be counted, averaged, graphed and compared over time. They may then be used to refer to expectations: are they are higher or lower than average; how do they compare with other places and different times of day or year.

Qualitative data do not necessarily involve numbers but refer to the wider exploration of a place. They could involve a sense of how safe people feel, which could, for example, be rated out of 10 but is not based on an actual 'value' that everyone would give. It could refer to a feeling that a place provides. Traffic counts or visitor numbers are, by contrast, quantitative data.

Questionnaires

Questionnaires can be used when you want to consult a group of people to find out what their thoughts and opinions are on a particular subject or issue. These may be physical sheets of paper or you could create a questionnaire online using a survey tool such as SurveyMonkey.

- Firstly, work out what information you need to find out. You may have an issue which requires people to have an opinion or perception, or you may be asking them to tell you some specific factual information.
- Each question should aim to collect a specific piece of data, which can then contribute towards the final conclusion.
- Do not have too many questions; even if they are quite brief, people may feel they don't have the time to answer them.
- Start off with a few easy questions to put people at ease. This might include asking them whether they are visitors or residents, for example.
- Have a mixture of open and closed questions. Open questions enable people to offer any answer or opinion. Closed questions may offer a choice of response, such as 'yes' or 'no', which are useful for later analysis.
- Avoid asking leading questions such as, 'What do you think of the horrible effects of noise pollution?', as this prompts people to answer in a particular way.
- You may want to ask some questions which require people to rate or score something, perhaps on a scale from 1 to 5, or 1 to 10. Be aware that if you have an odd number of scores, there may be a tendency for people to give the middle answer and 'sit on the fence'.
- Think carefully about where to stand. Some supermarkets may not like you to stand near the entrance to their store. Also, by standing outside a particular shop, it may add a bias to your questions on which supermarkets respondents most often use.
- Think carefully about the sampling method that is used to identify the people who will complete the questionnaires. A questionnaire is designed to provide a sample from the total population so the people you approach need to be representative of the population as a whole.

▲ **Figure 5:** Questionnaires are a useful way of collecting primary data

Using mobile devices

Tablets and smartphones are increasingly being used during fieldwork. This could include:

- apps to record sounds or interviews with people
- apps to collect data at particular points, which are then added to mapping tools
- apps to transform or label images (e.g. Skitch)
- video apps to record and then slow down a physical process (e.g. a wave breaking, so that it can be analysed as to whether it is a destructive or constructive wave).

How can you use secondary sources?

Secondary sources can provide support and offer further insights to help develop your enquiry. These are increasingly digital in nature. The Office for National Statistics (ONS) releases census data and a range of other information from time to time. Other downloads and data are produced by organisations such as Natural England and the British Geological Survey.

Using geographical information systems

Geographical data may have a location, which means that they can be mapped. By mapping the data, patterns often emerge. Maps can be obtained from the trace of a base map or by finding an existing map. You may need to use interactive maps which have been produced for a specific purpose. The Environment Agency, for example, produces flood risk data for specific addresses. This information could be used alongside some practical fieldwork involving questionnaire surveys of householders in areas which have (and haven't) experienced recent flooding (Figure 6 on page 278).

Students and teachers also have access to a free version of Google Earth Pro, which allows for the production of high-quality images showing cross sections across a path which the user has created. Figure 7 shows a cross section across Llyn Idwal in Snowdonia. The line is drawn as a path and the elevation profile along the path is then added and displayed. Students may be able to explore cross and long profiles of river valleys, or the changes that glaciation makes to upland landscapes before they go out and experience these places.

▲ **Figure 6:** An interactive map from the website of the Environment Agency, https://flood-warning-information.service.gov.uk/

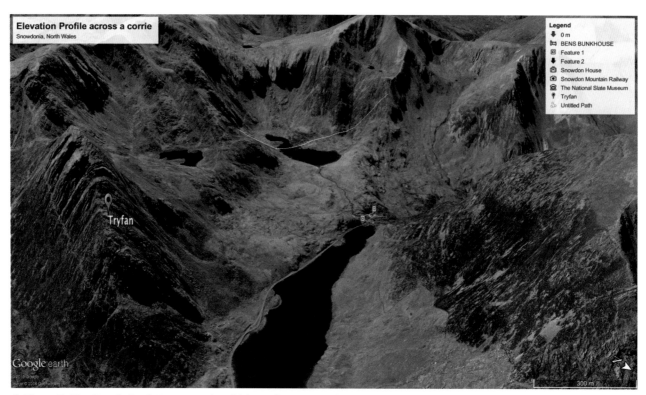

▲ **Figure 7:** Use Google Earth Pro to produce high-quality cross sections

How can you present your findings?

You will be studying and using a range of geographical skills during your GCSE course. Some of the presentation and interpretation of data skills can be best covered as part of your fieldwork enquiry. You can be tested on these skills in all of your exams.

Figure 8 shows some of the ways that you could present your data.

How do you analyse your findings?

You will need to analyse the primary data that you gather during your fieldwork trip, along with any secondary data you may gather from other resources, such as through websites.

You may analyse the data in various ways.

- Look at relationships between different sets of data that you collect.
- Make predictions from trends that can be seen in your data.
- Look at the trend lines on scatter graphs.
- Draw lines of best fit.
- Look at a map that you have created using the data and analyse any relationships that you see on that map between different types of data.

When analysing maps, use the acronym GAS to explore and critique what they are showing.

- Look at the **general** pattern that you can see (**G**).
- Look for **anomalies**; areas which don't quite fit the expected pattern (**A**).
- Finish by being **specific** about something that the map is telling you about one or more areas (**S**).

Maps	Sketch maps of the area
	Annotated Ordnance Survey maps of the area
	Choropleth maps
	Flow-line maps
Graphs and charts	Bar graphs
	Line graphs
	Histograms
	Scatter graphs
	Dispersion graphs
	Pie charts
	Climate graphs
	Proportional symbols
	Pictograms
	Cross-sections
	Population pyramids
Other visuals	Annotated photographs
	Sketches and diagrams

▲ **Figure 8:** Data presentation methods

Health and safety

Taking students off site can be nerve wracking but, with appropriate preparation, everything will go smoothly. Your school's fieldwork protocols should be followed to the letter. Risk assessments must be carried out on the chosen area to identify hazards and ways that they can be dealt with effectively. The location may need to be changed, even on the day itself if circumstances change.

You should be properly briefed and have practised techniques in advance if possible, so that you don't waste time learning how to use pieces of fieldwork equipment when you could be more active and actually collecting data.

Here are some brief suggestions for specific locations that might be visited as part of GCSE geography fieldwork.

River fieldwork

You must stick to the measurement area at all times, and not push people or otherwise mess about in water. You should take extreme care near river banks, especially where the ground is steep or wet, and wear suitable footwear. Remember that electrical equipment such as iPhones don't like water.

Coastal fieldwork

On the beach, don't climb on groynes or sea defence structures. Be careful not to handle beach litter. Agree on a particular distance that you must stay away from the tide line and keep an eye on the waves. Do not enter the sea under any circumstances. Check tide times carefully and ensure that it is going out before entering low-lying coastlines. These can be found at www.tidetimes.org.uk.

Town centre

Stay in your designated group and make sure you have contact numbers for your supervisors. Familiarise yourself with the area. Only question people you are comfortable talking to, and who are happy to help. Avoid asking the same people as another group working in the same area, particularly if there are lots of groups operating within a small area. Avoid blocking pavements, and cross the road at designated points.

How do you reach conclusions and evaluate your work?

Conclusions are not just the end of a fieldwork write-up, they are also the beginning of your understanding and also the start for further exploration, which can be suggested even if there is no time to actually carry it out. You may be asked what you would do differently if you were to start the process again and should consider the limitations of the methods used.

- Fieldwork should be summed up using the main themes which were introduced at the start of the process, and the extent to which the main enquiry questions have been answered.
- How robust are the conclusions that have been reached?
- What unexpected results have you come across? How far did this change your conclusion?

You should always evaluate the work you have completed. This means assessing the value of it. In order to do this you should ask yourself the following questions.

1. Were the methods I used appropriate?
2. Did the methods I used help me to answer my question?
3. Was I able to answer my original question given the primary and secondary data I collected?
4. How could I improve my study?

Useful weblinks for fieldwork

- The Royal Geographical Society website has a well-developed fieldwork section, complete with ideas for enquiries, recording sheets and suggestions on places to visit: www.rgs.org/ OurWork/Schools/Fieldwork+and+local+learning/ Fieldwork+and+local+learning.htm
- The Geographical Association has published a very useful book called *Fieldwork through Enquiry*. This book details ten fully worked fieldwork ideas and included ideas for using modern technology and apps to help collect and analyse fieldwork data. It has also collated a number of useful links

for helping with statistical analysis of fieldwork data: http://geography.org.uk/resources/ conductingstatisticaltestsforfieldwork/
- Google Earth Pro can be downloaded from here: www.google.co.uk/earth/download/gep/agree.html
- ArcGIS Online can be accessed via: www.arcgis.com/ home/. Click on MAP to get started.
- Details of Digimap for Schools can be seen here: http://digimapforschools.edina.ac.uk/
- Look for fieldwork providers that display the Learning Outside the Classroom Quality Badge: http:// lotcqualitybadge.org.uk/

Practice questions

Physical geography fieldwork

1. Figure A shows a data collection technique being used by a group of students carrying out a physical geography fieldwork investigation.

▲ **Figure A:** Students carrying out primary data collection

   a) Name this data collection technique.   **[1 mark]**
   b) Evaluate how effective this technique would be to compare the ecosystems found in deciduous and coniferous woodlands. **[2 marks]**
   c) Suggest one sampling method you could use to decide which specific locations you would use this technique within your study area.   **[2 marks]**

2. Name a primary data collection technique suitable for carrying out a physical geography fieldwork investigation looking at the impact of groynes on the movement of sediment.   **[1 mark]**

3. Figure B shows part of a data collection sheet from a physical geography fieldwork investigation. The students were asked to sample sediment sizes at several locations on Cromer Beach. These were the sizes of one sample of ten randomly selected pebbles, measured 20 m south of the pier.

92	86	156	49	215
73	68	90	83	73

▲ **Figure B:** Sediment sizes from a sample measured 20 m south of Cromer Pier

   a) Calculate the mean.   **[1 mark]**
   b) Calculate the mode.   **[1 mark]**

   Figure C shows the average sizes of sediment with distance south of the pier.

Distance south of the pier (m)	10	20	30	40	50	60
Average sizes of sediment (mm)	44	98.5	112.5	140	154	103.5

▲ **Figure C:** Results of a beach sediment survey

   c) Draw a graph to present the data in the table.   **[3 mark]**

4. You will have carried out some physical geography fieldwork as part of your GCSE Geography course. Briefly describe the fieldwork, and explain how your fieldwork conclusions improved your understanding of a geographical question or issue.   **[8 marks]**

Human geography fieldwork

5. Name a primary data collection technique suitable for investigating how the quality of the environment changes with distance from the city centre. **[1 mark]**

6. Study Figure D, part of a survey sheet used by a group of students to investigate the environmental quality of an urban area. Complete the three remaining rows with appropriate categories for this type of survey. **[2 marks]**

Negative	1	2	3	4	5	Positive
Shops are closed down and boarded up						Shops are open and well maintained
Buildings are derelict and falling down						Buildings are new and well maintained

▲ **Figure D:** Environmental quality survey sheet

7. Is this type of survey designed to collect quantitative or qualitative data? Explain your answer. **[4 marks]**

8. State two types of data that could be used during an investigation into changing land use in a CBD over the last ten years and give reasons for your choices. **[4 marks]**

9. For a human geography fieldwork investigation that you have completed, evaluate **one** technique that you used to collect **quantitative** data. **[2 marks]**

10. Study Figure E, a graph from a data presentation part of a human geography fieldwork investigation. Residents of a town were asked to give a score for their views on the plans for a proposed new supermarket being built. A score of 0 indicated they were very much against, and a score of 5 meant they were very much in favour.

    Suggest what Figure E indicates about variations in views on these plans. **[3 marks]**

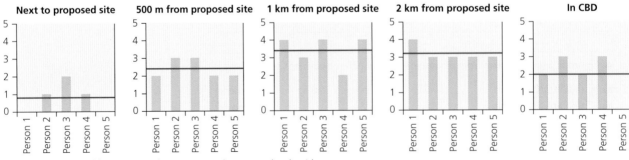

▲ **Figure E:** Approval for a proposed new supermarket among local residents

11. You will have carried out some human geography fieldwork as part of your GCSE Geography course. Briefly describe the fieldwork and evaluate the methods that you used and the accuracy of the results that you obtained. **[8 marks]**

18

Geographical exploration

The impact of Typhoon Haiyan in the Philippines

In this geographical exploration, you will look at the effect that Typhoon Haiyan had on the town of Guiuan in the Philippines in November 2013. Using the resources provided you will answer some practice questions similar to those that you will find in Paper 3: Geographical Exploration. The final question is a decision-making exercise, where you will create a short-term and long-term plan to help the population of Guiuan after Typhoon Haiyan has hit the town.

Resources

- Guiuan is 109 km south of Borongan and 154 km from Tacloban in the province of East Samar.
- It has a total land area of 175 km² (four times the size of Exeter).
- The total population is approximatley 47,000 people (including 16,000 children). The average family size is ten.
- On 8 November 2013, the city suffered heavy damage and numerous casualties as it was hit by the eye of Typhoon Haiyan with peak winds near 350 kph. The winds were described as the equivalent of standing next to a jet engine.

▲ **Figure 1:** Guiuan factfile

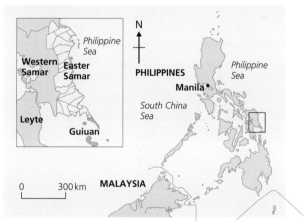

▲ **Figure 2:** Location of Guiuan

Geographical exploration

➜ **In this section you will:**

➜ look at the effect that Typhoon Haiyan had on the town of Guiuan in the Philippines.

✚ Geographical skills

To calculate the population density, you need to divide the total population of an area by the total land area:

$$\text{population density (per km}^2\text{)} = \frac{\text{total population}}{\text{total land area}}$$

1. What is the population density of Guiuan?
2. The population density of Exeter is 461.7 per km². What is the population?

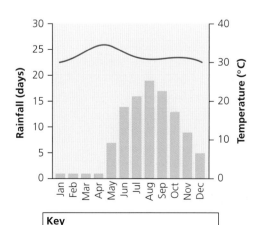

▲ **Figure 3:** Climate graph for Manila in the Philippines

Key
▢ Rainfall (days) —— Temperature (°C)

Development indicator	Philippines	UK
Life expectancy (years)	72	80
Birth rate (per 1000 people)	25	12
Infant mortality rate (per 1000 live births)	18	4.5
Number of doctors per 1000 people	1.153	2.765
Literacy rate	95.4%	99%
GDP per capita	US$4,500	US$37,500
Mobile phone use	103 million (12th)	81.61 million (17th)

▲ **Figure 4:** Development indicators

The storm shattered not just houses and lives but also the hundreds of fishing boats on which 80 per cent of the 45,000 population depend for a living.

Most of the coconut trees were also destroyed, cutting off a source of income for the villagers who sell coconut meat to be processed into refined oil.

Officials estimated that the super typhoon destroyed 95 per cent of the town's buildings.

The typhoon destroyed the municipal government office, the sports centre and the public market. It ripped rooftops apart, smashed walls, lifted vehicles off the ground and dumped them several metres away. Even the sixteenth-century Catholic church, one of the oldest in the Philippines and which had previously withstood earthquakes, was ruined.

The death toll in Guiuan was 99, with almost a thousand people injured. The town was ripped apart, sparking fears among officials that the typhoon could further impoverish people in an already very poor region.

▲ **Figure 5:** The impact of Typhoon Haiyan on Guiuan

Mosquito net	£5
Three hygiene kits (containing soap, shampoo, toilet paper, toothbrushes, nappies and underwear to keep families clean and healthy)	£45
Ten computers with an internet connection put into the hospital	£5,000
One tarpaulin (plastic sheet) to shelter one family	£10
Fifteen blankets	£30
Water kits to give safe water to five families	£50
Enable a phone company to set up an emergency mobile phone network	£2,000
Build a new school for 500 children	£40,000
Medical team of four doctors	£3,000
Earth mover (JCB)	£15,000
Vital food package for ten families containing rice, noodles and sardines	£80
Clear and reopen the airport	£8,000
Medical centre	£35,000
Fishing boat for one fisherman	£1,000
Coconut tree	£30
Build a place of worship	£30,000

▲ **Figure 6:** Aid price list

Tip

The last question in the Geographical Exploration exam requires you to make a decision and is worth 12 marks. To achieve the highest level of marks you need to:

- make reference to specific facts and statistics from the figures to fully justify (give reasons for) your decisions
- apply geographical terms accurately.

Think like a geographer

Make clear and explicit links to your knowledge and understanding from across the course. These are known as synoptic links. This decision-making exercise links to both Topic 1: Global Hazards and Topic 6: Dynamic Development. The best answers will explore the links between many aspects of geography.

Practice questions

1. Using Figures 1 and 2, describe the location of Guiuan. **[2 marks]**
2. Figure 4 gives development indicators for the Philippines and the UK. The life expectancy at birth for the UK is 80 and for the Philippines it is 72. Write the ration 80:72 in its simplest form. **[1 mark]**
3. Using the development indicators in Figure 4, explain the difference in development between the Philippines and the UK. **[3 marks]**
4. Use Figure 3 to describe the climate for Manila in the Philippines. **[2 marks]**
5. You are the managing director of a small charity that has received £100,000 in donations to help in the aftermath of Typhoon Haiyan in the Philippines. You have chosen to focus your efforts on helping the people in the town of Guiuan in Eastern Samar, one of the first places to be hit by the full force of the typhoon. Create a short – and long – term plan for delivering aid to Guiuan, using the information in Figures 1 to 5 and the price list in Figure 6. Explain your decisions. **[12 marks]**

Activities

Complete the two activities below to help you answer Question 5.

1. What will you do in the first three months after Typhoon Haiyan hit the town? Copy and complete the table below to help you with your answer. You have £50,000 to spend.

Aid needed	Why did you make this decision?	How many?	Sub-total

2. What will you do after the first three months have passed until two years after the typhoon hit the town? Copy and complete the table below to help you with your answer. You have £50,000 to spend.

Aid needed	Why did you make this decision?	How many?	Sub-total

→ Take it further

3. How might the extensive damage to Guiuan affect its economic development in the long term?

Glossary

Abiotic – the physical, non-living parts of the ecosystem, including temperature, water and light

Abrasion – the scraping, scouring or rubbing action of materials being carried by moving feature such as rivers, glaciers or waves, which erode rocks

Advanced country (AC) – countries that share a number of important economic development characteristics including well-developed financial markets, high degrees of financial intermediation and diversified economic structures with rapidly growing service sectors; ACs are classified by the IMF

Ageing population – population structure that becomes distorted with a high and increasing proportion of people in middle and old age

Albedo – the amount of incoming solar radiation that is reflected by the Earth's surface (and the atmosphere); fresh snow and ice have a high albedo with up to 90 per cent of energy being reflected back

Anomalies – data values which don't match the pattern of a sample

Atmospheric air pressure – the force exerted on the Earth's surface by the weight of the air, measured in millibars

Attrition – a reduction in the size of material

Backwash – the movement of water down the surface of a beach and through the beach sediment as a result of gravity after a wave has broken

Bedding planes – within a sedimentary rock, these represent the points where layers of sediment accumulates; they may later form horizontal weaknesses within the rock along which water may penetrate them

Biofuel – a fuel that comes from living matter, such as plant material

Biological processes – processes that result from the action of living organisms, whether plant or animal, in nature

Biomass – the total mass of plants and animals in an ecosystem

Biome – large-scale ecosystems that are spread across continents and have plants and animals that are unique to them

Biotic – all of the living elements of the ecosystem including plants, animals and bacteria

Birth rate – the number of live births per 1000 population

Bottom-up development strategy – an improvement scheme led by the local community on a small scale, such as digging new wells

Built landscape – the human-made surroundings that provide the environment for human activity; may also refer to towns, cities and other urban environments

Calories – a measure of the food energy provided by a foodstuff

Carbon sink – a forest, ocean or other natural environment that is able to absorb carbon dioxide from the atmosphere

Carnivore – an animal that eats other animals

Cash crop – crops grown and produced to be sold for a profit, such as wheat or cotton

Cave – a natural underground chamber or series of passages, especially with an opening to the surface; may also refer to the extended cracks at the base of a cliff

Chemical processes – processes that result from chemical reactions and interactions

Circumpolar winds – flows of air around the Earth's poles

Climate change – changes in long-term temperature and precipitation patterns that can either be natural or linked to human activities

Climate zone – divisions of the Earth's climates into belts, or zones, according to average temperatures and average rainfall. The three major zones are polar, temperate and tropical

Condensation – the process whereby rising water vapour becomes a liquid

Coniferous – trees that are evergreen and have needle-shaped leaves

Consumption – the act of using up resources, or purchasing goods and produce

Continental drift – the movement of continents and tectonic plates, which is driven by convection in the mantle

Continental plate – the lithosphere (crust) upon which sits our continents and land

Continental shelf – the area of seabed around a large land mass where the sea is relatively shallow compared with the open ocean

Contour lines – a line on a map joining places of equal height

Conurbation – a large urban agglomeration that results from several cities merging over time, forming a continuous urban area

Convection – the constant churning of the mantle through heat energy (radiation) passing out from the core

Convectional rainfall – occurs frequently in the tropics where it is hot; hot air close to the ground rises, cools and condenses to form rain; if the air is hot enough, it rises very quickly and can lead to thunderstorms

Co-operative – a farm, business or other organisation that is owned and run jointly by its members, who share the profits or benefits

Core – the centre of the Earth, with a solid metal inner core (at 6000°C temperature) and semi-solid outer core (4030–5730°C) from which heat is radiated outwards through the mantle

Coriolis effect – the result of Earth's rotation on weather patterns and ocean currents, making storms swirl clockwise in the southern hemisphere and anticlockwise in the northern hemisphere

Corrasion – an alternative word for abrasion

Corrosion – an alternative word for solution

Counter-urbanisation – the movement of people from urban areas into rural areas; these may be people who originally made the move into a city

Crust – the solid, rocky shell layer (lithosphere) over the mantle around the Earth, upon which sit our continents and oceans; the Earth's crust is fragmented into tectonic plates that float on the mantle

Culture – the values and beliefs of a particular society or group of people; often associated with the arts and creativity

Death rate – the number of deaths per 1000 population

Deciduous – trees that shed their leaves during winter to retain moisture, also known as broadleaved trees

Deforestation – the cutting down of trees, transforming a forest into cleared land for other uses such as building or growing crops

Demographic transition model – a theoretical model based on the experience in the UK showing changes in population characteristics over time

Desertification – the process whereby fertile land degrades to become more arid and desert-like, usually because of drought, deforestation, over-cultivation or over-extraction of water

Development – the state of growth or advancement whereby people and places improve over time

Drought – a prolonged period of time with unusually low rainfall; droughts occur when there is not enough rainfall to support people or crops

Economic hub – a central point or area associated with economic success and innovation

Economic indicator – ways to measure development that focus on money, such as GDP per capita or poverty

Ecosystem services – the services that are provided by a natural ecosystem to people; these can be seen as benefits of keeping the ecosystem functioning efficiently

El Niño – climatic changes affecting the Pacific region and beyond every few years, characterised by the appearance of unusually warm water around northern Peru and Ecuador, typically in late December; the effects of El Niño include the reversal of wind patterns across the Pacific, causing drought in Australasia, and unseasonal heavy rain in South America

Emerging and developing country (EDC) – countries which neither share all the economic development characteristics required to be advanced or are eligible for the Poverty Reduction and Growth Trust; EDCs are classified by the IMF

Endemic – plant or animal species that are unique, or native, to a particular area

Enhanced greenhouse effect – the exaggerated warming of the atmosphere caused by the emission of gases from human activities resulting in the natural greenhouse effect becoming more effective

Epicentre – the point on the Earth's surface directly above the focus

Eutrophication – the process of excessive nutrients (particularly nitrogen and phosphates) building up in water sources, usually because of leaching and surface runoff

Evapo-transpiration – the process by which water is transferred from the land to the atmosphere by evaporation from surfaces, e.g. lakes, and by transpiration from plants

Fault – like a fissure, this is a split in the rock; in plate tectonics this is where the plates are moving, e.g. the San Andreas Fault

Fauna – another term for the animals in an ecosystem

Fissure – a narrow opening in the Earth's crust caused by splitting (e.g. because of tectonic movement)

Floodplain – the flat area of land either side of a river channel forming the valley floor, which may be flooded

Flora – another term for the plants in an ecosystem

Focus – the location in the Earth where earthquakes start

Food price volatility – sudden changes in the price of foodstuffs as a result of external factors, which may lead to food insecurity

Food security – the ability of a population to access adequate supplies of foodstuffs and quality nutrition to meet dietary needs for an active and healthy lifestyle

Fracking – hydraulic fracturing; a controversial practice for extracting gas and oil from shale rocks

Freeze–thaw cycle – the daily fluctuations of temperature either side of freezing point; when repeated they contribute to physical weathering

Friction – when plates rub against one another to create heat and stress, which will lead to rock melting and snapping

Front – a boundary separating two masses of air with different densities, usually heavier cold air and lighter warm air

Fuel poverty – a situation that occurs when people's income means that spending money to heat their home would take them below the official poverty line; having higher than average fuel costs

Function – a role performed by something; in the case of a city, this may be administrative or related to a sphere of activity

Gabions – metal cages filled with rocks which can form part of a sea defence structure or be placed along rivers to protect banks from erosion, and example of hard engineering

Geology – the study of rocks and their formation, structure and composition

Geomorphic processes – processes that result in a change in the shape of the Earth; from 'geo' meaning the earth and 'morph' meaning to change shape

Glacial periods – historic cold periods associated with the build-up of snow and ice and the growth of ice sheets and glaciers

Glacial processes – processes resulting from the action of ice, often in the form of glaciers or other landforms but can also involve the cold temperatures associated with glacial periods

Glacier – a frozen river of ice formed by snow and ice accumulating in mountains or polar areas, which can even form on top of volcanoes (e.g. in Iceland)

Global warming – a trend associated with climate change involving a warming trend (0.85°C since 1880)

Globalisation – the process whereby places become interconnected by trade and culture

GM foods – foods that have had their genetic material (DNA) modified in the laboratory rather than naturally; this is done to give the plant or animal some additional 'benefits'

Goods – an item that people can source or gather from an ecosystem

Green belt – an area of land around several major urban areas, given protection under the Town and Country Planning Act of 1947, to prevent urban sprawl

Green energy – the use of renewable resources, such as sunlight, wind, rain, plants, geothermal heat, etc., which are considered eco-friendly

Green Revolution – refers originally to the work of Norman Borlaug in India; a large increase in crop production in LIDCs

Greenhouse effect – natural warming of the atmosphere as heat given off from the Earth is absorbed by liquids and gases, such as carbon dioxide

Greywater – recycled waste water from showers, baths, wash basins and washing machines

Hazard – a danger or risk; tectonic hazards include volcanic eruptions, earthquakes, landslides, etc.

Headland – an area of land that extends out into the sea, usually higher than the surrounding land; also called a point

Heatwave – a prolonged period of abnormally hot weather

Hemisphere – a half of the earth, usually as divided into northern and southern halves by the Equator

Herbivore – an animal that feeds on plants

High pressure – when there is more air pressing down on the ground, caused by air sinking; air descends as it cools, leading to high pressure at the surface

Hotspots – weaknesses in the Earth's crust where rock is thinner, which allows magma to the surface even though it is not at a plate boundary

Human Development Index (HDI) – a scale that measures development and gives a score from 0 to 1, with 1 being the highest

Hunter-gatherers – nomadic people who move from place to place, hunting, fishing and harvesting (gathering) wild food

Hydraulic action – an erosive process which involves the pressure of water hitting a surface, compressing air in any cavities which exist, and resulting in the removal of rock fragments over time

Hydroelectric power – electrical energy generated from the rapid movement of water through turbines; a renewable energy resource

Hydroponics – a method of food production that involves plants growing in nutrient-rich water pumped through a material other than soil

Ice age – a glacial episode characterised by lower than average global temperatures and during which ice covers more of the Earth's surface

Igneous – when referring to rocks, this means rocks formed within the interior of the Earth, and shaped by heat

Impermeable – a surface or substance that doesn't allow water to pass through it

Industrialisation – the process whereby factories, industry and manufacturing increase and dominate

Informal sector – refers to jobs that don't offer regular contracted hours, salary, pensions or other features of more formal employment; may refer to illegal or unlicensed activity

Infrastructure – the basic structures and facilities needed for a society to function, such as buildings, roads and power supplies

Interdependence – the reliance of every form of life on other living things and on the natural resources in its environment, such as air, soil and water

Inter-glacial periods – historic warm periods in-between glacial periods where conditions were much the same as they are today

Internal growth – growth within a city that results from births among the resident population rather than people moving into the city

Internally displaced people – people who have been forced to move from their homes but have resettled within their own country rather than migrating to a foreign country

Intertropical convergence zone – a low-pressure belt that encircles the globe around the Equator; it is where the trade winds from the northeast and southeast meet; the Earth is tilted on its orbit around the Sun, causing the ITCZ to migrate between the Tropics of Cancer and Capricorn with the seasons

Jet stream – A jet stream is a narrow band of very strong wind currents that circle the globe several kilometres above the Earth

Joints – vertical cracks within a rock, such as limestone, which result from the natural shrinking of the rock over time as it was formed; these may form weaknesses allowing water to penetrate the rock

Katabatic winds – movements of cold dense air that flow downhill and along valley floors; in Antarctica, most winds blow towards the coast from the centre

Landform – a natural, recognisable feature of the Earth's surface

Latitude – the imaginary lines that surround the Earth ranging from 0° at the Equator to 90° at the poles

Latosols – a name given to soils found under tropical rainforests with a relatively high content of iron and aluminium oxides

Levees – raised banks along a river that help to reduce the risk of flooding

Litter – the total amount of organic matter, including humus (decomposed material) and leaf litter

Local – tends to refer to a small area or region when considering the scale of a study but can also be used to refer to one's own neighbourhood or an area known to a person; a local scale can be either local to the learner or another small-scale location

Longshore (littoral) drift – the movement of sediments along a stretch of coastline as a result of wave action

Low pressure – caused when the air is rising, so less air is pressing down on the ground; air rises as it warms, leading to low pressure at the surface

Low-income developing country (LIDC) – countries that are eligible for the Poverty Reduction and Growth Trust from the IMF; LIDCs are classified by the IMF

Mantle – hot, dense liquid rock (magma); it is continuously moving due to heat from the core (convection), which drives plate movement

Meanders – a sinuous bend in a river that results from the flow of water along it

Mechanical processes – physical processes that act mechanically on a substance

Mechanisation – the process whereby machinery is introduced to complete work normally done by hand, for example washing machines, tractors, industrial robotics, engines, automated tools, etc.

Media – the communication of information and ideas, commonly involving newspapers, magazines, TV and the internet, but also involving music, theatre and even video games

Megacity – usually defined as a city that has a population of over 10 million, although the exact number varies

Metamorphic – rocks that have been changed as a result of heat and pressure being applied to them over long periods of time

Microclimate – the climate of a relatively small area, which is likely to be different from the climate of the surrounding area

Migration – the movement of people from one place to another; may be voluntary or forced, permanent or temporary, domestic or international

Mitigation – the action of trying to reduce the impact of a hazard, by planning, predicting and preparation (e.g. building earthquake-resistant buildings)

Monsoon – heavy rainfall that arrives as a result of a seasonal wind, notably in southern Asia and India between May and September

Multilateral – action taken, often in the form of aid or sanctions, involving several different countries

Multiplier effect – the chain of consequences in which investment leads to wealth, which leads to more investment, leading to more wealth; a spiral of improvement

National – referring to a nation or country; a scale of looking at things where particular countries are the subject of study

Natural – existing in, or derived from, processes that do not involve humans

Natural arch – an arch-shaped structure formed as a result of natural processes within a rock feature such as a cliff

Natural increase/decrease – the difference between the birth rate and death rate, usually expressed as a percentage

Natural landscape – a landscape that is the result of natural processes and has not been shaped or changed by human activity

Non-governmental organisation (NGO) – a not-for-profit organisation that is not under government control, for example charities

Non-renewable resources – resources that cannot be readily replaced, such as fossil fuels (oil, coal, gas) whose use is unsustainable because their formation takes billions of years

Nunatak – a peak that sticks up through an overlying layer of ice; the top of the peak is often affected by frost erosion

Oceanic plate – the lithosphere (crust) that is underneath our oceans

Omnivore – an animal that eats both plants and animals

Over-cultivation – the process of excessive agriculture, exhausting the nutrients of the land by over-use for crops or animal grazing

Over-extraction – using up more resources than can be replenished by nature, e.g. taking too much water

Ox-bow lake – a horse shoe-shaped lake that forms when a meander is separated from the main river channel as a result of erosion

Oxidation – a chemical reaction between a substance and the air; it can change its appearance or weaken it

Parent rock – the upper layer of rock on which the soil layer forms

Plate boundary – the area where two or more tectonic plates meet, and where many hazards such as earthquakes and volcanoes, and mountain building, can be found

Plunge pool – a pool formed at the base of a waterfall

Population density – the number of people in an area, usually expressed as people per square km

Population explosion – the sudden, large and rapid increase in the world's population; often considered to have been in around 1950

Population pyramid – a diagram, essentially a bar graph, that shows the structure of a population by sex and age category that may resemble a pyramid shape

Precipitation – the collective term for moisture that falls from the atmosphere; this could be in the form of rain, sleet, snow or hail

Prevailing wind – the most frequent, or common, wind direction

Primary data – data collected by students personally during fieldwork as a result of measurement and observations

Primary effects – the immediate consequences of a hazard, for example an earthquake causing a house collapse

Primary industries – an economic activity that involves collecting raw materials, such as fishing, farming and mining

Pull factor – a positive factor that attracts people into an urban/rural area

Push factor – a negative factor that results in the movement of people away from an urban/rural area

Qualitative data – data involving the quality or nature of something rather than its quantity; can be used to refer to observations or opinions of people rather than something that can be given a numerical value

Quantitative data – data involving numerical values

Quaternary geological period – the most recent geological period covering the last 2.6 million years, during which time there were several cold and warm periods

Rain shadow – an area or region behind a hill that has little rainfall because it is sheltered from rain-bearing winds

Refugee – a person who has been forced to leave their home country and move to another country, often in response to persecution or natural disaster

Regional – used to refer to the characteristics of a defined area within a larger area; the scale can vary but within geography regions could include East Anglia or a district within a county; a region is an area of land that has common features, which may be artificial, such as dialect, language, religion, industry or administrative boundaries, or natural, such as climate or landscape

Renewable resources – organic and natural resources that can be replenished constantly when used, e.g. wood, hydropower, solar energy, biomass and wind

Re-urbanisation – the use of initiatives to counter problems of inner-city decline

Rip-rap barriers – a type of sea defence involving a wall or pile of boulders, often igneous, along the sea front; an example of hard engineering

Rock slide – the movement of loose rocks down a slope as an avalanche of material, and the resulting mass of stony material that is produced

Rotational slumping – a process that involves the base of a slope failing, resulting in the rest of the landform falling down and moving in a curve along a plane as it does, so that the base of the feature extends outwards

Rural – areas which are not urban; characteristic of the countryside rather than towns and cities

Rural – urban migration – the movement of people from the countryside into towns and cities; occurs as a result of push and pull factors relevant to both locations

Scale – can refer to maps that are drawn at particular levels of detail; in geography, this often refers to whether something is looked at from the local, regional, national or global level

Sea walls – curved concrete structures placed along a sea front, often in urban areas such as the front of a promenade, designed to reflect back wave energy; an example of hard engineering

Secondary data – data collected from sources other than the student; may include published material, reports from public bodies and the work of other people

Secondary effects – follow-on consequences of hazards, for example a fire from a gas pipe broken during a house collapse

Sedimentary – rocks that have been produced from layers of sediment, usually at the bottom of the sea

Seismic waves – a wave of energy passed through the Earth or along its surface due to plate movement

Services – a function, or 'job', that an ecosystem provides

Slash and burn – a form of shifting cultivation where the natural vegetation is cut down and burned to clear the land for cultivation; when the plot becomes infertile the farmer moves on to a fresh plot and does the same again

Social indicator – ways to measure development that focus on people, such as life expectancy or birth rate

Social inequality – the extent to which people have unequal opportunities and rewards as a result of the position they occupy within the society; different groups, characterised by age, gender, 'class' and ethnicity, may have different levels of access to employment, education and healthcare

Social premium – part of the support to farmers offered under the Fairtrade system; a payment to communities to spend on projects that help them in some way, such as improvements to water supply or education

Solution – a type of erosion that involves rock being chemically changed such that it is taken into solution and removed, e.g. the action of acidic water on limestone

Spot height – the height of a specific point on the land, which is added to an Ordnance Survey map

Stack – a coastal feature that results from erosion; a section of headland that has become separated from the mainland and stands as a pillar of rock

Stakeholders – individuals or organisations who have a viewpoint or concern about something, e.g. local residents, government, tourists, business, etc.

Stump – a coastal feature that results from the collapse of a stack to form a protrusion of rock close to the sea surface

Sub-aerial processes – processes that aid weathering and the mass movement of material; they include the action of the weather

Subduction – the sinking of a dense plate into the mantle

Subsistence – only producing enough goods to meet your own basic needs, with no extra to trade

Suburbanisation – a change in the nature of rural areas such that they start to resemble the suburbs

Sunspot – a spot or dark patch that appears from time to time on the surface of the Sun and is associated with an outburst of energy from the sun

Sunspot cycle – a period lasting eleven years during which sunspot activity increases from a minimum to a maximum and then back to a minimum

Super typhoon – a storm that reaches sustained wind speeds of at least 150 mph

Sustainability/sustainable development – this approach places emphasis on improving the current quality of life but still maintaining resources for the future; it is a balance of providing social, economic and environmental benefit long term

Swash – the movement of water up a beach following the breaking of a wave on the coastline

Tectonic plates – the crust is broken up into seven large sections and various smaller sections, which are floating on the mantle and moving towards, away from and past each other

Thermocline – the point at which the temperature changes from warmer surface waters to deeper, colder water

Tides – changes in sea level as a result of the Moon; regular movements which occur every day

Top-down development strategy – a large-scale, expensive initiative (usually controlled by the government and often requiring loans from organisations such as the World Bank) to improve development, such as the building of a dam

Trade winds – the prevailing pattern of easterly surface winds found in the tropics, within the lower section of the Earth's atmosphere

Trans-national corporation (TNC) – businesses that operate all over the world, usually with their headquarters in an advanced country and their manufacturing branches in emerging countries

Trophic cascade – the transfer of energy down through an ecosystem as a result of food chains; at each level some energy is lost

Troposphere – an area of the atmosphere, from the Earth's surface to a height of 10–15 km, in which the weather takes place

Tundra – a vast, flat, treeless Arctic region of Europe, Asia, and North America in which the soil is permanently frozen

Unilateral – action taken, often in the form of aid or sanctions, involving a single country

Urban – refers to areas that have been built by people; towns and cities

Urban belt – an area of land which has become more urban in character

Urbanisation – the process of towns and cities developing and becoming bigger as their population increases

Volcanic winter – cooling trend caused by volcanic particles in the atmosphere blocking out some of the Sun's radiation

Water security – the ability of a population to access safe and affordable drinking water to sustain health, socio-economic development and ecosystem stability

Water stress – pressure on water supplies caused by demand exceeding or threatening to exceed supply

Waterfalls – a steep fall of river water where its course crosses between different rock types, resulting in different rates of erosion

Wave-cut notch – an area at the base of a cliff that has been eroded back further than the higher sections by erosion, and may result in a later collapse

Wave-cut platform – a flat area along the base of a cliff produced by the retreat of the cliff as a result of erosive processes

Waves – elliptical or circular movement of the sea surface that are translated into a movement of water up the beach as they approach the coastline

Weathering – the breakdown of material *in situ* by physical, chemical and biological processes; if movement is involved, this becomes erosion

World city – a city considered to be an important node in the global economic system, and one which has iconic status and buildings, e.g. London and New York; also known as a global or alpha city

Xerophytic – a type of plant that can survive on very little water

Index

The Publishers would like to thank the following for permission to reproduce copyright material.

Photo credits

p.1 © C. Sherburne/Photodisc/Getty Images/ Environmental Concerns 31; **p.4** t © Tony Eveling/Alamy, b © BANANA PANCAKE/Alamy; **p.5** t © David Noton Photography/Alamy, b © age fotostock/Alamy; **p.10** © Corbis; **p.13** © Xinhua/Alamy; **p.17** © Ashley Cooper pics/Alamy Stock Photo; **p.18** © Martin Bennett/Reuters/Corbis; **p.19** © Mark Pearson/REX Shutterstock; **p.20** t © Marc Hill/Alamy Stock Photo, b Image courtesy of Nicholas Pearson Associates; **p.21** © Hugo Michiels via Getty Images; **p.23** © 505522751 – Thinkstock/ Getty Images; **p.26** © Jo Debens; **p.28** © Jo Debens; **p.32** © Jo Debens; **p.35** t © ARCTIC IMAGES/Alamy Stock Photo, b © Jo Debens; **p.36** © Meteosat, 2010; **p.37** © Jonny White/Alamy Stock Photo; **p.38** t Cartoon by Rob Pudim © Natural Hazards Center, 1999, b © Federal Emergency Management Agency (FEMA); **p.41** © Guilhem Baker/LNP/REX Shutterstock; **p.44** l © Patrick Guenette/123RF, r © ARCTIC IMAGES/Alamy Stock Photo; **p.45** © Akademie/ Alamy Stock Photo; **p.46** t © NASA Goddard's Scientific Visualization Studio, b © U.S. Geological Survey; **p.47** both © NASA images by Jesse Allen and Robert Simmon, using Landsat 4, 5, and 7 data from the USGS Global Visualization Viewer; **p.49** t © Alberto Garcia/Corbis, b © NASA; **p.53** t © ton koene/Alamy Stock Photo, b © Ashley Cooper pics/Alamy Stock Photo; **p.55** l © Juliana Spinola/Demotix/Corbis, r © Paulo Fridman/Bloomberg via Getty Images; **p.58** © E.Westmacott/Alamy Stock Photo; **p.59** © PearlBucknall – Thinkstock/Getty Images; **p.60** t © Richard Allaway, cl © Alan Parkinson, cr © Alan Parkinson, b © Alan Parkinson; **p.63** © Alan Parkinson; **p.64** both © Alan Parkinson; **p.67** t © Forestry Commission , b © Helen Dixon/Alamy Stock Photo; **p.69** © Alan Parkinson; **p.70** t and background © Ian Ward, bl © Alan Parkinson, br © Alan Parkinson; **p.71** both © Bryan Ledgard; **p.73** © Alan Parkinson; **p.74** t © Val Vannet, b © Alan Parkinson; **p.76** © Guillermo Avello/123RF; **p.77** © APEX NEWS & PICTURES; **p.81** © Ian Ward; **p.83** © MikeLane45/Thinkstock/ Getty Images; **p.84** © Alan Parkinson; **p.86** © Matthew Dixon/123RF; **p.88** l © Alan Parkinson, r © Jo Chambers/Fotolia; **p.89** © attiarndt/Thinkstock/Getty Images; **p.93** © Francois Gohier/VWPics/Alamy Stock Photo; **p.95** © Pcha988/ Thinkstock/Getty Images; **p.97** © Paola Giannoni/123RF; **p.99** t © Nazzu/Fotolia, b © SerengetiLion – Thinkstock/Getty Images; **p.101** © Ilo-Pok – Thinkstock; **p.102** © Savageslc – Thinkstock/Getty Images; **p.103** © Steve Byland/123RF; **p.104** © szefei/123RF; **p.106** © National Geographic Creative/Alamy Stock Photo; **p.107** l © Jan Sochor/Alamy Stock Photo, r © blickwinkel/Alamy Stock Photo; **p.108** © Fotos 593/Fotolia; **p.109** © Hailshadow – Thinkstock/Getty Images; **p.110** t © RSM Images/Alamy Stock Photo, b © robertharding/Alamy Stock Photo; **p.111** © Mike Goldwater/ Alamy Stock Photo; **p.112** © Warmlight – Thinkstock/Getty Images; **p.113** t © fabio lamanna – Thinkstock/Getty Images, b © mazzzur – Thinkstock/Getty Images; **p.114** © HappyToBeHomeless – iStock – Thinkstock/Getty Images; **p.115** © Mark Brandon; **p.120** © Wayne R Bilenduk via Getty Images; **p.121** t © Alan Parkinson, b © Mark Brandon; **p.123** © staphy – iStockphoto via Thinkstock/Getty Images; **p.124** Christopher Michel: CC2.0 licensed image from Wikimedia Commons; http://en.wikipedia.org/wiki/Union_Glacier_Camp#/ media/File:Antarctica_(11254517513).jpg; **p.125** © Nigel McCall/Alamy Stock Photo; **p.126** © Karl Tuplin, British Antarctic Survey; **p.127** © Secretariat of the Antarctic Treaty, March 2016; **p.129** Rio+20 summit logo designed by the Graphic Design Unit of the United Nations Department of Public Information in New York; **p.131** © IRStone – Fotolia; **p.132–3** © Bryan Ledgard; **p.133** inset © Courtesy Everett Collection/REX Shutterstock; **p.135** © Steve Rosset/ iStockphoto.com; **p.140** © Photodisc/Getty Images/World Commerce & Travel 5; **p.141** © Andrew Holt/Digital Vision/Getty Images; **p.144** l © Mohammed Elshamy/Anadolu Agency/Getty Images, r © PIUS UTOMI EKPEI/AFP/Getty Images; **p.146** © PinkBadger – iStockphot via Thinkstock/Getty Images; **p.147** © Greg Balfour Evans/Alamy Stock Photo; **p.148** t © Universal Images Group North America LLC/DeAgostini/Alamy Stock Photo, bl © Diana Jarvis, br © Diana Jarvis ; **p.152** © Ian Dagnall/Alamy Stock Photo; **p.153** all © Diana Jarvis ; **p.154** © Diana Jarvis; **p.156** t © A.P.S. (UK)/Alamy Stock Photo, b © Ian Dagnall/ Alamy Stock Photo; **p.157** © Guy Corbishley/Alamy Stock Photo; **p.158** t © HS2 Ltd (www.gov.uk/hs2), b © Gehl-Arup; **p.162** t © TNT Magazine/Alamy Stock Photo, cl © Harriet Cummings/Alamy Stock Photo, cr © Photon-Photos – Thinkstock/Getty Images, bl © Patrik Stedrak – Thinkstock/Getty Images; **p.164** © Tim Whitby/Alamy Stock Photo; **p.165** Courtesy of Pablo D. Flores via Wikipedia (https://en.wikipedia.org/wiki/GNU_Free_Documentation_License); **p.166** © Gehl-Arup; **p.167** © Jo Debens; **p.169** tl © Jo Debens, tr © Jo Debens, bl © Jo Debens, br © Starcevic – Thinkstock/Getty Images; **p.173** all © World Mapper; **p.174** © Sam Tarling/Oxfam; **p.180** © Hu Yanhui/Xinhua Press/Corbis; **p.181** © Florian Blümm/Alamy Stock Photo; **p.183** both © Darren Thompson; **p.189** both © Darren Thompson; **p.192** © Darren Thompson; **p.194** both © Darren Thompson; **p.195** © JENNY VAUGHAN/AFP/Getty Images; **p.197** © Christ Hammond/Alamy Stock Photo; **p.198** t © DEREKMcDOUGALL – iStock – Thinkstock/Getty Images, b © Les Gibbon/Alamy Stock Photo; **p.202** l © greenwales/Alamy Stock Photo, r © Photodisc/Getty Images/ World Landmarks & Travel V60; **p.203** © LCM2007 © NERC (CEH) 2011; **p.205** t © LondonPhotos – Homer Sykes/Alamy Stock Photo, c © Philip Halling via Geography.com (http://creativecommons.org/licenses/by-sa/2.0/), b © Ebbsfleet Development Corporation; **p.211** © kzenon – Thinkstock/Getty Images; **p.212** l © Alex Raths – iStockphoto; **p.212** r © Adrian Brockwell/123RF; **p.214** l © FURLONG PHOTOGRAPHY/Alamy Stock Photo, r © Washington Imaging/Alamy Stock Photo; **p.215** t © Hulton-Deutsch Collection/CORBIS, b © scenicireland.com/ Christopher Hill Photographic/Alamy Stock Photo; **p.216** © Marcus Rowland via Wikipedia Commons (https://creativecommons.org/licenses/by-sa/3.0/deed. en); **p.218** © Monkey Business – Fotolia; **p.220** © Skyscan Photolibrary/Alamy Stock Photo; **p.223** © STFC Innovations via ESA.int; **p.224** © Valery Sharifulin/ ITAR-TASS Photo/Corbis; **p.226** © Juan Teixeira/NurPhoto/REX Shutterstock; **p.227** t © Francesca Volpi/SIPA/REX Shutterstock, b © Stanislav Krasilnikov/ ITAR-TASS Photo/Corbis; **p.228** © Oli Scarff/Getty Images; **p.229** t © Mohamed Abdiwahab/AFP/Getty Images, b © Gallo Images/REX Shutterstock; **p.230** tl 'The Hay Wain' by John Constable, photograph © Steve Vidler/Alamy Stock Photo, cl © John Kellerman – Thinkstock/Getty Images, bl © Zoonar RF – Thinkstock/ Getty Images, c © Miroslava Markova/123RF, tr © Lukassek – Thinkstock/ Getty Images, br © Col Pics/Everett/REX Shutterstock; **p.231** tr © Ken McKay/ REX Shutterstock, bl © REX Shutterstock, tl © Ray Tang/REX Shutterstock, br © Jonathan Hordle/REX Shutterstock; **p.232** t © Adolph/ullstein bild via Getty Images, b © Dean Murray/REX Shutterstock; **p.234** © ZUMA Press, Inc./Alamy Stock Photo; **p.235** t © MGM/Everett/REX Shutterstock, b © Carl Court/Getty Images; **p.236** © Justin Kase z09z/Alamy Stock Photo; **p.237** l © Robert Judges/ REX Shutterstock, r © Colin Underhill/Alamy Stock Photo; **p.239** © Agencja Fotograficzna Caro/Alamy Stock Photo; **p.242** © Jo Debens; **p.249** © chungking – Fotolia.com; **p.252** t © Jo Debens, b © NASA; **p.254** l © Robert Harding/ Alamy Stock Photo, r © Global Warming Images/Alamy Stock Photo; **p.255** © Jo Debens; **p.262** © Alan Parkinson; **p.264** both © Alan Parkinson; **p.266** © Bryan Ledgard; **p.267** t © Jeffrey Blackler/Alamy Stock Photo, c © IET community team, b © IET community team; **p.268** t © Alan Parkinson, b © Fairtrade Foundation; **p.270** © Carolyn Cole/Los Angeles Times via Getty Images; **p.271** © Oxfam; **p.273** © Simon Ross; **p.274** © Simon Ross; **p.276** t © Alan Parkinson, b © Simon Ross; **p.277** © Alan Parkinson; **p.281** © Simon Ross; **p.284** © epa european pressphoto agency b.v./Alamy Stock Photo

Key for Ordnance Survey 1:50,000 maps

Communications / VOIES DE COMMUNICATION / STRASSEN UND WEGE

ROADS AND PATHS

Not necessarily rights of way

Service area (S)
Junction number 1
Elevated / En Viaduc / Erhöht
M 1

Motorway (dual carriageway)
Autoroute (chaussées separées) avec aire de service et echangeur numeroté
Autobahn (zweibahnig) mit Servicestation und Anschlusstelle sowie Nummer der Anschlusstelle

Motorway under construction
Autoroute en construction
Autobahn im Bau

Dual carriageway
Chaussées separees
Zweibahnige Strasse

Untenced / Sans clôture / Nicht eingezaunt
A 470

Primary Route
Itinéraire principal
Fernstrasse

Primary route under construction
Itinéraire principal en construction
Fernstrasse im Bau

A 493
Main road
Route principale
Hauptstrasse

Main road under construction
Route principale en construction
Hauptstrasse im Bau

B 4518
Secondary road
Route secondaire
Nebenstrasse

Narrow road with passing places
Route etroite avec voies de dépassement
Enge Strasse mit Ausweichstelle

A 855 / B 885
Road generally more than 4m wide
Route generalement de plus de 4m de largeur
Strasse, im allg.über 4m breit

Road generally less than 4m wide
Route generalement de moins de 4m de largeur
Strasse, im allg.unter 4m breit

Other road, drive or track
Autre route, allée ou sentier
Sonstige Strasse, Zufahrt oder Feldweg

Path / Sentier / Fussweg

Footbridge / Passerelle / Fussgängerbrücke

Gradient: steeper than 20% (1 in 5) / 14% to 20% (1 in 7 to 1 in 5)
Pente: Supérieure à 20% (1 pour 5) / 14% à 20% (1 pour 7 à 1 pour 5)
Steigung über 20% / 14% bis 20%

Bridge / Pont / Brucke
Road tunnel / Tunnel routier / Strassentunnel

Gates / Barrières / Schranken

Ferry P / Ferry V
Ferry (passenger) / Ferry (vehicle)
Bac pour piétons / Bac pour véhicules
Personenfähre / Autofähre

PRIMARY ROUTES

These form a network of recommended through routes which complement the motorway system

PUBLIC RIGHTS OF WAY / DROIT DE PASSAGE PUBLIC / ÖFFENTLICHE WEGERECHTE

Footpath
Road used as a public path
Bridleway
Byway open to all traffic

Public rights of way shown on this map have been taken from local authority definitive maps and later amendments. The map includes changes notified to Ordnance Survey by 1st August 1997. The symbols show the defined route so far as the scale of mapping will allow.
Rights of way are not shown on maps of Scotland

Rights of way are liable to change and may not be clearly defined on the ground. Please check with the relevant local authority for the latest information

The representation on this map of any other road, track or path is no evidence of the existence of a right of way

OTHER PUBLIC ACCESS / AUTRES ACCES PUBLICS / ANDERE ÖFFENTLICHE WEGE

◆ National Trail, European Long Distance Path, Long Distance Route, selected Recreational Routes

• • • • Other route with public access { not normally shown { in urban areas

The exact nature of the rights on these routes and the existence of any restrictions may be checked with the local highway authority. Alignments are based on the best information available. These routes are not shown on maps of Scotland

National/Regional Cycle Route
Surfaced cycle route

4 National Cycle Network number
8 Regional Cycle Network number

Danger Area
Firing and Test Ranges in the area. Danger! Observe warning notices.
Champs de tir et d'essai. Danger! Se conformer aux avertissements.
Schiess und Erprobungsgelände. Gefahr! Warnschilder beachten.

RAILWAYS / CHEMINS DE FER / EISENBAHNEN

Track multiple or single
Track under construction
Light rapid transit system, narrow gauge or tramway
Bridges, Footbridge
Tunnel

Station, (a) principal
Siding
Light rapid transit system station
LC Level crossing
Viaduct

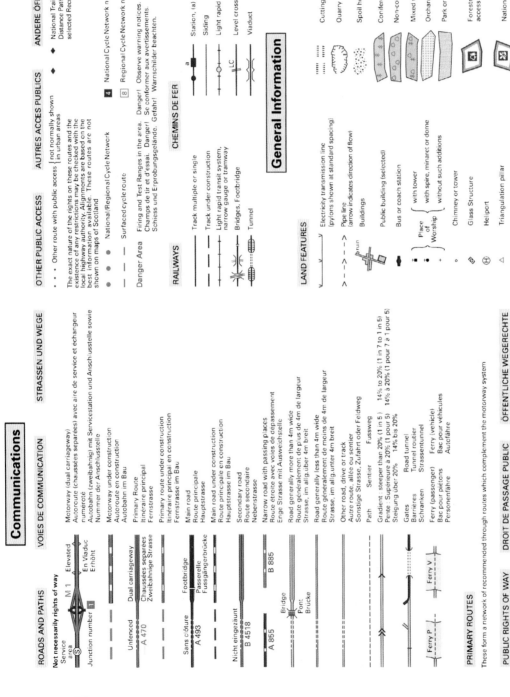

General Information

LAND FEATURES

Electricity transmission line (pylons shown at standard spacing)
> > - > - > Pipe line (arrow indicates direction of flow)
Buildings
Public building (selected)
Bus or coach station
Place of Worship { with tower / with spire, minaret or dome / without such additions
o Chimney or tower
Glass Structure
(H) Heliport
△ Triangulation pillar
Mast
Wind pump/wind generator
Windmill with or without sails
Graticule intersection at 5' intervals

Cutting, embankment
Quarry
Spoil heap, refuse tip or dump
Coniferous wood
Non-coniferous wood
Mixed wood
Orchard
Park or ornamental ground
Forestry Commission access land
National Trust-always open
National Trust-limited access, observe local signs
National Trust for Scotland

Tourist Information

TOURIST INFORMATION

⚠	Camp site Terrain de camping Campingplatz
⚏	Caravan site Terrain pour caravanes Wohnwagenplatz
⚜	Garden Jardin Garten
⚑	Golf course or links Terrain de golf Golfplatz
ⓘ ⓘ	Information centre, all year / seasonal Office de tourisme, ouvert toute l'année / en saison Informationsbüro, ganzjährig / saisonal
⚑	Nature reserve Réserve naturelle Naturschutzgebiet
P&R P&R	Parking / Park and ride, all year / seasonal Parking / Parking et navette, ouvert toute l'année / en saison Parkplatz / Park & Ride, ganzjährig / saisonal
✕	Picnic site Emplacement de pique-nique Picknickplatz

RENSEIGNEMENTS TOURISTIQUES / TOURISTENINFORMATION

PC	Public convenience (in rural areas) Toilettes (à la campagne) Öffentliche Toilette (in ländlichen Gebieten)
	Selected places of tourist interest Endroits d'un intérêt touristique particulier Ausgewählter Platz von touristischem Interesse
✆ ✆	Telephone, public / motoring organisation Téléphone, public / associations automobiles Telefon, öffentlich / automobilklub
✺	Viewpoint Point de vue Aussichtspunkt
V	Visitor centre Centre pour visiteurs Besucherzentrum
⚇	Walks / Trails Promenades Wanderwege
▲	Youth hostel Auberge de jeunesse Jugendherberge

Technical Information

NORTH POINTS

Difference of true north from grid north at sheet corners

NW corner	NE corner
1° 03' (19 mils) E	0° 33' (10 mils) E

SW corner	SE corner
1° 02' (18 mils) E	0° 32' (10 mils) E

To plot, the average direction of magnetic north join the point circled on the south edge of the sheet to the point on the protractor scale on the north edge at the angle estimated for the current year

True North
Grid North
Magnetic North

Diagrammatic only

Magnetic north varies with place and time. The direction for the centre of the sheet is estimated at 3° 19' (59 mils) west of grid north for July 2004.

Annual change is about 13' (4 mils) east

Magnetic data supplied by the British Geological Survey

Base map constructed on Transverse Mercator Projection, Airy Spheroid, OSGB (1936) Datum. Vertical datum mean sea level (Newlyn)

HOW TO GIVE A NATIONAL GRID REFERENCE TO NEAREST 100 METRES

SAMPLE POINT: Goodcroft

1. Read letters identifying 100 000 metre square in which the point lies....NY

2. FIRST QUOTE EASTINGS
Locate first VERTICAL grid line to LEFT of point and read LARGE figures labelling the line either in the top or bottom margin or on the line itself 53
Estimate tenths from grid line to point 4

3. AND THEN QUOTE NORTHINGS
Locate first HORIZONTAL grid line BELOW point and read LARGE figures labelling the line either in the left margin or on the line itself 16
Estimate tenths from grid line to point

SAMPLE REFERENCE NY 534 161

For local referencing grid letters may be omitted

IGNORE the SMALLER figures of the grid number at the corner of the map. These are for finding the full coordinates. Use ONLY the LARGER figure of the grid number. EXAMPLE $3\vert7\vert$000m

INCIDENCE OF ADJOINING SHEETS

The red figures give the grid values of the adjoining sheet edges. The blue letters identify the 100 000 metre square

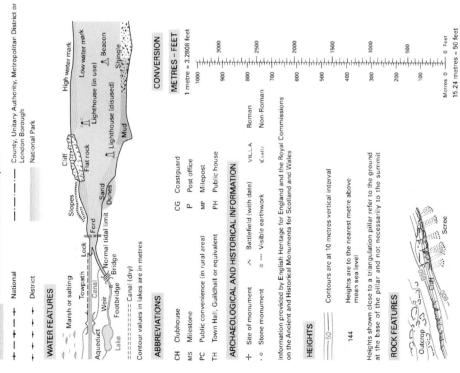

BOUNDARIES Administrative boundaries as at January 2002

–+–+–+ National	County, Unitary Authority, Metropolitan District or London Borough
–+–+– District	National Park

WATER FEATURES

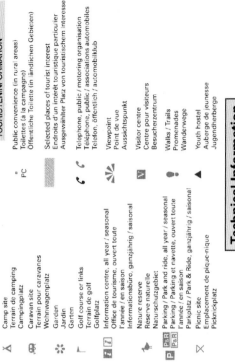

Marsh or salting

Aqueduct Canal Weir Towpath Lock Normal tidal limit
Lake Footbridge Bridge
Canal (dry)

Ford Slopes Cliff Flat rock Sand Dunes High water mark Low water mark
Lighthouse (in use) Lighthouse (disused) Beacon Shingle Mud

Contour values in lakes are in metres

CONVERSION

METRES – FEET

1 metre = 3.2808 feet

1000	3000
900	2500
800	2000
700	1500
600	
500	1000
400	
300	500
200	
100	0 Feet
Metres 0	

15.24 metres = 50 feet

ABBREVIATIONS

CH	Clubhouse	CG	Coastguard
MS	Milestone	P	Post office
PC	Public convenience (in rural area)	MP	Milepost
TH	Town Hall, Guildhall or equivalent	PH	Public house

ARCHAEOLOGICAL AND HISTORICAL INFORMATION

+	Site of monument	VILLA	Roman
∘	Stone monument	Castle	Non-Roman
✕	Battlefield (with date)		
✕	Visible earthwork		

Information provided by English Heritage for England and the Royal Commissions on the Ancient and Historical Monuments for Scotland and Wales

HEIGHTS

—50— Contours are at 10 metres vertical interval

144 Heights are to the nearest metre above mean sea level

Heights shown close to a triangulation pillar refer to the ground at the base of the pillar and not necessarily to the summit

ROCK FEATURES

Outcrop Cliff Scree

Key for Ordinance Survey 1:25,000 maps

BOUNDARIES

- National
- County (England)
- Unitary Authority (UA), Metropolitan District (Met Dist), London Borough (LB) or District (Scotland & Wales are solely Unitary Authorities)
- Civil Parish (CP) (England) or Community (C) (Wales)
- National Park boundary

HEIGHTS AND NATURAL FEATURES

Surface heights are to the nearest metre above mean sea level. Where two heights are shown, the first height is to the base of the triangulation pillar and the second (in brackets) to the highest natural point of the hill.

- 52 Ground survey height
- 284 Air survey height
- Vertical face/cliff
- Contours may be at 5 or 10 metres vertical interval

Loose rock   Boulders   Outcrop   Scree

Water   Mud   Sand; sand & shingle

ARCHAEOLOGICAL AND HISTORICAL INFORMATION

- + Site of antiquity
- ✗ Site of battle (with date)
- Visible earthwork
- VILLA Roman
- Castle Non-Roman

Information provided by English Heritage for England and the Royal Commissions on the Ancient and Historical Monuments for Scotland and Wales

General Information

VEGETATION
Limits of vegetation are defined by positioning of symbols

- Coniferous trees
- Non-coniferous trees
- Coppice
- Scrub
- Bracken, heath or rough grassland
- Marsh, reeds or saltings
- Orchard

GENERAL FEATURES

- Place of worship
  - + Current or former place of worship
  - with tower
  - with spire, minaret or dome
- Building; important building
- Glasshouse
- Youth hostel
- Bunkhouse/camping barn/other hostel
- Bus or coach station
- Lighthouse; disused lighthouse; beacon
- Triangulation pillar; mast
- Windmill, with or without sails
- Wind pump; wind turbine
- Electricity transmission line
- Slopes

- Gravel pit
- Other pit or quarry
- Landfill site or slag/spoil heap
- Sand pit

- BP/BS Boundary post/stone
- CG Cattle grid
- CH Clubhouse
- FB Footbridge
- HP; MS Milepost ; milestone
- Mon Monument
- PO Post office
- Pol Sta Police station
- Sch School
- TH Town hall
- NTL Normal tidal limit
- W; Spr Well; spring

Selected Tourist and Leisure Information
RENSEIGNEMENTS TOURISME ET LOISIRS SÉLECTIONNÉS   AUSGEWÄHLTE INFORMATIONEN ZU TOURISTIK UND FREIZEITGESTALTUNG

- P&R / P&R Parking / Park & Ride, all year/seasonal
  Parking / Parking de navette, ouvert toute l'année/en saison
  Parkplatz / Park & Ride, ganzjährig/saisonal
- Visitor centre / Centre de visiteurs / Besucherzentrum
- Forestry Commission visitor centre
  Commission Forestière Centre de visiteurs
  Staatsforst Besucherzentrum
- PC Public convenience / Toilettes / Öffentliche Toilette
- Telephone, public/roadside assistance/emergency
  Téléphone, public/borne d'appel d'urgence/agence
  Telefon, öffentlich/Notrufsäule/Notruf
- Camp site/caravan site
  Terrain de camping/Terrain pour caravanes
  Campingplatz/Wohnwagenplatz
- Recreation/leisure/sports centre
  Centre de détente/loisirs/sports
  Erholungs-/Freizeit-/Sportzentrum
- Theme/pleasure park
  Parc à thèmes/Parc d'agrément
  Vergnügungs-/Freizeitpark
- Preserved railway
  Chemin de fer touristique
  Museumseisenbahn

- Walks/trails / Promenades / Wanderwege
- Cycle trail / Piste cyclable / Radfahrweg
- Mountain bike trail / Chemin pour VTT / Mountainbike-Strecke
- Horse riding / Équitation / Reitstall
- Public house/s / Pub/s / Gaststätte/n
- Viewpoint / Point de vue / Aussichtspunkt
- Picnic site / Emplacement de pique-nique / Picknickplatz
- Country park / Parc naturel / Landschaftspark
- Garden/arboretum / Jardin/Arboretum / Garten/Baumgarten
- Nature reserve / Réserve naturelle / Naturschutzgebiet
- Fishing / Pêche / Angeln

- Water activities / Jeux aquatiques / Wassersport
- Slipway / Cale / Helling
- Other tourist feature / Autre site intéressant / Sonstige Sehenswürdigkeit
- Cathedral/Abbey / Cathédrale/Abbaye / Kathedrale/Abtei
- Museum / Musée / Museum
- Castle/fort / Château/Fortification / Burg/Festung
- Building of historic interest / Bâtiment d'intérêt historique / Historisches Gebäude
- National Trust
- English Heritage
- Historic Scotland

Communications

ROADS AND PATHS
Not necessarily rights of way

- 7 Service area / Junction number
- M1 or A6(M) Motorway
- Dual carriageway
- A35 Main road
- A30 Secondary road
- B3074 Narrow road with passing places
- Road under construction
- Road generally more than 4 m wide
- Road generally less than 4 m wide
- Other road, drive or track, fenced and unfenced
- Gradient: steeper than 20%(1 in 5);   14%(1 in 7) to 20%(1 in 5)
- Ferry; Ferry P - passenger only
- Path

RAILWAYS

- Multiple track / standard gauge
- Single track
- Narrow gauge or / Light rapid transit system (LRTS) and station
- Road over; road under; level crossing
- Cutting; tunnel; embankment
- Station, open to passengers; siding

PUBLIC RIGHTS OF WAY
(Rights of way are not shown on maps of Scotland)

- Footpath
- Bridleway
- Byway open to all traffic
- Restricted byway (from 2nd May 2006 roads used as public paths were redesignated as restricted byways. They provide a right of way for walkers, horse riders, cyclists and other non-mechanically propelled vehicles)

Public rights of way shown on this map have been taken from local authority definitive maps and later amendments.
Rights of way are liable to change and may not be clearly defined on the ground.
Please check with the relevant local authority for the latest information

The representation on this map of any other road, track or path is no evidence of the existence of a right of way

OTHER PUBLIC ACCESS

Other routes with public access (not normally shown in urban areas)
The exact nature of the rights on these routes and the existence of any restrictions may be checked with the local highway authority. Alignments are based on the best information available

- National Trail / Long Distance Route ; Recreational Route
- Permissive footpath
- Footpaths and bridleways along which landowners have permitted public use but which are not rights of way. The agreement may be withdrawn
- Permissive bridleway
- Traffic-free cycle route
- National cycle network route number - traffic free
- National cycle network route number - on road

Scotland

In Scotland, everyone has access rights in law over most land and inland water, provided access is exercised responsibly. This includes walking, cycling, horse-riding and water access, for recreational, educational purposes, and for crossing land or water. Access rights do not apply to motorised activities, hunting, shooting or fishing, nor if your dog is not under proper control. The Scottish Outdoor Access Code is the reference point for responsible behaviour, and can be obtained at www.outdooraccess-scotland.com or by phoning your local Scottish Natural Heritage office.   "Land Reform (Scotland) Act 2003

- National Trust for Scotland, always open / limited opening - observe local signs
- Forestry Commission Land / Woodland Trust Land

England & Scotland

Firing and test ranges in the area. Danger! Observe warning notices
Champs de tir et d'essai. Danger! Se conformer aux avertissements
Schiess und Erprobungsgebiete. Gefahr! Warnschilder beachten
Visit www.access.mod.uk for information

- DANGER AREA

ACCESS LAND

England

Portrayal of access land on this map is intended as a guide to land which is normally available for access on foot, for example access land created under the Countryside and Rights of Way Act 2000, and land managed by the National Trust, Forestry Commission and Woodland Trust. Access for other activities may also exist. Some restrictions will apply; some land will be excluded from open access rights. The depiction of rights of access does not imply or express any warranty as to its accuracy or completeness. Observe local signs and follow the Countryside Code. Visit: www.countrysideaccess.gov.uk for up-to-date information

- Access land boundary and limit
- Access land in woodland area
- Access information point
- Access permitted within managed controls for example, local byelaws Visit www.access.mod.uk for information
- MANAGED ACCESS